The Wrong Side of the Room

A Life in Music Theater

N<small>ORMAN</small> M<small>ATHEWS</small>

E<small>BURN</small> P<small>RESS</small>
N<small>EW</small> Y<small>ORK</small>

THE WRONG SIDE OF THE ROOM
Copyright © 2018 by Norman Mathews

Incidents and stories in this book reflect the author's recollection of events.
Some names have been changed to protect the privacy of those depicted.
Dialog has been recreated from memory.

ISBN-13: 978-1-7323671-0-4 (paperback)
ISBN-13: 978-1-7323671-1-1   (ebook)

Cover Design by Darlene K. Swanson
Cover Photograph by Duncan Steck
Back Cover Photograph by Rick Schwab

CONTENTS

For Todd and Tony

The Child Who Never Was

HUH? NO! NO! LEAVE ME ALONE. What time is it anyway? I'm sleeping for god's sake. A little peace, PLEASE. It's the crack of dawn for crying out loud, barely ten AM. I didn't fall asleep until five this morning. Have a heart, will you?. . . That's better. Mmm. . . uh huh. . . ah. . .okay now. So cozy—almost back in dreamland.

Ugh! Now what? Get that cold thing off my head! What the hell is it, a pair of pliers? Ouch! That hurt. Now you're tugging at me with it? What's going on here? I'm slipping down. I'm going to crash. Somebody catch me. Ahhhh. Whew!

What's all this light? It's blinding. Ow! Who's slapping my ass? Ow! Looks like some dirty old man. What a brute. Sex pervert. I'm warning you, don't even think of leaving marks on my butt, mister! Jesus. it's freezing in this place. Goodbye sleep; hello, pandemonium. All these people. What in god's name are they doing?

And what's all that white stuff out there? Snow? Snow on September 12? That makes no sense; it's still summer. I'm sorry, this is not working for me at all.

ST. ANTHONY'S HOSPITAL, ROCKFORD, ILLINOIS,
SATURDAY, SEPTEMBER 12, 1942. MY FIRST DAY.

Hardly an auspicious start, but eerily prescient for my future. "Instrument" baby, born too early in the morning for my own good (on a sleep-late Saturday no less), and the ominous incongruity of snow in the summer. In the often-repeated words of my mother, the former Mary Giovingo, "That damned Russian horse doctor scarred me for life." And me, too, mom. The "horse doctor" was all that my father, Matthew Cancelose, could afford.

As it was, the twenty-two-year-old couple, married only a year, was still living with his parents in an upstairs bedroom in an undistinguished wooden house on Longwood Street, soon to be covered with an unsightly brown asphalt tile.

Why on earth bring a child into the world under such conditions? Well, we can blame the Catholic church. It seems the only birth-control options Rome allowed were abstinence or the rhythm method, popularized by a Catholic Chicago doctor named Leo Latz. He advised avoiding intercourse for eight days, beginning five days before ovulation. His book sold more than 200,000 copies by 1942. Although the church was ambivalent about the morality of the technique, parishes were not above distributing instructional pamphlets as prizes at church-basement bingo games.

In my case, it didn't work. Either someone miscalculated or in my preferred imagined scenario, my father, a light drinker, had a little more than he could handle at the annual extended family Christmas party nine months earlier. That debauchery led to an off-schedule and uncharacteristically amorous evening when they got home from the festivities. So, no two ways about it—I was a mistake.

Ignatius Norman Cancelose. Talk about mistakes. What kind of name is that? Ignatius, because they were obliged to pay homage to my paternal grandfather. Okay, it's hideous, I know, but it makes sense, though the name was never once uttered in the family or anywhere else, even by my grandfather, Ignazio. (How much nicer it sounds in Italian.) In fact, I didn't know it was my name until I was five years old. But Norman? What Sicilian calls a son, Norman? How romantic if only I had been named after the very worldly and multiculture-loving Norman kings who ruled Sicily from 1071 to 1194, but I doubt my parents, both born in Rockford, had a clue about Sicily's remarkably colorful history. And Cancelose? Don't even start! The labyrinthine explanations for the various surnames and their myriad spellings will be revealed in due course. As Mary Giovingo would have said, "Hold your horses. I'll get to it when I'm good and ready and not until then."

All three of us are now in the upstairs bedroom on Longwood Street. With the lack of privacy, my parents probably dispensed with the rhythm method entirely and went whole-hog Christian abstinence for the next two years. Most people are incredulous when I describe vivid memories from those two years, but it's their own tough luck that they can't recall a thing from their early childhoods.

I'm puzzled that my strongest memory is of the five of us having breakfast in the kitchen. Not only have I always hated mornings, but also have I had a life-long antipathy toward breakfast, a meal seemingly designed to cause a queasy stomach for the rest of the day. Once I began school, I reluctantly consented to a glass of fresh-squeezed orange juice and a vitamin capsule. Occasionally, my mother would coax me into an eggnog made with the ultra-rich Golden Guernsey milk, delivered in glass bottles by our milkman, to fatten up my scrawny frame. Yet there I was, seated in my high chair, pounding my tiny fists on the feeding tray and demanding that I be served the same thing as my grandfather, Ignazio, who soaked chunks of crusty Italian bread in a bowl of *caffe latte.* How my parents permitted me this indulgence at such an early age is a mystery. Although I'm sure I enjoyed the soggy bread at the time (mostly because I was emulating adults—a questionable habit begun almost at birth), I was inoculated against any craving for coffee for the rest of my life.

My other vivid memory was incessantly asking my mother in the middle of the night to retrieve my little pillow (she pronounced it, "piddle"), which had slipped to the floor as I kept turning it over to find the cool side. I always slept on my stomach, hugging my piddle to my body. The science showing that infants should sleep on their backs had probably not yet developed—alas, even in sleep, I was always on the wrong side.

Never mind the wrong side, I was in the wrong town. Rockford was a conservative, industrial city that no one ever heard of—the second largest city in the state at that time—ninety miles northwest of Chicago, but light-years distant in attitude. What on earth were Sicilians doing in a place like this—dreary and run mostly by intolerant and ultra-religious Swedes who first came to Rockford in 1852. That year, the Reverend Erland Carlson, pastor of the Immanuel Lutheran Church of Chicago, suggested that recent Swedish immigrants "take the train as far west as it went." At the time, the end of the line was Rockford. To me, it was still the end of the line. Initially they came to farm the land before they elevated themselves to factory owners by the turn of the century.

Ignazio Cangialosi was born in Partinico, Sicily, a town nineteen miles southwest of Palermo. in 1881. Francesca Spera was born in Belmonte Mezzagno, Sicily, almost directly south of Palermo in 1886. Although they were second cousins, they married in 1905, a not unusual arrangement in that era. To my eye, it never resulted in any bizarre physical deformities in their progeny. How they got to know each other is unfathomable, considering the formidable distance between the two towns, either probably reachable only by mule cart at the turn of the century. I visited Belmonte Mezzagno in 2012, and the hour-long, four-mile bus trip from Palermo is a punishing swirl of hairpin curves up a steep mountain. The only plausible explanation: family members must have arranged the marriage. Belmonte is a small, dusty town that probably never saw a prime, but if it had, was certainly well past it.

The couple moved to Palermo immediately after marriage. Francesca was in heaven. The beauty and excitement of the city after her circumscribed existence in Belmonte was euphoric. In their small apartment, she seized on the luxury of not having to cook dinner every day. No need even to leave her apartment. Street vendors peddled toothsome, prepared dishes that could be hoisted up to her balcony in small baskets attached to pulleys. She would send the payment down the same way.

Ignazio found work as a clerk in a *farmacia*. This was certainly a step up from his small-farm existence outside Partinico. He now wore a white shirt and starched collar to work. Within a year, their first child, Gaetano, was born. Strolling through Palermo's luxuriant parks with her newborn son and shopping in the bounteous outdoor food markets and the *pasticcerie* with their inviting baroque-decorated pastries, Francesca had never known such happiness. Sadly, it was not to last.

Ignazio, a slight man of five-foot-three inches, took a dislike to his boss, the *farmacista*. "No matter what I do for him, he's never satisfied," he complained to Francesca, who cautioned him that all bosses were probably like that. They were now in the best position of anyone in their families, and she begged him to overlook any indignities until he found a better job, something she knew was unlikely given the severe scarcity of employment in the city.

Always a very hardworking man, Ignazio was essentially quiet and mild-mannered, but like most of the men in our family, he could be fiercely stubborn when he believed he was in the right. A few months later, after suffering one too many disparagements from the *farmacista*, he uncharacteristically let loose a barrage of Sicilian expletives and quit on the spot.

When the distraught Francesca asked what they would do now, he said, "We'll emigrate to Argentina." "Argentina, why would we go there?" "Because there's plenty of work and the pay is good.." "Who do we know in Argentina?" "No one," he admitted, "but a lot of Sicilians are moving there, and they are very welcome by the government. We'll make friends." Francesca was completely unnerved by the idea of leaving her beloved Palermo, and Argentina was simply out of the question.

"Why not America? At least I have brothers there? They can help us get started," she countered. She put her foot down. America it was. They sailed on a new ship, the SS Re d'Italia, with $50 and the year-old Gaetano in tow. Not one of them had ever been on a boat, much less at sea. The trip was grueling, with 1,900 frightened dirt-poor passengers tightly packed in third class. Ignazio and Francesca were both sick when they hit rough seas.

On June 27, 1907, they arrived at Ellis Island in New York. Francesca's brother, Tony, who lived in New York at the time, was supposed to meet them. They called "Tony, Tony" up and down the platforms, but he was nowhere to be found. Confused and not knowing what to do, they decided to take the train to Rockford, where her brother Benny was living. They stayed with him until they found a place of their own in South Rockford, the ghetto for Italian immigrants.

At the time, Rocford was a haven for manufacturing in the furniture, textile, and machine-tool industries. Ignazio found a job quickly. Francesca packed a lunch and sent him off for his first day. As evening approached, a soot-covered apparition came to her screen door. Afraid of strangers, she asked crossly, "Who are you? What do you want?"

"*Sei pazza?* (Are you crazy?) *Apri la porta subito! Sono io.*" (Open the door now! It's me.) It was Ignazio returned from his first day in a factory foundry. Stunned, she got his clothes off and shoved him into the bathtub. Then she collapsed in a paroxysm of sobs. "Is this why we came to America, so you can look like a chimney sweep? In Palermo, it was white shirts and ties. You were refined. Now look at you."

It took many months for her to acclimate herself to this strange new life, but eventually she found her groove. Many new friends were made among the Italian expatriates. In 1908, her second son, Paul, was born, followed by a daughter, Jennie, in 1910, and after several still births, finally my father, Matt, in 1920. She had at last assumed the role she was destined to play—matriarch, the queen of the family. She was addressed by everyone outside her family as *Donna Ciccia* (pronounced chee-cha), a nickname for Francesca. The emphasis was always on the "*Donna*," a woman of consequence.

My grandfather secured a long-term job at the Roper Stove Company, after it opened in 1919. When I was born, my father was employed in a newly formed tool-and-dye company, Nylint Tool and Manufacturing, which made anti-aircraft magazines and torpedo components for the war effort. With both men gone at work, my days during my first years of life were spent under the care of my *Nonna* (my grandmother), my mother, and my Aunt Jennie. I was fawned over and plied with many of the colorful words of the Sicilian dialect, which I absorbed, though curiously I never learned to speak the language, perhaps because my parents, scarred by discrimination, preferred that I learn good English. I had a predilection for neologisms: My *Nonna's* stool with its fold-away steps became an uppity-down, and her scrumptious potato croquettes became teddy bears. I had inherited my father's childhood teddy bear, and the browned breadcrumb coating on the croquettes appeared so much like the now ratty and worn brown nap of my beloved stuffed animal. As a result, everyone in our family adopted my invented terms.

As for playmates, there were none. In fact, I can't recall a single child with whom I had any extended contact until I started kindergarten. The result: I was a miniature adult from the beginning. I don't think I understood or even tolerated children at all. I was comfortable with grownups, enjoyed hearing their concerns and the stories they told. Oh, there were the occasional unruly children of distant cousins who would visit my grandparents' house, much to the consternation of my *Nonna*, one of which in later life turned out to be a child molester.

My mother made certain I was not assigned to the same undesirable category as these diminutive savages, who ran rampantly through every room of the house. She had no intention of enduring the raised eyebrows or snide remarks about parents who were negligent in disciplining their children. No, there I was seated snugly next to her on the sofa, wearing my immaculately clean white-and-baby-blue knit romper, my tiny feet in little white socks and little white lace-up, soft-soled shoes, dangling off the edge of the couch. If I so much as adjusted my position, I'd hear very definitely, but unobtrusively, through clenched teeth, "You make one move from here, and I'll break your neck."

Not that she was in any way an abusive mother. In fact, she was intrinsically kind and self-sacrificing. She rarely if ever spanked me in an age where "spare the rod and spoil the child" was gospel. It was all words, but her words and her warnings were inviolable, and that was that. She always believed that my father's clan saw her family as less-desirable stock, so she had much to prove. Her reward came from the other relatives: "Look at Norman, he's such a good little boy." "Nothing like the others." " He listens and talks just like a little grownup." My *Nonna* was equally proud to hear these encomiums. Thus I was robbed of a childhood so adults could gain esteem.

These gatherings were not all grim, restrictive affairs for me, however. My grandfather would surreptitiously provide me with a tiny cordial glass of sweet vermouth or anisette, which I loved—not with my mother's approval, of course. As with the coffee drinking, having been allowed small tastes of alcohol at an early age immunized me against the obsessive binge drinking that so many teenagers feel compelled to experience. I even recall glasses of Mogen David wine at Christmas. Mogen David? In an Italian family? That's absurd. This was a concession to those who couldn't stomach the "sour tasting" dry wine my grandfather made in the basement.

In 1944, at age two, everything changed. My father received his orders to report for basic training in Oscoda, Michigan. The war was raging. My *Nonna* and my mother reacted with teary outbursts in their fear for Matt's life. The whole family displayed the typical Sicilian derision for conscription and for the military in general. An old Sicilian proverb states: "It's better to be a pig than a soldier." Sicilian families would resort to all sorts of subterfuges to avoid having their sons drafted into the Italian armed services, including dressing them up as girls (god forbid) or having them disappear into the sparsely populated interior of the island, where they often became brigands. But no, Matt went willingly, or more likely begrudgingly, to war.

My mother determined at this point that we should move back to her family home in South Rockford. She took a job as a sales clerk at Mangel's, a small but fashionable women's clothing shop in downtown Rockford, which was almost exactly midway between my two grandmothers' homes. Off we went to the brick bungalow on South Central Avenue. My grandfather, Tony Giovingo, kept a substantial garden in the back of the house where he grew asparagus, peppers, strawberries, raspberries, and *cucuzza*, the obscenely long, pale-green, somewhat sweet-tasting squash that Sicilians love so much. There were also several fruit trees: sour-cherry, sweet golden plums, and seckel pears. The fresh-picked fruit and vegetables were manna, and the yard allowed me more room for outdoor activities, though I can't recall actual play and certainly no playmates, just like on Longwood Street.

Tony immigrated from Sambuca, Sicily, close to the island's south coast. The Palermo side of the family saw Sambuca as somehow vastly inferior to the more refined northern coast of the island. Tony first worked in the coal mines around La Salle, Illinois, before moving to Rockford. He married my grandmother Rose, whose maiden name was also Giovingo, though they were not related.

Rose Giovingo was born on a remote farm near Baton Rouge, Louisiana. She never attended school, was illiterate, and much to my embarrassment as I grew older, spoke English worse than any of my other grandparents, who were all born in Sicily. This was always a great mystery to me. My mother explained that their farm had little or no contact with other Americans, so she only ever heard the Sicilian dialect spoken. Her parents had recently immigrated from Sicily, but no one ever discussed when or from where. Poor Rose was singled out in childhood to be the homemaker or, more likely, house slave to her parents and several siblings. She did the washing in an old galvanized tub, all the cleaning of what was certainly a little farm shack, much of the cooking, and took care of her

7

younger siblings. I detected rumors that she had been sexually abused by her father, whom she despised. When or why she and her brothers and sisters moved to Rockford, I never learned.

When my mother and I moved in with them, Rose was employed in one of Rockford's hosiery factories, as was her daughter, my aunt Lena, who was six years younger than my mother. Lena was the wild daughter who had always been given more freedom, which generated a poisoning resentment in my mother she was my never able to conquer. Lena ran around with men, wearing provocative dresses and Kelly-green platform shoes, her hair piled high in typical 1940s fashion. My grandfather held a factory job, although he did some freelance barbering at home for friends and relatives. He once shaved my mother's head bald when she was a little girl, in the mistaken belief that her hair would grow in stronger. In an old photograph of her at that time, she could easily have been the poster child for a pathetic and destitute little refugee.

With everyone working, where was I to spend my days? My mother, who never learned to drive, found the solution. Every morning she took me by bus across town to my grandmother Francesca's, getting back on the bus to go to her downtown job, returning to Longwood Street to pick me up after work, and once again taking me back on the bus to the Giovingo's. I was to learn the horror of this scheme on the first day, when I had to get up at six AM to allow for the forty-minute bus trip to the other side of town. Will no one ever let me sleep in the mornings when I most need it? My mother had no easy task getting me up at that hour every weekday morning. She resorted to bribery. If I would get up, she offered to buy me Twinkies or devil's food cream sandwiches (an earlier version of Hostess Suzy-Q's) from the corner store, while we waited at the bus stop. Contrary to the pattern of inoculation against coffee and alcohol, this unhealthy habit was not stemmed by it's early-in-life introduction. Rather, it solidified my already ravenous addiction to sweets and pastries, though I acquired a taste for higher-quality goods as I aged. Now if I want Twinkies, I make them myself from the finest ingredients. Mary Giovingo certainly gained no marks of distinction in the official ledger of exemplary parenting for such a ruse.

A few weeks after we began this routine, my mother realized just how hard this was on her. One day she decided to leave me at a daycare center run by nuns near her parents' house. She hadn't prepared me for this abrupt change until that morning. Extreme turbulence best describes my reaction as we entered the center. Here were evil-looking women wearing rimless glasses, dressed in black, with sinister, anachronistic wimples on their heads. They appeared a coven of witches to me, hovering over a pack of screaming wild-eyed children. I began to cry immediately and begged my mother not to leave me there. I knew I'd never survive such an environment. She also was in tears as the nuns convinced her to go. They would handle me, they promised. Trust me, they wouldn't and they couldn't. I carried on to such a degree that they called my mother at work and told her to pick me up on her lunch break. That was my first and last encounter with the nursery-school crowd and the terrifying nuns.

So it was back to the comfortable and familiar days with my *Nonna*. One day she needed to do some shopping downtown. I was already enthralled with city downtowns, despite the fact that Rockford's was is no way designed to make anyone's heartbeat race. We boarded the bus and sat across from a large African-American woman. I began to stare rudely, never having seen a black person before. *Nonna* tried in vain to distract me with everything in her arsenal. Undaunted and wide-eyed, I continued staring, and finally blurted out full-voiced to my grandmother, "Doesn't that woman ever wash herself?" My *Nonna* wanted to crawl under the seat. The black woman got up angrily and said, "You should teach that child some manners, woman!" The memory of this incident still causes me extreme mortification.

One Friday evening, to save an extra trip, my mother decided to spend the night at *Nonna's* rather than take me back to the Giovingo's, because she had been asked to work on Saturday. Several of the relatives came over to play penny-ante cards, and I discovered how words could frighten. Losing consistently, mother said, "I'm going in the hole." I interpreted this to mean that someone was going to bury her alive. That same night I asked her why she wouldn't stay home from work on Saturday. "They'll fire me if I do." I grabbed on to her and began crying, assuming that this meant she would be roasted whole over a roaring flame.

Across a driveway from the house on Longwood Street was a redbrick four-family apartment building on the corner of State Street (Rockford's main drag). On both the front and backsides, the building had porches extending most of the width of its two floors. On the front side, each apartment had a wooden swing for three, hung from thick metal chains. There were only two slivers of yard, each encircled by thorny shrubbery and separated by a pair of stone steps leading to the first-floor entrance. My grandparents bought this building, along with their house, at the end of the Great Depression with the plan that one apartment would be given to each of their four children. In this way, my *Nonna* could reign supreme over her family. During the war, three of the apartments were occupied by her offspring: Uncle Paul and his wife, Rose, on the corner of the first floor; Aunt Jennie, her husband, Andy Scianna, and their daughter, Jo, on the other first-floor apartment; Gaetano, who had changed his name to Tom, his Brunhilde of a German wife, Ruby, who towered over him by at least five inches, and their four children on the second floor. The corner upper-floor apartment was being rented out, though kept in reserve for my father when he returned from the war.

Uncle Paul unexpectedly was seized with the spirit of entrepreneurship. He wanted to turn his apartment's dining and living rooms into an Italian restaurant. There was only one other in town and that was on the opposite side of the Rock River that separated the east from the west side. He convinced my grandparents to do the cooking; my mother, my aunt Jennie, and my cousin Jo to be waitresses, while he and Rose would "manage" the eatery. The menu was limited to spaghetti and meatballs, plus a couple other Italian specialties. A red neon sign was hung in the front window on State Street, and The Cancelose Spaghetti House was in business. No one left his or her day job because the restaurant served only from six-thirty to nine PM.

What did my family know about the food business? Actually, quite a lot. My grandparents had opened a small vegetable store in South Rockford before the Depression, with the idea of building a family enterprise in which each of their four children could work, establishing careers for themselves, under the supervision of my *Nonna*. Ignazio, my *Nonno*, would take over when he returned from the day's work at the Roper Stove company. The business was moderately successful, but the three sons, who were very Americanized, turned up their noses at the idea of being Italian shopkeepers. It seemed so old country to them. They preferred to work in factories, much to my *Nonna's* chagrin. Talk about a distorted sense of what endows prestige. Without her boys' commitment and only her daughter, Jennie, to help, the shop became too difficult to manage, and it closed.

More significant was my grandparents' experience in the kitchen. They were both excellent cooks. They had a secondary income cooking for many of the Italian weddings in Rockford. In fact, they cooked the entire wedding dinner for 150 people in the church basement when my parents married.

So here they were back in the kitchen at the Spaghetti House. Almost from the inception, it was an enormous success. In mild weather, diners waited in lines on the front porch and many had to be turned away. It was particularly popular with the Swedes, who had tasted nothing like it. Some apparently had more on their minds than Italian cuisine. One lone male diner made an untoward request of my mother. "After dinner, I'd like you to arrange for me to go across the driveway." "Across the driveway?" "Yes, I saw the red light in the window next door, and I'd like to use that service." Mary Giovingo, a virtual saint of Catholic morality, was frozen speechless. She ran to my grandmother in the kitchen and quite out of character began giving orders to her. "You go next door this minute and get that candle out of the window now. Do you know what one of the diners thought that was?" My *Nonna*, religiously kept a votive candle in a clear red glass in a bedroom window. How would our family ever live this down?

Everyone worked so hard in the restaurant, except for Rose and Paul who enjoyed playing the grand hosts and especially relished collecting the money. Other family members, and particularly my mother, suspected that they also hoarded the tips, which were supposed to be shared equally, though no one ever confronted them about it.

And what did Mary Giovingo do with her little Norman while she was busy waitressing and washing dishes? It goes without saying that she put him in the closet in one of the bedrooms. The sad fact is, I quite literally grew up in the closet. Well, at least it was a walk-in closet. Mary placed a thick quilt on the floor, along with my little "piddle," where I could sleep and be out of everyone's way. In true humanitarian spirit, she left the door open so I could breathe.

Those hours of the evening could hardly be deemed my sleeping time (even though I'd been cruelly deprived of my coveted morning slumber). So I wandered around the restaurant, sometimes talking to diners (many claimed they were delighted with me, that I was a little charmer, and Mary Giovingo was gullible enough to swallow that line whole), other times making a nuisance of myself in the kitchen. Truth be told, I was an annoying little brat. Mostly, I had to be coaxed back into my closet like some recalcitrant puppy remanded to the doghouse.

When I think back at the enormous potential for this restaurant and how it was so easily squandered, I become apoplectic. To say that Rose and Paul were not easy to get along with would be a gross understatement. My grandparents came to the end of their rope with their incessant arguing, which often seeped out from the kitchen embarrassingly into the dining rooms. In a fit of pique, they threw up their hands and refused to cook any longer.

Rose took over the kitchen. It would be generous to call her culinary skills unspeakable. Overdoses of cinnamon (what was she, a Greek?) and needless quantities of sugar were added to the tomato sauce, which was now hastily concocted with inferior ingredients. The onions were chopped much too coarsely and the garlic burnt, making the *salsa pomodoro* an insult to the nose and an assault to the taste buds. The crowds quickly dwindled away and the Cancelose Spaghetti House shuttered within a few months.

Despite all the disagreements, my grandparents did everything they could to smooth over bruised feelings among all those who had worked with Rose and Paul at the Spaghetti House. In fact they spent much of the rest of their lives mending fences for anyone who had run-ins with the irascible couple, just to maintain peace in the family.

What could have produced this incongruously contentious pair in an otherwise congenial family? Uncle Paul was an embittered and cranky man whose speech resembled a guttural growl. Everyone described him as always having a *fungia*, a sourpuss. At family gatherings, he would sit silently, his elbow resting on the arm of the chair, his right index finger against the side of his nose, and his thumb hooked under his chin. Before long, you would hear the same snarling phrase directed to his wife: "*Ma* (but or why in Italian), when we goin' home?" Rose's high-pitched shrieking reply was always the same, "When I feel like it. I'm having a good time." The fights between them were practically nonstop. There was a several-octave span between his basso-pitched snorts and her ear-piercing screeching, which projected all over the neighborhood. They were not very affectionately known among the family as the dog and the cat.

"I'm telling you, my Paul was never like that when he was young. Not until he married Rose," Nonna reassured us, or at least herself. Once, the young Paul caught his younger sister, Jennie, playing with Rose, whose family lived several blocks away in the Italian ghetto. He gave her a spanking that she never forgot. "I don't ever want to see you with her again. That family is bad, rotten—all of them. Stay away from them!" Rose's relatives were known to be forever squabbling and fighting amongst themselves, cheating each other and everyone else at cards and out of money. Guns and knives were sometimes drawn. Several of Rose's brothers had already served jail time.

It's hard to imagine the shock his mother received when a few years later Paul abruptly announced that he was going to marry Rose. No one understood the reason. Everyone begged and pleaded with him not to make such a disastrous mistake, to no avail. The reason revealed itself a few months later when Rose discreetly disappeared to Chicago to consult a physician. She returned, claiming the "problem" had been solved. My grandmother, relieved that there need be no shotgun marriage, told her son, "See, there's no reason you have to marry her now. Just back out of it." The Cancelose stubbornness again reared its ugly head. "I said I'd marry her and that's what I'm going to do."

Incompatibility on nearly every level led to hostility between the two from the wedding day on. Though resentment set in quickly, Paul's foolish pride prevented him from acknowledging the extent of his blunder, much less taking the obvious steps to end the marriage. When no children were born (for which the world should be grateful), it became generally known that Rose was barren. Everyone realized that she saw in Paul an opportunity to elevate her social position, so she tricked him into marriage by feigning the pregnancy. Resentment turned to loathing. He took revenge in a myriad of ways: never allowing any of her family into his house; even forbidding her from visiting them, though she did so on the sly; and slinging a shroud of surliness over the smallest happy moment.

Paul took great pride in his job as an inspector of highly specialized textile and milling-machine parts at the Barber Coleman Company. Earning a good salary, he was able to amass an ample savings and still indulge in some showy luxuries: an aquamarine Packard sedan, expensive jewelry, and eventually a prime-neighborhood ranch house, sporting marble fireplaces and one Philippine mahogany wall, that had been owned by the city's foremost dealer in tombstones. Rose knew she couldn't hope to replicate their lifestyle were she to leave him. Her intelligence clearly did not permit her to excel beyond the dry-cleaner clerk that she remained throughout her work life.

In his late fifties, Paul developed early-onset Alzheimer's, which forced a premature retirement from his beloved job. He had one final and ironic revenge against Rose.

"Who the hell are you?" he'd ask her almost every day.

"Who am I? You know perfectly well who I am. I'm your wife, Rose," she shrieked in exasperation.

"You're not my wife. You're just some whore from Chicago."

This would send her into a screaming rage. It did appear almost willful on his part, since he recognized everyone else in the family.

Family dissension over the Spaghetti House was eclipsed in 1945 when my mother learned that my father was being shipped overseas, first to Hawaii and then who knew? As it turned out he was sent to the front in Okinawa, site of one of the bloodiest battles in the Pacific theater. The fear level among family members became palpable. Even I sensed it from all the whispering, though no one gave me any information. We learned only much later that Matt's arrival on the war-torn island occurred luckily just after the battle had ended on June 22, 1945. The next year he was discharged and returned to Rockford, nearly twenty pounds heavier than when he left. His position as supply sergeant saved him from any combat.

Everyone was so glad to have him safely back home, but not everything went smoothly. There were the usual adjustments from two years of the regimented military life, back to a civilian existence. The Klint family, owners of Nylint, kept his job open for him despite the fact that they had transformed the company from making military equipment to making toys. My father was everlastingly grateful for the favor. Nights were not always peaceful. He often awoke in a sweat, experiencing nightmares over his term in Okinawa. Though he had not seen any major battles, the constant threat of sniper fire, and the grim task of having to dig graves for the thousands of decaying bodies found in caves haunted him deeply.

I was another problem. Until I came along, he had been the family darling. By the time he returned from duty, I had replaced him in that coveted role and resentment and jealousy were inevitable, perhaps, in both of us. I was not instinctively aware of this, but my mother made it clear to me whenever there was a disagreement between my father and me. Also, I was not growing up to be the son he imagined. I was a mama's boy and from infancy, a crybaby to boot. Neighbors came to inquire whether my parents had been beating me, my howling through the night was so ear-shattering. A photo taken just after he returned from his Army Air Corps duty as a noncommissioned sergeant is telling: He's in uniform holding me in his arms, I'm wearing shorts with the famed World War II visored officers' hat carelessly perched on my head. We both look extremely ill at ease.

What my father thought about my incessant singing and dancing, I cannot fathom. I began talking even before I started crawling, and soon I began imitating what I heard on the radio. I had a dismaying penchant for inane popular tunes such as the Andrews Sisters' wartime hit, "Pistol Packin' Mama," which I could deliver pitch-perfectly, correctly pronouncing every word of the lyric, and adding my own inimitable choreography. Strange and embarrassing that I should choose a song based on a country tune, since there is no more loathsome music to me than country and western. I believe my relatives were charmed by my show-off routines because they often demanded that I entertain them. I'm not sure what my father's reaction was. He liked popular music and variety shows so it's possible he was pleased. At this point my childhood memory fails me. I'm certain that someone either made too big an issue of these little floor shows, causing me to be self-conscious or, perhaps, even humiliated me about them because after the age of four I could not have been coerced into singing for them for any reason.

Then there was the vomiting. My parents desperately wanted a standard-issue normal child. I was definitely not accommodating them. My generally nervous disposition manifested itself in nausea. It might be triggered by unfamiliar food or situations, a poorly timed or harsh reprimand, and most bizarrely by the singing of "Happy Birthday." I refused to attend my own birthday parties unless I was assured that the offending song would not be sung.

I've tried to determine what could be so objectionable about this banal little tune to no avail. The effort has engendered wild flights of imagination. Perhaps in a former life I had been a little girl with long blond hair. When the singing stopped and I bent over the cake to blow out the candles, my hair caught on fire and I was burned beyond recognition, karmic retribution for an even earlier reincarnation as an evil child abuser. Was it any wonder my parents were at the end of the their rope with me? My mother dragged me to our family doctor for diagnosis. "Doctor, can you do something for him? Is he really sick?" He told her there was nothing physically wrong with me, that I would probably end up either a genius or a bum. Unhappily, she subscribed to the latter result.

Years later upon leaving a job, my colleagues took me out to a farewell dinner in a nice restaurant. I had told them about my "Happy Birthday" problem as a child. In the middle of dinner, several waiters came over to the table next to ours and began singing the odious tune. My coworkers turned sheet white in fear that I would begin vomiting. I had quite a time assuring them that I had long ago outgrown this absurd quirk. I will admit, however, that though today I can join in singing the song, I still get an unpleasant visceral reaction at the sound of it—generally the hair on the back of my neck stands on end. Go figure.

The money my mother had saved up as a salesclerk and a waitress, went toward the renovation of the apartment my grandparents had reserved for my father. The family that had been renting the place had been "a bunch of pigs," my mother declared. She even had to get an exterminator to fumigate the place. Roaches were something my family had never been exposed to. We moved into the apartment as soon as my father returned from the war. There we were living right above Rose and Paul.

Because of their reduced incomes after the closing of the Spaghetti House, they rented the spare bedroom out to an itinerant, long-haul truck driver named Sammy. It was a convenient arrangement because he was away much of the time. However, on one occasion Paul came home unexpectedly early from work and found Rose in bed with Sammy. Though not prone to violence, he nevertheless beat her mercilessly. *Nonna* begged my father to go downstairs and break up the altercation, which he did reluctantly. This was an unheard of scandal in my family and it had to be hushed up completely. Sammy was exiled and no further borders were ever permitted.

My mother decided that dancing school was just the thing for me. One afternoon just after my fourth birthday, I was taken to this large studio, painted in that noxious institutional pale green that was so prevalent in dentist's offices at the time. Ominously, the repellent room was filled with about twenty-five young children, their mothers proudly doting on their little future *prima ballerinas* and *premier danseurs*.

The teacher, an overly giddy and exuberant older woman, dressed in flowing lavender chiffon announced in her chirpy voice, "Now, children, today we will be airplanes, starting low and flying high into the sky." To demonstrate, she glided ethereally about the room. "We all feel light, light, light." She then indicated the counterclockwise direction of the flight pattern. At this announcement, my left eyebrow arched so high that I felt pain in my forehead. Arms were fully extended out to the sides. Beginning in a slightly crouching position, we began to run.

After the first turn, legs were straightened, and then light, light, light, we began reaching for the stratosphere. I observed the swarm about me as we ran and was reminded more of a flock of small birds of prey rather than graceful aircraft soaring in the clouds. After the third turn around the studio, I abandoned the flight plan, marched determinedly over to my mother who was smiling, so pleased with her Norman, and informed her in no uncertain terms that it was time to leave. She erroneously assumed that I simply hated dancing school when in point of fact my mini-adult self could not abide the idea of running around a room like a silly airplane. How utterly childish, I thought. Foolishly, I never communicated this to her, creating a misunderstanding that would have life-defining implications.

Other Children at Last

HALL SCHOOL WAS HOUSED in a dilapidated old red-brick building. The students were mostly from poor to lower-middle-class families, and the faculty was less than stellar. My first day in kindergarten made my mother cry. She was in the hospital about to give birth to my younger brother, and it pained her that she missed the opportunity of escorting me to school. My Aunt Jennie was enlisted in her stead.

I was at my grandmother's sitting on the toilet, my short pants down around my ankles when I heard *Nonna* yell that I had a baby brother. I was so excited that I ran out of the bathroom without even bothering to hitch up my pants. I wanted all the details. My father could now afford someone better than the "horse doctor." This second birth had gone much easier for my mother. Larry was born September 7, perfectly healthy and happy, no scars, physical or psychological, on either of them this time—and no ominous unseasonal snowstorms.

When Larry came home, we were all back in our apartment. I thought he was so adorable that I could hardly be coaxed to leave the side of his crib. My mother occasionally allowed me to hold him, under her supervision, which I considered a real honor—another chance to play the little adult.

Kindergarten was a traumatic adjustment for me. Never used to being around children, I didn't know how to act and kept to myself as much as possible. The requisite afternoon nap on the little throw rugs that we were required to supply was a challenge. Little did I imagine that as an adult working in offices, I would have killed for such a break in the dull routine. But as a child, this was not my time of day to be tired, so I couldn't be made to understand the enforced rest period.

Cookies-and-milk-time was a far bigger issue. Having to eat in front of strangers engendered great anxiety and often untimely vomiting, which drove the teacher to distraction and caused me untold embarrassment. The only saving grace seemed to be music period, when we sang songs and banged on triangles and tambourines, while marching about the room. My teacher informed my mother that I was uncommonly musical and that she should consider instrumental lessons for me.

My mother had already noticed when we went downstairs to my Aunt Jennie and Uncle Andy's apartment that I was picking out tunes on their daughter Jo's old upright player piano. The piano, an old ebony Clarendon whose cracked surface had developed an alligator-like finish, was made in Rockford. It had been in the family for years, first at my grandmother's, before it was given to Jo. I don't believe any family member other than Jo could play, It was bought because the old piano rolls provided needed entertainment in my *Nonna's* house. We had boxes upon boxes of the rolls, some of which were so old that the hooks to connect them to the rollers had torn and were reinforced by various makeshift devices. Grandmother's favorite was "Yes, We Have No Bananas." I delighted in pumping the pedals so we could sing along with the tune.

Piano lessons seemed to be in order for me. The Clarendon was moved to our upstairs apartment, and off we went to Leola Arnold's studio. Miss Arnold was a skinny, pinched-nosed spinster with rimless glasses. She may have been a good teacher, but clearly she was wrong for me. She despised popular music and scoffed at the idea of teaching me any of the songs I loved hearing on the radio, music that might have induced me to practice. Curiously, I don't recall ever being introduced to a single piece of serious classical music either. She relied exclusively on those dreary piano-teaching method books that seemed designed to snuff out anyone's love of music. Filled with mind-numbing exercises for finger, pedal, and note reading, the books avoided offering even the semblance of a pleasing musical phrase, and what's worse failed to help realize their own stated goal of developing technique.

Who on earth wrote these things? I can only imagine that thousands of children were needlessly turned off to music because of them. Miss Arnold came armed with all the accoutrements of the truly uninspired, including bright red-orange lesson-assignment volumes that complemented the method books. In these she would vehemently scribble the pages I was to study for the next lesson, always followed by the threatening phrase, "READ AND HEED." I can't recall an instance that I enjoyed in my few years of lessons with her.

I often asked my mother if I could quit, but she had no tolerance for people who veered from one interest to another and was therefore adamant that I continue. She often sat with me at the piano because I had an aversion to practicing any of the assignments and made only minimal progress. Once I nearly succeeded in quitting, but Miss Arnold told my mother she was moving to a wonderful new two-story studio with a balcony overlooking the two grand pianos. She was confident that I'd be inspired by the new setting, and begged mother to let me continue for another year. Mary Giovingo relented, much to my disappointment. Though I was vaguely intrigued by the studio's architecture, I made certain it was my last year with Leola.

Miss Arnold made homemade soups, which she canned in large Mason jars, in those spare hours when she wasn't engaged in stifling all musical instincts. She would often proudly present my mother with a jar, for which she was profusely thanked. I was startled the first time we brought one of these home and she immediately dumped it down the toilet. "Why did you do that?" "How do I know whether she's even clean? And god knows what she may put into that slop?" Mary Giovingo had a mania for cleanliness, and even my brother's prospective brides, were given a thumbs-down because she suspected the worst. One of her favorite expressions was, "A little soap and water never hurt anyone."

If on any Saturday afternoon during winter, I crossed the driveway to *Nonna's* house, I could be sure to find my grandfather, Ignazio, with his ear pressed against an old Zenith radio, listening to the Metropolitan Opera broadcast. It might well be Bidú Sayao and Ferruccio Tagliavini starring in *La Boheme* or any other of the Italian operas he adored. He'd plead with me to sit with him and listen to the music of his country, which I was certain he deeply missed. No doubt the opera was a heartwarming escape from his tediously stultifying job at the Roper Stove Company. I sensed his disappointment as I'd squirm about, unable to sit through much of the performance, even though I was struck by the beauty of the voices and the glorious melodies of Puccini and Bellini. The fact that the broadcast was coming directly from New York interested me more than the opera, with which I had little patience. If I could have seen into the future, I would have been more attentive.

Our extended family huddled around my grandparents' radio, however, on Tuesday nights to listen to "Life with Luigi," a series about an Italian immigrant in Chicago named Luigi Bosco. We howled at his mangling of the English language. On one show, Luigi approaches an information desk in a department store and says, " I wanna speaka to da manager." The attendant points and says, "Escalator." " Ma, I no wanna aska later, I wanna aska now." Although today any ethnic group would take great offense at such humor at its expense, the thought never occurred to us.

After my first year at Hall School, the school board approached my mother about a transfer to Jackson School because Hall was overcrowded. We lived on the border of the two school districts, and Jackson's began across the street from us. Seeing this as an excellent opportunity for me, she quickly consented. The transfer played a significant role in the quality of my education and in the development of my social skills because the school was staffed by excellent teachers and the student body came from somewhat more affluent and better-educated families.

I was nervous about the change, and I insisted that my mother speak to my first-grade teacher, Miss Wonser, on the first day of school about my food-eating phobia, and inform her that I must be excused from the ritual. I dreaded the thought of throwing up in front of a whole new group of kids. I began to tremble on the first day when cookies-and-milk time came. Miss Wonser said, "Norman, I want you to come with me." She took me by the hand out of the classroom and closed the door. In the hallway two chairs had been placed. "Do you like graham crackers and milk?" "Yes, I do." "Well, the two of us are going to sit out here and just talk while we eat some together. Does that sound okay?" Though the idea scared me, I nodded in consent. Miraculously, I made it through several crackers without a hint of nausea. I was nearly, though not completely, cured, and both my mother and I were eternally grateful to her.

In an age where kidnapping and sexual predators with a taste for children were not on anyone's radar, I was allowed to walk the eight blocks to school by myself. Dogs seemed to be the only threat. A large Irish Setter, a Dalmatian, and a German Shepherd barked, menaced, and chased me. They sensed my helpless fear as I passed them, and it emboldened their ferocity. When I told my mother I was scared, her advice was to pray hard to the Virgin Mary and she would certainly protect me. A few days later as I approached the German Shepherd's abode, I begged the Virgin Mary to keep the snarling beast at bay. I crossed to the other side of the street hoping to avoid him, but the dog began following me. Foolishly, I started to run, and he took off after me and bit me on the back of my calf. Though the wound was not serious, I had to endure a painful rabies injection. Clearly, I was not the Virgin Mary's sort of boy. I needed to find a different saint.

I excelled at school work from the beginning. Because I had a mortal fear of making mistakes, I had my mother check every homework assignment before turning it in. This lasted until about the third grade when it became obvious that I had gone beyond what either of my parents could help me with. I was on my own now.

I began making friends with children my own age. A classmate named Ritchie invited me to spend a Saturday afternoon at his house. In his bedroom were two handheld chalk boards, and we spent much of the day happily scribbling and drawing on them, though I had no flair for drawing whatsoever. What possessed me I can't imagine, but for some unfathomable reason I drew a full-frontal male nude with the correct anatomical attributes. Carelessly, I failed to wipe clean the slate before I left for home. That evening my mother got a call from Ritchie's mother, accusing me of subjecting her son to filthy pornography. I was mortified when I realized what a faux pas I had made. I was never invited to Ritchie's house again.

There were the three Swedish Terrys in my life: Terry A., Terry B., and Terry C. Terry B. for Bryan became my closest friend through childhood. Terry A. for Anderson would play a larger and unexpected role later in my life; and Terry C. for Carlson, whom I met in high school, played a role far greater in my imagination than in reality.

Terry Bryan was a stocky but bright boy. In his basement, we planned glorious trips to the West on the great Streamliner trains of the 1940s and '50s. Neither of us had traveled any farther than Wisconsin. We were engrossed in railroad calendars, train schedules, and brochures depicting the national parks. The spectacular panoramic views we might witness from the domed passenger cars kept us mesmerized for years. We conspired to find ways to convince our parents that our families should take these trips together, with the hope that by the time we were in high school they would allow us to travel by ourselves. Never happened. There were two small problems with our fathers: lack of money (Terry's father was a postman) and an even deeper lack of interest on their part. Dad did, however, buy me a model Union Pacific train set one Christmas.

In fifth grade, we both took a passionate interest in the astronomy section of our science textbooks. Terry B. had a small, but powerful, hand-held telescope. We formed an astronomy club with three other boys from our class, including Terry Anderson, and on clear nights we would scan the skies for the wondrous sights. We had all memorized the names of the planets in our solar system in order, beginning with Mercury, the closest to the sun and working outward, so sighting one of them caused great exhilaration. The apex of our astronomical pursuits came when the club took a trip with our parents to the Yerkes Observatory in Williams Bay, Wisconsin, about sixty miles from Rockford. Naively, we thought the tour would include a peek through the great telescope. We were left sadly disappointed. Not one of us ended up in astrophysics, but Terry B. did become a meteorologist, and Terry A. a chemist.

I even joined the Cub Scouts and Mary Giovingo became our den mother. I enjoyed wearing the dark blue and chrome-yellow uniforms and had a good time in the meetings with the other boys. Cory was the new friend that I made through scouting, and our mothers also became close friends. Was I at last becoming a normal boy? Not a chance. One bizarre scout gathering held at school required that I wear a grass-skirt and perform a hula dance. My father brought the skirt back from Honolulu, along with a crocheted bra-type top, which I also wore. From Okinawa he brought a silk kimono. Did he really expect Mary Giovingo to parade before him in these duds? Given her hyper-modest personality, the very notion is ludicrous. One Halloween my mother costumed me in one of her below-the-calf 1930's dresses and a hat with a veil. I remember her applying my makeup, bright red rouge and lipstick. What was she trying to accomplish? Never into drag, I was extremely uncomfortable and self-conscious at both occurrences.

Good storytelling riveted my attention from my earliest years, whether a yarn about our family, a schoolmate, or one told in a theater. I loved being taken to the movies. Sitting in those darkened cavernous palaces with hundreds of other wide-eyed voyeurs brought me ineffable pleasure. I was so deeply immersed in the lives of those beautiful people in beautiful settings on the huge screens that I felt a part of them. These scenes took me far away from Rockford. The more serious the drama, the better I liked it.

My father, in contrast, could not bear to sit through a dramatic film. Though he and my mother dated for four years prior to their marriage, the only movies he would take her to were silly comedies, Laurel and Hardy or Abbott and Costello films, which she hated. So mother took me alone. "I like a good story," she would say. *Laura, Gone With the Wind,* and *Leave Her to Heaven* were some of the films that left lasting impressions—not exactly the sort of fare little boys usually like.

If handsome movie stars, such as Robert Taylor, Gregory Peck, or Cornel Wilde, took off their shirts, I would suddenly get the strangest feeling in the pit of my stomach. I crossed my legs, with my left foot hooked behind my right calf, and became very fidgety, feeling there was something taboo about my mother watching this. The first time it happened, I turned to her and complained, "I have sand in my shoe." "How could you have sand in your shoe? There's no sand here?" "I don't know how. Just look in my shoe." She took my shoe off and of course found nothing. She then noticed how tightly my legs were entwined. "Your foot just fell asleep. Uncross your legs and move them around a bit, and it will go away." I dared not mention the naked torsos.

It wasn't just the moving pictures that intrigued me but also radio plays. My enforced weeknight bedtime was nine PM, ludicrously early to my taste. At age six, I negotiated with my mother that on Monday nights I could stay up until ten. *The Lux Radio Theatre,* which presented live one-hour performances of Broadway plays and Hollywood films, often using the original stars, before a studio audience, was not to be missed under any circumstances. I was required to get into bed to listen to the broadcasts so that I might fall asleep instantly when the program was over. Fat chance. Picturing the scenes of these scripts in my mind made them more compelling than seeing them on the big screen. Often I spent hours replaying favorite moments in my imagination, before I could get to sleep.

Knowing how much I loved the movies, Uncle Andy, Aunt Jennie, and Cousin Jo, always invited me to join them. One Friday night when I was six years old, we were driving home from a film and Jennie suddenly screamed, "Oh my god, look out." An instant later we were hit head-on by a speeding drunk driver. My breath was completely knocked out of me. My cousin and I were wedged in between the front and back seats. I started wailing melodramatically, "I'm dying. I'm dying." Jo, who couldn't see anything because she had lost her glasses, said, "You're not dying. You're okay." Well, not exactly okay, because I began throwing up. I was not yet completely cured.

The car, which looked like a folded-up accordion, was totally de-molished and was hanging precipitously on the edge of a ten-foot-high embankment over the Sinnissippi Park Lagoon, a duck pond that was also a popular ice-skating rink in the winter. An ambulance soon arrived, and we were freed from the wreckage and taken to St, Anthony's Hospital. Amazingly, there were no serious injuries. My aunt and uncle, who bore the brunt of the impact, required some stitches in their heads, nothing more. The nurses found Jo's glasses in her mother's hair. She and I were treated for some minor cuts and bruises. I have always believed that this accident permanently knocked any love for driving and automobiles out of me.

Andy, Jennie, and Jo were by far my favorites among all my relatives. They helped me overcome the next level in my food-phobia saga, eating in restaurants. Because my parents were relatively poor, eating out was mostly for special occasions. Until I was six, we never dined out, not be-cause I was unruly in restaurants—god forbid—but because I threw up. My mother got a break from daily cooking only through carry-out foods: the Coney Island Hot Dog, made by Greeks, with a special hot chili sauce and the Maid-Rite, a popular Midwestern franchise that offered sand-

wiches of braised ground beef cooked in stock and herbs and served on a
soft bun with pickles and ketchup. I relished both of these foods, and later
made my own version of the Maid-Rite.

One Saturday night when my parents attended a wedding in
Chicago, I stayed at Jennie and Andy's. It was rare that they ever went
anywhere without me, and I hated when they did because it triggered
abandonment panic. Did I have some dim awareness of what a nuisance
I was to my poor parents? Maybe "we're going to a wedding" was just a
euphemism for "we're ditching you, you impossible child."

My uncle decided that we would go out to dinner. The very thought
brought volcanic churning to my stomach. We ate in a restaurant whose
specialty was fried chicken in the basket. They suggested that I order this
and just take a small taste. If I didn't like it, I didn't have to eat it. I found
the idea of chicken propped up in a basket over a pile of french fries in-
triguing. Cautiously, I nibbled a tiny piece of the drumstick and was immediately smitten. End of restaurant phobia. Fried chicken became my
meal of choice. In fact, at thirteen, when we took our first extended road
trip, I ordered fried chicken twelve of the thirteen nights we were away.
The result: I had such intense pains from constipation by the end of the
journey that I had to be taken to an emergency room.

Uncle Andy, who also worked at the Roper Stove Company, always
took me to the company's annual picnic in Sinnissippi Park every summer.
It was a whole day of food stands, rides. games, and fireworks at night. Jo
and I loved the ferris wheel, especially when we were stopped at the very
top and we could look out over the entire panoply of activities. Although
I enjoyed the showy fireworks, I dreaded and abhorred the noisy ones,
and covered my ears through the entire display.

Without question I had developing issues over the male torso, including my own. I made my mother speak to the Sciannas and warn them
not to ask me to take off my shirt no matter how hot it got. I had an irrational dread of appearing in public without a shirt.

Cousin Jo was definitely my closest companion. Our relationship
was baptized early in my life when she leaned over me while changing my
diaper and I peed in her face. We shared so many interests. Although she's
thirteen years older than I am, I firmly declared that I intended to marry
her when I grew up. I was crushed to be told in no uncertain terms that
you could not marry your first cousin. She was a private secretary to one
of the top officers at the National Lock Company and as such achieved a
certain status in a family of factory workers. She almost never went out
on dates, though she was personable and attractive. In the rare event when
she did, she would vomit—an unfortunate trait we shared—several times

before the man arrived to pick her up. So I was her date and I eagerly anticipated those adult outings for just the two of us.

With a good job and living with her parents, she had more discretionary income than my family. She took me shopping and often bought me some pricey piece of clothing I fancied. She always asked my opinion before she bought something for herself. One day while trying on hats, the saleswoman declared, "I must say, Miss, you look very sassy in that hat." It was all we could do to keep from bursting out laughing in front of her. The rest of the day was spent repeating that phrase and emphatically stressing the word "sassy," then laughing ecstatically.

We went ice skating, to the movies, and to performances of operettas—Sigmund Romberg's *The Student Prince* and Victor Herbert's *The Red Mill*— performed by high school students. We adored the movie musicals and anything set in New York City or Paris. Jo played an outsized role in revving up my desire for a showbiz career and a life in a big city. My date nights with her continued until my teenage years.

Chicago, that toddlin' town. How I loved it. Here was a city where real life was lived, nothing like the pale imitation that was Rockford. Any reason to go there was a good reason as far as I was concerned. I loved the Christmas-time visits to Marshall Field's, where we would gawk at the elaborate window displays, marvel at the enormous Christmas tree, and aimlessly ride the escalators up and down all nine floors. In the 1940s, Rockford didn't have a single escalator. We rarely bought anything. "Why pay Chicago prices when we can get the same thing cheaper at home," both my parents agreed. And State Street that great street: this was real glamor, throbbing with bustle, excitement and tremendous marquees.

Most of our excursions were to Wrigley Field because my father was a rabid life-long Cubs fan. We would cheer on his heroes at least ten times every summer, always going to double-headers. This was fine with me, too, and in the 1940s there was the added treat of the big bands and the brassy female vocalists who performed during the seventh-inning stretch, until they were sadly replaced in later years by an organ. When the vocalists sang, I craned my neck to see over the right-field wall onto North Sheffield Avenue toward The Loop, imagining what exciting venues these musicians would be performing at that same evening, wishing I could be there.

The excitement of anticipation began as we drove along old Route 20, which ran right in front of our apartment. The Northwest Toll Road, built in 1958 to skirt all the towns, made the trip much faster, but robbed it of untold pleasure. Belvidere was the first town we hit, then Marengo, and Elgin. Excitement intensified as we reached Oak Park and at last

Chicago. My heart was pounding. Three miles west of Marengo we passed The Shady Lane Theater, housed in a former barn, and its restaurant in the old farmhouse. The theater sat right next to an enormous pig farm. In summer, with the car windows open, we all began laughing as we drove by the farm, inhaling its pungent fragrance. My family termed it "the giggle smell." I wondered if it also made the actors crack-up during serious scenes.

Then came our rest stop in Elgin. We always went to the soda fountain at the Walgreen's across the street from the famed Elgin Watch Company for Green Rivers, a drink of lime syrup and soda water. Just before we reached the Chicago suburb of Oak Park was a farm stand that sold cherry cider, an ambrosia of ruby-colored liquid so cherished that we always bought a two-gallon glass jug to take home. Finally, the excitement of reaching the city limits, with its magnificent skyscrapers looming in the distance.

Chicago made me realize just how wrong Rockford was for me. As we were returning home, I sat in the back seat praying so hard and so futilely that my father would somehow get lost so we would have to remain in Chicago forever.

In 1950, the extended family took a trip to the Windy City, a moniker that some claim refers not to the icy wind blowing in from Lake Michigan, but rather because of the notoriety of its hot-air politicians. The reason for this excursion was not explained to me until we were en route. We piled into four cars and the caravan started off early on Saturday morning. "Where are we going?" I kept asking. Not until we passed the Shady Lane Theater did my mother answer. "All of us women are going to the matinee at the Shubert Theater to see Janet Blair in a musical called, *South Pacific*. You get to go with the men to see the Cub's game," expecting that I would be thrilled. "What? But I want to see *South Pacific*." I protested though I had no idea what it was. "If I'd known. We thought you would want to go with the men to the game."

I could not understand how my parents could have been so unperceptive about my interests to think this. It soon hit me. This was strictly a gender issue—the men did men things, the women did women things. I simply didn't fit the mold.

Another one-time full-family event involved renting a cottage for a minor disaster-plagued week at Lake Wabesa near Madison, Wisconsin. One of my cousins in an attempt to hook a fish managed to hook my shoulder instead, causing a bloody mess. Arguments between families continually threatened the Arcadian peacefulness that a lakeside cottage was supposed to afford. Of course, Paul and Rose were at the center of these disagreements. When fire broke out in one of the upstairs bedrooms, we had to evacuate for a couple hours. Except for the smell of smoke, damage was so minimal we were able to return to the bedlam.

The cottage came equipped with a row boat and my father took me, my ten-month-old brother, and my mother out onto the lake. None of us could swim, and my mother was a nervous wreck. As we returned to disembark, I got out of the boat onto the dock first. My mother, cradling Larry in her arms, was next. As she rose, the boat rocked. She became dizzy or frightened, shifting her weight frantically from one foot to another, until she managed to tip the boat over. All three began screaming, my mother holding Larry up over her head so he wouldn't drown. I looked on, frozen in horror, until it occurred to me to run for help. The whole family came out to save the drowning victims. Fortunately, the water was only five feet deep at the dock. My parents had had quite enough of Lake Wabesa and we left that evening.

My captivation with the New York depicted in the movies, was augmented when an unexpected new Spera relative surfaced during the war. Rockford had a small army base called Camp Grant. On Saturday nights, the lonely and homesick soldiers were drawn to the ballroom of the Lafayette Hotel, where live bands performed for dances. One young recruit checked his hat and got into a conversation with the coat-check girl. He asked her what her name was, and she said, Jennie Spera. She was married to my grandmother's nephew, Tony Spera.

"Spera?" said the soldier. "I can't believe it. That's my name, too. I'm Jerry Spera."

"Really? Where are you from?"

"Brooklyn."

"And what about your father, was he born in Brooklyn, too?"

"No, in Sicily."

Jennie Spera phoned my grandmother immediately from the hotel.

"Invite him to my house for dinner tomorrow,"

On Sunday Jerry, who was finding army life lonely, showed up at Francesca's house.

"What town in Sicily did your father come from?" inquired my grandmother almost as soon as he walked in the door.

"Oh, just a little village near Palermo called, Belmonte Mezzagno."

My grandmother immediately asked him to call his father, Pete, from her house, a long-distance call that was no small expense during the war. The phone conversation established that they had never known each other, but *Nonna* invited him and his wife, Theresa, to come and visit so they could discuss the old country and see Jerry at the same time. It was a lovely gesture of kindness, extended to parents who missed their son. *Nonna* lamented that there was no possibility of seeing her own son, who was somewhere in the faraway Pacific.

The Brooklyn Speras arrived a couple weeks later, and though we were living with the Giovingos at the time, my mother and I were invited to meet them. After much parting of the leaves and examining every branch and twig of the family trees, it was discovered that *Nonna* and Pete were actually third cousins. I had committed some rare minor infraction during dinner, and my mother meted out her standard punishment: I had to sit in the corner facing the walls. Jerry's mother, Theresa, noticed my shoulders rising and falling and realized that I was quietly sobbing.

"Mary, he's such a good boy. Please let him come back to the table. I can't watch him crying." My mother relented. I listened attentively to the stories about Brooklyn, and asked not very informed questions about New York, based on what I had seen in the movies. All three delighted me with their descriptions. This intensified my interests and sowed the seeds that created the trajectory that would lead me to New York.

My mother and the mother of my scouting friend, Cory, decided that the two of us should be sent to camp for a week during the summer after third grade. We all went to check out Camp Rotary to see whether we liked it. Cory and I were both excited when we saw the secluded, bucolic setting in the woods along the Kishwaukee River and the large oval pool nestled among the trees. I was born fully equipped with an intrinsic longing to commune with nature, something my parents had no interest in, so here was my chance. A month later, off we went, name tags all carefully sewn into every garment.

Little did I suspect that the retreat, which was for boys only, was run like an army boot camp. We slept in barracks on straw-stuffed mattresses, lining bunk beds. Reveille was blasted at six in the morning— the middle of the night for me—and there was no option to remain in bed. Having so looked forward to the pool, I was shocked to learn that the first thing required when we got out of bed was to run down the hill like recently released convicts and plunge into its icy waters, until you turned blue and became so numb you could barely move. I hadn't yet learned to swim and rest assured it was not going to happen at Camp Rotary.

The canoes that I had hoped we would paddle ever so placidly among the weeping willows on the river were reserved only for those who could demonstrate they were excellent swimmers. The sight of the pool, which had seemed so inviting on our visit, now struck terror in me that can be compared only with what a war prisoner must feel facing waterboarding. All movement seemed to require lining up and marching in lock step to a drill sergeant's commands. Following pool torture was mess hall (a more perfect name I can't imagine) torture.

The usual breakfast was a bowl of oatmeal. I preferred a more descriptive term, gruel, for this tasteless, sticky paste, which we were required to finish to give us the requisite energy to survive the loathsome activities that would fill the remainder of our day. I had never eaten oatmeal before and vowed never to again, though strangely as an adult I developed a fondness for it. Each meal was more stomach-churning than its predecessor. Luckily, I had overcome my penchant for spontaneous vomiting or I would have been brutalized.

Inane games and sports were on tap for the afternoons. It was here I first sensed that team sports would become the bane of my existence. I was abysmal at them and therefore quite naturally despised and tried to avoid them. Not to worry, there was no choice to be made, "You will participate and that's final."

Dante's Ninth Circle of Hell has nothing on nighttime in the barracks. Yelling, fights, vicious, dangerous pranks, and roughhousing prevailed until the commandants threatened severe corporal punishment. I lay face down on my lumpy, smelly straw mattress in tears. The next morning I wrote a postcard to my parents bemoaning how homesick and miserable I was, pleading with them to come and get me. Of course, they didn't receive it until three days later.

They finally appeared on the weekend and begged me to stay until after the final ceremony when I was to receive some stupid award for god knows what, considering I never did anything. I adamantly refused and we left. It's only fair to report that all the other boys, including my friend Cory, treasured every moment at Camp Rotary. A reporter on the Rockford newspapers described the camp—now mercifully shuttered like Auschwitz—as "a place designed to build real men." Oh, dear.

My parents never let me forget the homesickness business. They assumed that they would get a call to come pick me up whenever I left the familiar safety of home, even when I went off to college.

That summer I was talked into joining a softball team at the neighborhood playground. I had failed to internalize at Camp Rotary that team sports were not for me. My father was so delighted with this decision—finally his son was doing what boys are meant to do. It's not that I was uncoordinated in any way. When I played catch with my dad, I didn't throw like a girl (I was good at mimicking the pros), and I had no trouble catching the ball. It was more a paralyzing fear of letting down the team or worse, making a fool of myself that resulted in my ineptness. I lasted for three games. I never made any terrible errors. I rarely swung the bat and was always walked because the opposing pitchers were not very good. The team sensed, however, that I was not an asset, and I was asked to leave.

That night at dinner, I told my dad what had happened. "Why, what did you do that they kicked you off the team?"

"I don't know. I walked every time I came to bat," unable to find any specific reason.

"You must have been bad at something," he said growing angrier.

"I don't know. It doesn't matter. I didn't like it anyway."

He began yelling at me. "What do you mean you didn't like it? It's not normal for a boy not to like sports. How can you not be good at it when I taught you how to catch and bat. All the men in our family love sports. You're just not normal."

Nothing could have cut through me more than the "you're not normal." I'd already suffered so many doubts about myself over this issue, and to have my father screaming at me was unbearable. Deeply wounded, I had no words to defend myself so I began to sob, left the table without eating a thing, and cried myself to sleep. I heard my mother say, "Matt, you should never have said that to him."

I suddenly realized just what a disappointment I was to my father. His family was obsessed with sports—it was in their DNA. He would love to have been a pro athlete, but claimed he was too small. At five-foot seven, I doubted that was the case. It's more likely that he wasn't good enough and thus projected all his unrealized hopes onto me, the way stage mothers do. He did play on a shop softball team and was secretary of his bowling league, small stuff that in no way fulfilled him.

His brother, Tom, who was much smaller—about five-foot three—than he, was a prominent local sports promoter. He brought the Harlem Globetrotter's basketball team to Rockford every year for decades, and proudly was inducted into the Globetrotter's Hall of Fame. This exhibition team featured African-American players, who combined the sport with comedy, music (their signature tune was "Sweet Georgia Brown"), and theatricality. They were hugely talented and hugely popular because the National Basketball Association did not put its first African-American under contract until 1950. Once Uncle Tom dragged me out onto the court to have our picture taken next to some of the Trotters stars, including the famed "Goose" Tatum. We looked like two pathetic white pygmies dwarfed by black giants.

Tom also promoted boxing, wrestling, hockey, and even brought the Ice Vogues, a lesser ice spectacular to the Rockford Armory each season. He was a local promotor of the Rockford Peaches, part of the women's hardball league that was assembled when the drafting of so many star players during the war threatened to shut down major-league baseball. The Peaches were the team featured in the 1992 film, *A League of Their Own,* which starred Geena Davis, Madonna, and Tom Hanks. The women were astounding players and we, of course, attended nearly every home game that was held at Beyer Stadium.

Overcompensating for my lack of athletic ability, I worked even harder to become a top student. I would proudly show my report card to my father and would receive an unenthusiastic and perfunctory, "Yeah. All right, good." I was so disappointed that he didn't seem impressed. Mother told me that he always bragged about me to others. Why never to me? As I grew older, I began retaliating childishly by pointing out his intellectual deficits. Dad dropped out of high school in his junior year. He had been a terrible student, and one teacher belittled him: "You are one of the dumbest students I've ever had."

"Dumb? I'll show her dumb," he thought. That term he applied himself as never before and came out with a B-plus average. He shoved his report card in her face, "You call that dumb?"

"I can't believe it," she said. "Well, believe it!" He threw the card in her face and said, "I quit." His mother was chopping vegetables when she heard what he had done. She was so enraged that she went after him with the knife, until Jennie calmed her down.

Despite being a dropout, he was an excellent worker and was promoted to shop foreman. Nylint Toys had developed a national reputation—some calling their toys the finest ever made in America. The scale-model versions of construction equipment, trucks, and cars were made of the same heavy-gauge pressed steel that was used in automobiles, then painted with a baked enamel finish. Larry and I got almost every toy they made as Christmas gifts.

A couple weeks before Christmas we loaded up dad's trunk with boxes of these toys and headed for St. Vincent's Catholic Orphanage in Freeport, Illinois. We brought the toys into the administration's offices, but a few children were invited to open one or two boxes on the spot. Their joy when they saw the toys was infectious. One year as we began to leave, a little boy of three or four years, who had been particularly exuberant over a toy, ran up to my mother, grabbed her, and began pleading, "Take me with you. Take me with you. Please."

A nun intervened and began prying him away from my mother. The boy cried hysterically holding out his arms to us, as we left the front door. In the car on the way home, there was total silence. I looked around to see that we were all in tears. It was my first painfully poignant awareness of just how cruel and unfair the world can be to some people.

In sixth grade I was assigned to be a traffic-crossing guard for the younger kids, along with a boy named Steve. We shared many of the same bizarre tastes. While standing on the corner wearing white canvas belts fastened around our waists and diagonally across our chests, we would enact little improvised dramas set in ancient Rome, which were inspired by the sword-and-sandal movies of the fifties, such as *The Robe*. Adopting English accents (why would the Romans have English accents?), we took turns playing one or the other of the Caesars. After school, we would have cocktails at his apartment—Coke with an olive in it. How sophisticated we were at age eleven.

My fascination with foreign accents began early in life, but my abilities to imitate them began to flower in sixth grade. While studying French geography, I was asked to portray a Parisian tour guide for a classroom skit. Excited about this opportunity, I bought a French phrasebook for tourists, brushing up on the major sites and fine-tuning my Charles Boyer imitation. With a French beret on my head and a scarf tied around my neck, I led the imaginary tour, announcing, "Ze next visite will be le Louvre Museum."

Mrs. Thompson, our teacher, who was also the principal of the school, stopped me cold. "I must ask you to pronounce the name correctly. It's Louver," she said in no uncertain terms.

"But the guidebook says, 'Louvre,'" and I pulled it out of my pocket to show her the phonetic pronunciation.

"Norman, please do as I ask. It's pronounced Louver, not Louvre. Now say it correctly."

"Louver," I repeated most reluctantly under my breath. Steve and I turned to each other, both rolling our eyes. I was aghast that this otherwise intelligent woman could possibly be so ill-informed, and it pained and angered me for weeks after to think that I had been forced to concur with this unforgivable error.

A major scandal rocked Rockford and Jackson School that year. Laurie, a schoolmate, invited our sixth grade class to her home during class time for a demonstration. She lived in an elaborate mansion that could be described as pseudo-Tudor, far grander than any other student's house. Her father was the district attorney in town. Laurie fancied herself a ballerina. We all sat in the oversized living room. Laurie's mother served delicate petits fours. Her father played on a large pipe organ that he recently had had installed in the room. This was accompaniment to Laurie, who performed awkward arabesques and *pas de bourrées* on point for us, all the while emoting feverishly with her arms. At the time, I thought ballet was a very silly art form, and Laurie did nothing to dispel that notion.

A month after the performance, only a local scandal newspaper reported that Laurie's father was being charged with sexually abusing a young boy he knew. Not having begun to read newspapers, I asked my mother what this was all about. Hesitant to be explicit, she simply said, "He did things to that boy that ruined him for life." "What kinds of things?" I pressed on. She refused to elaborate, and I sensed that I should stop asking. For weeks I tried to imagine what exactly he had done that could "ruin him for life" but could not formulate any picture in my mind. I was very disturbed by the incident and sensed that it somehow related to my discomfort over male torsos. In the end Laurie's father was not prosecuted. Rather, he was quietly asked to leave town and the whole sordid affair, which never made the mainstream press, was hushed up.

Storytelling was a major pastime in the Cancelose family. On Friday nights around ten, all four families, including the children, assembled at my grandparent's house for a coffee party. Each week a different family was charged with supplying pastries, generally from the wonderful Swedish bakeries in the neighborhood. We all sat around a large table, discussing the family happenings for the week and reminiscing about good times past, while nibbling Swedish coffee cakes. On Saturday nights, often following a restaurant dinner, a similar coffee party took place in one of the four apartments or at one of *Nonna's* Spera relatives' houses.

One of the favorite topics, spun again and again, was about Uncle Tony, who by then had passed away. No one ever tired of hearing these tales, and curiously, my sourpuss Uncle Paul was often the raconteur. These were the only times I ever remember him laughing and enjoying himself. Uncle Tony was my grandmother's brother, the one who failed to show up at Ellis Island, though we were never provided with an explanation for his negligence.

After moving from New York to Rockford, Tony became known as Uncle Hopples. Why Hopples? Because his first job in town was as a pushcart fruit vendor. With his very poor English, he peddled his fruits up and down the streets yelling, "Hopples, horangez bonahnnahs."

When he graduated to freelance construction worker, Dr. Magnelia, who was virtually every Italian's dentist, hired him to pave his driveway. Uncle Hopples was busy mixing the cement when the dentist came out to inspect his progress. He scrutinized the mixture carefully and declared, "That cement looks too watery, Tony." *"Scusi dottore,"* he warned, holding up his hand to stop the dentist's critique, *"ma* you frixxy da teets,—I mixxy da chement."

My grandfather's English also left much to be desired. He would ask non-Italian neighbors, "How you today?" They often launched into a litany of complaints about deaths in the family, sickness, and losing a job. Ignazio nodded, smiled, and said in his sweetest voice, "Ahtsa nice-ah." He hadn't understood a word they said, and with a totally befuddled look, they turned and walked away, shaking their head.

Once when my grandparents were away, dad was able to tell a story about his mother. *Nonna,* who was short and rather stocky, had extremely bowed legs, which got worse as she grew older causing severe arthritic pains. Her favorite expression in her later years was, "I'm no good for sheet anymore." One day dad was driving down State Street with one of his coworkers. "Look at that little old lady. Did you ever see such bowed legs?" "Yes, I have. That's my mother." Oops!

As the evening wore on and the stories of reminiscence and tales of current woes dwindled, there was suddenly a pregnant silence. No one in my family could handle extended silences—they must be filled and filled they were. I'd begin smiling to myself, knowing the evening was coming to an end as I waited for someone to deliver the inevitable exit line: "Yehh-hhp! It's a great life, they say, if you don't weaken."

Perilous Pubescence

ST. ANTHONY OF PADUA church was the hub, the nerve center of life for the Italian community in South Rockford. My parents grew up embraced by the parish. Mary Giovingo even attended the adjoining school for eight years, until she transferred to the public Central High School, where she met my dad through mutual friends. When Mary mispronounced a word, such as "pupcorn," which she was wont to do, dad would say, "What do you expect? She's a graduate of St. Ant'ny's School." Catholic schools apparently had poor reputations in those years.

In his youth, Matt, spent hours playing ball in the school's gymnasium or in the church basement, which until the 1950s housed a four-lane bowling alley. These were designed to keep tough Sicilian boys off the streets and into healthy all-American sports under the umbrella of the parish. As a teenager, my dad spent much of his time working as a pinsetter (this was before automatic setting machines) at the bowling alley, another reason he did so poorly in school.

Although the family no longer lived in South Rockford, St. Anthony's was still their church of choice. They had so many ties to it: memories, weddings, baptisms, funerals, relatives, and old friends. It's Italianate Renaissance-like architecture and the Italian and Polish priests, who were of the Franciscan order, offered a warmer and more welcoming environment than the austere and chilly ambience at St. James's Church, which was near to our house. This meant getting up earlier on Sunday mornings for the drive across town to attend mass. In our family, no one ever missed mass unless you were so sick you couldn't get out of bed.

Attending church, not to mention believing in its doctrine, was like attending sporting events. You never thought to question whether you liked it. You just simply did it. And as a child, I most definitely was a believer. The belief could not be considered innate to my personality or indicative of some nonthinking individual who always bows to authority. Rather, it was the triumph of the church's propagandist approach to brainwashing children at a very young age. I was taken to mass even as a baby, and initiated into church doctrine as soon as I developed language comprehension.

When it came time for me to receive the sacraments of communion and confirmation, St Anthony's was no longer a practicable option. Because these milestones each had to be preceded by a year or more of education, my parents were forced to join St. James's parish as well, so that I could walk to the weekly catechism classes. Horrors! During these instructional periods, I had to get up early on Saturday mornings, my one day to sleep late. My only memory of first communion was that one boy vomited all over the altar rail as the priest placed the eucharist wafer on his tongue. The priest nearly dumped all the other hosts out of the chalice as he lurched backward to avoid the barf. Aha! Now it was my turn to look askance at those cursed with delicate stomachs.

Lincoln Junior High School, an enormous institution, was another major adjustment for me. There were a few very bright students at Jackson, but now I was confronted with many more, who seemed even smarter to me. Many of them came from far wealthier and more sophisticated families, the school encompassing the entire east side of town. One of the smartest, who was part of my homeroom class, was Connie Carlson, a tall attractive blonde Swede. My desk was always directly in front of hers because we were seated alphabetically. We were friendly immediately, and she became a sort of role model for me. I aspired to be her intellectual equivalent all the way through high school, though I never quite made the grade. She always responded to teachers' questions with the smartest answers, wrote better papers in a superior penmanship, aced every exam, and was more popular than I could ever hope to be.

There were many bright kids in that class, and Mr. Costello, our homeroom teacher, who later became principal of the school, commented to Connie at a class reunion a few years ago, that we were the smartest and most promising group of students he taught in his whole career.

I had been plagued by frequent and severe sore throats since childhood. In my second semester at Lincoln, my doctor suggested a tonsillectomy to solve the problem. My tonsils were so swollen that they required a week of antibiotics to shrink them before surgery could be performed. A rubber mask was placed over my nose and mouth to deliver the cloyingly sweet odor of ether. I immediately began hallucinating that I was strapped to a very long moving conveyer belt. The belt started inching slowly forward, and I felt I was being pelted by tiny, evenly spaced metal balls that made a popping noise as they struck me. The farther the belt moved, the larger the balls became, with a concurrent increase in the volume of the popping sound. When they reached golf-ball size, I felt myself begin to laugh. The balls caused no pain, only an eerie sensation. Now they reached the size of baseballs and the noise sounded like bombs exploding. I was becoming very frightened when I overheard the doctors and nurses talking.

"What do you think? I believe he's out."

"You're right. Let's begin the procedure."

I knew that if I was hearing this, I couldn't be "out." I began shaking my head and trying to move any body part not strapped to the operating table so they would know I was still conscious. Imagining the excruciating pain of surgery, I thought to myself, "Please don't let them start yet." The next thing I knew I was in the recovery room. The pain of swallowing even water was like nothing I'd ever experienced. As a result I was out of school for ten days. Mary Giovingo shook her head in exasperation as she watched me try to eat, "You're just too *delicato*."

That term I was required to take a course in mechanical drawing, in which we designed household implements, drew them at various stages of manufacture, and turned the drawings into blueprints. These were the days when boys were required to take shop courses, and girls were routed into home economics. Our current assignment was to design and draw a metal sugar scoop, which in the next year's home-mechanics course had to be executed. This was not an area where I excelled at all. I was slow at completing the drawings—erase, redraw, recalculate. My ten-day absence from school put me even further behind. As a result I received the grade of "D" in the course. I never had had such a bad grade and it terrified me. When Mr. Costello passed out the report cards, he asked me to remain after homeroom period.

"I'm very disappointed in you, Norman. How did you manage to get such a poor mark?"

I tried to explain to him.

"Well, it's not at all like you to do this badly. I want you to promise me that it will never happen again."

And it never happened again.

For months I couldn't think about this incident without experiencing extreme shame. My mother was also disappointed, and it pained me that I'd probably dropped down a notch farther in my father's estimation, though he never mentioned it.

The sports issue began to loom larger at Lincoln. We now had team-sports coaches for gym teachers, and they were unforgiving to the athletically challenged. Unlike in grade school, gym class was now gender-separated. Every day was basketball, football, or wrestling, which I despised. I always seemed to get the meanest and toughest boys as an opponent, who were determined to inflict maximum pain for the sheer joy of it.

Swimming class was thankfully not traumatic. I had taught myself basic swimming skills from a self-help television show. "You can easily learn to float simply by standing in waist-deep water and trying to touch your toes," the instructor assured. It worked. I could swim, though never extremely well. The breathing technique held me back. I had an excellent crawl stroke as long as my face remained in the water. When it came out to breathe, I was more like Esther Williams, slowly inching forward in an ungraceful water ballet.

The shirts-off phobia came to a sudden end. All the shirts versus skins basketball games in gym class cured that. Then there was swimming class, which in those days was mandatorily naked because of state health laws about the dangers of wearing trunks. Also, there were the communal showers.

Today when I'm in my gym's locker room, it's all I can do to keep from laughing at the false puritan modesty, everyone wrapping a towel around their waists, while they valiantly struggle in and out of their undershorts, in a Sisyphean effort to keep from, god forbid, dropping the towel. I attribute this to mass homophobia, despite the purportedly enlightened progressiveness of the younger generation. It's only the old guys who grew up with forced nudity or the young exhibitionists who dare expose anything.

I was fortunate to escape the dreaded paddle in junior high phys. ed., though I witnessed this barbaric ritual applied to several boys. The four-inch wide wooden paddle had holes drilled into it to make the blows more painful and to leave large circular welts. Often the sadistic coaches would insist on administering the beating as the boy exited the showers and while his butt was still wet, adding even more zing to the whacks.

One of the most paddle-crazed coaches also taught swimming class. One day he removed his trunks (teachers were allowed to wear them) to demonstrate the backstroke across the pool. All the boys nearly gagged as they stifled laughter when it became obvious that he was sporting a full erection. Perhaps, the paddling was indicative of a serious sado-masochistic personality

My worst gym nightmare came when we were informed that for one-week we would be playing mixed volleyball with the girls. My serves always went in every direction except toward the net, and I dreaded more than anything having the girls, and especially Connie, witness how pathetic I was at sports. Bad enough the boys knew about my lack of athletic prowess, but now the girls, too? The night before the first match it began to snow heavily. How I prayed that school would have to be canceled, a totally unrealistic expectation, considering that in my entire Rockford school career, there was never a cancellation even following a snowstorm of several feet. So I staggered through the snow drifts with a hang-dog expression only to have my most virulent fears confirmed—I was worse than many of the girls. My only consolation was that no one ever said a word.

Sports mania was far more than a family trait. It was intrinsic to a midwestern town like Rockford. Sports was the major entertainment. Friday night high-school football and basketball games were the hottest ticket in town. Everyone attended and whether your team won or lost was a matter of life and death. If you wanted to be popular in Rockford, you needed to excel as an athlete.

I received a one-semester reprieve from gym class in ninth grade. I contracted verruca warts on the bottom of my foot, most likely from the school pool or shower. The podiatrist dug them out with a sinister-looking tool, then squeezed around the resultant holes until a hideous brown substance was exuded as though it were toothpaste. The pain they caused was nothing compared to the pain of gym class. Because these warts were contagious, I was excused from physical education for five blissful months, the time better spent in study hall.

Junior high brought into focus another issue Rockford faced—it had an ethnicity problem. I began hearing ethnic slurs toward Italians, the words "dago" and "wop" (an acronym for "without passport") were the choice putdowns of that era. Although the insulting terms were never flung in my face directly, I had a stomach-clenching reaction whenever I heard them, knowing that I was certainly included in their scorn. There were only a few Italians in the school, and it was clear to me that they were not part of the in-group unless they were either very rich or an athletic star.

This was a subject I heard my parents, and especially my mother, mull over many times. They clearly had suffered the stings of bigotry far more than I ever did because it had significantly diminished by the time I was in school. Swedes had inhabited the city decades before the Italians arrived and thus had become the ruling class—in business, the professions, and government. Like all ruling elites, they had a condescending haughtiness toward those who came to town as uneducated, unskilled laborers, struggling with the English language and local customs.

My parents maintained that the Swedes were tight-fisted, as well. Dad complained that they always blocked every attempt to give the city a little life, either for religious reasons or because they refused to allocate the money. Swedes who belonged to the Evangelical Free Church, and certainly not all did, often eschewed, drinking, dancing, and theatrical productions. There were many Swedish restaurants in Rockford that would not serve alcohol because their customers refused to patronize any establishment that did so. Ironically, dad would often repeat, "Rockford only has two things, churches and taverns." Many Swedes, it seems, were heavy drinkers.

Mary Giovingo, endured many slights, particularly when she transferred to the public high school. "All the Italian kids were given lockers in a filthy basement, called, 'Rat Alley.'" One teacher cruelly remarked, "You Italians who came here from St. Anthony's School are about as stupid as they come. What on earth did they teach you there?" Poor Mary had to present a marketing plan for any chosen commercial product. When her presentation was one of the best received, a student named John B. Anderson approached her after class, "I had no idea that an ITALIAN could possibly come up with such a good plan." Mr. Anderson later became a Republican U.S. Congressman, and in 1980 he ran for president as an independent against Ronald Reagan. Would Mary Giovingo vote for him? Not on your life. He fit handily her often repeated, "Those damn Swedes." It must be stated, however, that almost all of her best friends in adulthood were Swedes.

I was an adult when my mother told me a story that made me very proud, indeed, of Ignazio and Francesca. In the 1930s, when they wanted to move out of South Rockford and into the east side of town, which was almost strictly Swedish, no bank would issue them a mortgage, despite the fact they could demonstrate financial solvency. They became so disheartened they were about to give up on buying the house on Longwood Street and the adjacent apartment building. The Italian lawyer who represented them insisted they must under no circumstances relent. They needed to fight on for the sake of all the other Italian families who were eager to move. He drove them to a bank in Freeport, twenty-seven miles from Rockford, which offered them a mortgage. Their new neighbors were incensed that they would be living next to a bunch of dirty dagoes.

This was a clear demonstration that redlining, as has been practiced against African-Americans to keep them out of certain neighborhoods, was not a recent phenomenon at all, but dates back at least to the Depression or certainly much earlier. There was a period before I'd heard this story that I wondered whether all this moaning over discrimination was not to some degree just a sign of victimization and jealousy felt by any underclass struggling against a ruling class.

I was dissuaded from this notion when a Jewish friend in New York told me the following tale after learning that I was from Rockford. "Rockford?" she said, incredulously. "What a strange place. They have a serious racial problem there, but it's not between blacks and whites. It's between Italians and Swedes. I went to school at Beloit College (a few miles north of Rockford across the Wisconsin border). I had a boyfriend who worked in Rockford so I spent all my weekends there. I could hardly believe what I was seeing." So the bigotry continued well beyond my years there; her college days were in the early 1970s.

Never consciously did I deny or obliterate my ethnicity, and yet I certainly didn't trumpet it, either. I didn't look especially Italian, and even the name Cancelose did not by any means scream "Italian." I didn't have a single Italian friend so I undoubtedly internalized the demeanor of the Swedes I spent my time with. It's not unusual for people who are marginalized to emulate the dominant culture, to feel more a part of it, to "fit in." Not having a deep understanding of my own culture and heritage until much later in life, I couldn't debate a Swede over what was obvious: Italian culture had contributed more to Western civilization, to food, to literature, to music, and especially to art than theirs did. Today I might have asked, "Who is the Swedish equivalent of Leonardo da Vinci?"

I certainly didn't hide my ethnicity with regard to food, however. Unlike in grade school, where I walked home for lunch everyday, this was not possible in junior high, so my mother packed my lunch because I refused to eat the cafeteria food. This often included fried eggplant sandwiches on a bun, which to this day is one of the most prevalent street foods in Palermo. Also, I loved wedges of asparagus *frittata* between two slices of bread, which turned green before I unveiled the delicacy in the lunch room. My lunch mates shouted, "What the hell is that you're eating?" I didn't mind a bit because I loved this food, so superior to the disgusting fare shoveled out in the cafeteria.

My mother told me that she'd heard about a good piano teacher who was receptive to popular music. "Please give it another try." Irene Glasford had a studio right downtown, above the city's major piano retailer. She was married, middle-aged, but younger than Miss Arnold, and with a much cheerier disposition. As we spoke, it was evident to me that there was a great rivalry between the two teachers, and she reveled in my description of how I had disliked my lessons with Miss Arnold—and especially my closing phrase for why I had quit: "Enough is enough."

I was happy that exercises were ignored in favor of music. The easy classics were introduced, as well as some popular tunes that I liked. I had the distorted notion that if one were truly good at something, one needn't spend hours working at it. I was simply mediocre at best, so I spent minimal time practicing. I had excellent musicality and interpretive ability, but no real technique. My biggest regret regarding my time with Mrs. Glasford was what she never said to me: "You obviously have talent, and you owe it to yourself to put forth the effort and practice to make the most of that talent." I'm sure she recognized a certain gift because when I quit a few years later, she began to cry at the thought of losing me.

After about a year, I had learned to play Beethoven's *Für Elise* quite respectably. One day she invited some of her students to play for Guy Maier, with whom she had studied. He was a concert pianist who had performed at Carnegie Hall, an author of respected piano pedagogy books, and later a teacher at the Juilliard School. When I finished playing the Beethoven, Maier said to me, "I have never ever heard a boy play that piece so prettily." I suspect he meant it as a compliment, but at the time I thought to myself, "My god, I even play the piano like a girl, and it shows."

Mrs. Glasford offered a music theory class on Saturday afternoons, and she asked me to attend. I had no idea what anyone was talking about in the class. I had never learned key signatures, chord names, or even scales. Suddenly, Mrs. Glasford pointed to me and demanded, "Norman, what is the dominant seventh chord in the key of G Major?" I looked at her with blank stupidity. I detected her disappointment as she directed the question to a brighter student. I was not at all used to looking dumb in class, and I hated the feeling intensely. I assumed I was a moron when it came to music theory, and I refused to attend another class. Oh, how sadly we misread events in childhood to our own detriment in adulthood.

Terry Bryan and I never got to travel on a train together, but Cory's mother suggested that we go by rail to Chicago for a weekend. Finally, I would ride a train. Okay, it was the dumpy old Illinois Central that was on its failing final years—nothing at all like the domed streamliners Terry and I had fantasized about. Still it was a train, and we were on our way to Chicago, Cory and I sitting in one seat, our mothers in the seat behind. The thrill of arriving at the cavernous Union Station with its glass-arched ceiling, directly in The Loop, was even greater than that when approaching the city by car. Two whole days in downtown Chicago would be absolute nirvana.

This was to be my first ever night in a hotel—the Allerton—an old but distinguished lodging on the fashionable Magnificent Mile, which became my Chicago hostelry of choice as an adult. I was a bit disappointed that our room didn't have a stunning view of the skyline. A hamburger at Toffenetti's Restaurant became a singular Proustian experience simply because it had lettuce in the bun. I had never had lettuce on a burger before. If they do it in Chicago but not Rockford, it must be *de rigueur*. It made such an impression that I would insist on it forever after. If only one could recreate the intense surge of emotion one feels as a child in experiencing a new adventure—even one so mundane and banal as lettuce on a burger— for the first time. Alas, it's impossible except in fond reminiscence.

The strange feelings I got when looking at men's bodies suddenly turned brutally consummatory—SEX! It was so overpowering. I had no idea what it meant, much less how to handle it. Sex education was nonexistent in those years, and neither of my parents could muster the courage to talk with me about it. As a three-year old, one day I began reciting a series of rhymed words: duck, luck, tuck, buck, fuck... "What did you say?" my mother screamed. "Don't you ever use that word again. It's filthy. It's sinful and if you ever say it again I'll wash your mouth out with soap." "Why, what does it mean?" "It's disgusting. It means—uh—well, it means kissing someone's private parts." As an adult, realizing how sheltered she had been, I wondered, "Did she really think that's what it meant or was she just avoiding having to explain it to me?"

Wet dreams. Wow! I was so naive and so far removed from street-boy talk that I thought a few drops of urine had oozed out during my dreams, which were of course all about men. And how those dreams overwhelmed me every time. Our apartment had a very small second bedroom, so my brother and I had to share a three-quarter-sized bed. There was a strict invisible line down the center of the mattress, which neither of us ever dared cross. In the morning, I would wait until Larry got out of bed, then I would try to wash the stain out of the sheet and my underwear so my mother wouldn't see what I had done. I never stopped to consider that it had already soaked through to the mattress pad. None of my friends ever mentioned such things, and I certainly didn't have the audacity to bring up the subject. As a result, I remained totally, and unblissfully ignorant.

The first time I discovered that if I touched myself I got the same reaction, I let out a yell. Thank heaven no one was home at the time. What was that stuff? Most definitely it wasn't urine. Pus, perhaps? But I was certain I wasn't diseased. And what, what was that smell—like the Linco bleach my mother used? Oh, how the sensation intensified if I concentrated on some man while I indulged in it.

On Seventh Street, a secondary shopping area near to our house, was a very sleazy-looking store that had a pool hall in the back and in the front sold, cigarettes, cigars, and magazines. The store smelled of cigar smoke, sweat, and sin. The latest issues were displayed in the window and at one inconspicuous spot was Joe Weider's *Muscle Builder* magazine. I walked back and forth in front of the store, unable to take my eyes off its cover. I certainly didn't have the nerve to go in to buy one. A couple months later, nature supplied the nerve. I stayed outside the store until I saw that there were no customers inside, making sure I had the exact purchase price in my hand, so that I wouldn't have to wait for change. When the store was free of customers—and sometimes this took as long as twenty minutes—I'd dash in, pick up a copy, wait nervously while the clerk put it in a brown paper bag, hand him the money, and tear out into the street, my heart beating so wildly I could hardly breathe.

The magazines could in no way be considered pornography, still I hid them deep within a box of old papers in my closet. I knew they would arouse suspicion. The competition body builders of that era—Steve Reeves and Reg Park—were pre-steroid-crazed and had more natural looking physiques than those over-pumped monstrosities who came later. Those body builders became my idealized heroes. They looked so young and virile that it never occurred to me that these guys were merely five or six years younger than my father.

In my catechism classes before confirmation, it was made clear that "spilling seed" outside of marriage was considered a mortal sin, meaning that if you were to die in this state, you went directly to hell. There was no get-out-of-purgatory free card. The thought of this struck such terror in me that I began going to confession almost every Saturday to "purify" myself. As I walked to church, I was so frightened that I might be struck by a car and killed in my blackened state that I waited at every corner until there were no moving vehicles in sight before crossing. After confession—huge sigh of relief—I could walk home normally. Hell was again off the table—temporarily. My family and relatives noted my blossoming piety and began teasing, "Norman is so religious. I'll bet he's going to be a priest someday."

Little did they know, I was no longer the good little boy they imagined, but rather a degenerate sinner on the fast track to hell. My efforts to stop these damnable acts took on herculean proportions equal to those body builders I lusted after. Could reason triumph over religious dogma? My logically oriented mind embarked on a Byzantine quest to make it work for me. Certainly, god could never be evil or capricious, could he? Why would he endow us with such a powerful force, then send us to hell for bowing to it? This was illogical to me. Maybe it was a test we were meant to overcome. No, we've entered a capriciously mad world with that thought. Still, he provided us with the spontaneous release of the nocturnal emission. Why would he do this? The seed was spilled outside of marriage whether we participated in it or not. Perhaps the problem was not the discharge, but the touching. If there was no touching involved, would it still be a sin? Maybe not. Could I bring it about without any physical stimulation, simply by staring at the magazines? Great effort expended, no satisfactory result.

Now what? Prayer? Is there a special saint to help with this? I couldn't locate one. No, I needed to develop a firmer resolve, turn myself into sterner stuff. Willpower alone kept me going for a few weeks. I thought about my relatives' line: "It's a great life if you don't weaken." I weakened.

Plan B. I was a hopeless romantic from as early as I can recall. I adored the movies with love stories. I would cry at all the sad love songs—especially the torch songs—in the musical films: Ava Gardner singing "Bill" in *Showboat* (though I didn't know at the time that her voice was dubbed by Annette Warren); Doris Day singing "You Made Me Love You" and "Ten Cents a Dance" in *Love Me or Leave Me*. All of this provided vibrant material for me to create magnificent romances in my mind when I went to bed. Never one of the lucky ones who go out like a light as soon as the head hits the pillow, I used these improvised dramas to lull me to sleep gently. The romances always involved girls, never the men I worshipped. Somehow I did not equate love with sexuality. I never had been exposed to the idea of love between two men and apparently wasn't imaginative enough to envision such a thing. It occurred to me that if I could meld the erotic thoughts with the romantic episodes involving girls, I could forget about men, transfer the desire to women, and solve the problem. Not even close, and certainly no cigar. It just didn't work. Back to square one.

One day in the summer after seventh grade, my friend Cory invited me over to his house. Though it seemed highly unlikely coming from him, he suggested that we play a game of strip poker, something I had never considered, surely something sinful, illicit. "It's just a game," he assured me. I relented after much coaxing. Somehow I seemed to be losing almost every hand, so more and more clothes kept coming off. Was Cory cheating? Finally, down to my undershorts, I realized I was being seduced, and I was powerless to resist. I did not find Cory attractive in the least. Thoughts began swirling around my mind, creating a state of utter confusion. I'm not the only person in the world with such temptations, as I had feared. The fact that this was happening with another boy excited me to such a degree that I completely lost control. Premature ejaculation certainly understates the dissatisfying finale.

When it was over, Cory gave me an even greater shock. He told me that a whole group of boys often got together for "a game of cards." He began naming names, and included in this group were some of the toughest jocks in our class. I could hardly believe what I was hearing. Did I want to join them next time? The very idea of group sex was abhorrent to me, but I didn't want to appear the prude that I, in fact, was so I said, "I'd think about it."

Leaving his house, the confusion grew worse. What had I just done? If I was in mortal sin before, this was surely a degree far worse in the eyes of god and the church. How could I confess such a thing? I couldn't think how, but of course, I must. There was no way I could survive with such a stain on my soul. I thought about how disgusted my parents would be if they ever found out about this. No, they definitely never would. Whatever would I say to the priest? Would the prayers of penance be so extensive that I'd never be able to leave the church? Could prayer even be sufficient as penance for such a sin. It was only Tuesday, and I'd have to wait until Saturday for confession. I must be very vigilant in keeping free from harm until then or else HELL.

My parents generally confessed no more than once a month, and when they did my father drove us all to St. Anthony's. The coming Saturday would not be their time yet, which meant I had to go to St, James's. The Irish priests there, part of the Dominican order, were infinitely more severe and punitive than the much warmer Italian and Polish clergy at St. Anthony's. I hadn't yet read Joyce and had no idea that guilt, especially with regard to sex, was common among many Irish.

Saturday finally arrived and never had I walked to church more slowly and deliberately, or with a greater sense of dread. As luck would have it, I drew as my confessor the Monseigneur, the ancient, stone-faced, and stern man who headed the parish. After the scripted opening of "Bless me father for I have sinned," in a most quavering and subdued voice I mumbled, "I committed an impure act."

"A what?"

"An impure act."

"Alone?"

"No."

"With whom?"

"Another boy."

"Say it again. I can't hear you."

Oh, god, I have to repeat it. I did, nearly choking on the words.

There was a long painful silence. What was happening? I waited nervously. Not a sound. Then the floodgates opened.

"Is it not enough that you are a disgusting and depraved boy yourself? A sinner of great magnitude in the eyes of god? A disgrace to his beneficence? And to your family? No, apparently not. You must go about corrupting and bringing other innocent people down to your contemptible perverted level."

The penance was only about double the length of the prayers that I usually received, much less than I had anticipated.

"I don't ever want to hear you come to confession with such a sin again. Now go. And may god have mercy on your evil soul."

I said the penance as quickly as possible. I couldn't breathe. I needed to get out of that church now! When I came out into the sunlight, I was shaking all over. Never in my life had I been so devastated. My head hanging, I straggled toward home as slowly as possible.

Was I really that evil? I never meant harm to anyone. Why was I the corrupter? I wasn't the one to initiate the act. Could god ever forgive me? What could I do now? Then the deadliest thought of all struck me. Had I already, at thirteen, become like Laurie's father, "ruining someone for life?" Would I be run out of town if anyone found out about this? Somehow I had to restore my sense of calm in a hurry. The last thing I needed was to have my parents wanting to know what happened to me.

My mother often asked, "Why don't you ever get together with Cory any more. You two used to be so close. His mother has been asking me if anything is wrong." "No, no, I've just been busy doing other things," I lied. Cory and I were never friends again.

When the evangelical Christians of today maintain that homosexuality is merely a choice, I go ballistic. "How dare you suggest that you know what I experienced?" Choice, indeed. Would I possibly have made such a choice at that age? Did I choose to be aroused by male movie stars at the age of three? Did I choose for my dreams to be about men? I will concede that there may be those few who on the continuum of sexuality between zero and ten—with zero being completely heterosexual and ten being completely homosexual—fall precisely in the center and thus are able in their bisexuality to choose one or the other. But for the majority, it's twaddle. And if you insist that it is a choice, you must own up to the inverse— that every heterosexual could just as easily have chosen to be homosexual. Hmm, why am I unable to convince myself they'd be willing to do so?

And as for the Catholic Church, I honestly believe that sexual abuse by a priest would have been far less harmful than what that Monseigneur did to me. Which of us did more harm in this case—me or him? I concede he won a certain pyrrhic victory; I didn't have another sexual experience for almost eight years. But at what cost? Much has been written about sexual abuse by priests, but I suspect there are many equally gruesome tales to be told about the psychological and emotional damage done to sensitive and vulnerable children by nuns and priests who, in their eyes are simply enforcing church doctrine.

Looking up something in my set of red-leather-bound *World Book Encyclopedias,* I discovered an old sex manual my mother had hidden behind the volumes. Surprise! "Fuck" has nothing whatever to do with kissing. It was a chapter on homosexuality, however, that drew my rapt attention. It explained how young teenage boys often experiment sexually with each other until their "true" heterosexual natures kicked in. What a relief! So this is just a phase I am passing through. I'm perfectly normal. It would all be mercifully over in a few years.

Post-tonsillectomy, I was still getting sore throats, and they were even worse than before the surgery. Only years later did the medical community discover that unless the tonsils were the source of the infection, they should be left in place because they serve as a protection against throat illnesses. This was to be the first of several medical protocols that proved to be dead wrong for me.

My father was an officer of St. Anthony's Senior Holy Name Society, a men's club that met once a month after mass for breakfast in the church basement. Dad was called upon to engage sports celebrities to speak at the annual Father and Son Breakfast because he had appropriate contacts through my Uncle Tom. For the first time, I was sick in bed with a sore throat on the Sunday of the breakfast and was unable to attend. My father was disappointed because he assumed that I was so looking forward to it. He had managed to engage Johnnie Lujack, the star quarterback for the Chicago Bears. I was still in bed when dad returned from the breakfast.

"I have a surprise," he said. "Look who I brought to say 'hello' to you." Lujack came into my room and wished me a speedy recovery, saying he was sorry that I had missed his speech. Dad was always trying to please me with gestures like this. He was truly a good father, and I knew it, despite our many differences in temperament and interests. I was touched that he must have gone to much trouble to get Lujack to agree to come to our house. Still I couldn't help thinking: "If only it could have been Ethel Merman instead of some sports star."

Mother was both Mrs. Malaprop (the character in Richard Brinsley Sheridan's 1775 play, *The Rivals*) and a serial mispronouncer of words. I was, of course, obsessive about using the right word in the right place, and most definitely about pronouncing it correctly. As such, mother became a great source of laughter (which, happily, she took very good-naturedly), but also a source of embarrassment, when she mangled language in public. I attributed this to the fact that she had not grown up hearing well-spoken English and to the fact that she just didn't have a good ear for such things. I turned the situation into my very own version of the Pygmalion drama. I would become her tutor, patiently and phonetically correcting her English, until she was a polished and erudite speaker. It pains me to report that I was no Henry Higgins and was an utter failure at this endeavor.

We were often subject to such howlers as: "What are you, the Gestapolo?"; "I don't give one coyote what she thinks"; "Lord and behold"; "Your brother just shruggled his shoulders"; or my personal favorite, "When he showed up at the door, I was just fiberglassted." Neither she nor her sister Lena could say the word, anxious—it was always antchus—nor could they pronounce words that had "ts" or "tes" endings. Tastes became taysez; costs became caussez; and an often-repeated line was, "She trusses no one."

As many women in the 50s did, she attended Tupperware parties, where those plastic food-storage containers were sold. Tupperware, tripping, no flopping, off her tongue, became Tumperware. One of our pronunciation seminars involved the following typical exchange:

"Mother, can you say the word, supper?"

"Supper."

"Good."

"Now say, supperware."

"Supperware."

"Excellent." I was certain we were about to scale the mountain.

"Now say, Tuh—per—ware, one syllable at time, very slowly."

"Tuh."

"Yes."

"Per."

"Good."

"Ware."

By George, she's got it!

"Now say, Tupperware."

"Tumperware."

I threw up my hands in total defeat.

A few years ago, my Taiwanese friend, Tony Lin, who identifies completely with Mary Giovingo, insisted that she be referred to by her maiden name (and she has been ever after). Though he never met her, he'd chide, "You were such a horrid, precocious little monster. You're going to burn in hell someday." Why are people always trying to send me to hell?

I lived for the summers: the freedom to do what you want, the sleeping late, the lazy days—the utter boredom. Rockford offered little in the way of diversion for young people. Terry Bryan came to my house one day, and we couldn't find a single thing to occupy us. That week we had already exhausted going to movies, spending the day at the public pool, riding our bikes, and discussing our dreams for the future. What was left? Nothing.

I decided to call the Rockford Chamber of Commerce and register a complaint. I got some poor unsuspecting woman on the phone and began my lament. "My friend and I are sitting here during our summer vacation with absolutely nothing to do. We're thirteen years old, and we can't think of a single thing that Rockford has to offer young people." "Well, let's see. Have you thought about joining the Boy's Club," she suggested. "The Boy's Club? Do you have any idea what sort of boys go there. It's all troublemakers and hoodlums—hardly appropriate for us. Our parents would never allow us to join." "Well, let me think. What about the swimming pool or games in the park?" "But we just did those things yesterday. Surely, the city has an obligation to provide some recreational facilities for its youth." "I don't know what to suggest to you," she began to stammer. "No one has ever called here with a question like that before." I sensed in her voice that tears were about to flow. "I'm so sorry. I just don't have any ideas for you at all." "That's just as I suspected," I snapped before hanging up.

Todd Lehman, my life's partner, said to me many years later, "If you'd been practicing the piano instead of wasting your time calling the Chamber of Commerce, today you might be somewhere." Mary Giovingo would have concurred and added, "The truth hurts." And indeed it did. Though I moaned and complained about the town, it would have been the perfect place to polish my piano-playing or theatrical skills, if only I had been disciplined and had had some foresight. With little to distract one, a singular concentration on constructive practice and study was actually facilitated. To this day, one of my greatest regrets is that I wasted so much valuable time in my youth with trivial concerns. Lucky the child who's aware that a life in the arts demands serious preparation and training, and it must begin at an early age.

Temporary relief from the boredom came in the form of travel. With dad's promotion to foreman, we could now afford to take a two-week vacation. Until then, during the two weeks in July that Nylint shut down, we could afford only short day trips. These were fun and dad tried to please all of us by interspersing a variety of jaunts in between the mandatory trips to Wrigley Field. There were days at Lake Geneva in Wisconsin.

One year, we discovered a small coin-operated recording booth there. My parents wanted Larry and me to record something. I apparently saw this as an opportunity to make my star debut as a recording artist. I chose to sing the theme song from the 1952 movie, *Moulin Rouge.* Unknown to me then, the song was written by the French composer Georges Auric, one of the famed Les Six, a group of six serious composers from Montparnasse, who would have a minor influence later in my life. I eagerly listened to the recording when we got home, and it's painful to admit that a major record-label contract was not in my future. I was the only one who enjoyed our time on the beach at Lake Geneva because no one else could swim; they were all terrified of the water.

Dad also insisted each year on a visit to Chicago's Midway Airport. Though he'd never been on a plane, he was like a child in awe as he watched the aircraft take off and land. Actual flying was another story entirely. A supplier at Nylint invited dad for a flight in his Piper Cub. Dad asked me if I wanted to go. "Yes," I screamed. We drove out to the tiny Rockford airport on a clear summer day and boarded the plane. I sat next to the pilot in the copilot's seat. Dad sat behind me, with his right foot stretched out beside me. Every time a wind current made the plane dip a bit, dad's right food slammed into the floor as if he were hitting the brake. I realized how scared he was. "I hope he's not going to pee his pants," I thought. I was enjoying every moment in the air. Within about fifteen minutes, dad said to the pilot, "Okay, well, I— well, I, I think we've seen enough." Here I was—his sissy son—and I'm the brave one.

Real travel, however, was of a different order all together. On our first trip to Colorado, where dad had been briefly stationed before being sent to Hawaii and Okinawa, he invited Andy, Jenny, and Jo to go with us. All seven of us crammed into his 1950s mist-green Styleline Deluxe Chevrolet with gleaming whitewall tires. Jo and I always sat together in the back seat, studying the American Automobile Association tour guide, conspiring over which sights to visit, and putting in our bids for better restaurants and motels with swimming pools, though we were often overruled because they were too expensive.

I was so overexcited the night before the trip that I couldn't sleep at all and still didn't mind having to depart at seven in the morning. Mother bought Larry and me leather travel diaries so we could keep a record of each day or more likely to keep us occupied and quiet on the long drives.

I'm astounded when I look over those journals today, just how utterly banal my observations were, considering how deeply exhilarated I was by the rushing mountain streams in Big Thompson Canyon, the majestic peaks in Rocky Mountain National Park, and the dizzying view from the Royal Gorge bridge, perilously suspended like a necklace 1,000 feet above the canyon. None of the women had the nerve to look down. Despite my love of language, I had obviously not yet developed the nuanced vocabulary needed to describe the intensity of what I was experiencing. Rather my evocative and scintillating journal entries read, "Today we saw Pike's Peak. It was beautiful." Lord, have mercy!

Each year my father would say, "So where do we go on vacation?" My vote was always for New York City, but that idea was nixed. Michigan's Upper Peninsula, Mackinac Island, Toronto, and Niagara Falls became vacation number two. Traveling with the Sciannas was such a pleasure that we invited them again. Our first night was spent in Escanaba, Michigan. The next morning we had breakfast at Marco's Restaurant, so typically midwestern in its 1930s, two-story rounded-corner structure, with a huge EAT sign on the roof. Larry invariably ordered more food than he could down. Wasting food was a sin to Mary Giovingo, and she did not in the least tolerate it.

"What are you ordering, Larry?" she asked.

"I'm having the pancakes."

"Okay, then order the children's stack."

"No, no, I want the stack of five."

" Larry, you know your eyes are bigger than your stomach."

" No, I'm hungry. I'll get the five."

"All right, but if you can't finish every bit of it, you'll have to pay for it yourself. We're not going to spend hard-earned money for you to waste food any more."

As a child, my brother was notoriously tightfisted with the few coins he received as an allowance. My father, Larry, and I were all addicted to Cokes at that time, and on vacation we would often take three dimes out to the motel vending machine and drink a bottle each before bed. Definitely a health warning required here. Dad established the rule that we must take turns buying the Cokes. Strangely, whenever Larry's turn came around, he suddenly was not thirsty.

The pancakes arrived, and the stack of five was mountainous. Larry poured a deep puddle of cheap syrup over them and dug in. He did pretty well with about a quarter of these gigantic dough disks. After that, we watched him chew very, very slowly, mimicking a cow masticating cud, and then with great effort swallow what looked like, from the pain in his face, a mouthful of nails. By the time he reached the half-stack mark, the rest of us had finished eating, and it was certain he was never going make it to the finish line.

"Just pay for the pancakes, Larry, then you don't have to eat them." mother offered.

"No, I'll finish them." He was adamant.

Every bite became more onerous than the one before.

"Mary, let him quit, please. I can't watch him struggling like this any more," Aunt Jennie pleaded.

"No, I said he'd have to eat them all or pay for them, and that's what he will do."

"I'll pay for them myself," Uncle Andy offered.

"That won't help at all. He's got to learn his lesson. He's pulled this so many times, but this is going to be his last."

And a lesson he did learn. We sat for an hour watching him turn a pale shade of green as he agonizingly forced down the final bite. Unsurprisingly, Larry never ate another pancake in his life.

Not even on vacation did our family ever miss mass. Wherever we happened to be on a Sunday, we would find a church—in this case, it was St. John's in Kingston, Ontario, our first mass outside America. The service was exactly the same in Canada, but when the ushers began collecting the donations, we all choked back laughter, because rather than using a collection basket on a long pole that reached across the entire pew, as we had always known, the ushers wore old-time coin changers around their necks, just as bus drivers used to use.

After mass, we went to a restaurant for a very quick breakfast (no pancakes), because we had less than half an hour before embarking on an eight-hour cruise through the Thousand Islands. We woofed down the food and barely made it to the ship on time. Jo began complaining almost immediately after leaving the dock, "My breakfast didn't go down too well." Within an hour, she began vomiting over the side of the boat and continued to do so for most of the trip, inciting the disfavor of the pleasure-seeking passengers on this intimate vessel. I felt a bit queasy myself but managed to hold my food down. What a man I'd become!

The tour to nowhere was endless. Take it from me, you've seen one of those islands, you've seen them all. But on this no-exit expedition, the ship of shackled prisoners endured the draconian punishment of witnessing all 1,800 of them TWICE, going and coming. About a half hour before returning to port, Larry began a vomiting duet with Jo. First one, then the other in imitative counterpoint, building to a stunning crescendo in close harmony. As we were pulling into port, Larry ran to the bow of the ship for his grand-barf finale. The crew tried in vain to steer him to the stern because they didn't want the people who were waiting on the dock for the night cruise to witness such an inviting spectacle.

When we returned from vacation mother gave Larry and me a nasty surprise. She had arranged for the two us to go across town to visit my father's aunt, Fannie. She was married to my grandmother's brother Benny, with whom they stayed when they first arrived from Palermo. Fannie and Benny still lived in the same house. Fannie was also my uncle Andy's sister, making the whole thing seem rather incestuous. Fanny detected certain physical deficiencies in the skinny physiques of both my brother and me, and she pleaded with my mother to send us to her house for one of her special treatments. She saw herself as a kind of healer. Many Sicilians have a serious superstitious streak. They believe in *malocchio* or the evil eye that can deliver a curse. Even Mary Giovingo, who had worms as a child, was convinced that one of these faith healers cured her. She swore that the woman put some threads in a bowl of water, and as she rubbed a potion on her belly, chanting prayers, the threads began swimming like worms in the water, and she was freed of crawly critters. Really, mother.

Larry and I both complained about this visit, but we were told we had to go. Fannie asked me to lie down on her couch and raise my shirt. She proceeded to rub some smelly warm ointment on my stomach, while she began chanting horrid, primitive-sounding prayers in Sicilian. What was she, a witch doctor? She declared that she could feel tremendous nervousness in my stomach. No doubt, considering the anxiety I had about what was coming next. A little more rubbing and a few more chants, and I was thankfully "cured." Now it was Larry's turn. The minute her hand touched his stomach he began laughing and squirming. He was very ticklish from the time he was a baby. She tried again, and again, but he started laughing. "Stop that. Stay calm or I can't do this." He gritted his teeth, but the minute she touched him, he laughed so hard his feet started kicking. She got very angry. *"Basta, basta, non lo posso fare"* (Enough, I can't do it.)

When we got on the bus to go home, everyone began looking at us with strange faces. Then they started moving to the other side of bus, and we knew why. Fannie's potion contained voluminous amounts of raw crushed garlic, and we reeked to the high heavens. I was completely humiliated. We both let mother have it in no uncertain terms for subjecting us to this barbarism. She apologized, but maintained that Fannie wouldn't take "no" for an answer, and mother feared offending the relatives.

Another diversion from the doldrums of summer boredom came

from an unlikely source. Uncle Andy, who began golfing regularly, decided to buy a new set of clubs. Years earlier, he had been given a used set by a friend. He told me that I could have the old set and that he would teach me how to golf, if I was interested. Although my swing in baseball, and consequently in golf, was naturally left-handed, the clubs were for a right-hander. It was somewhat of challenge to make the switch, but I managed it, probably to the detriment of my game. At first, Andy and I went to the local golf courses together. Terry Bryan also had an old set of clubs and we became friends with Kent Finger, a fellow student, who was quite a good golfer, making a twosome or threesome. I don't think I ever really loved the game, but it was so pleasant to be out on the links on a beautiful day, and I was so pleased with myself that I could finally participate in a sport without feeling mortified about my ineptness.

Around the same time, Uncle Tom was put in charge of the Sinnissippi Park golf course during the summers. His sports promoting didn't bring enough income to support his family, so he often took odd jobs. He always helped facilitate our getting onto the links. I think my dad, also a left-hand swinger, felt excluded so he bought some inexpensive clubs and joined us whenever I went out with Andy. Dad didn't last very long at this because even though I was not great at the game, I was much better than he was. I could see how it rankled when I beat him time after time. His hopelessly sports-challenged son now had three different athletic feats over him. I could swim and ice skate, neither of which he could ever do, plus I beat the pants off him at golf. Much too humiliating for the wannabe-jock father.

One summer the Speras from Brooklyn came again to visit. Jerry had now married a very warm and wonderful woman named Ann. She took an immediate liking to me, and I to her. Once again I started pumping them for information about New York. When they returned home, they mailed me a book all about New York City. It detailed almost everything I wanted to know, all accompanied by wonderful and enticing black-and-white photos. Before long, I had memorized most of the book, including the address of every landmark, the street and subway maps, and the names and histories of the major mansions on Fifth Avenue.

Around the same time, my cousin, Jo, introduced me to the recordings of jazz pianist, Joe Bushkin and his orchestra. Two of his records were entitled, *Midnight Rhapsody*, with a photo of the nighttime New York skyline on the cover, and *Skylight Rhapsody*, with a photo of a formally dressed young couple in an elegant studio with a skylight and a grand piano. This was archetypically New York for me. I played the two recordings, which featured many Gershwin tunes and the Rodgers and Hart song, "Manhattan," over and over again, while thumbing through the photos in the book. These songs and the sound of these arrangements seemed so quintessentially Manhattan that the aural imagery conjured up an even more powerful visual image of the city. My future as a New Yorker came vividly to life in these reveries.

I loved my brother, but I found it a bit annoying that he had to hang around us whenever I had friends over. Sometimes, however, he entertained my friends as much as he entertained my parents and me. He was always funny: making ridiculous faces; imitating TV variety-show impresario Ed Sullivan with his shoulders hiked up near his ears, his thumb and forefinger grabbing the elongated chin, "Tonight we have a really big shew"; or rummaging through an old trunk of my mother's and popping out dressed in some of her old wardrobe. He was more into drag than I ever was.

Diminutive hardly did justice to Larry's size. Even as a teenager he looked like a little boy—so much so that old ladies would offer to help him cross the street. When we were in Denver, a restaurant menu promised a prize to any children under five who finished their dinners. Larry was already eight and on this rare occasion he easily ate everything on his plate. We watched him surreptitiously trying to sneak out of the restaurant before anyone spotted him. He got right to the door when the waiter came rushing after him, "Here, little boy, you forgot your prize." He nearly died of shame.

Once mother gave us each money and told us to go to a local bakery and pick out some pastries for ourselves. Larry could not make up his mind. He looked so small, so forlorn, so pathetic that the clerk was practically moved to tears. "Here's a free donut for you, little boy," she said with a deeply concerned look, so proud of herself that she had done a charitable deed for a poor starving child. "Thanks," he said, ever so sweetly, taking a bite out of the donut. He then took the cash out of his pocket and ordered, "I'll take two of those, two of these, and two of those Napoleons back there," much to the clerk's horror.

Sadly, school was not a laughing matter for him. He was a very poor student, and he did not get the same opportunity I had been given to transfer to a better school. During his Hall School days, my mother was called in on dozens of parent-teacher conferences to discuss his deficiencies. When he began junior high, he had many of the same teachers I had had five years earlier, and they had the despicable habit of comparing him to me. By the time I moved to New York and Larry was in high school, he grew so angered by the unfavorable comparisons that he came home crying to my parents, "I hate my brother. I'm sick of hearing how much better he was."

His size became an excuse for much taunting by the time he reached high-school age. He was nicknamed, "fly," which stuck through his adult years. Once a group of boys grabbed him, slicked down his hair with oil, and carried him over their heads through the school hallways. He laughed about it, but it was obvious how much it pained him.

He wanted to quit high school in his junior year, but my parents wouldn't hear of it. My dad, I'm sure, saw this as a reprise of the dreadful mistake he had made in high school. Larry used his ingenuity to get through his last year and a half. He paid other kids to write his papers, do his homework, and I suspect on one occasion even take a test for him. Somehow he made it through graduation.

Larry got the tap-dancing lessons that I should have had. Though his performances were not embarrassing, they were not inspiring. He was not very musical, and he always looked cute but a bit awkward at his recitals. I had the job of taking him to his weekly lesson at Jinx Brown's studio. I watched the class intently, marking the steps with my feet while seated. Just as in *A Chorus Line*, I'd say to myself, "I can do that." I kept hoping that Jinx would notice my enthusiasm and ask me to join in. She never did.

When no one was home I was always dancing around the living room to Sammy Davis recordings or to Doris Day singing, "Shaking the Blues Away." A few times my mother caught me and would yell, "Stop that prancing around in there." It wasn't cute any longer. Fred Astaire and Gene Kelly movies were a must. I so much wanted to quit piano lessons and study tap, that I took a pair of penny loafers to the shoemaker and had taps put on them. I tapped a bit on the linoleum floor in our hallway, hoping my mother would get the hint and ask if I wanted lessons; she never did. I was afraid to ask her because I was aware of the tremendous sacrifice my parents made to pay for the all those piano lessons. She'd view dropping piano as a terrible waste of money. And I knew how she deplored people who went from one interest to another. Her line would be: "What do you want to be, a jack of all trades and a master of none?" When I told her about this years later, her response was, "I had no idea. If only you'd said something." Ah, yes, if only I had.

Another of my interests reared it's head for the first time—cooking. Mother and her sister had a shower to attend, so Lena left her daughter, Gloria, in my care for the afternoon. Gloria was a bad girl, always getting into things. I was irrationally possessed with the idea of cooking something. Let's see, what about a chocolate cake? I took down my mother's *Betty Crocker Cook Book* and eagerly began, with Gloria acting as sous-chef. Everything was going swimmingly until I unmolded the creation. To my shock and horror, the bottom of the cake was entirely lined with egg shells. I couldn't figure out how this had happened. I couldn't have done that. It's not possible. It must have been Gloria. Several years went by before I got the urge to cook again.

Near the end of ninth grade, my theatrical aspirations came more into focus. The school play for that year was something called, *Huckleberry Finn, Detective*. I was cast to play one of the leads, Tom Sawyer. I did a creditable job in the role, but backstage before every entrance I would feverishly review my lines for I had a phobia that I'd have a memory lapse, not a desirable personality trait for an aspiring performer. I suffered the same terror at every piano recital, my foot shaking so badly I could hardly keep it on the pedal. The dreaded lapse thankfully never occurred in either instance.

My Tom Sawyer was apparently impressive enough that Miss Nyman, the drama coach, encouraged me to pursue acting as a career. Wow, she honestly thinks I could be an actor—maybe I'd be the next Laurence Olivier? She told me I should begin preparing immediately. She had me write for catalogs to the two schools she thought I should attend: The Goodman Theatre School in Chicago and Pasadena Playhouse. I was fascinated by the courses in the curriculum, which included dance, voice lessons, stage fighting, as well as acting and directing. So it was settled; this is what I would do, what I would become. When I declared my intentions to be an actor to adults, the skepticism—the "right," "sure," "I bet" expression—was deflating. I began tempering my pitch by saying that I wanted to be a director, though at that point I wasn't clear about what a director actually did and was certain they didn't know, either.

When Miss Nyman said, "Prepare immediately," I thought that writing for the catalogs was sufficient. My dreams of a showbiz career veered more toward a castles-in-the-sky approach. I once sent my photograph to 20th Century Fox Studios in the hope that they'd give me a screen test. When the negative response came in the mail, my father opened the letter, and I was mortified because I had done this on the sly. At the same time I heard about the famed High School for the Performing Arts (the one depicted in the TV series *Fame*). I fantasized that perhaps I could live with the Speras and attend the school. No thought about the preparation for the audition crossed my mind. And there was no way in hell my parents would have allowed such a thing, in any case.

The summer after junior high I finally got my wish. We were going to New York, this time without the Sciannas. Jennie had developed tiny, unidentifiable sores in her mouth, which began spreading to her face and neck. No one could diagnose the problem, but she was not well enough to travel.

We took a southern route because my dad wanted to see Washington, D.C. and Atlantic City first. We crossed from Ohio into Kentucky and stopped at a public bathroom at a scenic overlook. I looked up and saw the word WHITE carved in granite above the door and thought: "That's strange. I guess the White family donated the money for the facility." When I came out and crossed to the other side of the structure, I saw the word BLACK carved over that doorway, and the obvious hit me. I'd heard about such repugnant segregation but didn't think it still existed in 1957. I was so shocked and outraged about this, I couldn't rid the thought from my mind, and it poisoned much of the ride through West Virginia and Virginia.

Washington, D.C., made little impression on any of us, and we decided to forgo the tours through the White House and Capitol. Atlantic City was my first look at an ocean. There wasn't time for a swim, so I insisted on walking from one end of the boardwalk to the other, with our box of pastel-colored salt-water taffy. At the Steel Pier, we witnessed the grotesque diving-horse act, in which a female rider mounted the animal atop a sixty-foot tower, from which both dove into the water below. This atrocity, probably the most frequented attraction on the boardwalk, was thankfully stopped in the 1970s. The Marina Ballroom at the Pier was luckily featuring Tony Bennett, with the Maynard Ferguson Orchestra and Gene Krupa during our visit. Bennett sang his hits of the day including my favorite, "One for My Baby." There was, of course, dancing but Dad hated to dance, probably because he was so bad at it. He often took mother to the famed Aragon Ballroom in Chicago, but never to dance. She'd force him reluctantly out onto the floor then remark: "You dance like you have shit in your pants, Matt." He went to the ballrooms because he adored the big bands and especially Gene Krupa on drums. He had begged his mother to let him play the drums, but she forbade it, knowing she couldn't bear all that banging in her house.

We never argued on these trips, but the drive from Atlantic City to New York was an exception. Dad wanted to visit relatives in Franklin Square, Long Island, before going on to Manhattan. I wasn't happy with this plan because New York meant Manhattan to me. I assuaged myself knowing we would have to drive crosstown first. I had it all planned in my head. We'd approach the Lincoln Tunnel from New Jersey and exit into paradise on Thirty-Fourth Street, where we would drive by so many of the great landmarks I had fantasized over.

Dad hated driving in big cities, especially ones he didn't know. He hoped to avoid what was sure to be horrible traffic in Manhattan and find some alternate route to Long Island. I was incensed when he announced this. I had imagined the thrill of approaching the city for years, and he was thwarting my dream. Things got rather nasty and mother tried to calm us both down without success. Dad announced that we would stop at the next gas station so he could get directions on how to skirt the city. I sat in the back seat fuming, hoping we'd never find a station. But, no. There's one straight ahead. Rotten luck. My fists were clenched and I began sweating as we approached. We both got out of the car, because I wanted to hear what the attendant would say. Dad explained what he wanted to do. There was a nerve-racking silence for a moment, while the attendant pondered the question. "Nope. Can't be done. No such route. You have to drive through Manhattan." I was wise enough to keep silent and not look too pleased, but inside I was smiling from ear to ear.

When we emerged from the Lincoln Tunnel, I couldn't see the tops of the skyscrapers through the side windows, so I stretched out my body, threw my head back as far as it could go, and looked up through the rear window. As we began crossing Thirty-Fourth Street, "Oh my god, look, it's Macy's. There's the Empire State Building. Did you see it? And B. Altman's," I began screaming. My mother turned around to look at me with an expression that read, "Who is this maniac in the back seat?" Traffic happened to be very light on a summer Saturday afternoon, so the trip across the island flashed by in less than fifteen minutes. I hardly got the chance to savor what I had seen before we entered another dark hole, the Queens Midtown Tunnel, and headed to Long Island.

At the Cinici's house (I had never met these people and couldn't figure out why we had to visit them), I stood outside on tiptoe trying desperately to get a view of the Manhattan skyline. Not a chance. Too far away. After mass on Sunday, dad asked to see a Long Island telephone directory. He wanted to look up an old army buddy, who lived in Babylon. He found the name and with great anticipation called:

"Is Red there?

Someone yelled for him to come to the phone.

"Red, this is an old buddy of yours. I'm in the area and I'd like to come over and visit you for awhile," dad said eagerly.

Silence, while Red is obviously asking who was calling.

"You'll see when I get there. Is it okay to come over? Long pause. "All right, I'll be there in about forty-five minutes."

Red apparently was a redheaded Italian that dad met while in Okinawa, where they became very close. It had been eleven years since they'd seen each other. They communicated only by exchanging Christmas cards each year. We arrived at a ranch-style suburban house.

"Wait in the car while I go talk to him first," dad told us. He went to the door and rang the bell. A woman answered. There was some discussion and Dad returned to the car.

"What happened? my mother asked.

"She told me to wait outside, and he would come out."

"Why didn't you just tell her who you are and be done with it?"

"I want to surprise him.

Instead, we were the ones to get the surprise. The house door opened and out stepped five of the tallest, burliest, toughest-looking Italians I'd ever seen. They approached Dad menacingly, arms crossed against their chests, biceps bulging.

"Who are you and what do you want with Red," one snarled threateningly. Dad suddenly looked extremely nervous.

"I'm just an old army friend. We were together in Okinawa," he was stammering.

"Then why didn't you just say so?"

"I just wanted to give him a little surprise."

"Surprise, huh? What's your name?"

"Matt Cancelose," he began to tremble.

"We'll go in and see if he knows you. You wait out here."

When they were back inside, Mary Giovingo, in her most intimidating tone of voice said, "Don't you EVER do that again, Matt. This is so embarrassing."

Finally, Red came out, the two buddies hugged, and we were invited into the house for coffee.

"You scared the hell out of me. I thought it was someone gunning for me, so I asked these guys to come over for protection."

When we got back in the car, mother said, "They looked like a bunch of mafiosi to me, Matt. Who knows what could have happened to us there?"

Our family, honest to a fault, sparing no effort to look upright and respectable, lived in terror of being associated, even tangentially, with the mafia. The Brooklyn Speras were away during our trip, so that afternoon we headed to Manhattan, where we stayed at the New Yorker Hotel, a block from Macy's on Thirty-Fourth Street. How horrified I was in 1972 when this renowned hotel turned into the headquarters of the Moonies, who thankfully sold it in the 90s.

Everything in Manhattan enchanted me. So often coming face to face with the real thing, after having fantasized about it for years, is disillusioning; for me, Manhattan become even more vibrantly compelling. Standing in front of the Astor Hotel on Times Square, I marveled at the gigantic Pepsi Cola sign above the Bond Clothing Store across the street: Two enormous Pepsi bottles on either side of building flanked a real waterfall, crowned by a magnificent lighted bottle cap. On the building to its right was the famous Camel's sign in which a large painted man blew smoke rings the size of an automobile tire every four seconds.

What truly seized my attention, however, was one block to the west of Times Square—Shubert Alley. So many theaters in one place, each presenting a Broadway show I would love to have seen. The alley itself housed two theaters, the Shubert and the Booth, with inviting posters of myriad plays along the outer walls. We walked by the Shubert and there on the marquee was Judy Holliday, one of my favorite Hollywood stars, starring in *Bells Are Ringing*.

"Please, dad, can we go see this? Please." The box office was closed on Sundays.

"I'll check with the ticket agent at the hotel and see what it costs."

I could tell he wasn't excited about the idea. I don't think he knew what musical theater was. So many things in the show he would have loved: the big band in the pit; the pretty girls; one of his favorite songs, "Just in Time," would soon be recorded by both Frank Sinatra and Tony Bennett; Peter Gennaro and his dancers would delight him on TV's *Your Hit Parade* the following year. My hopes were so high about seeing a show as we walked down Shubert Alley. When we reached the Booth Theater, a kindly-looking stage doorman (generally they're nasty tyrants) was standing outside. The door was wide open and I stood on tiptoe trying to get a peek inside.

"Would you like to see the theater?"

"Oh, yes, yes, I would."

He led all four of us onto the stage, where an ornate living-room set was in place. I could hardly believe this. I was actually on Broadway, on a stage, and gazing out into the audience, imagining what it would feel like if the house were packed and they were applauding my stunning performance. As we walked back out into the alley, he said. "If you want to see the show, come back tomorrow night, and I'll get you all in free." This was a stroke of luck beyond any hopes I'd had. The play was Gore Vidal's *Visit to a Small Planet*, which I'd never heard of. However, it starred Cyril Ritchard, whom I had known from the movies, but more so from his performance as Captain Hook in the television production of *Peter Pan*.

"Wow, isn't this great?" I jumped up an down, as we walked back to Times Square.

"Great? We're not coming back here tomorrow night for sure," my mother said firmly.

"Why not? It's free!"

"Free," she said with great contempt. "Nobody gives strangers something for free. It's just a trick to get money out of us."

"But, mom!"

"Don't 'but mom' me. No ifs, ands, or buts about it, we are not going, period."

A huge weight of disappointment crushed me. Still a faint smile stole over my face when a thought about Mary Giovingo crossed my consciousness, "She trusses no one!" Anyway, there's still *Bells Are Ringing*, and I want to see that much more than the play. Dad went to the ticket agent when we got back to the hotel. The unpleasant-looking surly man barked, "The cheapest seats I can get you are $10.20, which includes the ticket-broker fee."

We walked away from the desk, and dad whispered, "We can't afford that." They saw how crest-fallen I was so they conferred. "We'll get you a ticket and you can go by yourself."

I thought about it a moment, and the whole thing seemed unfair to them and spoiled for me, so I said, "No." "We don't care about seeing it anyway, so why don't you just go?" "No, that's all right. I don't want to go alone." I desperately did, but I was totally demoralized.

As I learned in later years, we could easily have found seats for around $2 each, if we'd only gone straight to the theater box office rather than a ticket broker, who sold only the most expensive seats, plus an added commission. At the time, I wasn't aware of just what I had missed. The show was directed by Jerome Robbins and choreographed by Robbins and Bob Fosse, two of the greatest creative talents that Broadway has ever seen. And they never worked together again.

Also, we missed the other play because we just weren't savvy, so typically midwesterners. Summertime in New York in those days (that is, unlike modern times when swarms of tourists invade the city like locusts at all seasons) meant that the theater was in deep doldrums. The stage doorman was simply "papering the house," in other words, putting butts in the seats rather than having the actors play to a half-empty theater, which is bad for performer morale and sends audience enthusiasm crashing.

We spent only two days and nights in Manhattan, hardly enough time to get a real feel for the city. Dad was getting antsy to leave the place so we departed for New England, meandering aimlessly through several states. The only memorable moment was my first-ever plunge in the ocean at Orchard Beach, Maine. The sea beckoned to me, and I eagerly abandoned myself to it, madly diving into the surf. And quite a shock it was, too. The water was so cold that I instantly turned blue—redolent of my days at Camp Rotary.

More aimless driving through tree-covered hills that New Englanders brazenly refer to as mountains. Have you ever seen the Rockies, guys? We were in the Catskills when I spotted a sign saying New York City, 120 miles. That was just a couple hours away. At a rest stop, I pulled ma aside and begged her to plead with dad to let us go back to the city and escape the boredom I knew we were all experiencing.

"Check through the AAA book and see if you can find a really cheap place to stay." I did and Dad reluctantly agreed to return for two days. The Hotel Excelsior was an interesting find, across the street from the American Museum of Natural History and the Hayden Planetarium, and less than a block from Central Park. The price was very reasonable, and we actually were given a rather nice suite—bedroom, living room with a sofa bed, and kitchen (not that Mary Giovingo had any intentions of cooking on vacation.) I opened a window to look out on what I hoped was Central Park, only to discover an air shaft. As I was drawing back inside, the window fell without warning and hit me on the head.

The sofa bed, where Larry and I slept, was strangely made, folding in half, rather than the usual thirds. Also, it was longer in width than length so you had to sleep parallel, rather than perpendicular, to the couch. When Larry got out of bed in the morning, the bed snapped shut like a bear trap, with me in it. I looked like a hot dog on a bun. Thankfully, others were in the room because I was unable to release myself from the bed's vice-like grip. I could have been trapped there for hours before someone found me. It took all three of them to get me out.

The two days consisted of more touristy outings. One to the United Nations and a guided tour through the NBC Studios. We were offered free tickets to that evening's broadcast of "The Price Is Right," the silly game show hosted by Bill Cullen. This time Mary Giovingo didn't turn it down; she trusses NBC. I found it interesting to watch the technical aspects of the broadcast, but I winced when we were asked to applaud and ooh and aah on cue.

The sad part was that I had the chance to see two fine Broadway shows, and ended up with a stupid TV game show. It was as though I was tempted with fine French champagne served in Baccarat crystal flutes but was instead served flat, cheap beer in a rusty can. I learned that if I wanted to see New York in my own manner, I would have to go there alone.

Those Low-Down, High-School Blues

"YOU NEVER GET OVER HIGH SCHOOL" is a truism that haunts many lives. East Rockford High School, which was nearly a three-mile walk from home, was a larger and more imposing institution than Lincoln Junior High—there were nearly 2,600 students. Here the rigid social stratifications in life came into sharp focus for me. The in-group was referred to as "the clique," always spoken in reverent tones. Nearly everyone aspired to be in the clique. These were the people who mattered, who seemed to have all the fun, ran everything from student government to the various clubs (oh, I became president of the French Club, but there was no prestige in that), and generally dictated the rules for socializing.

To be admitted to the clique, you needed to be able to put your check mark in most of the following boxes: good looking; from a good, and preferably well-off, family; of acceptable, if not superior, intelligence; well-dressed, but within a very strict code of suitable taste; extremely sure of yourself; at least fun-loving, if not fun-inducing; and most important, an athlete if you're a boy; and a cheerleader if you're a girl. Those not admitted spent their high school years on the other side of the glass, enviously peering in, their sweaty palms and noses unappealingly flattened against the pane.

Pairing off became much more marked and far more important. The number of students "going steady" increased dramatically. Unlike in the musical, *Bye Bye Birdie*, where the teenagers "got pinned," at East High, the accepted way to make public such a commitment was to give your letter sweater, a bright red cardigan with a large black "R" emblazoned on the front, to your girlfriend. Of course, only athletes received these letters, so the ritual conferred elevated status on both the giver and the recipient. I, naturally, had no letter sweater, no girlfriend, and was certainly not a member of the clique. Most of my friends were in the same

65

position, all outsiders, barbarians at the gates. We listened with envy to the fervid discussions about weekend parties at the country clubs and various homes to which we were never invited.

The most painful element for me was knowing that most of the boys who had been named to me as participating in the strip-poker games in junior high school were now going steady, including my former partner-in-crime, Cory. This meant to me that they had moved on from the experimental early-adolescent, homosexual phase and assumed their rightful place as "normal," well-adjusted heterosexual boys. I had not. I completely lost confidence that it was just a phase for me. Because I knew of no one else who shared my proclivities, I was left isolated and alone, with no one to talk to about it.

In my sophomore year, I developed my first crush on another boy, Terry Carlson. Whenever Connie Carlson was not in a particular class, Terry C. sat behind me, because of the continued alphabetical seating. He was my idealized Nordic god: blond, extremely handsome, a smooth, muscular body, very bright (smarter than I was), and on the basketball team. We became very friendly, but it was strictly a classroom friendship that lasted throughout high school. Whenever I was near him, school took on a particularly radiant luster it lacked at any other time. The only remembrance of spending time with him out of class was when I once ran into him by chance at the public library, and we ended up researching and studying together for an exam. Studying was never so compelling for me. I so hoped he would suggest we could get together again, but he never did.

I loved watching him play basketball. Uniforms for that sport in the 1950s were so much more revealing than those of today, especially the tiny satin short shorts that slid provocatively against his skin. By the end of the year, he was going steady with a girl named Sharon, whom he ended up marrying after graduation, so that completely separated him from me socially. It intrigued me also that my three Terrys—A, B, and C— were each the captains of their respective ROTC companies. I was always a bit puzzled that Terry Carlson was involved in ROTC because it had a reputation for attracting nerdy types, which he definitely was not.

Another incident, which confirmed that my obsession with men was not simply a phase, occurred during the summer after my sophomore year. I was walking down Seventh Street (where the magazine store was located—a street of sex and sin, it seems), and I looked up and saw this man high up on a telephone pole, making repairs. He was stripped to the waist, in his late twenties, and overwhelmingly appealing. I stood for one long moment on the other side of the street transfixed, unable to take my eyes off him.

Once he looked down and noticed me and I became very self-conscious so I kept walking. His physical presence was a powerful flesh-to-flesh magnet, forcing me to walk back and gape again. I hope my mouth wasn't hanging open, too. How many times did I imagine I could get away with this, without alerting him? I had to stop; I couldn't stop. I believe I paced back and forth five times, always pausing across from him and pretending to look in store windows. What possible hopes did I have for this encounter—that he would eagerly descend the pole, take me in his strong arms, and carry me far away from Rockford to a world that was more congenial to me? Again, he noticed me, and this time I thought I detected a look of disgust, though I may have imagined it in order to break the magnetic spell he had cast. I ran home completely shaken, but exhilarated, unable to get him out of my head for weeks.

Hours of study expanded exponentially in high school in my desperate need to keep up with my peers. Did these brainy kids have to work as hard as I did? I never knew. East High was, at the time, rated one of the best high schools in the country, and the demands were intimidating. Studying until three or four in the morning was not unusual. At the same time, Dad was promoted again, this time to plant supervisor. His bosses, the Klint brothers—both of whom had stellar sons in my class and, of course, members of the clique—thought he should take a correspondence course to strengthen his management skills. Dad was still not disposed toward scholarship of any kind.

The added responsibilities of his new position seemed to frighten him. Some of his nervous tics became more pronounced. When sitting, his legs opened and closed as rapidly as butterfly wings. He began chewing the knuckle on his right thumb, creating an angry red bump. "Matt, stop that chewing right now. Your knuckle looks like a monkey's *culo* (behind)," Mary Giovingo ordered. We became concerned when clumps of hair began falling out. He already suffered from the Spera family's male pattern baldness syndrome. (Please, god, spare me this curse.) He saw a doctor and when we asked what was diagnosed, he answered, "I've got the nerves." The blotchy hair loss made him look frightful. Both my mother and father were far and away the best-looking members of their families, so this was disconcerting. The hair grew back as predicted, but a certain unease remained.

Why this was I couldn't ascertain because he was clearly far beyond merely competent at his job. Whenever our family ran into his bosses at school functions, they always were effusive in their praise of his performance. I believe it was shaky self-confidence, a plague that hung over our whole family. He was falling behind in his course study, so mother asked me to please find some time away from my own studies to help him. Now I became his tutor. I'd explain words and passages that stumped him in the reading assignments, help him take the exams, and give him advice on writing papers. Unfortunately, I was no more successful with him than I had been as Henry Higgins with Mary Giovingo. He just couldn't apply himself and never completed the course.

When Larry began school full time, mother decided to go back to work half days as a sales clerk. She got a job selling women's sportswear, at D. J. Stewart and Company, one of Rockford's swankiest department stores. In a few years, she began working full time and remained there until she retired. She was offered a promotion to buyer, which meant trips to Chicago to select new clothing lines, something I was sure she would have relished. She turned it down out of fear, again because she lacked the confidence that she could handle the job. What is it about our family? I suspect, in addition to the lack of self-confidence, there is an inherent Sicilian mistrust of the future. Better to be satisfied with what you have than risk a change. The Sicilian language interestingly has no future tense. A nation that had been dominated and exploited by one group after another simply could not envision anything better about tomorrow than today, so they summarily dismissed it.

Changes came to East State Street, however. Rose and Paul moved out of their apartment and bought the house from the monuments dealer. They rented out their flat to a Jewish family with two children, much younger than I. *Nonna* never said a word, but I sensed that she was anxious about losing her matriarchal status, even though I know she was happy that they were moving up in the world. Then Tom and Ruby bought a house and rented their apartment to a childless Evangelical couple—no makeup, no fashion flair, *no joie de vivre,* but very sweet.

Curiously, we saw more of Rose and Paul after they moved than when they lived directly below us. We almost never were invited to their apartment, but eager to show off their new house, we were frequently asked to visit. Paul's overflowing pride with his new-found status as a homeowner in an upscale neighborhood seemed to lighten his dour demeanor ever so slightly. They especially liked to have us over in the summer to enjoy their "breezeway," an enclosed structure connecting the house with the garage that was aired on both sides with jalousie windows.

Rose had hideous taste in clothes, furniture, and decor, which unfortunately diminished the stateliness of her lovely new home. In the apartment, she had two large, grotesque table lamps with shiny black vinyl shades, emblazoned with gaudy red roses, which sat on either side of an equally grotesque turquoise sofa. She transferred these to the new house, completely oblivious to how inappropriate they looked in the new setting. Never one to leave bad enough alone, she had two faux old-Dutch-masters-style oil paintings of forest scenes. In their glorious new setting, Rose donned her artist's smock and highlighted the leaves with gold paint. "I'm very talent," she immodestly boasted, always leaving off the "ed," as she exhibited her painterly brush strokes.

That talent was now broadened most emphatically to music. She bought herself a small Hammond chord organ and began lessons. Naturally, she had to regale us with her new-found keyboard skills. The organ seems to be the perfect instrument for the distinctly unmusical. When one can't locate the next note (oh, yes indeedy, it does take many glances back and forth between the sheet music and the keyboard), one simply holds down the pedal, to provide a continuity of tone until that damned key can be found.

We never accepted dinner invitations to her house, knowing all too well her culinary travesties. But, one Sunday afternoon we were invited over for coffee, and she had baked chocolate cupcakes. I was hungry, and I thought, "How bad could they be?" I was certain she had used a box mix. What could possibly go wrong? You just add egg, water, and oil, *et voilà*. My, how deeply I underestimated her expertise. I took one bite and one chew and had a panic attack, "She's trying to poison me." I had never tasted the likes of this concoction. What could she conceivably have done to produce such a noxious lump. What to do? What to do? There was no dog I could feed it to, except perhaps, Uncle Paul. Besides, I'm totally against cruelty to animals. There was no way I could swallow even this one tentative bite, so I daintily took out my napkin to wipe my mouth, spit out the offending turd-like substance, squeezed the remainder into a rubbery ball, which could easily have bounced, and stuffed the entire jumble into my pocket.

My parents exhibited a totally atypical mercenary attitude toward Rose and Paul. We had to be nice to them because they had MONEY and no one to leave it to. Larry and I were definitely their favorites. In fact, except for Jo, they kept all their other nieces and nephews at arm's length. They even alluded to the fact that we would be the recipient of their largesse after their demise. Ah, the best laid plans. . .

Mary Giovingo, with her tough talk, often needled my father, but there was a good-naturedness about it, and dad sloughed it all off with a laugh. "Matt, when you're listening to that damn ball game you're dead to the world." During Cubs' games, first on radio and later on TV, Dad could not be moved to do anything or focus on anything else. Another of her favorite lines came when they went out together: "Matt, you go to your damn bowling banquets and you get all sheiked up; you go out with me and you look like an old farmer," apparently "farmer" was as dowdy as you could get. If she asked him to do something he didn't want to do, it was, "Matt, if you don't like it, you know where the door is." The tough-talking woman who hadn't the power or will to kick anyone out of the house. We all laughed.

The departure of the two brothers from State Street, however, fomented an element of dissension between my parents I had not seen before. Mary Giovingo basically loved her mother-in-law, but Dad was still a mama's boy and *Nonna's* matriarchal status made my mother feel that her life was not completely her own. "Your brothers can move away from here; why can't we buy a house?" "Because we don't have the money for a down payment." Mother didn't buy this argument, and she sensed that he just didn't want to leave his mother, which, I believe had an element of truth in it. The arguments became intense. She began belittling him in ways that even I could see were unwise. Dad rarely got angry, but when he did it was scary. Once, the situation got so bad that I thought he was going to strike her. It frightened me so that I ran out of the house, which thankfully distracted them and eventually calmed them down.

Mysterious diseases and the Mayo Clinic made unwelcome appearances in our lives. Mother, who had been plagued with arthritis pain in her neck and shoulders, found no relief in chiropractic or analgesics. Dad decided to take her to the Mayo Clinic in Rochester, Minnesota. Nothing new was offered for her discomforts, but during the physical exam, doctors began calling in about twenty of their colleagues.

"Look into her eyes. You won't see many examples of this."

The diagnosis was areolar sclerosis, a hereditary eye disease in which the retina begins to shred over time. What was so unusual was that she was only in her thirties and the degeneration was already observable. She manifested no symptoms yet, but she was warned that there would be a long progressive decline. As it turned out, before seventy, she became functionally blind.

The more serious disease was discovered in my Aunt Jennie, who was in her late forties. The strange, painful blisters and sores that began in her mouth had now spread to other parts of the body. This rare immune-system disease, called pemphigus vulgaris, at the time could be found in fewer than 100 cases in the medical literature. She made many trips to the Mayo Clinic, and on her final visit, she spent months in residence there. To this day there is no cure, and poor Jennie was subjected to all sorts of experimental treatments, most of which involved steroids, some of which affected her mentally. This extremely gentle and kind woman was said to have become so violent she had to be restrained for a period, all because of the medications she was given.

Nonna was so upset at the thought of losing her only daughter that she made a solemn promise and commitment to St. Joseph in the hope that he would spare her life—she created a St. Joseph's altar. This joyously beautiful tradition was very popular among Rockford's Sicilian community, though it has all but disappeared today even in Sicily. On March 19, the feast of St. Joseph, those elderly Italian women, who were asking some favor from the saint, cleared out the living rooms of their houses. They enlisted the help of relatives, who cooked elaborate dishes beginning at least a week in advance of the feast.

On the evening of March 18, the bounteous food, which filled the entire room, was elaborately displayed on white linen- and lace-covered tables. Tiers were built in the middle of one wall to resemble an altar; each tier was covered with food, and a painting or statue of St. Joseph was placed at the apex, lighted with candles. In the center of the room was a round table, also covered in white linen, with three place settings of the finest china, crystal, and silver. The local papers listed all the homes that had prepared the altars, so that anyone could come to view them in an open house the night before the feast day. Generally, there were about eight to ten each year. The rooms were roped off so you could not enter. However, the women served the visitors cookies or small pastries, as they marveled at the altars.

I loved being taken from house to house to witness the remarkably inventive ways in which the food was presented. There is no word to describe the intoxicating fragrance that wafted through the room from the mingling scents of the wide variety of foods created. To this day, I can summon up the memory of that perfume, though I've not seen a St. Joseph's altar in sixty years. No meat was cooked—only ornately decorated whole fishes, piles of beautifully presented vegetables and *frittatas*, varieties of colorful pastries, including cream puffs in the shape of swans, and highly ornamented cookies, wreaths of fresh-baked braided breads, two feet in diameter, with wide red bows tied about them, and enormous sheaths of spaghetti, two-feet in length, also tied with red bows.

On the feast day, three children were selected from the orphanages to play the roles of Jesus, Mary, and Joseph, and they were costumed appropriately. No one ate until they took their places at the center table. They were expected to taste—if only a single bite—every one of the foods in the room. Once they had sampled each dish, festivities began: The family and invited guests, often as many as fifty people, began eating all that was left on the altar. It was my first time to partake as a guest at the feast, and how lucky I was to have had this opportunity.

Around this time Jo, who was now twenty-nine, was engaged to be married to Jack, a very tall man seven years younger than she. It seemed curious to me, recalling that I had planned to marry her myself as a little boy, that Jack was only six years older than I was. She was warned by many against this guy, who was a real playboy, but she was not to be dissuaded. After the St. Joseph's altar, her mother was taken back to the Mayo Clinic for her extended stay.

The question loomed as to whether Jennie would be released in time to see her only child married. From the reports we got from Rochester, prospects were very grim. Then a couple days before the wedding, we were told that Jennie made a miraculous improvement—was it the St. Joseph's altar?—and would be able to return for the wedding. There had been no miracle. The dreadful sight of her literally being dragged up the aisle of St. Anthony's Church to her pew by Andy and my father is seared into my memory. It was obvious to everyone that in no sense was she any better.

At the reception, she looked so weary that family members asked if she wanted to go home and rest. But no, she was determined not to miss a moment. We all noted that she drank bottle after bottle of soda pop through the evening, which was very unlike her. When the reception ended, Jo and Jack left for their honeymoon. In the middle of the night Jennie had to be rushed to the hospital. The next day, a Sunday, we went to visit her. Not having seen her for months before the wedding, we sorely missed her. I was nearly in a state of shock when we got to the hospital. They were just turning her from her back to her side when the blister that covered her entire back peeled off, oozing all the vile smelling liquid that had accumulated under it. She screamed in pain. My parents took us out of the room and Jennie died shortly after.

I had never experienced a death of someone so close. I had loved this woman, who had been so good to me, and to everyone, since my infancy. I was deeply devastated by the whole series of events leading to this tragic end. I overheard the adults saying, "All this after *Donna Ciccia* at age seventy-two made a St. Joseph's altar to save her daughter." Others countered, "But St. Joseph is the patron saint of a beautiful death." "Beautiful?" I thought. "Who are they kidding?"

Plans for the funeral began immediately when someone asked, "Who's contacted Jo?" Everyone looked about blankly. "Where is she?" another asked. More blank stares. No one knew. What were we to do? Surely, it was inconceivable that she would miss her own mother's funeral while honeymooning. Uncle Tom, who had connections at the local TV station was able to get an announcement on the news that if anyone knew Jo's whereabouts they should contact the family immediately. No word for a whole day. Then someone who was a friend of her husband, Jack, phoned Tom to inform him that the couple was at a resort lodge in Wisconsin. Dad was elected to call her and deliver the bad news. She made it back just in time for the funeral, a bad start to a bad marriage that ended several years later when Jack left Jo with three small children for another woman.

A year after Jennie died, Andy met another woman and moved out of their apartment. We were now the only Cancelose family remaining in the apartment building. This prompted Mary Giovingo to begin further pressing my dad to move, "Why should we be the only ones left living here?" She met even more resistance because if we moved now my grandparents would be left alone in the house next door, with no relatives around to help them.

Dad was so pleased that he could afford to buy me two gifts that played important roles in my life. I was never much of a materialist, but objects that were both utilitarian and could advance my interests held me captive. The first was a VM hi-fi. Mother was none too pleased that I had picked out a blond Danish-modern model on wrought-iron legs. Admittedly, it clashed with her walnut and mahogany furniture. I now heard the music I loved with clarity and presence. Dad enjoyed listening to the Sinatra, Sammy Davis, Jr. and Ella Fitzgerald records in hi-fi, too. I was now able to begin collecting original-cast recordings of Broadway shows. Broadway came vividly to life for me in my own living room. I studied the liner notes and occasionally bought the scripts so I could fully understand the context of the songs. I also purchased the music to play on the piano. *Kismet, My Fair Lady,* and my favorite, *Gypsy,* were productions I felt a part of as I danced and sang along when no one was home.

Larry discovered the music that makes him dance during this era—Elvis Presley and "Hound Dog." What on earth was this stuff? What happened to the sensual melodies, the emotional or witty lyrics, and the surprising and elegant harmonic progressions? All gone! Surely, it's just a fad that will fade in a year or two. Jimmy Durante said, "The problem with rock and roll is that it only uses three chords and two of them are wrong." This was not the last time I would be totally off-base about popular tastes. Here was the nascent indication that I was not a man of my own times.

The second gift was a Royal portable typewriter, which was accompanied by a book and instructional recordings to teach one how to type. S,S,S,S with the fourth finger of the left hand; L,L,L, L with the fourth finger of the right hand. Over Christmas vacation, I was already typing 40 words per minute. A typing class at school brought me up to 70 words per minute. In later years when electric typewriters became the norm, I was a whiz at 120 words per minute. Typing is a cinch for anyone who can play the piano. This gift taught me a marketable skill that would open new doors for me in a few short years.

In my junior year of high school, I enrolled in an elective dramatics course taught by Adelaide Hoagberg. This was my chance to brush up my skills before I went to acting school. A few weeks into the class, auditions came up for the junior class play, *Onions in the Stew,* by Cornelia Otis Skinner. I hoped for a decent part, but was cast as a plumber, with a measly two lines in the second act. This was a very poor omen for my aspiring acting career. How could I consider professional acting when I couldn't even get a decent role in a high-school play?

The dramatics class provided a basic but thorough grounding in theatrical arts. We began by reading a lot of plays: Moliere, Shakespeare, Aristophanes. I loved them all. We were asked to write a radio script in the form of an interview with celebrities. I was paired with a senior student, Joan Lindstrom, who was a star in high school theater and went on to sing at the New York City Opera. The script we wrote had Joan as the interviewer and me as both David Niven and Maurice Chevalier, another chance to use my British and French accents. Miss Hoagberg was very impressed with our performance.

The class play was performed at the end of October, and I was embarrassed to have my parents come to hear my two lines. The whole situation made even the mention of my attending acting school ludicrous. They did come to the performance and afterward Miss Hoagberg said to them, "I'm so sorry that I completely underestimated Norman's talents." This was the first of many times in my life I was to hear the same phrase. What triggered this underestimation? Was it my lack of self-assuredness? I never understood it.

With Miss Hoagberg's words, acting school was back on the table. Our next assignment was to take a play of our choice and create lighting, costume and set designs. I chose Moliere's *Le Bourgeois Gentilhomme.* I could do the lighting plot and set designs, but costume designing meant drawing. Mary Giovingo to the rescue. I chose the kind of costumes I wanted, and mother executed most of the drawings, the first time she'd been able to help me since third grade. I was astounded at how good her renderings were and told her so. "When I was a girl I always dreamed of being a fashion designer. I wanted to go to school in Chicago to study. But when I asked my mother, she said, 'Yeah, go to Chicago and come back with a big stomach? No you're not.'" She didn't fight for herself, and that was the end of it.

In the second semester, Miss Hoagberg spoke to me after class about entering the Illinois State speech contest, in which she thought I would acquit myself admirably. She asked me to learn the opening prologue from Sheridan's *School for Scandal.* "Come back next week and we'll start rehearsing it after classes." I looked over the text, knowing this was something I could handle and went to the first rehearsal. She began showing me a series of foppish gestures—bows with one leg extended forward; a lot of limp-wristed motions, using a lace handkerchief—that would accompany the speech. That night I began to ponder what my father would say if he saw me doing this, and I panicked. The whole thing was so obviously effeminate that it made me shudder. I backed out, much to Miss Hoagberg's disappointment and probably much harm to myself.

At the same time my moods became morosely despondent over my sexuality. My parents kept asking me what was wrong, and I didn't know how to respond. Finally, mother insisted on an explanation. I said, "I need to see a psychiatrist." "What? Why, what's wrong with you?" "I can't tell you, but I need to get help." She talked it over with my father, who thought the whole idea was ridiculous. "There's nothing wrong with his mind," he told her. I persisted, so mother called our family doctor and asked him for a recommendation. An appointment was set up with Dr. P. the following week.

This was 1958, not the age of analysts and therapy. One needed to be mentally deranged to see a psychiatrist. I was warned not to say anything about it to anyone, including my brother. "What will people say?" was a question I heard from childhood. Most people are concerned about how they are perceived by others, but Sicilians make an obsessive study of this. There's even a term for it, "*bella figura*," which means no matter what happens within the family, a veneer of decorum and respectability must be presented to the outside world. They were horribly disappointed and embarrassed by me. My parents exerted every effort to look like upstanding, average Americans, and here I was making it impossible for them.

My biweekly sessions were in the early afternoon on the other side of town. Notes had to be provided to my teachers, indicating that I had a standing doctor's appointment so that I could be excused from class. My father had to make his own excuses to take off from work to drive me. I felt like a criminal every time we went through this routine. I was a total wreck by the time we got to the doctor's office, which was in his home. Mother warned me not to let anyone see me enter or leave his house, which was only a block away from my piano teacher's house. I looked everywhere to be certain no one was about before I opened the car door and dashed into his office. No one was to find out about this shameful episode—ever!

Dr. P., a stocky, unattractive man in his forties with coke-bottle-thick glasses, lived in this house with his wife and children, none of whom I ever saw because his office had a private entrance.

"What brings you here?" he asked. I froze and couldn't say a word.

"Well?" Still nothing.

"If you want me to help you, you have to talk to me, you know. Now, what is it?"

"I just can't say it," I stammered.

"Okay, then write it down for me."

"I can't unless you promise me that you will never tell my parents why I've come here."

"All right, I promise."

He handed me the paper and pen. My hand was shaking violently as I scribbled, "I am a homosexual" in a handwriting I didn't even recognize as my own.

He considered the note, looked at me soberly, and said, "So what's wrong with that?"

"What's wrong with that?" I echoed almost in shock that he would suggest such a thing.

"It's terrible. It's a tragedy."

"Does that mean you want to change?"

"Oh, yes, yes, I do."

"Good. I can help you do that then." An enormous sense of relief came over me.

First he asked me to draw a picture of my family.

"But, I can't draw."

"It doesn't matter. Just do whatever you can do."

When I finished with my childish-looking renderings, he asked, "How tall are you?"

"About five-eight and a half."

"How tall is your father?"

"About five-seven."

"Then why did you draw your father as taller than you?"

I wasn't aware that I had done so and couldn't answer the question.

No doubt this meant that I saw myself as small and inferior to my father. But did I?

"Have you ever had sex with a male?" Oh, god do I have to do this?

"Only, once about three years ago," I stammered.

"How did it happen?"

I was so embarrassed to explain the strip poker.

"So who blew whom?"

I was mortified. And how did he know?

"Well?"

"He did," I mumbled.

"Just as I suspected, the passive role," he noted in his book. "What most attracts you about a man's body?"

My, god, this is torture, I thought to myself, squirming in my seat.

"Shouldn't I be lying on a couch?" I tried to divert him.

"I prefer to have my patients sitting, rather than lying. You haven't answered my question."

"A muscular chest," I murmured in my embarrassment.

"Look, I have a big chest. Are you attracted to me?"

"No!" I blurted out emphatically. I didn't know anything much about psychiatrists, but this question seemed completely out of bounds to me. I noted his stocky unappealing frame and wondered, "Does he honestly think he's well-built? Was he hoping that I was attracted to him?"

"Why can't you just give me a shot of narco-synthesis?" I inquired in desperation. I had seen far too many movies of the era where the patient received an injection of some mind-altering substance, went into a subconscious reverie, then unloaded secrets that were not accessible to their conscious mind, and was miraculously cured when the psychiatrist interpreted what had been revealed. I assumed that's what the session would be. Instead, it was all these embarrassing questions. I hated every minute of it.

"Because that's not an effective way to get at the problem. Talking is the method we use."

The only positive thing I took away from our first session was, "I can help you."

Dad was much too embarrassed to ask how the session went, but mother did. All I could answer was, "fine." They received a call the following day from the doctor who said he needed to speak to them alone in the next appointment. I was terror stricken. What would he tell them? As it turned out, I was convinced that he had kept my secret. However, the conversation they had actually made it far worse for me than if he had told them outright.

"And you think you've got problems?" Dad said on returning home. "Do you know what your psychiatrist said was wrong with him when he was young?"

"What?"

"Something really bad. He was a homosexual."

I began hyperventilating. I covered my mouth and nose to hide it. I'm sure I turned white as a sheet. They didn't seem to notice.

"What do you think of that? I'll bet your problems are nothing compared to his. This is probably just a waste of time and money."

I couldn't think of any sensible answer to this. My mind was reeling. I just shrugged my shoulders. I was so relieved when they left the room so I could be alone to process what had just happened. "Why on earth would he tell them such a thing?" I wondered. "Was he? —really? Is that why he asked me if I found him attractive? No, no, he must have been testing them, trying to see how they'd react to it. He probably didn't like the response he got. I'm sure of it. Just the way dad described it is enough to prove that."

The next session was just dad and me alone. I was wishing I had never suggested going to see this guy. It was turning into a nightmare, and I was petrified as we walked into his office together.

Bizarrely, the session began with, "Tell me what you think of Norman's looks."

What? Now where are we going with this?

"Pretty darned good," dad answered.

"Well, I should say so," said Dr. P. Did he have the hots for me? That may have been the best compliment I ever received from my father. Strange, because I saw myself as looking average to mediocre at best, and I admitted as much to them.

"I'll bet you've noticed both your sons sitting with their legs spread apart and their hands on their crotches."

Oh, my god, we've just slipped down the rabbit hole.

"No, no. I've never seen either one do that.

Thanks, Dad!

"And what about his sex organ. Does it look normal to you?" Is he itching to see it?

"Well, it does seem a little small for his age,"

Is there a hole I can crawl into? What? Dad thinks I'm stunted?

"Norman, do you know what knocked up means?"

"No." I had never heard the term.

"Mr. Cancelose, do you know?"

"Sure, it means pregnant."

What on earth does this have to do with my problem? Dad's looking at me as if he has a son who's lived under a rock all his life. At this point, Dr. P. brings out two pairs of boxing gloves. Oh, no. Now what?

"I want you two to put these on and just do a little boxing."

I'm trying to figure out if there's any purpose, any logic whatever to this charade. I'm not sure which of us is feeling more humiliation at this point, Dad or me? Isn't there an SOS signal for therapy patients caught in an undertow?

The boxing match is a total dud, no more than a couple perfunctory jabs. Neither of us can bring ourselves to it. We looked at each other in despair, as if to say, "Why in the hell are we doing this?" I had the suspicion Dr. P. was trying to demonstrate a raging antagonism between us that was highly exaggerated at best.

The remainder of the sessions, which continued for several months, but were interrupted during the summer, are a blur to me. They definitely were not some mid-century version of reparation therapy, mostly useless chatter. The only other thing I recall is that he wanted me to go to a hospital and apply for a job. "Just go fill out an application and take any job that's available, even washing bedpans. What you need, right now, is to be around a bunch of nurses. They'll change you in a hurry," he chuckled lasciviously. He also thought I needed to take more responsibility for myself and help pay for the therapy. I did go to St. Anthony's Hospital, but they told me no positions were available, much to my relief.

My parents never asked me to take an after-school or even a summer job because they saw how overwhelmed I was by schoolwork. But mother arranged for me to sell boxes of Christmas cards, beginning in junior high, to relatives and friends. She thought I might learn valuable business skills, while earning some extra spending money. I didn't mind it, but I was not a salesman by any means, and I had the nagging suspicion that people were making purchases only because they knew me, which I found humiliating.

Ironically, I did end up in St. Anthony's hospital for a few days that summer. I began experiencing severe chest pains, that caused me to pass out briefly—I was reminded of those Southern women in the movies, who get the vapors. After the second time, I was taken to the doctor, who sent me to the hospital for tests, all of which indicated that nothing was wrong. I had shot up in height all at once that year, and the doctor said it was probably just "growing pains." I suspected it had more to do with my emotional state. The nurses always seemed to be hanging around my bed. "You're so cute. Don't you have an older brother you could introduce to us?" Is this what Dr. P. was talking about?

Sensing my despair, mother decided to do some confessing herself. "When I was a girl, I knew nothing about sex at all. One day Aunt Gertie (a large Swedish woman who was married to her mother's brother, Jasper) took me aside and told me the facts of life. 'Sex with a man is the most disgusting thing a woman will ever go through. You'll just have to grin and bear it.' When I married your dad, I hoped there would be more romance to it than Gertie said, but your dad's not that kind of man. I started dreaming about what it would it be like to have a romantic affair with a man. I knew this was a sin, and I had to stop it so I prayed to the Virgin Mary to help me. She did help me and it stopped. You should think about trying that, too."

I'd already given up on the Virgin Mary after the dog bite. Maybe if my appeals went straight to the top. Mother had hung a picture of the Sacred Heart in our bedroom, showing Jesus pointing to his bleeding heart. When alone, I stood staring at the picture, focusing my concentration fervidly and praying with such impassioned devotion that my own heart felt entwined so tightly it could scarcely beat. My attentive and lengthy stares led me to believe that Jesus's finger was moving back and forth toward the heart. I took this as a sign that he heard my prayers, rather than seeing it for what it was, an obvious illusion from riveting my eyes on the image.

I began thinking about my mother's romantic fantasies and their startling similarities to my own bedtime romantic story telling since I was a child. We are obviously much more a product of our genes than we care to recognize. Many in the family would say to me, "Norman, you remind me so much of your dad's uncle, Matt." He had died before I was born. When he emigrated from Sicily, he lived in New York and Chicago for awhile before moving to Rockford. He never married and was a theater and opera fanatic. When he lived with my grandmother, I was told that he kept a series of dolls on his bed. I may have been his reincarnation, but with the dolls, we part company genetically.

I was aware, as I believe mother was, that dad was not in any way a cold and distant person. He was, in fact, a very warm, loving, and caring father and husband. He simply couldn't demonstrate his affections the way most people did. I don't believe I ever saw him kissing my mother, and he never kissed Larry or me. He showed tenderness by teasing, by grabbing our arms and pinching us warmly. Mother had chosen a chintz fabric for her bridesmaids' gowns and dad, who had never heard of it, found the word amusing. He never called her Mary; it was always "chintz" or "Mrs." as he teased, and fondled her arms. Sometimes he was more crude and would goose her. "Matt, you know I don't like that one bit."

Neither the therapy nor the fervent prayers to the Sacred Heart seemed to be working for me. It wasn't that I didn't like girls. I loved watching pretty girls, especially when they were beautifully dressed. I especially enjoyed socializing with them. But it was strictly esthetic, not erotic. I had no desire to see them undressed. In all, I had four dates in my high-school years, two movie dates plus the junior and senior proms. It was just enough to mute the questions about why Norman doesn't have a girlfriend. In those days, if you dated a "nice" girl, you were expected to act like a gentleman and sexual advances were not welcome, so they were safe and so was I.

On the other hand, was my crush on Terry Carlson diminishing as a result of all this therapy? In a word, no! Another red flag was my spending time watching TV shows that had little appeal for me, except for their handsome male leads: Clint Walker in "Cheyenne"; Ty Hardin in "Bronco"; and Gardner McKay in "Adventures in Paradise." I tried doing homework while I watched because my only interest was in the scenes where they undressed.

I was never addicted to television. Our family loved the variety shows: "Your Hit Parade," with Dorothy Collins and Giselle MacKenzie, was a Saturday night ritual. "Stranger in Paradise," the number one tune for more than fifty-two weeks, enthralled me because they had to create a different setting and dramatic context for the song on each episode, no small feat; Sunday night was the "Ed Sullivan Show." My parents enjoyed "The Lawrence Welk Show," but I recognized this as schlock and hated it. But it was the late-night weekend movies that were my refuge from emotional turmoil. When everyone went to bed on Saturday nights, I sat in the dark all alone—the other-worldly, bluish glow of our Sylvania TV's halo light enveloping me—and transported myself to the magical world of 1930s and 1940s musicals, screwball comedies and film-noir favorites. That era seemed so much more glamorous and seductive than my own.

In the movie theaters, the musicals of the 1950s were favorites—of course the Rodgers and Hammerstein works. But the three films that left the most marked impression on me were: *Love Me or Leave Me,* with Doris Day starring as the Broadway celebrity Ruth Etting; *I'll Cry Tomorrow,* with Susan Hayward, one of my all-time favorite movie stars, playing Lillian Roth: and *Pete Kelly's Blues,* starring Jack Webb, Ella Fitzgerald and Peggy Lee. I learned to play the music from all these films on the piano. The movies and their scores, flickered with the lights of showbiz, but all had a veneer of sadness that seemed to mirror my despondent moods so closely.

In my junior year, when I should have taken driver's education at school,

Dad decided to teach me how to drive. He had tried to teach mother with no success, and it didn't go much better with me. He was fanatical about his cars. They were always cared for, cleaned, and polished. We didn't have a garage at the apartment building, but he was not about to leave his baby on the streets, exposed to the elements. Instead, he rented a garage from an old woman in the next block. The slightest scratch on his car was as painful as a wound to his body.

On a Sunday, he took me out on a deserted country road. Mother and Larry were in the back seat, the car parked on the dirt shoulder. As I took the wheel and put my foot tentatively on the gas pedal, the car lurched forward. Dad screamed at me and grabbed the wheel, scaring me half to death. I knew I had to drive but had no enthusiasm for it. Mother later said, "You should have learned at school; no one could learn from him." It took me three tries to get my license. I always failed in the first block because the front wheels crept over the crosswalk stripes on the street, the first time out of ignorance, the second, because I couldn't see the crosswalk since it was buried in snow. Again, dad was disappointed in me because he prided himself on being an excellent driver.

I think his discouragement with me reached a tipping point because at one of our Friday-night coffee parties he humiliated me brutally in front of all the relatives. I was dumbfounded and could make no retort. I remained silent for what I thought was a suitable interval, then excused myself and went next door to bed, though it was only 10:30. I sobbed violently and for the first time in my life hoped that I would fall asleep and never wake up.

Public humiliation is something I have no defenses against and consequently find it both terrifying and unendurable. Because it was so painful, what he actually said is beyond the reach of my memory—singularly unusual for me because I have the unfortunate ability to remember in sharp detail every slight I've ever suffered. It was so unlike him to be mean, and it only happened twice throughout my childhood. When my parents came upstairs, I overheard my mother asking him why he felt the need to do that in front of everyone, but I couldn't hear his response.

Counselors, teachers, and adults who learned that I planned to attend acting school did everything they could to discourage me. Teachers asked why I insisted on wasting my life pursuing so tenuous a career. "You're a top student. Go to college. You've got a brain. Don't waste it." My parents said, "If you really want to go to acting school, we will send you, but we can't afford to spend all that money to have you come out a bum." There was that prediction from our family doctor again come back to haunt me.

Yes, I lacked self-confidence. But what was worse, I could point to nothing significant I had achieved theatrically, even to myself, that would indicate I had a future as an actor. I was thus dissuaded from following through on my dream. I had stopped taking science and math courses after my sophomore year because they seemed superfluous for acting school. I was woefully unprepared to take the SAT exams and ended up with very mediocre scores. What a poor predictor of college achievement they turned out to be. I began looking at college catalogs without enthusiasm.

The summer after my junior year, we traveled to California. En route we stopped in Denver to look at the university there. I was more interested in attending a school in a big city than I was in the school's academic distinctions. Dad liked the idea of my going there, and it was pretty much decided.

My senior year English class was by far the most demanding class I'd ever taken and perhaps ever would take. Twenty-five of the best students in the school were chosen to be in an honors division, taught by one of the finest and most severe teachers, Adele Johnson. If she had chosen to grade on a curve, a ninety would have meant nearly failing. We began with *Beowulf* and had to memorize extended passages from Chaucer's *Canterbury Tales* in Middle English to be recited before the class. Our senior paper was a year-long extended project that included submitting a full-outline, an annotated bibliography, all our note cards organized categorically, and the text with footnotes, following strict guidelines.

Foolishly, I chose a comparison of Tennyson's and Browning's poetry, using two poems to illustrate my points. It would have made so much more sense to have chosen Shakespeare as a topic. Never had I put so much effort into a single assignment. When I got my paper back, I was horrified to see that I had received a B minus, the paper covered in great red scrawls of criticism. Two years later, out of laziness, I retyped the same paper and submitted it for a college literature course and received an A plus, with the remark that this was one of the best papers the professor had ever received. I graduated from East High School with a class rank of 24 out of more than 800, not exactly humiliating but definitely humbling.

In the middle of the year, auditions were held for a production of the musical, *The Boyfriend,* in which Julie Andrews had appeared in her first major role. I sang "Oh, What a Beautiful Morning," for the school's choir director. His response was, "And where exactly have you been hiding for the past three years?" We were given a dance audition, consisting of the Charleston, which I already knew how to do. No boys in my class had studied dance formally so I was hands down the best. Then I read for

Miss Hoagberg, who was directing the show. I did scenes using both my English and French accents, as the piece required. It was looking as though I would get one of the male leads. If only this could happen—please, god—it was not too late to revive the acting-school plan. It didn't happen. The lead was given to Jim Klint, the son of my father's boss, Barney Klint. As it turned out, he couldn't sing in harmony so those sections had to be cut. Also, being a jock, he couldn't dance at all, so the choreography had to be dumbed down for him. I was cast in the chorus, putting an end to any hope of a theater career. That was the best I could do, chorus in a high-school production? Pathetic. Was I really that bad? Was this Miss Hoagberg's revenge because I had backed out of the state speech competition. Mother was sure the Klints had paid money to ensure their son got the lead. I doubted this scenario.

In the spring, I at last got to see my first professional production of a musical. My father always drove to Chicago on a Saturday at this time of year to purchase the trophies for his bowling league. Terry Bryan and I had tried the year before to see *The Most Happy Fella* but no tickets were available. Dad asked if Larry and I wanted to drive with him to Chicago. I begged him to let us go to the matinee at the Shubert Theatre of *Redhead*, starring Gwen Verdon and Richard Kiley, as well as the rest of the original Broadway cast. I knew nothing about this show, had never even heard the music, but I knew Gwen Verdon from the movie of *Damn Yankees,* and I knew Richard Kiley's gorgeous voice from my cast recording of *Kismet.* We went to the box office just before curtain time and were able to get two inexpensive seats that were remarkably in the eighth row of the orchestra. They must have been unloading last-minute tickets at deep discounts. Dad went to buy the trophies while Larry and I watched the show.

As the house lights went down, the hot, white spot beamed onto the conductor, and the overture began. The opening tympany drum roll was followed by an explosion of brass. My body began to tingle from head to toe in excitement from the very first notes. With the ballad, "She's Not Enough Woman for Me," I began to soar, and when the uptempo waltz, "I Feel Merely Marvelous," played, I felt so marvelous I launched for the planets. I was already sophisticated enough to know that this was not a great musical, despite stunning performances and a very good score. It was a Broadway musical; what more could I ask. The choreography by Bob Fosse, whose work I had missed in New York, was so dazzling my feet began moving under my seat in imitation. When the curtain came down to thunderous applause, I had a sense of exhilaration I had never before experienced. When we got in the car to come home the elation wore off, and I suddenly turned despondent. Why couldn't I have seen a professional show years before? Why didn't my family take me to see *South Pacific* instead of the Cubs game? This was exactly what I wanted to do. If I had known, maybe I would have pushed to study dance, maybe I would have studied voice and acting. The technically difficult dancing in this show was clearly achievable only with years of training. Now it was all too late. I was doomed to some mundane, dreary job for life.

The summer after graduation I got my first job so that I could earn money for college. Dad arranged to get me summer work at Nylint. At first, I worked all alone in the plant at night, because nothing else was available. Nylint made a model water-sprinkling truck that cleans city streets. My job was to take the nozzle, which consisted of two plastic parts glued together, attach it to a hose, and run water through it, marking any spot that leaked at the seam where the two halves met. It was incredibly mind-numbing, but I didn't care because I could contemplate my future in peace as I worked. When that line of toys was completed, I was transferred to the day-shift assembly line, where I snapped two metal headlights into the cab of a model Ford Highway Emergency Truck.

The assembly line was staffed almost entirely with women who had the quickest, most nimble fingers imaginable. Toys came down the line at a terrifyingly furious pace, and I had a mere couple seconds to get both headlights in. I began to look as fumbling as Rosalind Russell in the movie version of *Auntie Mame,* where she couldn't manage the customer receipt book as a clerk at Macy's. Pages and carbons kept unraveling, mixing up madly, and falling out all over the counters.

In my case, the trucks began piling up as I fell further and further behind. I endured the superior smirks on these women as they watched the boss's son, a supposedly bright college-bound student, unable to handle this simple, moronic task. Dad was beside himself as he was forced to help me catch up. That night he drove me back to the factory after dinner to practice getting up to speed, all so humiliating.

Well, is it my fault that inanimate objects inevitably take a vengeful dislike to me and thwart my every attempt to bend them to my will? The headlights simply refused to fit into the slots in the cab or if they did they obstinately refused to hook in securely and fell out directly. I got better with the practice, but it was obvious that I was slowing down the line. Dad moved me to a spot-welding machine where I could work at my own pace, as long as I met the unreasonable quotas. Rumors swept through the factory that Dad was favoring me with the easiest jobs, and I sensed resentment from all quarters.

I survived the summer on the thought that I'd soon be out of this dehumanizing environment. I watched those poor women who were doing this repetitive, unrewarding work and wondered how they could bear the tedium, knowing there was no end until they retired or died.

I determinedly saved almost every penny I made that summer so I would have the funds to enjoy the pleasures of a big-city life, recompense for being condemned for lack of talent to study something that held no interest for me.

Out of Rockford, Into the World

MY HEART IS POUNDING. I'm about to leave Rockford. Everyone is silent in the car as dad drives to some remote outpost railroad station in Illinois called Davis Junction, where I will board the train to Denver. This is the only place nearby to connect with the railroad heading to the West. Dad wanted so much to drive me to college, but he couldn't take off from work in September. Mary Giovingo, in her inimitably supportive way, breaks the silence, " I hope this isn't going to be like Camp Rotary when you got homesick and wanted to come home." I don't answer, but I'm wondering if that's what she's hoping for. Most Sicilian boys we know do not leave the bosom of their families for a new town. Again, I'm an outlier, and they're none too happy about it.

We arrive at the station early. Nervous pacing back and forth on the platform by all. It's twilight and beginning to get dark as I spot the revolving headlight of the Streamliner engine approaching. A lot of rushed goodbyes and kisses. Dad actually hugs me—wow, that's new. The train pulls in and there's a mad dash to get all my luggage, plus a large foot locker on board. I look out the window and watch them waving at me as the train pulls out of the station. Mother is in tears. Even with the promise of a new and exciting life ahead, partings are sad occasions. I'm a bit frightened that I'm leaving the safety of this loving family for what—I'm not certain.

When they are no longer in sight, I concentrate on what's happening around me. I'm finally on a Union Pacific Domeliner, ten years after Terry Bryan and I first fantasized about this. My seat is not in the dome, but as I search for the dining car, I'm directed by the conductor to climb the stairs to the dome, where dinner will be served. All right, it's already dark, and I really can't see anything. But still, I'm in the dome having a lovely dinner on a white-linen table cloth all by myself, and I'm thrilled.

The overnight trip doesn't allow for any interesting views from my window, but it doesn't matter. There's not much to see between Rockford and the Rockies.

I try to sleep, but train stops in every little town jar me awake. When morning comes we're in Colorado, and I go up to the dome again and this time I see the glorious Rockies in the distance. I'm a bit agitated as we pull into Union Station. How am I going to get all this luggage to a taxi? Not to worry. The minute I step off the train, three young men approach me. "Are you going to DU?" "Yes." "We're all students from Illinois, and we'll drive you to school." They're members of some jock fraternity. They even take the luggage up to the dorm room for me.

My room is on the second floor of a new three-story building. The room is spartan—interior red brick walls, vinyl-tile floors, built-in desks with Eames-style molded orange chairs, and two beds— but very bright and inviting. How exciting. From the huge plate glass window, I have an expansive view of the Rockies. It's spectacular. My roommate had not yet arrived, so I begin unpacking. Within an hour, there he is, Joe. from Pittsburgh. Joe's a tall, unappealing Italian, who came to Denver on a football scholarship. Breathe easy. No need to be concerned that I'd find his athletic body attractive; it's huge, but shapeless and floppy. The school maintained that they paired roommates by several criteria: similar backgrounds, common interests, enough divergent interests to expand our horizons. What possible common interests had the administrators detected from the forms we had submitted? I never could figure it out except that we were both Italian.

A welcome-to-incoming-freshman party was held that first night. I knew no one, so I went alone. Joe went with his football buddies, some of whom he knew from Pittsburgh. I was probably looking forlorn when I was approached out of the blue by Wade, a native Denverite. He was nearly a replica of Terry Carlson in height, build, and hair. His German heritage gave him a very handsome look, not unlike Terry's Swedish features. We thoroughly enjoyed each other's company and became friends immediately. I could hardly believe my luck.

The next day Wade invited me to sit with him and some friends in the cafeteria. The coat-and-tie dress code at this first meal was enforced only during Wednesday evenings and Sunday afternoons, hereafter. I was worried that the food would be like the high-school cafeteria, but was relieved that it was actually quite good. Wade's friends were all Centennial Scholars, as was he. They had all earned full-tuition scholarships as part of the school's centennial celebration. Later in the term, these Centennial's couldn't understand why I had not applied for the scholarship. Me? I never had even inquired about scholarships, believing I wasn't nearly bright enough to get one.

I called my parents to tell them that not only was I not homesick, but that I was having a great time and had already made several new friends. A whole new environment, a whole different group of people who knew nothing about my background renewed my hope that I might still change my sexual desires.

"What do you plan to study?" my parents kept asking. I wanted to be an actor. I had no idea whatsoever what I wanted to do as a second choice in life. In fact, there was no second choice—nothing, so I took the easy way out and said I would study business. The business school was not located on the main campus but rather in the middle of downtown, right next door to the Denver Hilton. This meant I had to commute by bus each day. The business students were a very different lot from my scholarly friends and clearly I was out of place.

Denver was on a trimester schedule, and fortunately the first two terms meant mostly courses from the core curriculum. I did take enough business courses to learn this what not for me. I was bored senseless with accounting and business law, but it was a class in management during second term that dissuaded me from pursuing this path. One day, the professor delivered this warning: "If you have any hopes of being successful as a business executive, you had better be married before the age of thirty." This was the red flag—time to move on.

A few good things came from my two terms in business school. I joined the men's glee club (most of the students in business were male in those days), which was directed by a wonderful professor from the music department, Gordon de Broder, who became a friend and a mentor. In the glee club, I met Brian, who shared my interests in theater and was as out of his element in business as I was. The school encouraged business majors to take part-time jobs, so I got a position at a major bank as a check sorter, alphabetizing canceled checks. I kept the job for more than a year, helping my parents out and giving me extra spending money.

The most important benefit came as a complete surprise. After the first term, I received a letter in the mail saying that my academic performance was so superior that I was being awarded a half-tuition scholarship. I was having to spend far less time studying than I had done in high school to get more accolades. Needless to say, my parents were delighted because the tuition, which was only $900 per year, was nevertheless somewhat of a strain on their finances.

Two of the Centennial Scholars I met through Wade became our dates. Wade dated Linda and I dated her roommate, Johnnie, whose real name was Ruby. The four of us ate dinner together every evening. Johnnie was the sort of girl I could never have hoped to date at East High. She had been a runner-up in the Miss Nebraska contest, she was a talented and very bright singer, majoring in music, and her father was an inordinately wealthy cattle rancher. We hit it off because of our common interest in the arts. It was a strange but delightful experience for me to be the envy of the other guys in our dorm. My roommate, Joe, actually asked me, "How did *you* get so lucky to date one of the most beautiful girls in school?" He held the attitude that girls of her calibre were reserved specifically for jocks. Unlike high school, I was now part of the in-group, and the people I associated with were more interesting culturally than many in East High's clique.

The four of us often double-dated, and one of our first dates, which I suggested, was to the homecoming football game. I did this only because I always went to the school games in Rockford, so I assumed that's what one did. All of us seemed bored to tears with the whole thing, and the crowd exhibited less enthusiasm than we did. After the game, it struck me that I didn't actually have to like sports, and these people, unlike the Rockfordites, couldn't care less about it. I never went to another sporting event in my life.

Because Johnnie and I had a stronger interest in the arts, while Wade and Linda were more science-oriented, we often went our separate ways. The highlight of my dating spree came when Johnnie told me she would love to see England's Royal Ballet, which was coming to town. Though I had no interest in ballet, I was eager to expand my cultural horizons. Johnnie insisted on paying for her own ticket, "My dad is rich, and I know yours isn't." We went to a Sunday matinee, and I was floored by how exciting the performance was, especially the male dancers. A whole new world opened to me. I had no idea of the athleticism involved, and was certain I would never have been capable of such feats, no matter how much I trained. The program was a series of *divertissements*, rather than a full-length ballet, so I got to see a variety of styles and periods of dance, all of which enthralled me.

I had decided to make a day of this, so after the performance I took Johnnie to the elegant and historic Brown Palace Hotel for dinner. We were both dressed in our finest clothes, and after the sumptuous meal, we danced the night away to the small band the hotel had engaged. I began smiling to myself at how much my life had been transformed in a few short weeks from my dreary Rockford days. I thought, "My, Norman, you've become quite the young man about town," and was exceedingly pleased with myself. Then the check for the evening came. I opened my first checking account in Denver, and I had grown used to paying for everything by check. All the stores and restaurants around the campus readily accepted checks. Naturally, I thought the same would be true here. When I proudly placed my check on the silver tray along with the bill, the waiter said, "I'm sorry, sir, the Brown Palace does not accept personal checks." I rummaged frantically through my wallet to see if I had enough cash but was far short. Johnnie hadn't brought much money with her, so she couldn't bail me out.

The waiter said, "You'll have to come with me to the manager's office, I'm afraid." I was panicky. Are they going to throw me in jail? Will I end up in the kitchen washing dishes for weeks? "You need to give us your parents' phone number and address, as well as the person in charge of your dormitory. We have a telephone number for the university's administration should the check fail to clear." "You don't need to worry, sir. There are funds to cover the check, and besides I'm employed by the bank." "Okay, you can go." Huge sigh of relief.

The dashing-young-man-about-town feeling, swirled ingloriously down the drain, and I was ashamed to have to face Johnnie. I thought I had made a terrific impression. I had felt so adult; now I was a pathetic child again.

I made another very good friend whom I met in the laundry room, Barry Booth. He was a pharmacist's son from Iowa, who was studying library science and was far more cultured than I. He had a stereo and we listened to classical music for hours. I quickly developed a love for this music, about which I had been so ambivalent as a child. Why was this, I wondered? When I played classical pieces on the piano for family members, my father and most of my relatives would say, "Play something popular instead." Was I so unsure of my tastes that I needed the encouragement of my peers to permit me to enjoy these works? We actually began comparing and criticizing Bruno Walter's conducting of Beethoven symphonies with Arturo Toscanini's. The Italian won hands down, as determined by our untrained ears.

Barry convinced me to join him in a subscription to the Denver Symphony, which gave us the privilege of hearing great soloists including Van Cliburn and Isaac Stern. Stern played the Brahms Violin Concerto brilliantly, but the thing I most remembered was that during an orchestral tutti, when he wasn't playing, he turned his back to the audience for a moment, and someone flashed a photo. Stern turned around with violent force, and his bow suddenly became a saber as he glared into the audience with such fire in his eyes, I thought the auditorium would go up in smoke.

Quite unexpectedly, I began to miss the piano very much. I had hardly touched it since I quit lessons in my sophomore year. I went to the music department and asked if I was allowed to rent a practice room for an hour each day, not being a music major. They agreed, and I taught myself Chopin's "Military Polonaise" in A Major, which had seemed beyond my reach when my teacher tried to get me to play it.

Denver also helped me fulfill my theater cravings. I went to every single national touring company of every show that played the town, with either Johnnie, Barry, or Brian. I got better at discerning what made for good theater over what was strictly mediocre. As with *Redhead* in Chicago, the musicals excited me the most, and I'd get the same adrenalin rush, whenever the overtures began.

If Barry visited me in my dorm room, he always came armed with a can of air freshener because Joe was less than fastidious about washing his clothes. His method was to throw all his dirty laundry into the chest of drawers. He took copious showers, doused himself in a cloud of Cashmere Bouquet talcum powder, then took out a soiled and smelly pair of underwear from the drawer—ah, the mingled fragrance of sweet and stink—and off he'd go on a date. Pity those poor girls.

Living with a football player brought back memories of my fretful nights in the barracks at Camp Rotary. While I and my friends were striving valiantly to become sophisticated adults, these jocks acted as though they were still in kindergarten. Barry and I had both shunned the fraternity system because we sensed that frat boys were of the same ilk, not our kind of people. Also, my family could never have afforded fraternity life for me. We developed a dismissive little saying for ourselves, "Too chic to go Greek."

I never knew what to expect in my room from Joe's football buddies. One night I walked in, and the entire room was covered in shaving cream. How, I never knew because we kept our door locked. Another night I was sound asleep and my hand slipped off the bed onto the floor, "Why are my socks floating?" I wondered, barely conscious. With a jolt, I jumped out of bed. Our room was flooded with three inches of water. One of Joe's buddies had opened the fire hydrant, which was just outside our room, allowing all the water to flow our way.

All of these players were so unattractive, except one, a handsome Swede named Curt, from Minneapolis, who lived two doors down from us. Curt was already married, though he left his wife back in Minnesota. He told me that while he was asleep some guy came into his room and flopped down on top of him. "Oh, god, I'm getting queered," he yelled out. It turned out to be Joe, who was so drunk he didn't know whose room he was in.

Joe loved to lie in bed in nothing but his stinky undershorts and talk seductively on the phone to one of his many girlfriends—a precursor to phone sex. He obviously thought of himself as an Adonis. Why do people who have the least to brag about have the biggest egos? I found these little chats both distasteful and very appalling to have to watch. Once, a girl, who was probably as repulsed as I was, hung up abruptly on him. Then out of nowhere Joe asked me, "Would you give someone a blow job for a million dollars?" "No," I screamed much too vociferously. Did he suspect me? Was this some sort of oblique proposition? I had no interest in pursuing the topic, in any case.

Barry was less than thrilled with his roommate, as well, so we went to the dorm administrators and requested that we be allowed to room together, beginning the next trimester. I thought Joe would be relieved since we did not connect on any level. Much to my surprise, he was very hurt. "Don't you like living with me?" he said with the saddest look on his face. I lied, "Sure I do, Joe. It's just that Barry and I have become very close friends." A bigger blow to Joe came a week later when the university decided to abandon football all together, and the players' scholarships were to be discontinued at the end of the year. Someone scrawled on the stadium wall, "Largest Intramural Field in the World."

After dinner one evening, Wade and I sat with our two girlfriends in the lounge. He was holding Linda's hand. When the girls decided that they had to go study, Wade and I went to his room to continue our conversation. Once inside, he pointed out a prominent wet stain on his crotch. "I'm so oversexed that this happens to me just from holding hands." This generated much confusion for me. First, the sight of it excited me. "This is not supposed to happen to me any longer. I have a girlfriend now. I certainly never got such a buzz holding hands with Johnnie."

That summer Wade decided to be circumcised because he had been told this would lessen the sexual tension. The surgery caused him much pain, but also gave him a permanent erection for two weeks. And here we sadly watch these poor, tired old guys today with their erectile dysfunction, popping away Viagra to maintain their false virility.

On one of our double dates, Wade and Linda were in the front seat of his car, making out. I was growing very uncomfortable with Johnnie in the back seat. I thought "I need to do something fast so I don't look abnormal. Maybe I should try to kiss her, though I have no desire to do so. Who knows, maybe that will awaken me sexually." I had never kissed a girl—or anyone but my family before—and I made an awkward pass. Astonishingly, Johnnie rebuffed me and pushed me away. She explained that she had been taken advantage of by some guy back in Nebraska, and she wasn't comfortable even with kissing.

"Is she dating me only because she thinks I'm safe, nothing to worry about with me?" I didn't know what to think, but a few days later she said that we should stop seeing each other and that we should no longer have dinner together in the cafeteria. I was completely taken aback and felt so rejected watching the three of them eating together without me. So soon and I'm an outcast again. A week later I heard that she was leaving Denver at the end of the term and returning to Nebraska. I wasn't sure if I had anything to do with this or whether something was going on in her life I knew nothing about.

Curiously, about two weeks later, Wade got dumped by Linda, without explanation. We went to Wade's room and he lay down on his bed and began to cry. I didn't know what to do. I desperately wanted to go over to him and just hold him and comfort him, but I couldn't work up the nerve to do it, which I later regretted. I wasn't sure how he would interpret the gesture, afraid that he might see it as only an excuse to have intimate physical contact with him—which was, in fact, the case.

Wade was rather mysterious, as well. He was an orphan since a young child, but he refused to discuss it. This orphan had his own car and more spending money than any of the rest of us had. This seemed incongruous until one day he said that he knew a man who had become a sort of patron to him. This guy pulled strings so Wade could get the Centennial Scholarship, though I was certain he was bright enough to have earned it without assistance. He was also placed by this patron in well-paying part-time jobs, and it appeared that he had bought Wade the car. Very suspicious, I thought.

The first hairline cracks appeared in the fortress walls safeguarding my religious beliefs during late-night bullshit sessions with these friends. Never had I heard people question the existence of god before. Their arguments cast a pall of doubts in my mind. I still went to mass every week, but I grew envious of those who felt no obligation to rouse themselves on a Sunday morning and trudge through three feet of snow to attend a service. In fact, I believe I had always held a resentment against those who were lucky enough to be unburdened by religion.

At the end of the second term, I had to decide on a new major since I was leaving the business school. I had taken an introductory psychology course and found it very interesting, so that became the likely choice. If nothing else, at least I thought I would gain more insight into my own problems. I was especially fascinated with the abnormal psychology class. The American Psychiatric Association did not remove homosexuality from its Diagnostic and Statistical Manual of Mental Disorders until 1973, so it was still treated as an illness when I took the course. Until that course, I had not been exposed to the idea that it was not a matter of "you are" or "you aren't" homosexual (the term "gay" was not in use yet in Rocky Mountain states), but rather it was a continuum from 0-10. Though I was sure I was a 10, this new information made me look at other less-certain guys, such as Wade, in a different light.

I satisfied my physical education requirements by taking swimming and social dancing. For the final exam, Elspeth, a sultry theater major, clenched a long-stemmed rose in her teeth and the two of us wowed the professor with our tango. But it was the swimming class that left a raw scar. The instructor had been in the navy, and he inexplicably decided to favor us with a tale: "When I was an officer at sea, we discovered we had some queers on the ship. There was only one solution. We just tossed them overboard. We had to do it, otherwise they might contaminate the whole crew." I was so shocked by this that I was frightened and uneasy for weeks. Could it be true that they did such a thing? Did they really think that homosexuality was a communicable disease? Did he bring this up because he suspected some of us in class? I was certain I'd done nothing to arouse such suspicion but was seriously on my guard throughout the rest of the term.

By the third trimester anxiety struck regarding what I would do in the summer. The thought of returning to Rockford and working at Nylint was repugnant. Barry got the idea that we should rent an off-campus apartment together and spend the summer in Denver. Would my parents allow me to do this? I needed a plan. I would take psych courses during the summer to catch up on my late start on that major. Also I had my job, boring but better than the pressure in the factory. We found a very inexpensive furnished apartment. I told my parents about the plan, assured them it would cost them no money, and that, besides, I would be able to save money for next year. They agreed.

Brian, who was from Arlington Heights, Illinois, became very close to Barry and me. He had not been living in our dorm but had been sharing one of the university's on-campus apartments with a bunch of other guys. The three of us spent a lot of time together, our interests being so similar. There were even some moments of silly adolescent fun, very unlike me. We often listened to music in the apartment, never terribly loud and always classical or show tunes. I was still so unsophisticated that I played Stravinsky's *Firebird*, finding it so utterly atonal and unlistenable that it didn't distract me from my studies. One day our crotchety upstairs neighbor came down to complain that the music was driving him crazy. We turned it down, but he was not satisfied. In the next week he came down several more times, pleading that he couldn't stand the sound of music.

One Sunday, when Brian was visiting, Barry had had enough and sought revenge. He owned a recording by Yma Sumac—the freakish-sounding Peruvian-American soprano with the five-octave range—called *Legend of the Jivaro*. Her sometimes ear-shattering music, part of the exotica movement, was an attempt to evoke the image of a wild-eyed princess from some pre-Columbian sect about to be delivered in human sacrifice. Barry had several Mesoamerican artifacts on the wall, which we lit with candles. We burned quantities of incense, filling the room with smoke. The three of us wrapped orange fabric about ourselves like shawls and sat cross-legged before the god-like artifacts, as if in prayer.

Barry then played Madame Sumac as loud as he possibly could. Within a few minutes our nemesis was pounding furiously on our door. Barry cautioned Brian and me to maintain our prayer-like positions while he answered the door. The poor man was in tears, pleading with us to cease and desist. In his calmest drone-like voice, Barry said, "As you can see, sir, we are part of the Jivaro religious sect. Today is a very holy day for us and we are obliged to observe it. I'm certain you would not care to interfere with our religious rites, which you are presently and rudely interrupting." The poor man left completely defeated, and we never heard from him again.

Professor Gordon de Broder somehow came to know Van Cliburn, who offered to give a private recital in the professor's house. Gordon called to invite me, as well, but I was unfortunately at work at the time and never received the call. He described the afternoon as "illuminating" in its difference from Cliburn's public performances. "What rotten luck to have missed such an opportunity," I thought.

The professor then asked me if I would be interested in accompanying him on a weekend trip to Glenwood Springs. I was a bit leery at first, but the idea of a weekend in the mountains sounded too enticing to pass up. He picked me up after my job, and when it grew dark he asked me if I would drive the rest of the way. Never a fan of driving, and particularly on unfamiliar mountain roads at night, I was nervous, but said, "Of, course." Within five minutes, on this pitch-black hairpin-turn highway, a deer jumped right in the front of the car. I slammed on the brakes and thankfully just missed hitting him, before he bounded off across the road. We both had the breath completely knocked out of us. Somehow I managed to get us to Glenwood without further incident.

I had a moment of panic when we got to our motel, wondering what the sleeping arrangements would be. I wasn't sure, but I suspected that he might be gay. Although I was extremely fond of Gordon—he was bald, in his early forties, and not bad looking—but I was not attracted to him and hoped I wouldn't be put in an awkward position. I was so relieved when we entered and saw that the two double beds were on opposite sides of the room. He was very gentlemanly and never made any advances toward me. I suspected he wanted to when the next morning he claimed that I had been talking in my sleep and had mumbled rather risqué things, which he wouldn't define. I had never talked in my sleep to my knowledge and believed this was some awkward ploy on his part.

We so enjoyed the beautiful setting and especially bathing in the hot springs. While lying sunning, he said "I was hearing Cliburn playing the Schumann Piano Concerto in my head." "That's interesting because I was just thinking of his performance of the Rachmaninoff Third Piano Concerto," I responded. Hardly the stuff of a sultry seduction. I was sure, however, that he was eyeing me very closely in my swimming trunks and, perhaps, just to look was all he really needed.

My parents and Larry came to visit that summer, and it gave me my first chance to act as tour guide through the university and the city. I took them to some fine restaurants that they would never have considered on their own. They met Barry and Brian, and I felt that they were impressed with my friends and especially the progress I had made toward adulthood in just ten months.

One weekend, Barry was away, and I asked Wade if he would like to stay overnight at our apartment. I had ulterior motives. He had told me that he was very upset because people were gossiping about him, implying that he was gay. They knew about his patron, who apparently was a notorious homosexual in Denver, and the assumption was that if he was helping out Wade financially, there had to be sexual payback. I don't know which people were saying these things because I had never heard any such rumors from anyone, despite my own suspicions. I couldn't figure out why Wade told me about it, but I thought it might be to get me to open up about my own sexual inclinations.

I was still battling against my impulses, which were now held in check mostly by religious, rather than societal, taboos. However, the thought of a liaison with Wade was more enticement than my willpower against it could withstand. The rumors indicated to me that he might be perhaps a five or six on the continuum. Who knew what might happen? Our apartment had two twin beds in the bedroom and a sofa in the living room. He agreed to spend a Saturday night with me. I wanted at least to have him sleeping in the same room with me, even if not in the same bed, but he refused and slept on the couch. He probably didn't want to add any more fuel to the rampant gossip. I was both disappointed and relieved that I still had not succumbed to my sinful passions.

Denver had a couple art cinemas, and I had read a review about a new British film called, *Victim*, starring Dirk Bogarde, which was very controversial because it depicted homosexuality and used that term for the first time ever in cinema. I was strapped to a seesaw about my own sexuality—one day almost accepting it, the next vowing to continue the battle against it. I had to see this film so I went alone. It was refreshing to learn that in a big city, unlike Rockford, one could attend a movie alone without appearing a weirdo.

The film riveted me with its depiction of a prominent, married barrister, who was having an affair with a younger man. It showed a range of gay men who were being blackmailed by a ring of toughs, which was easy to do because homosexuality was a criminal act in Britain until 1967. It never occurred to me that law was involved in such things, and I wasn't sure about Colorado. I only learned years later that it didn't overturn its sodomy laws until 1971. In any case, I knew I had to be very careful, and legal issues became a new obstacle.

For the fall term, Brian suggested that the three of us live together, We found a much nicer apartment, with a roof deck and a swimming pool, though it was unfurnished. I couldn't imagine how we could live without furniture, but Brian had it all worked out. "We'll basically live on the floor, since it's already carpeted wall-to-wall. We'll buy large pillows to sit on and mats to sleep on." "But what will we eat on or type papers on?" I questioned. "Easy, we'll remove the closet doors and the bedroom door, and set them up on fabric-covered cardboard boxes."

I was skeptical, but kept my doubts to myself. Splitting the rent three ways made our expenses even cheaper, so I was saving my parents even more money. Brian discovered a frozen-meat-locker storage company between school and the apartment. We bought a half side of beef, had it cut into steaks, roasts, and ground meat, all of which cost only $.30 per pound and gave us enough to eat for six months.

The landlord insisted on seeing our apartment after we moved in, and he was fit to be tied, "What happened to the doors?" he asked frantically. We pointed out the dining table and the work tables. "This stuff better be replaced exactly as you found it when you moved in, or you're going to be hit with a huge fine when you leave. I'm warning you guys." Warning taken.

Barry and Brian both had experience with cooking; I had only my egg-shell-lined chocolate cake. Brian said, "If you think we're going to cook for you, you're nuts. Here's a knife. Start chopping these vegetables."

Soon I was promoted from sous-chef to one of three equal head chefs. Our cooking was simple, but delicious.

On the floor below us lived one of the young stars of the theater department, Ric DiCicco, who was from New York. We had already seen Ric perform as Ariel in *The Tempest*. He was a senior with serious ballet (he had studied with Robert Joffrey) and musical-theater training. He was the model for what I had hoped to be—he could dance, act, sing, and he played the piano much better than I did. He made no bones about the fact that he was gay, but to my surprise he was also sleeping with a girl, who turned out to be Elspeth, my tango partner. Through him we made friends with several other theater majors, including a gay couple. I had never considered that two men actually could be coupled, almost like a marriage. I was fascinated by this, and listened intently to any discussion of their relationship.

Brian suggested that he and I take a theater-dance course as an elective, just for the fun of it. We shopped for tights and dance belts and enrolled in the class. It wasn't serious dance training, but rather a class in movement for actors. Martha Wilcox, the instructor, had danced in Hanya Holm's company, the choreographer of *My Fair Lady* and *Camelot*. Brian and I were evidently the two best boys in the class, and Martha was very pleased with us. One day she approached me after class and said, "I think you should consider studying dance seriously. You have ability." All those missed dance-class opportunities as a child suddenly struck me with a blow. Was it too late? What she suggested tumbled about in my mind like clothes in a dryer throughout the two terms I studied with her, one day dismissing it as nonsense, the next thinking maybe it was possible.

For Christmas, Brian suggested we fly home after finding a flight as inexpensive as the train. It was my first commercial flight so we got all dressed up (remember those days?), stepped aboard United's chic French Caravelle jet, and off we went to Chicago. I spent a couple days with him in Arlington Heights, then went home to Rockford.

Mother asked me if I would mind having a talk with Larry about the facts of life. "You know your dad won't do it, and I don't feel I can with a boy. We did a bad job with you, and I'm hoping this will be better." They went to a wedding and left Larry and me at home. I was a bit nervous about it, only because Larry was much more of street boy than I ever was, and I thought he probably knew more than I did. I was stunned to discover that he knew nothing at all. We had a very sober and interesting talk, Larry asking many questions. When it was over, I pondered why parents find this such a difficult task. I found it gratifying.

For one term I also studied voice with Gordon de Broder, not for credit and again just for fun. The lessons were not that serious; mostly, we talked. He told me he had begun working on a Ph.D. in psychology. Was he using the field as self-examination, as I was? The one thing I wanted out of our lessons was to develop a vibrato like the Broadway singers that I worshipped. Gordon gave me a series of exercises to practice, and *voilà*, a vibrato. Because Brian and I were no longer in the business school and consequently no longer in the Men's Glee Club, Gordon suggested that we audition for the University Choir, an almost professional-level group made up primarily of voice majors. "I think you two might just get in."

I nervously went into Dr. Roger Dexter Fee's studio, being certain I would be rejected. He asked me to sing some scales and arpeggios. Then he handed me a piece of music, gave me just the opening note on the piano, and said sing this. "I can't do that," I said. "I don't know how to sight sing," which meant singing cold a piece you'd never heard, with no help from the piano. "That's fine. I'll play it for you once, and then you'll try to sing it." I listened very intently and sang the piece back perfectly. "Good, you're accepted," he said. Brian also made the grade. I had little use for my vibrato in the choir because much of the music we sang was from the Renaissance and required a vibrato-free "white sound."

Working with Dr. Fee, who was recognized as one of the finest choral conductors, and with that choir, I would rate as one the most glorious musical experiences of my life. The chorus was devoted mostly to the finest religious music, generally sung a cappella. A majority of the singers were from the opera department and had magnificent voices. Most a cappella choirs use a pitch pipe to find the opening pitches. Not the University Choir. Each section had at least one person, strategically placed, with absolute pitch, who hummed the note very softly, inaudible to the audience. The person with perfect pitch is able to identify any note, simply by hearing it. Those with absolute pitch can produce any desired note out of thin air. Sadly, I had neither skill and was so impressed by those who did. These abilities are generally nature-given or must be learned before the age of four, or they are unteachable.

The centerpiece of our repertoire was the glorious Palestrina *Stabat Mater*, but we also sang a Bach *Missa Brevis* and 20th Century works, such as Randall Thompson's beautiful *Alleluia*. A highly respected composer-in-residence, Norman Lockwood, wrote a very dissonant work specifically for our choir. Being surrounded by such incredible voices gave me the illusion that I could actually sing well. The real joy, though, was working with Dr. Fee, a consummate musician, who had the ability to make the choir respond to his slightest gesture as if it were a single instrument.

I listened intently when the music majors discussed their classes, my interest especially piqued by their worries over the intricate difficulties of counterpoint. I couldn't imagine what this was, but I assumed it had something to do with music theory. We have already demonstrated I was hare-brained about that particular subject, so I was careful not to flaunt my ignorance publicly.

During spring break we toured the Rocky Mountain states, singing mostly in churches, and were popular wherever we went. Our first engagement was at a Seventh Day Adventist high school in a very isolated area of Wyoming. We were all starved by the time our bus arrived there. Brian and I roused the chorus into singing "Food, Glorious Food," from *Oliver*. In the school cafeteria, what we were served was most definitely not glorious food, and I would hesitate to call it "dinner." It consisted of a single slice of toasted bread, topped with a couple broiled slices of tomato over American cheese. Hungry to bed we were to go, just as in *Oliver*.

We were housed in the dormitory with the students, and what we learned from them was startling and disturbing. They had been sheltered from virtually everything in life, isolated from any influences other than those of their church. When we asked how they would cope when they went to college, the answer was, "Oh, we will all go to Seventh Day Adventist colleges, so it will be just like this." Never mind the work world that would follow college. The girls were not allowed makeup of any kind, so our female vocalists began painting them up very heavily, which delighted them.

They also tried on items of clothing, which would have been forbidden to them. They weren't allowed to listen to any secular music and had no means of doing so, but some of our chorus changed that with portable radios. We were warned to shut them off almost immediately for the most terrifying reason. Every room had a speaker-looking contraption mounted on the wall, and the authorities could listen in on everything that happened in those rooms—eager to punish for the least infraction. We all hoped that we had corrupted these kids to some degree so that they might stand up for themselves and reject this dreadful 1984-like reign of terror.

Sometimes we slept in parishioners' homes, and once Brian and I had to share the same bed. He made some untoward advances, which he tried to camouflage as teasing. I pushed him aside. I had no intention of making my gay debut with Brian. I believe Barry, Brian, and I were each aware that we were all gay, though none of us would have admitted it for the world.

At the end of the tour, we played a large church in Colorado

Springs. Somehow Dr. Fee was able to get us rooms at the famed Broadmoor Hotel for just a couple dollars each. Brian and I had a room with a fireplace and French doors that looked out onto the lake. It was luxury as I had never known. I had desperately wanted stay there on my family's first trip to Colorado, but it was completely out of our price range. In celebration, I decided to splurge with a fine room-service dinner and a plate of petits fours.

After the tour, the choir recorded a large part of its repertoire on an LP, a disk I was proud to have been a part of. All my life, I've been a very late bloomer at everything. Could it be that with the dance class and the choir, the first petals of that bloom were beginning to open?

Martha Wilcox told me that she was choreographing the theater department's spring production of Rodgers and Hart's 1927 musical, *A Connecticut Yankee,* and she thought I should audition for it. I prepared Jule Styne's "Comes Once in a Lifetime," from *Subways Are for Sleeping,* which had just opened in New York. I thought I sang fairly well. Ric told me he heard through gossip that I was being considered for a small role, but a few days later when I went to check the posted cast list, my name was nowhere to be found. It seems that every time I venture, albeit gingerly, into performing, I get shot down. Ric, who was cast as the dance lead, tried to assuage me that I was not cast probably because they had to give theater majors the first chance. I didn't buy it. I had to face that I just didn't have the talent; the bud was not opening, after all.

My psychology courses were all going well for me, but I knew that a successful career in that field required a Ph.D. I liked the classes, but certainly not nearly enough that I wanted to pursue a doctorate degree. I loved so much being around the theater people and the music people. This was clearly where I belonged. Surely, there must be some way I could find a niche in those worlds. I went to the head of theater department and told him that I hoped to work in the business end of theater and asked him for advice. He had no ideas and nothing to offer. These were the days before arts administration programs came into being. Why I just didn't begin taking theater classes as a second major or as electives to gain some acting technique, I can't fathom.

Ric, who was graduating in the spring and knew of my fanatical fixation on New York, thought I should transfer to New York University. "You will come to New York," he kept insisting. The seed had been planted. Maybe I could go to New York, continue my studies in psychology to mollify my parents, while I took dance classes in my spare time. Now I needed a feasible plan to convince them. My plea was quite a piece of fiction. "Because I've changed my major, I need to be at a school that specializes in psychology. Denver's department just isn't that great. I'd be much better off at NYU." I knew they would never check this out, and besides the difference in the tuition was minimal, so why should it matter to them?

Just before the third trimester, I informed Brian and Barry that I was transferring to NYU in the fall. Things quickly began deteriorating between us. Barry had become friendly with David Griffiths, who was a student in both the theater and radio and television departments, and later became the director of Julia Child's "French Chef" television program. Brian and I watched them spend more and more time together, and we were suspicious of the relationship. Truth be known, we got rather catty about it. Were we jealous that Barry had the nerve to take the plunge into gay life and find himself a boyfriend? Finally, Barry announced that he would be moving into an apartment with David. Brian and I couldn't afford the apartment on our own so Brian went back to the on-campus apartment housing.

On last minute notice, I moved back into the dorm for my final term, and got stuck with an obsessive-compulsive science major named Ralph as a roommate. Ralph was a monitor in the dorm; he inspected everyone's room on the floor to make sure that a high degree of cleanliness and order was maintained. He was the SS of monitors, taking his job very seriously, indeed. In our room, even with a magnifying glass, you would not have been able to locate a speck of dust or a book or piece of paper out of place. I knew precisely what Ralph would be doing at any particular moment simply by looking at the clock. At 9:52 PM, he would slam his books shut, place them correctly on the shelf, rise determinedly from his desk, remove his pants, stretch them out full length, snap them violently, like a whip, against the closet to remove any wrinkles, carefully hang them, then go to bed exactly at ten. He drove me totally mad.

I had no choice but to return to Rockford for the summer and work at Nylint. Another monotonous three months in the factory was thankfully uneventful. Connie Carlson also worked there that summer, so we at least were able to commiserate with each other during lunch breaks. Only the countdown until September kept me going. As the end of the summer and my farewell to Nylint approached, over and over again, I repeated to myself the mantra, "Norman, you are not going to New York to become a homosexual." Hmmm.

Manhattan

SOMEHOW DAD MANAGED to get off work so that they could drive me to New York. We stayed with the Brooklyn Speras while we searched for a place for me to live. I hadn't foreseen that living in New York would be prohibitively more expensive than living in Denver. My parents had only two days to spend in the city, and in such a short time we couldn't find any apartments in the vicinity of NYU that were affordable. We checked to see whether the school had a list of reasonable accommodations. They had nothing, and at the time, NYU had no dormitories.

Dad suggested to Jerry that maybe I should live at the YMCA. I saw Jerry pull dad aside, and though I couldn't quite hear what they were saying, I knew he was warning him that he wouldn't want his son to be exposed to a lot of homosexuals in the Y. Out of desperation, my parents rented a room by the week in a small, dingy hotel on 8th Street, two blocks from school, called The Marlton. "Stay there for a couple weeks until you find a place."

My first day alone in New York was going to be all the things I'd ever dreamed about. I got dressed up in my navy-blue blazer, gray flannel trousers, and regimental tie and went uptown to buy theater tickets for that night. It was one of those early September days of coolish, yet oppressive, humidity and rain, so I wore my trench coat and bought an umbrella. I dashed happily in and out of the elegant stores along Fifth Avenue. When I came out of Saks Fifth Avenue to look for a place to lunch, it had begun to pour. I decided to wait under an awning until the rain let up.

A few minutes later, a nice-looking man approached me, "Do you have the time?" "Yes, it's 12:45," not suspecting that this was a terribly clichéd pickup line. "Where do you come from?" I must have had that forlorn out-of-towner look that New Yorkers can spot a mile away. "From

Rockford, Illinois." "Just visiting?" "No, I'm starting school at NYU at the end of the week. This is my first day in New York by myself." "Really? Well, in that case I'd like to prove to you that we New Yorkers are not all cold and heartless, as legend has it. May I treat you to lunch to welcome you here." I was a bit hesitant, but I thought, "Why not?" He took me to a small restaurant off Fifth Avenue, and we sat for nearly two hours just talking (do they get long lunch hours in New York?). "I'm the advertising manager at Lord & Taylor's, and I have to get back to work. Why don't you walk down with me. I'll show you my office."

Off we went to 38th Street. I had never been in Lord & Taylor's before and was struck by the elaborate white enameled and mirrored elevators on the way up to his office. He showed me around, then handed me his card. "You look so very innocent," he said, "and there are a lot of people in this city ready to take advantage of that. I live in Brooklyn. If you need any help or you'd like to get together, please call me. I'd love to see you again." I realized he had more on his mind than lunch, and I was flattered by the attention. "Norman, you did not come to New York to be a homosexual," I reminded myself.

That night I went to the show I'd been dying to see since I bought the album and the sheet music, Richard Rodgers' *No Strings,* starring Diahann Carroll and Richard Kiley. I bought cheap balcony tickets because I planned to see a lot of shows on the $200 I had allocated for that purpose from my Nylint earnings. I knew this musical had no overture, but the opening number, "The Sweetest Sounds," with the two leads standing alone on opposite sides of the stage, was just as breathtaking and exciting to me. I had played and sung this song a thousand times at the piano.

At intermission, I remained in my seat in the front of the balcony. As I watched the audience file into the lobby, the handsomest man I'd ever seen came up the aisle. He looked straight into my eyes with such laser-like intensity that I felt staked through the heart to my seat. I had never been looked at in that way before. I was startled, shaken, thrilled, flattered, and frightened all at once. "What should I do? Should I follow him? No, absolutely not. Remember your warning about coming to New York, Norman." I remained in my seat and didn't see him again. Little did I realize that all this attention from men was simply first-day beginners's luck. It wouldn't last.

The show, about an affair between a black fashion model and American novelist in Paris, with it's primarily black-and-white motif, was one of the most stylish things I'd ever seen. Joe Layton's direction and choreography were sleek, forward-looking, and in the height of fashion.

During registration for school, we were required to pass a speech test. I lined up behind at least 150 students. Each was asked to read a paragraph from a book. Everyone in front of me failed the test and was required to enroll in a remedial speech course. Finally, it was my turn. I read the paragraph, "You're fine. You needn't enroll in speech." I tried to figure out what made me different when I realized it was because everyone else had a thick New York accent, which apparently was undesirably *déclassé* even in New York. However, I learned to imitate the accent immediately because it amused me so.

What a remarkable change from Denver University. The classes were excellent but how was I to make friends here? I had no idea that NYU was a commuter school—virtually everyone was a New Yorker who lived at home, totally different from the international university it has become today. Classes ended and everyone disappeared. I thought, well, "I'll join the choir to meet people." At the first rehearsal, four students showed up and I was the only baritone. There were two sopranos and one alto. The director said, "We need at least one tenor to continue, so if anyone knows somebody, please talk him into joining." I never returned for a second rehearsal.

This was one of the loneliest periods of my life. The Speras were kind enough to invite me to Sunday dinners, so I took the long subway ride to Bay Ridge, Brooklyn, nearly every week. I was introduced to Sicilian foods that were new to me, such as *arancini*, the deep-fried rice balls with cheese and prosciutto. My family never ate rice. On my birthday, they took me to Chinatown, the first time I'd ever eaten Chinese food, a wonderful new taste experience.

In those first weeks, the Speras were practically the only people I ever talked to. Ric was living on East 63rd Street in a lovely apartment (he had a very rich father), so I saw him a couple times, but he was often busy or away. One day he introduced me to an actor friend of his, who startled the hell out of me by asking, almost after shaking hands, "Are you gay?" "No," I said very defensively. "Well, you will be," he shot back in a very sarcastic tone, which rattled me for the rest of the day.

The Marlton Hotel was very cheap for many obvious reasons. The room was dreary beyond description—had no air conditioning, no bathroom, no amenities whatsoever. I stayed there for nearly six weeks, while I studied the classified ads, trying to find an apartment. I luckily happened on a tiny cheap restaurant, a Greenwich Village institution called, The Bagel, where I could have a baked potato, a salad with a superb mustard and tarragon dressing I've futilely tried to duplicate, and a decent entrée for under two dollars. The two waitresses, Sonja and Mary, were the sweetest people I knew in Manhattan. They gave me free desserts almost every night. "Would you like whipped cream on that chocolate cake, dear?"

Naive person that I was, it was only after I left The Marlton that I learned from another student about its notorious reputation. "Are you kidding me? Your parents actually left you at The Marlton?" she asked incredulously. "You know that hotel's populated by prostitutes and drug pushers, don't you?" Actually, I didn't know and hadn't been bright enough to figure it out while I lived there. Today it's a completely different upscale, boutique hotel.

I had a romantic and totally unrealistic Hollywood view of New York real estate from having seen the movie of *Breakfast at Tiffany's* in Denver. I assumed that Holly Golightly's apartment was a poor person's abode, rather than the smart Upper-East-Side townhouse that it was. I pictured myself living in a similar place, with someone like George Peppard crawling through my window at night. It wasn't until I saw Shirley MacLaine's New York downscale tenement apartment in the movie of *Two for the Seesaw* that I had an awakening. "Aha, so that's how I must live here."

I began looking at apartments on the Lower East Side blocks that looked forbidding and dangerous. With all the rundown facades and rusty fire escapes, I thought, "This looks just like the movie of *West Side Story*." At last I found a tiny "recently renovated" studio about a mile from NYU on East 10th Street, between Avenues A and B, on Tompkins Square Park.

It was on the ground floor in a rear house, which meant you had to pass through the street-front building and cross a hideous cement air shaft to enter the back building. It had white-and-gold-speckled linoleum floors, the tiniest of kitchen facilities stuck in the corner, one shallow closet, requiring that everything be hung on an angle, and a bathroom for $60 a month—twice the amount I was paying for luxury in Denver. The kitchen had a small stove and a half refrigerator stuck under a formica counter, the likes of which I had never seen. I noticed a couple bugs crawling on the counter and wondered, "Could they be roaches?" I'd never seen one before, so I consulted my dictionary, and sure enough, I put bug spray on my shopping list.

I had no furniture, but the Speras provided me with an old formica dining table and four plastic-seated, chrome-legged chairs, plus a set of white-flowered drapes on a dark green background for my two narrow grimy windows, looking out onto the light-deficient and airless air shaft. I bought a rollaway bed at a cheap furniture outlet on First Avenue, and just like that, I was a New Yorker with my very own apartment. I was certain my parents would just die if they saw this dump.

The first week after moving into the apartment was financial hell. After paying the deposit on the rent and buying the bed, plus a few kitchen items, I had used up almost every cent of the several hundred dollars I had saved. It would be at least another week before my parents sent me my allowance. What to do until then. I refused to ask them for more money because I was already feeling guilty about not having done my homework regarding the cost of living in the city. I had no extraneous luxuries: no TV, no record player, and worst of all, no telephone. I had to go to a corner payphone to call my parents collect.

They gave me the only thing our family had ever won: a ghastly pink clock radio, so I could listen to music. I had just enough money left to buy a commercial loaf of bread and a package of bologna. I scrupulously portioned them out to last a week by having one sandwich at noon and another late at night, so I wouldn't have to go to bed hungry. I developed a maniacal craving for a chocolate-covered mint patty, but didn't have the two cents to buy one. When my family learned about this several years later, they chastised me for not asking for help. Deprivation for a week or so, I believe, was valuable training to deal with a harsh world.

Shortly after I moved in, I noticed a movie being shot on my block—*Inside Daisy Clover*, starring Natalie Wood. In the scene, she crossed from the park to enter one of the buildings, and she looked gorgeous. Someone in the crowd shouted: "Dat's Na'alie Wood? Dat? She's a dawg, nutin' but a dawg." I knew she had heard this, and I couldn't believe the egregious rudeness of it.

The only personal contact I had at school was with the girl who set me straight about The Marlton. She asked me where I was from. "The Midwest." "Well, you're fighting it, I can tell," she said sardonically, as only a New Yorker could. She was a theater buff and suggested we go see the new Albee play.

I had no idea who Edward Albee was but was eager to find out. The play was *Who's Afraid of Virginia Woolf*. I also had never heard of Virginia Woolf and couldn't understand how she figured into this piece. I was astounded by the power of the play and especially by an actor I'd never heard of, Uta Hagen. Her performance was so compelling it was immediately obvious to me that she had to be one of the theater's great actors. I learned that standing room was even cheaper than balcony seats and made for better viewing from the back of the orchestra section. I was so engrossed in the plays that I was totally oblivious to sore legs and feet. Even with the low cost of standing, the $200 allotted for theatre was gone in a few weeks, leaving me no extra money to think about the dance classes I wanted to take. And didn't I come here to study dance?

I still went to church every week, always dressed in a coat and tie. One Sunday while walking back to my apartment, a little boy, no more than ten or eleven years old and carrying a baseball bat, started walking beside me, completely uninvited. He put his free hand on my arm and began rubbing it rather lasciviously. "I like you," he said. "Yes?" not knowing how to respond. "I want to go home with you." It hit like a blow from a brick. I was so shocked I couldn't believe it. "You'd better go home, little boy, before you get into a lot of trouble doing this." My god, here was a little boy out cruising for sex, and I was completely incapable of bringing myself to it at age twenty. How long could I keep this up?

The loneliness spread a dark veil of gloom over me. Always, I had had people in my life. Now never having anyone to talk to about school or the plays I loved was dispiriting. I was not made to be alone. Eating by myself was the most painful. My family had dinner together every night, without interruption from radio or television. For Sicilians food and eating together are binding forces within the family. At Denver, I had friends to cook for. My cooking skills deteriorated because I couldn't bear spending time in the kitchen to eat alone. Thinking about that little boy and coming to the unwelcome realization that I was never going to change my sexuality was crushing me. The religious taboo was the only remaining stumbling block—or so I thought. During Thanksgiving weekend loneliness triumphed over religion.

I didn't know how to go about it. It had been two months since I met the guy from Lord & Taylor's, and I didn't feel I could call him. Men sometimes followed me on the street. Occasionally, I think I even led them on, but I always became frightened when they approached and I darted away. On Greenwich Avenue was a bar called the Old Colony. Only men seemed to go in or come out. It must be a gay bar. On the Friday after Thanksgiving, which I had spent with the Speras, I walked back and forth in front of that bar for half an hour. It was as though I was an adolescent again, scared to go in and buy a muscle magazine.

I eventually screwed up my courage and went inside. I looked around and felt relieved. It all looked so normal. It couldn't possibly be a gay bar. I don't know what I expected to find in there, a wild orgy? I sat down on a bar stool and ordered a drink (at that time in the city you could drink at eighteen). The bartender set the drink in front of me, and before I took my first sip, a nice-looking man in his early thirties came and sat beside me. He began talking to me, and I was so nervous I didn't hear a word he was saying. My responses, I fear, were completely incoherent. "Do you live alone?" "Uh, well, I . . .yes." "Well, let's go then." "Wow, so fast," I thought.

What am I doing? I don't know anything about this guy, and I'm taking him to my apartment? We walk across town. More conversation that I can't digest because my mind is reeling. Did he just say something about being an interior designer? Maybe, I'm not certain. Is this IT? No turning back? What is he going to expect of me? Will I be some fumbling, awkward, oversexed kid? I keep hoping we'll never reach my place? Maybe I can make up some excuse and back out of it before it's too late. I can't think of anything. We arrive at my front door. I can hardly get the key in the lock. Once we're inside, I have no idea what to do.

"Would you like some coffee?" Where in the hell did I think I was, at *Nonna's* for the Friday night coffee party? "Okay, yes." he says hesitantly, sitting on my bed. I make the coffee, pour it unsteadily into a cup, and carry it over to him. My hand is shaking so violently, I spill half of it into the saucer by the time I reach him. Now what do I do? He takes a few sips and puts it on the table, realizing he has to take the lead.

He's undressing me and I'm shaking even more. I'm completely naked, and he winces as he notices that nothing is happening where it's supposed to happen. I'm beginning to panic. Never have I felt less like sex in my life. I'm racked with bone-chilling cold, colder than I ever knew it to be in Rockford's sub-zero winters.

"Maybe I need to get even with you." he says as he undresses. I watch him, hoping for a spark. It's not the sort of body that sets fire to my imagination. God, I wish this were over. Hands and arms begin to entwine. He kisses me—it's my first kiss—and I feel nothing. How many years have I waited to be kissed. I expected the earth to shake and instead I feel an enervating numbness. He leads me to the bed. Nothing he does seems to make the slightest difference. I'm completely impotent and I'm dying of embarrassment. I thought, if anything, I would have the opposite problem, as with Cory when I was thirteen. So determined to get things right that I'm getting them all wrong. I have moments of being outside my body, watching myself like some severe theater critic, totally damning my performance.

"I'm really sorry. I've never done anything like this before." "Oh, come on, you're just saying that." "No, I'm not. It's true." It was true in the sense that he was a stranger. I can tell he doesn't believe me. He tries everything in his repertoire, to no avail. I'm letting him down. No, I'm letting myself down. He gives up and starts getting dressed. "Well, thanks for inviting me over. If you should happen to see me on the street with another guy, please don't say, 'hello,' because that will be my boyfriend. It would cause a lot of trouble if he knew." Great ending to a great evening. I see him to the door, and he's gone.

I sit down stupefied by the whole thing. My mouth hangs open. I'm a totally empty vessel, completely numb from head to toe. I'm trying to process what has just happened. How could this be? I'm generally so highly sexed. Ten-year-old boys can do this, but I can' t? What does this mean for my future? I can't have sex with women. Now I can't have sex with men, either? Where does that leave me? What kind of romance can I hope for—no, what kind of life can I hope for? Is it the religion? Was I seeing the faces of my horrified parents or hearing the Monseigneur chastising me in the confessional? I don't know. I just need to sleep.

I remain in bed all day Saturday. I can hardly manage to get up to go to the bathroom. I try to eat something, but the food won't go down. On Sunday, I skip church. I'm supposed to go to the Spera's for dinner. I just can't face them. I can't even make myself go to the corner to call and say that I'm too sick to come. I simply don't show up. I eat tiny morsels of food and practically gag on them.

Monday morning and I must go to school, but I can't make myself. What do I care about school when my whole life is crumbling around me? I leave the apartment and wander about aimlessly. I return and feel that I'm entombed. I'm struck by the idea that I will be alone for the rest of my days. All my life, I've dreamt about the fulfilling, loving relationship I will have one day, and this is how it ends? I can't possibly go on like this. I'd rather just die.

That seems the only solution, the only way out of this hell. But how do I do it? I'm too much of a coward to do anything that's going to cause excruciating pain. I'd probably botch it, anyway. I'll think about it for a couple days. I decide to see some shows, a last whirl of enjoyment before my final exit. I go to see Anthony Newley in *Stop The World, I Want to Get Off.* Does a title exist that better expresses how I'm feeling right now? I begin crying right from the opening. This is what I always wanted, the theater. That and a meaningful relationship. Now I can't have either. When Newley sings "What Kind of Fool Am I?" an embarrassing torrent of tears pours forth. Almost every word in the lyric speaks directly to me. At least the tears bring a temporary catharsis. But only temporary. Going to the theater is not going to solve this problem.

Friday night, a whole week has past in a blur. I've made a decision. How trite it all seems. In an "everything I've ever learned, I learned from the movies" moment, I decide gas is the best solution. I stuff rags under the doors and at the window sills, just as I had seen in the films. I turn on all the burners and the oven, without lighting them. I begin taking deep breaths, sitting in front of the stove, my head in the oven. The putrid smell of the gas is nauseating. How long will it take—minutes? hours?

Ten minutes and nothing is happening. Nothing. I take even deeper breaths. It feels as though hours have passed. Still nothing! What am I doing wrong? Why isn't this working? I can't even manage this. Voices in the hall: "Do you smell gas?" "Yes, I do." "Should we call someone?" "Oh, I don't know."

Oh, my god, they're going to call the fire department, and they'll break down the door. I'll be sent to Bellevue in a straitjacket. I had to turn off the gas fast. Now what? Just go to bed. Saturday goes by, I don't know how. Sunday, and again no church. I've never just skipped mass in my life. How many mortal sins have I committed in a week? What does it matter if I go to hell; I'm already in hell. For certain, I can't face the Speras. I try to focus on a future but can't conjure up one. It's night and this can't go on.

There's a heavy metal grate on the wall, high up next to the ceiling. It looks strong enough. I test it; it seems sturdy. I don't know how to tie a noose. Belts. I hook two together. I think it'll work. The belt just fits through the hole in the grate. I unlock the door so no one has to break it down. I stand my foot locker on end and climb onto it. I slide the belt over my head and onto my neck. Everything goes black. Off the locker is a fathomless netherworld. All I have to do is kick the locker out from under me. So easy. Just do it!

I'm scared. My bowels are raging. I close my eyes. My heart is beating violently and I'm hyperventilating. I tentatively begin to push the locker with one foot. Suddenly out of nowhere, I hear a woman screaming. Who can it be? It's my mother. She just got the news about my death. It's all in my head, but it's so real that it shocks me to my roots. I can't do it. I remove the belt from my neck and sit on the foot locker. I can't move. I can't think. I'm in a catatonic state. I'm completely lost. Hours pass.

There's a knock on the door. I don't move. Someone opens it. It's Ann and Jerry Spera. Jerry looks up at the belts hanging from the grates and starts screaming at me, "What the hell are you doing?" I hear him as an echo through a long black tunnel. He and Ann seem so distant. I still can't move or speak. Even if I wanted to reach out to them I couldn't. Jerry starts slapping me across the face to snap me out of it. They grab me by the arms and drag me to their car. We drive to Brooklyn and Jerry calls my father. I can't hear what he's saying. When he hangs up, he's very angry at me and says, "We're putting you on a plane tomorrow morning. Your father will pick you up at the airport in Chicago." Ann comes over to me, "Norman, I know what's wrong with you. I've known since the first time I saw you in Rockford as a little kid. My brother is gay, so I know what you've been going through." I don't respond.

My parents and Larry pick me up at O'Hare. Mother warns me not to say anything in the car because they don't want Larry to know. When we get home, they send Larry to bed and shut his door. They sit on either side of me on the living-room couch. "What happened to you?" I can't answer. I have no idea how to explain this mess I've made. An hour passes. They plead for an explanation, and I still can't talk. Mother says, "I know what it is, but I just can't say it." She goes and gets the dictionary and thumbs through it until she finds the word she's looking for. I'm thinking, "Ann knew. She obviously knows, too."

I'm sure of what I'm about to see when she points to the word. I look down and am startled speechless. She's pointing to "Masturbation." I break down in tears. I can't believe it. Finally I speak, "Do you honestly think I'm that stupid that I would cause all this trouble over such a silly thing?" They are at a complete loss. I've no choice but to tell the whole sordid tale. All the while, I'm thinking, "Will they throw me out? Will they get hysterical? Will they disown me?"

Mother says, "Why couldn't you have told us when you were in high school, when you went to that psychiatrist?"

"I just couldn't do it."

"Well, you're going right back to see him."

"Okay." I can't imagine what good this will do.

The next day we talk further. Dad is beginning to cry, something I've never seen him do. "I know, I know. It's all my fault."

"It's nobody's fault, dad."

It takes a few moments to recover before he says, "You know when I was young and hanging around St. Anthony's, Father B. used to chase after all the boys."

"What? No, Matt, no, not Father B." Mother is horrified. She worshipped Father B. since she was a little girl. He even married my parents.

Mother turns to me, "I don't understand. I had no idea. You went out with girls. You have a deep voice and broad shoulders. How can it be?" She can't take any more and leaves the room.

"Your mother doesn't get it at all. Last night she asks me, 'What does it mean, homosexual,' I had to explain it to her. And your uncle Andy. When we were on vacation in Michigan, remember how one night the women slept in one room and we all slept in the other room? Andy and I had to share a bed. Well, in the middle of the night, he starts grabbing my crotch, and I had to push him away." Even I'm shocked by this.

"You know, when I was in the service in Hawaii, guys used to come up to me all the time." Why is he telling me this? Are we bonding on the issue? Is he bragging about how handsome he was then, which he was?

Was he one of the boys Father B abused? I don't have the nerve to ask. So far, it's going a lot better than I expected, considering this is a deeply Roman Catholic family.

My visit to the psychiatrist yields nothing. When I told him about the suicide attempt, his response was, "Well, wasn't that a perfectly selfish thing to do. You don't think about anyone else but yourself." He throws me with this. Of course, he's right. Suicide is so devastating to those left behind because they blame themselves or infer that the act was some sort of revenge or punishment against them. It generates such reflections as, "What should I have done to help? Why didn't I see this coming? Did I contribute to it?" After I left his office, I thought to myself, "But isn't that exactly what I did? I stopped myself because I realized the terrible pain it would cause my parents? What is he blaming me for?"

Mother wanted me to continue seeing Dr. P., and I refused. "There's no point," I said. "I don't think you want to get better. I don't think you want to change." "You're right, mother, I don't." I knew I had to nip this train of thought in the bud. If I had learned nothing else, it was that such a change was impossible and that I had already endured years of pain for not accepting that fact. I wasn't going back, period.

In retrospect, the whole melodramatic affair appears preposterous. Under a curse of guilt, I had done everything I could to smother, no, to strangle my sexuality for eight years. How absurd to believe in light of this that I could pick up some stranger and not confront these demons of my past. Consequently, I punished myself as deficient and nearly doomed my future as a result. If the encounter had happened with Terry Carlson or Wade, it would have been so much easier.

Letters to my parents began arriving from the university, saying that I had been missing from classes for more than two weeks. They wrote back, explaining that I was ill and at home convalescing. Another letter arrived saying that my midterm grades were straight "As" and that I could come back and make up the missing work. I was still in such turmoil I had no idea what I should do. I couldn't muster the courage to go back just before Christmas and cram sufficiently to pass the courses with less than embarrassing grades. It may have been the most spoiled-child thing I ever did in my life, but I refused to go back and complete the courses. This meant my mother and dad forfeited all the money they had spent. I felt guilty but couldn't force myself to rectify the situation. Of the many mistakes I've managed to make in my life, I'm most ashamed of this one.

Just before Christmas my parents went to confession at St. Anthony's, and they insisted I go with them. I dreaded what I was afraid might be a replay of my confession with the Monseigneur when I was

thirteen. I had even more to confess this time: an illicit act, a suicide attempt, and missing mass for several weeks, each a mortal sin. To my surprise, the priest was very understanding and consoling. He implied that
sometimes one can't control these things and that under no circumstances
did the church feel one should inflict punishment to the point of harming
oneself, regardless of the sin.

I was relieved but, at the same time, perplexed. Wasn't this
hypocrisy? I had been called a depraved sinner eight years earlier, but now
when it nearly cost me my life, all was forgiven. I knew that part of this
was the difference between the gentler Franciscan priests at St. Anthony's
and the unforgiving clergy of St. James's. Nevertheless, it registered as another seismic shift, creating a much larger crack in the ground supporting
my religious beliefs.

On top of all the troubles I was causing my parents, they were in
the midst of building a new house, which was behind schedule. They
needed to move in right after the holidays because they had already rented
out the apartment, and it was uncertain whether the house would be ready
in time. Mary Giovingo was, at last, getting her life-long wish for a new
home, independent of my grandmother's influence.

To maintain the *bella figura* within the extended family, and particularly during the Christmas holidays, we had to lie and say that I had
contracted some respiratory disease that forced me out of school. Intermittent phony coughing. What was clearly emerging was that I could no
longer live with my family. I had been on my own too long and remaining
in Rockford meant sacrificing my independence and living a terrible lie.

We moved into an unfinished house just after New Year's Day. I
announced that I wanted to go back to New York and to school. I promised that I would not walk out on my responsibilities for completing
the courses this time. It was the only rationale I could offer for returning
to the city. They were reluctant to let me go, but I insisted, mostly as a
reason to get away from home. Mary Giovingo told me as I was leaving,
"I'll pray to St. Jude for you every day." St. Jude is the patron saint of
hopeless cases.

I enrolled without enthusiasm for the second semester. I could
barely bring myself to study for these courses that held no interest for me
and ended up with the most mediocre grades of my college career. Two
weeks after my parents moved into their new home, my grandfather, Ignazio, unexpectedly died of a heart attack. The three brothers got together
to decide what do with my grandmother. She couldn't live alone in the
house on Longwood Street, now that there was no one in the apartment
building to watch over her. The decision was made without Mary

Giovingo's input: *Nonna* would live with my parents. My poor mother, who had fought for twenty years for her own home, enjoyed only those two weeks of independence from her mother-in-law.

I had come to New York to study dance and that's what I intended to do. I took one modern-jazz class (the type of dancing used in musical theater) with Harry Woolever, who had been the dance captain for *My Fair Lady.* I spoke to him after class and he recommended that I get some ballet training first. I was unaware that most theater dancers had a ballet background and that generally the very first thing given for a musical-theater audition was ballet to weed out the untrained. Again, there was no extra money available for classes. I needed a new plan.

I decided to drop out of school at the end of the semester and find a job to support myself. In April, I noticed an announcement in the *New York Times* that the Fred Astaire Dance Studio was offering a free training course for future dance instructors. This was perfect. I could earn a living teaching ballroom dancing and take ballet classes in my free time. The class lasted about six weeks, which meant I'd finish just as I completed the semester at NYU and could begin work directly after. I told my parents my plan, knowing that they would hate it. Mother said, "Fine. If you leave school, you're on your own. We're not supporting you." I told them about the training class, but they were not impressed.

In the class I made two new friends, Anita and Ron. They were both college students but were taking the free class just to learn the dances, not to work as instructors. Anita had already been hired to teach school the next fall. In the classes we had to learn one hundred school figures (the required basic steps) to a variety of dances. It was very easy for all three of us, and we passed the course with flying colors. School ended and I began my job. At first, I had no students but was required to give a free demonstration lesson to anyone who came in off the street. Then it was my job to sell them a program of lessons, for which I would receive a commission. I especially recall one very heavy teenage girl who came in with her father. When I tried to move her across the floor, it was like Sisyphus trying to roll an immense boulder up a mountain. She wouldn't budge. No lessons were sold. Our initial pay was a pathetic minimal salary designed to motivate us to hustle students—easier said than done.

After my first week I had one student, a woman of about seventy. On the weekend I was expected to accompany her to two studio-sponsored events in a rented tux: one at the Latin Quarter nightclub, and the other dancing at the Roosevelt Grill. I also had to escort her home. When I got to her apartment, she asked me to come in for a moment. She looked at me with hungry eyes, "Do you have a TV?" "No, I don't." "Oh, good, you can have mine." "Oh, no, no thanks anyway." At that moment I realized that I was basically expected to be a gigolo, as well as a dance instructor. It was clear that it would take months to develop a clientele large enough to support myself. I couldn't even cover my rent on the basic salary. My mind sent me an urgent message, "Get out of this business now, Norman."

Aware that I wasn't supporting myself, Mary Giovingo said, "You have one week to get a job that pays enough to live on or you're coming back home." Now that's incentive! I began looking through the classified ads but couldn't find anything I was qualified to do. In fact I wasn't qualified to do anything. On Monday morning, I decided to register with an employment agency. I got there about ten, and this nasty, gruff man greets me.

"You're looking for a job?"

"Yes."

"We'll then where the hell were you at nine AM this morning?" Staggered by the question, I remain silent. "It says on your application you have two and half years of college. What did you study?"

"Psychology."

"Why the hell didn't you study something useful. What do you expect to do with that?"

"Well, I did take a few business courses."

"Not enough to place you in any job I have, that's for sure."

I'm twenty years old and completely unemployable. I look at the classifieds again. There's a job listed with a different agency for a department-store announcer. I'll bet I could do that. "Ladies, we're having a sale on lingerie today on the third floor." Yes, that sounds right for me. I go to the agency, and meet with a far more pleasant man.

"Have you ever been a department-store announcer?"

"No."

"Explain to me exactly what a department store announcer does?"

"I don't really know."

"I don't think that's the job for you. What are you hoping to be?"

"I'm looking for a job that pays enough to support myself because I want to study dance."

"Dance. Hm. Do you type?"

"Yes,"

"Sit over at that typewriter and let me hear you." I type at my seventy-word-per-minute speed on an antiquated machine. He doesn't even check to see that I've actually typed words and not just random keys.

"That was just terrific. I'll bet you worked on your school paper in high school."

"No, I didn't."

"In college?"

"No."

"But you've always been interested in publications, right?"

"Not really."

"I have the feeling that you enjoy writing."

"No, actually I never have." I'm being brutally honest with this guy, as I was always taught to do. And I don't want to give the impression I have skills that I don't have. "What are you an idiot, Norman? This guy is trying to get you a job, and you're not even bright enough to give him a helping hand."

"I think I have the perfect job for you at *Dance Magazine*." Remarkably, he's undaunted by my obstinance. "It's an editorial assistant position; they need someone who can type like a whiz."

I'm scheduled for an interview and meet with the news editor, Don Duncan. I can tell he likes me immediately. There's a real rapport between us. The job sounds interesting, and it will put me, at least peripherally, in the dance world.

"Can I call Fred Astaire's for a reference?" he asks.

"Yes, of course."

" I know Dagmar Jarvel there. Will she know you?"

"Yes; She certified me as an instructor." Dagmar was the head of the studio.

"I'll let you know tomorrow."

Dagmar gives me a glowing recommendation, despite my short tenure. I'm hired. I'm on a new path, a whole new promising future. My life takes on direction and purpose.

First Love and First Position

As Don's editorial assistant, I'm hired to do all his typing and help with proofreading. I'm also to be his assistant on the Annual Directory of Dancers and Dance Attractions. In addition, he is editor-in-chief of a sister publication, *Ballroom Dance Magazine*, on which I am to assist him and his associate editor, Helen Wicks Reid. Don, who is in his fifties, tall, heavy, with wavy blond hair and very thick glasses, is indubitably the best boss I will ever have—kind, generous, intelligent, and a true mentor. In the past, he had been Martha Graham's stage manager and later an associate of the top dance publicist, Isadora Bennett.

Helen is a woman in her early seventies, with bright red sausage curls, flame-red lipstick, far too much makeup over her wrinkledy face, but a trim body, often garbed in bright green dresses. She owned a dance studio on Long Island and is a big deal in the ballroom dance associations, though I never had the privilege of seeing her dance skills. She's separated from her husband and obviously worshipfully in love with Don, who is single and gay.

Soon after I began, Helen sprained her ankle and I was assigned to get her by taxi from her apartment on West 45th Street to the office on West 47th Street. The cab driver noticed her limping and said, "Hoit yourself, miss?" "Yes, I sprained my ankle. I'm dancer, you see." You're a dance-uh, lady?" he inquires incredulously of the seventy-year-old. "Oh, yes, indeed I am." She had a patrician Long Island accent, her father having been a prominent dentist. "I did it doing a fast cha-cha." I could see his eyes roll in the rearview mirror.

As with all entry-level editorial positions, the pay is minuscule but enough for me to live on and afford dance classes. Within two months, Don says, "Norman, you're much too smart to just sit and type all day. I'd like you to try your hand at editing one of our foreign correspondents.

You know our style. Just edit to adhere to that." We had correspondents in all the major capitals of the world, who reported on dance events in their city each month. "You have to be careful because their English is often a bit, shall we say, creative." From some of our German correspondents, we received reports about the latest production of the "Hazelnusscracker." Another described a famous ballerina, "She danced with such joy that she was smiling at both ends." Would love to have seen that.

After my first crack at editing, Don says, "All right, I give you a B minus on this." Then he carefully explained to me how I could improve the piece. Within a couple weeks, he's entrusted me with several writers. I'm even editing Clive Barnes, our London correspondent, and soon to become the head dance and drama critic of the *New York Times*. Gradually I learn the business, working with the art director on page layouts, approving the final "blues" before we go to press, and coordinating with the advertising department.

And I'm meeting famous dancers. Don sends me to Edward Villella's apartment (the starry principal dancer of the New York City Ballet who's as charming in person as he is dynamic on stage) to interview him. Peter Gennaro, whose choreography I had seen in *Mr. President* and a new musical, *Bajour,* comes to the office, and I'm elected to interview him, as well. I also get a press pass. Don says, "With this pass and fifteen cents, you can ride the subway." Free tickets to many major dance attractions are another perk, and I'm seeing styles of dance I knew nothing about, especially the major modern dance companies— Martha Graham, Paul Taylor, and Jose Limon.

Ballroom Dance Magazine, which interests me far less, hosts America's Ball of the Year, a formal dinner and dance at the Plaza Hotel, a gala celebrity event. Don asks me to go to the Shubert Theatre to deliver an invitation personally to Chita Rivera, who's starring in *Bajour*. As I enter the stage door, several young men ask me if I'm there to audition for a dance replacement in the show. Oh, how I wish. "No, I'm here to see Chita Rivera." I'm announced and told to go to her dressing room. As I enter, she rushes up to embrace me. "Norman, I'm so glad to see you," as if she's known me all my life. She thinks I'm a major figure at the magazine; instead, I'm the guy at the bottom of the masthead. As I hand her the invitation, she says, "Oh, yes, I'd love to attend the ball." I can hardly believe this. Just five years ago, I was so despondent not to have seen Judy Holliday and Peter Gennaro at this same theatre, now I'm being hugged by the star in her dressing room and interviewing Gennaro.

The ball is in honor of Irene Castle, half of the pre-World War I dance team of Vernon and Irene Castle. Don takes me to her suite at the

Plaza. He mentions Hollywood's film biography of their lives, which starred Fred Astaire and Ginger Rodgers. "Oh, yes, that woman—what's her name?" she says condescendingly and with great disgust, "that tap dancer who played me on the screen." She simply could not bring herself to mention the likes of Ginger Rodgers. At the ball, I meet Bette Davis and Dame Alicia Markova, the English prima ballerina. As she makes her entrance, the band plays, "There Is Nothing Like a Dame," and everyone laughs. At the dinner I'm seated next to the rising young modern dancer Louis Falco, who is my age, and a principal in the Jose Limon Company. He will soon become famous as the choreographer of the movie, *Fame*.

I'm somewhat disturbed that Falco at my age is already a rising star, and I've barely started studying. There are a few carping people who intimate that at twenty-one years of age I'm much too old to begin serious dance training. I refuse to listen. If only I had ignored all the warnings about going to acting school, I would have started dance training as part of the curriculum three years earlier. It may have been that I was not cut out to be an actor, but other talents might have surfaced.

The week after I start my job at the magazine, I enroll in beginning ballet classes at the Ballet Arts School in Carnegie Hall. After my first class, several young girls come up to me, "Can we please look at your feet?" I can't imagine what this is about. "Look at that arch. How beautiful. Would you mind if we just touch them." Who knew? It appears that I have a pair of feet to die for—small, square-toed, and highly arched—perfect for ballet.

For this I have Mary Giovingo to thank. She generously passed her well-arched-feet genes on to me. Also, because she suffered through the depression, stuffing newspapers in her shoes and fought fiercely at age twelve with social-service employees to get free winter coats for herself and her parents, my brother and I always had quality coats and even finer shoes. We were never allowed to go barefoot, even in the house, for fear of falling arches.

Going into any dance class for the first time is daunting. Everyone knows the teacher's *barre* exercises and what to expect of the combinations (a series of steps strung together) in the center of the floor. Never having studied, I knew nothing and was defiantly swimming upstream, trying to learn the five basic ballet positions, all the French names for the various steps, and how to execute them. Generally taking two classes every night after work, with a variety of teachers, I began to progress very rapidly.

Sex had been put in the very back of my shallow closet, mostly out of fear of another humiliating episode. Shortly after I began at the magazine, I ventured forth again. At the Old Colony bar, a distinguished-looking man in his early forties approached me, introducing himself as Don Appell. I knew immediately who he was because I had recently seen the musical he wrote with Jerry Herman, called *Milk and Honey*. "Did you like the show?" "Yes," I told a half truth. I loved the music and the performances but thought that his book (the play part of the musical) was wanting. "Well, I'm glad or we would have gotten off to a bad start. Would you like to go for a drive in Central Park?" "Yes."

We got into a flashy red sports convertible and drove around for nearly an hour before he invited me to his Central Park West apartment at the San Remo, a 1930s building that has been home to many celebrities including, Glenn Close, Dustin Hoffman, and Rita Haworth. This was the apartment of my childhood fantasies, high above the city with a heart-stopping view of the park.

I was nervous and thought I had better be upfront about my problems. He listened carefully, asking many questions, and we talked until I saw the dawn rising. He made me feel very comfortable. "I have no intentions of making any move toward you. If you want anything more to come of this evening than a lovely conversation, it's up to you to initiate it," he said. I did, and it all went beautifully this time.

A whole new world of wonder had just opened to me. I felt relieved, unshackled from my constricted past and had no sense of guilt or remorse whatever. So many Catholics are never able to rid themselves of the oppressive guilt over their homosexuality. I was lucky; for me it vanished as though it had never been. "Can I see you again?" he asked. We set a date for the following week.

I went to the library to read his play, *Lullaby*, which appeared on Broadway. He was a rather well-known writer and director for television, as well. I was unimpressed by his play, which had not been a hit, though it was later turned into a TV movie starring Eli Wallach and Anne Jackson. On the way to the second date, the subway was delayed. I ran manically as I emerged from underground to try to make up the lost time. I was out of breath when I reached his apartment. He opened the door and pointed to his watch, "You're fifteen minutes late. If it happens again, it will NEVER happen again, I can assure you!" Is this the same man who was so kind the other night?

I should have turned on my heel and walked out right then, but I was somewhat in awe of his position in the theater world. I have zero tolerance for being spoken to in that manner, especially when I am not at fault. Unsurprisingly, the evening went very badly. I shut down completely, probably a way to get back at him for the abrasive greeting. I was upset about another failed encounter, but this time I recognized the reasons for it and maintained my equilibrium.

That summer my parents came to visit. I so hoped that I would get home from my job before they arrived so I could prepare them. But no, there they were standing on the corner of 10th Street and Avenue A, as I approached. I could see that they were both shaking their heads in disgust before I reached them. "How could you?" Mary Giovingo said. "How could you live in a place like this, when you have a perfectly good home in Rockford?" If they were appalled at the neighborhood, what ever would they think of my apartment? Hesitantly, I let them in only to be startled by something I'd never seen before. I had left the windows open onto the air shaft because it was so hot in the summer. The moment we entered, four alley cats leaped off my bed and out the window. My father never recovered from this. "You're going to sleep on that bed after those filthy cats were on it?" Mary Giovingo asked in horror.

Shortly after they left, I met a tall, Waspish-looking man, in Washington Square Park one sultry evening. Frederick, was a couple years older than I am. He claimed to be an heir to the Revlon fortune, though I was never able to confirm this. We talked for several hours in the park before I invited him to come to my apartment. He was an Ivy Leaguer who had just begun a job selling luxury real estate at a leading agency. He had been crashing at various friends apartments, while on the lookout for a place of his own. We agreed that he could stay with me for awhile. Having the same person in my bed every night increased my comfort level with my new gay life. However, two in a single bed in a stifling apartment was hardly physically comfortable. Frederick said, "I expect you will achieve big things in life, but I'm not sure it will be as a dancer." We were not destined to be lovers, and a month later we decided it was best if we separated.

A new teacher, Joy O'Neill, joined the staff of the Ballet Arts School. A stunning dark-haired woman who had danced with American Ballet Theatre, she inspired me to reach for a higher level of dance. I was moving from beginner, to advanced beginner, then to intermediate classes. She was a tough task master, but a high-school girl named Nancy Klebanow and I were her favorite students. I learned to endure some harsh criticism because I knew she was eager to help me advance. In executing the position called "attitude," (said to be inspired by Giambologna's statue of Mercury), in which the leg, raised behind the body, is bent at a ninety degree angle, Joy screams, "Norman, you look like a dog watering a hydrant." This was because I had allowed my knee to sink below the level of my foot—extremely unattractive. If my arms were not creating a beautiful line, I'd be called out, "Fix those arms! You look like a fine painting in a terrible frame."

A few times after class, I took a vocal-coaching session with the old woman who was the ballet accompanist. I was fascinated when I learned that she had been for a time Ruth Etting's pianist. Etting was the '20s Broadway star who was portrayed by Doris Day in the film, *Love Me or Leave Me*. The accompanist told me that Etting was so terrified of her husband and manager, the Chicago gangster, Moe "the Gimp" Snyder (played by James Cagney in the film) that she wouldn't sing a note or venture a thought of her own without getting his okay.

Maria, a girl in my other class who was more advanced than I was, asked if I'd be interested in joining the Hal Grego Jazz Ballets, a Brooklyn dance company, to do a concert. Virginia Lee, who ran the school, got wind of this and told me in no uncertain terms that I was not ready to perform and that I should concentrate on my classes. I disregarded her advice, auditioned, and ended up doing some minor dancing in a ballet called *Cinderita*, a Hispanic version of Cinderella at the Brooklyn Academy of Music. I missed only a few dance classes because of rehearsals, so the diversion did no visible harm and gave me at least one credit to put on my résumé.

One night Joy announced that she was moving to the International School of Dance, which was also in Carnegie Hall, and she hoped that Nancy and I would follow her, which we did without hesitation. Several months into my training, Joy was out sick when I showed up for class. The woman who managed the school said, "You are not going to miss class for any reason. I want you to take Alexandra Danilova's pointe class," which is reserved for girls to learn to dance en pointe or on their toes. Madame Danilova had been one the greatest prima ballerinas of Diaghilev Ballets Russes. I noticed her watching me intently throughout the *barre*. When we came to the center floor, she asked in her heavy Russian accent, "How long you study?" "Nine months." "Nine months? No! Girlz, girlz, watch this. Only nine months."

At last, I had the initial makings of a social life—so much harder to achieve than in Denver. Anita and Ron and I became a trio. We went to the beach (Anita's family had a summer home in Far Rockaway), to musicals, and out dancing together. Anita's mother worked at the Metropolitan Opera, so we got free tickets for *Aida* and Samuel Barber's *Vanessa*, which convinced me that I was not a fan of opera. Another young man, Greg Watkins, was hired in the advertising department at the magazine.

We lunched together almost every day. Greg had a full-time boyfriend already, and I sometimes went out with the two of them.

On Valentine's Day, which fell on Friday, I ventured once more to the Old Colony. A man in a tweed sport coat, smoking a pipe, whom I pictured as a college professor, was watching me assiduously. When he approached, I realized from his slurred speech that he had been drinking very heavily. He suggested we go to a restaurant where we could talk more easily. Hal Shaw was not a college professor, but a non-college-educated payroll supervisor. He had picked up that tweedy look when he was stationed with the air force in England. After about an hour, he invited me to his apartment on 15th Street, between Seventh and Eighth Avenues. The small one-bedroom flat was modest but comfortable looking and had the luxury of a large eat-in kitchen, with its outer wall stripped down to the bricks.

At six-foot-two and thirty-years-old, he was attractive but very thin. Almost immediately, I sensed that he was a man damaged by life, despondent and somewhat embittered. Before he undressed, he turned off the lights and insisted that I face away from him. Why he was so self-conscious about his body I never understood because he had a quite attractive frame, marred only slightly by legs that were a little too long and slim. I felt extremely comfortable and desired with him. The next morning he didn't want me to leave and begged me to stay. The intensity of the situation was quite beyond anything I had ever experienced. We made love several times during the day, and I noted that he was not drinking, which I saw as a good sign. I remained with him the whole weekend, and he suggested that I go to my apartment to get a few clothes, so that I could stay over the rest of the week.

He told me that he had been in a relationship with a guy named Chris, who was a dancer. When Chris got a summer stock job at Pittsburgh Civic Light Opera, he met someone else and left Hal, who was apparently devastated by the loss. Hal, who was from a suburb of Pittsburgh, had a father, deceased, who had been a severe alcoholic and often beat his mother. Once his father threw her against a door, severely injuring her. Later she developed cancer in that area in her back, and Hal blamed his father for his mother's death.

The following week, after work and dance classes, I returned to 15th Street about 9:15, and we cooked dinner for each other. Evenings began to feel so homey to me, and for the first time in a year my loneliness vanished. By the following weekend, Hal asked me to live with him. Everything seemed to be moving so fast, I had no time for reflection. I thought relationships like this took months to develop. I needed time. On Sunday,

I said I had to go home, be by myself, and just think for a night. I promised I would return Monday night after dance class. He didn't like the idea at all and was convinced that I was either abandoning him or just wanted someone new because I was already bored with him. Assuring him that he was completely wrong was no easy matter. I don't think he ever forgave me for that Sunday night, always implying that I had slept with another guy during the absence.

My apartment never seemed drearier or more oppressive to me than on that night. Looking around at the unwelcoming walls, the tacky linoleum floor, and the pathetically inadequate kitchen sent a shudder through my body. Could I conceivably go back to living alone in this hovel after my week of bliss? Sleeping alone, rather than the relief I anticipated, felt alien and I tossed about through the whole night. By the next morning, I made my decision. I returned to Hal's place Monday night.

"We need to discuss my dancing. Will you be able to deal with my coming home after nine, night after night, eating these late dinners? Will you be able to accept that I probably will have to be away from home for periods at a time if I ever get hired as a dancer?"

"I have no problem with that at all. I don't mind eating a late dinner, and I'm happy to wait at night, knowing that you will be here with me."

"Are you absolutely sure about this?" I asked skeptically.

"Yes, absolutely."

"Okay, I'll move in with you, but I'm going to hang onto my apartment for awhile." I needed to protect myself in case this was all a big mistake and things didn't work out. Had I found paradise? His interests suddenly became my interests. He loved plants, especially growing bonsais, which he kept in a specially constructed terrarium in the living room wall under special lights. I had never shown any affinity toward botanicals, but I loved watching him shape and trim the bonsais and even began assisting him.

How stunned I was when I realized that feeling wanted—and particularly feeling needed—was a highly intoxicating and addictive drug, a warm and gentle tropical wave that swept over my being, rendering me totally pliant. I believed that I had already effected a significant change in Hal, his whole demeanor being vastly improved since that first weekend I met him. If nothing more, I convinced him that he had no reason to be ashamed of his body. I was in love, deeply and profoundly, and was startled at how fully and uninhibitively I was giving myself both physically and emotionally to another person. It made me aware that this is what makes us infinitely human, transports us into a realm beyond the mundane. Here was the realization of the romantic fantasies I held as a child, but stripped of the superfluous material luxuries that I had envisioned, right down to their essential and imminent nature.

The next few weeks were wonderful. Hal didn't understand why I was holding onto my apartment. His rent was even less than mine. Dividing it two ways would give us much more money to live on, so I gave in and abandoned my place and furniture, still with a bit of nervousness, knowing how vulnerable I would be if anything went wrong.

Because I had dropped out of school, I received a notice to report for my army physical. What was I to do? I'm in the midst of learning to dance. If I stop now, that will be the end of any hope for a career. And am I going to give up my relationship for the military? Absolutely not. I decided that being homosexual had caused me years of grief; now it was going to save me from the draft.

I wrote to Dr. P. and asked him for a letter, saying that I was a practicing homosexual. Hal seemed not to approve, I assumed, because he had proudly served his time. I took the doctor's letter with me and entered a large room with at least 500 guys. They began calling out names. I had had to register for the draft under my given name at birth. Suddenly, I heard yelled out, "Ignatius Norman Cancelose." Everyone in that room turned to look at me. I had never been called this in my life, and it was an embarrassing shock.

I handed my letter to the presiding officer and was directed to see the psychiatrist, a very kindly man. "Are you in a relationship now?" "Yes, I am." "Well, I'm very happy for you." He scribbled some notes. "Take this paper to the sergeant at the desk in the waiting room outside." I went into this room where hundreds more were waiting, and handed the paper to the sergeant. At the top of his voice, he screamed out, "Go over to that bench and sit down. And keep your hands to yourself." All eyes turned toward me. I thought I would die of embarrassment, but I got my 4F classification, which exempted me from military duty.

Good Friday arrived and Hal and I were both scheduled to get out of work early in the afternoon. Hal asked me to meet him for a drink after work, and I declined for a very foolish reason. I had given up going to church shortly after returning to New York and rather than feeling guilty about no longer being a practicing Catholic, I experienced an enormous sense of relief, a huge weight lifted off my shoulders. However, I still believed in god. I had always been very observant on Good Fridays, and I wanted to go St. Patrick's Cathedral after work, light a candle, and say a prayer of thanks that I had been blessed by this relationship with Hal. In my mind, I thought god would approve—how could he not sanction love—even though the church condemned me.

That night when I got home from dance class, the apartment was dark. Hal had not come home. What could be wrong? Had something happened? Was he all right? I paced about anxiously, not knowing what to do. By two in the morning, I was frantic. I tried to go to bed but couldn't sleep. When he finally returned late Saturday afternoon, he was still drunk from the night before. I asked him where he had been, but he refused to tell me. I, naturally, imagined he had been sleeping with someone else and couldn't even conceive of a way to cope with having been betrayed. He berated me for not bothering to take the time to meet him after work; I apologized and explained about going to church. But I was angry at myself for being so stupid and selfish. This was my reward for thanking god? I began losing faith that there was, in fact, a god. I didn't know what to expect would happen between Hal and me. Could I forgive him for the infidelity? Did he purposely wait to pull this disappearing act until after I had relinquished my apartment? Would he throw me out into the street? Somehow we made up.

He wanted us to have rings, evidence of more stability in our relationship, so we went out shopping and bought two simple, inexpensive gold-plated bands. We wore them on our right hands to avoid too many questions. At the magazine, several people wanted to know why I was wearing a wedding band. I explained that it was my grandfather's old ring, and I wore it on my right hand as a remembrance of him. The many layers of falsehoods we hid behind in those days!

The money we were both saving by living together allowed us more leeway for our free hours. Already we were eating well. Porterhouse steak was so inexpensive in 1964 that we often ate it twice a week. We were able to go out to dinner and take in an occasional show. He enjoyed musicals, but not nearly with the passion that I did.

We got tickets to see Barbra Streisand in *Funny Girl*. I had worshipped her from her very first album release. The show opened on Thursday night, and we attended the first Saturday evening performance, when the excitement over it was still at its peak. Never had I seen a performance in a musical that was as electrically charged as Streisand's was.

After the Good Friday incident, drinking crept back into Hal's life, and when he drank he became a different person, surly and at times downright nasty. I noted that he had only one friend, Bob, a Broadway dresser, who was his drinking buddy. From the moment I met Bob, I was aware that he disliked me intensely. I had cut into his friendship with Hal and his resentment toward me was palpable. I was slow to realize that Bob would be a strong destabilizing force in our relationship. There were more Friday nights when Hal would not come home. He claimed he was out with Bob, but where was he sleeping? I never knew. It became my most dreaded night of the week, not knowing what to expect.

Hal had a Cocker Spaniel, Amy, whom I grew to love. She was my only comfort on those long abandoned nights. The drinking at home got worse, too, and almost always ended up in a fight between us. I was never much of a drinker and so I became an object of ridicule to him. The problem, he claimed, was that I never went out drinking with him, so I began occasionally skipping dance class, meeting him in a bar. It almost aways ended the same way. He was fine until the second or third drink, when the Mr. Hyde side of his character began to emerge frighteningly from the chrysalis. Sometimes he created a scene in the bar, once taking off his ring and throwing it at me to the astonishment of everyone around us. Then he would storm out, only to disappear until the next day.

He insisted that I was the problem in this relationship, and I sensed that Bob egged him on in this belief. Was I so naive that I just didn't understand what was expected of one in a gay relationship? Did I want for it to be too much like traditional marriage? I began blaming myself and trying to find ways to make things right. I knew how almost everyone believed that a love affair between two men never lasted. I made it my mission to disprove this. I would make it work if it killed me.

Joy O'Neill said she would like to give Nancy and me a private ballet class on Saturday mornings. It would be free, but there would be no accompanist, just the three of us working on technique. Nancy's parents were rich, and I suspected that they were paying for the lessons. Though I was never certain, Joy probably asked them if she could include me. These lessons were very concentrated and difficult, with all the attention focused on just the two of us, but they helped us both progress even faster. Joy hinted that if we worked very hard over the next year, she would invite some of her Ballet Theatre associates to see how we had progressed in such a short time.

Why she was no longer dancing was unclear to me? She was still young enough, and when she demonstrated she always looked terrific, though she rarely did the steps full out. At times, I began to think that all her hopes in dance had now been transferred to Nancy and me, and I sensed that she desperately needed for us to be good. Unfortunately, these extra lessons put even more of a strain on my relationship with Hal, because I was now gone on Saturday mornings, as well.

Work was also taking up more of my time. Don had guided me through the essentials of publishing the Directory of Dancers and Dance

Attractions. and he put me in charge of the issue, which was double the thickness of the monthly magazine.

The world today is aghast at the amount of sexual harassment being uncovered on a daily basis. I had my own incident when I worked at *Dance Magazine*. Don asked me to go to famed dance photographer Jack Mitchell's studio to pick up some photos we needed. Jack yelled, "I'm finishing them up in the dark room. Come in here." The minute I entered he slammed the door shut and locked it. Then he assaulted me, grabbed me in a bear hug, and tried pulling my pants down. I protested vehemently that I was in a relationship and wanted no part of this. He refused to relent, grabbing my crotch and my butt. I had to fight him off until I finally got him to let me out of the room. In those days, it never occurred to us to say anything about such abuse. I can't claim that I was scarred by the incident, but I should have spoken up, though it probably would have elicited chuckles in the '60s.

One morning at five AM, the telephone rang. Hal answered, "It's for you." Half asleep, I grabbed the phone, "Hello." "Norman, this is Jean Gordon," she was the associate publisher of *Dance Magazine* and ran the operation. "Something terrible has happened. Don was found dead in his hotel room in Puerto Rico. Get into the office as soon as possible. We're a week from deadline. You're the only one who knows what's going on in the news department. You have to get the section done yourself. Lydia and Doris, I'm sure, will help you." Lydia was the editor, Lydia Joel, and Doris Hering was the principal critic. I was completely unnerved. Don was fine when he left for his week's vacation a few days ago. How was I, a twenty-one-year-old college dropout going to turn out a twenty-four page section of the magazine? Lydia and Doris, who were both very fond of me, were either too busy or they trusted that I would get the work done on my own. Somehow in a state of sheer panic, I managed to do it.

Poor Helen Wicks Reid was in shock over the death. She had lost her imagined lover. The whites of her eyes appeared to be floating in blood. "But how did he die?' everyone was asking. No one knew. Then we learned that his body would not be returned to the U.S. and that he would be buried in Puerto Rico. Dick, the circulation manager, who was gay, whispered to me, "I've heard rumors that he didn't die naturally. He was killed by a hustler he brought back to his hotel room. Now everyone wants it hushed up, so they're burying him there." I didn't know if Don had any family. He never revealed a thing about his private life. We never learned the truth about his death, and no one wanted to discuss it.

After two months of putting out the news section, I was called into Jean Gordon's office. "I want to tell you that you've done a wonderful job in keeping the magazine going. I've decided, since you're doing the work, to give you the title of news editor, and I will be taking care of you financially, as well." Taking care of me financially meant to her a miserly $10 a week salary increase. Helen was made editor-in-chief of *Ballroom Dance Magazine,* and I remained her assistant on that. My increased responsibilities at the magazine made me miss more dance classes than I normally would have. The longer intermediate-level classes only allowed for one class per night. I tried always to get to class, except at deadline time.

Dad called to tell me he was being sent to New York by Nylint to attend the annual toy fair. I knew how nervous he was about flying. As luck would have it, while the plane was circling the city, flight attendants began tearing up the carpeting next to his seat. "What's going on?" he asked the flight attendant, who reluctantly explained, "The landing gear is not going into place automatically, so we have to operate it manually." Passengers were informed that the runways were being covered in foam, emergency vehicles were on hand, and instructions were given on what to do in case the landing gear didn't hold. Poor Dad was a wreck by the time he got to the city.

He was on an expense account so we could live it up. I took him to the Empire Room at the Waldorf Astoria, we ate in fancy restaurants, but best of all we became closer than we had ever been. If there had been some rancor between us when I lived at home, it had vanished. He respected what I was doing and was impressed that I could show him such a good time, and I reveled in every moment I spent with him.

Hal began to complain that he was tired of waiting alone for me every night, that I was never home when he needed me. "Remember, I asked you when we got together if you'd be able to tolerate this, and you said, 'yes.'" "Well, I can't stand it any more." Was this the whole problem with our relationship? I started missing more classes to be home with him. Joy called me over after class one night and said, "I don't know what's going on with you. You're missing a lot of classes, even the private lessons some weeks. If the problem is your boyfriend, I want you to solve it. You've come too far to give this all up. Bring him to class with you if necessary." That seemed ridiculous, and besides I knew Hal would never agree to such an arrangement.

I was suddenly confronted with having to make a choice between my two loves—my relationship or my dancing. I was so torn between them I didn't know which way to turn. Then one Friday night, Hal didn't show up again. All day Saturday I waited like a wild cat in a cage. Still no Hal. "Should I call the police?" He finally staggered in Sunday afternoon, looking haggard. I told him I was just about to call the police, and I demanded to know where he had been. "I don't know." "You don't know? What do you mean you don't know?" "I woke up today in the back seat of a car parked in a garage, and I have no idea how I got there."

It hit me that this was a far more serious problem than I had imagined. I was reminded of Ray Milland in *The Lost Weekend*. Blacking out, if Hal's story was true, was a sign of severe alcoholism. I confronted him with it and said we had to work together to do something about it. This made him furious. "I'm not an alcoholic. I can't be an alcoholic because mostly I only drink beer." I knew this to be true from the astounding number of quart Rheingold cans he could guzzle in one evening. But I also knew that beer didn't inoculate one against alcoholism. There were the rare times when he didn't drink and he was still the wonderful man I had known. Once when I was returning from a visit with my family in Rockford, I walked into the apartment and there were all my friends seated at the dinner table. He was so glad to have me back that he wanted to surprise me. It was moments like this that kept me going, always thinking I could help him work out his problems.

Work was going well. I certainly didn't love doing the same thing month after month, but it was nevertheless a good job and more than a college dropout could expect. I began having serious doubts about my ability to be a dancer. I deliberated with myself for weeks until I made the painful decision to quit studying and devote myself to Hal and my work. I had chosen: relationships were more important to me than a dance career.

We made plans to redecorate the apartment. We both liked period furniture, so money that I spent on classes now went to lovely antiques: a bergère Louis Quinze love seat and a period armchair. We repainted the place, papered the areas within the decorative wooden moldings, and bought new window treatments. Working together brought us closer together, and we were proud of how we had redecorated the apartment. He was glad to have me home in the evenings, and our relationship improved. It didn't last long. Soon the serious drinking resumed. The Jekyll and Hyde aspects of his personality were so pronounced I never knew what to expect.

Perhaps it's my Catholic upbringing, but I am inherently a monogamous person. I couldn't bear that he was often cheating on me. For nearly two years I wouldn't allow myself the same privilege. I didn't want to contribute to his paranoia about me. But one more weekend of being abandoned broke my resolve. It happened only a couple times. I didn't enjoy it in the least. Perhaps I was doing it simply out of revenge. It basically just tore me to pieces because I could think about nothing but Hal the entire time I was with another man.

My parents came to New York and I cooked dinner for them so they could meet him. My cooking skills were improving again, and I could see they enjoyed the meal. They took an immediate dislike to Hal, though they tried to hide it. Was it Hal or would they despise any man I was involved with? I couldn't be certain. He also began alienating my friends. As a gift to him, I had bought tickets for a play I thought he might enjoy. I asked Greg and his boyfriend to join us. We were to have dinner together before the show. Hal got very drunk that afternoon and refused to go to the show. "It's a gift to you," I complained. "What kind of gift is that supposed to be? You wanted to see it, not me." We threw away the tickets, and Greg and his friend were not interested in socializing with us again.

What had I given up? What was I gaining by quitting dancing for this? I learned all too painfully when one drunken evening he began to complain that I was home with him all the time, and he couldn't stand it. "But I stopped dancing because you said I was never home." "Well, now it's annoying having you around constantly." Something had to give. I began putting away every penny I earned in the bank. No shows, no dinners, no gifts. Nothing!

For some inexplicable reason, that Christmas he bought me a beautiful chocolate-brown suede trench coat. I knew it was expensive and didn't understand why he had done it, because he rarely bought me anything. After the holidays, I told him that I was planning to quit my job shortly and devote myself to studying dance. This enraged him. "You told me you didn't want me around the house all the time." "Well, I didn't want this. Why on earth did I waste my money buying that coat for you. I'd take it right back if you hadn't worn it." There was no winning with him.

Just before I left the magazine, someone I had dealt with at Creative Artists Management asked me if I wanted a job there, writing biographies and publicity materials for the many stars they represented. It meant a significant increase in salary. I thought about it for a couple days and decided I wasn't going to be sidetracked again. I resumed studying dance the day after I quit *Dance Magazine,* but not with Joy. She was so angry at me when I stopped taking her class that I couldn't go back to her. I went to the Joffrey Ballet School and also started taking a few jazz classes with Luigi, probably the most important dance teacher for musical theater people of that era. I had lost so much in the eight months of not dancing, and I was fighting desperately to get it back. My body was stiff and inflexible. I had done much damage to my technique during the absence, and I'm not certain I ever completely regained what was lost.

My first audition was for a new TV variety show called, "Hulla-baloo." I was completely outclassed by the experienced dancers, and I began to question my ambitions. Michael Bennett and Donna McKechnie were hired. Also once out of my comfort zone of ballet, I was at a loss. Auditioning was another skill, and I had failed to learn the essentials. I persevered, going from one audition to the next, hoping to get a summer stock job. My money held out until April, when I had to take an office temp job, which allowed me the freedom to go to auditions.

Things were looking grim when I went to audition for Pittsburgh Civic Light Opera. Bob Tucker (who was an assistant to both Jerome Robbins and Bob Fosse and in a few years would be nominated for Tony Award for *Shenandoah*) conducted the auditions. I did well, got into the finals, then to my disappointment learned I was chosen only as first alternate, which meant I would be hired only if one of the other dancers backed out. In the meantime, I got an offer at Mt. Gretna Playhouse, a small theater in Pennsylvania.

Before I signed the contract, Bob Tucker called me and asked if I would mind taking his wife, Nanette Charisse's ballet class. Nanette, was one of the dancing Charisse family into which Cyd Charisse married. He needed to see me dance again. I survived the class and was hired for one of the top summer-stock jobs in the country.

Things at home had been very tense since I quit my job. It was on again, off again. To Hal, I couldn't have received a more threatening offer than the Pittsburgh job. He saw his breakup with his former lover, cruelly replaying itself. I still didn't want to lose him, and I assured him that I would remain completely faithful and would not abandon him as Chris had done. I would be gone for only nine weeks, and maybe this separation would even be good for our relationship.

Before leaving, I became terrified that I had never had the experience of dancing with a partner. I engaged a ballet teacher who specialized in partnering to give me one private lesson before I left. It was a crash course in doing simple lifts and supported pirouettes. What I learned was that a single lesson was woefully insufficient to gain even the basic skills.

Mother and dad celebrated their twenty-fifth wedding anniversary with a large party the week before I was due in Pittsburgh. I arrived in Rockford, and to my utter amazement, Mary Giovingo said, "Just so you know, we told everyone that you are going to Pittsburgh to work on something for *Dance Magazine*."

"Why would you do that?"

We thought you wouldn't want anyone to know you were going there to dance."

"Why wouldn't I want them to know?"

"We just thought it might embarrass you?"

"Embarrassed? I'm proud of the fact that I got such a good job for my first professional dance engagement."

"Well, don't make a liar out of us."

I was furious and was certain that my dancing was embarrassing them, not me.

The last week in June 1966, I showed up for rehearsals in Pittsburgh. Staying at the YMCA seemed to be the cheapest solution. The rooms were not air-conditioned, and it was so hot that summer that I had to get up several times during the night to take cold showers, which didn't really help because even the water was warm.

I hadn't realized that the first three shows would be choreographed by someone I had never met, Tony Nelle, an old Russian ballet master. Several of the dancers were from the Chicago Opera Ballet, one had danced with the Joffrey Ballet. Everyone was so seasoned compared with me. After the first rehearsal, I stood alone on the stage of the 6,000-seat Civic Arena, thinking to myself, "Norman, what do you think you are doing here. You are definitely not ready for this." Tony Nelle must have been observing me because he came up behind me and said in his heavy Russian accent, "Don't be scared. You goin' to be just fine."

Tony was tough, but he seemed to like me. The choreography we did that summer was some of the most difficult dancing of my whole career. The dances were well beyond the usual summer stock level because they had so many terrific ballet dancers to work with. In fact, one of my partners, had already been engaged by the Royal Danish Ballet for the next season. Repertory stock is one of the best learning experiences and also one of the hardest dance assignments ever.

We did seven shows that summer, each getting only one week's rehearsal. (We had one week off from performing when Robert Goulet and Carol Lawrence did their club act, which I found disappointing given their enormous talent.) While performing one show at night, you rehearsed the next week's show during day. You worked extremely hard for long hours and had to learn very fast. Pittsburgh engaged major Broadway talent and even some stars. The enormous orchestra was symphonic in size, with many of the musicians pulled from the Pittsburgh Symphony. The chorus consisted of twenty-one singers and eighteen dancers.

The strangest part is that we were told not to sing, just mouth the lyrics. I'd never heard of such a thing; they were taking half the fun out of it. They claimed they didn't have time to teach us the songs, but I expect it was partly because they had such a large chorus of singers our voices were not needed, and also because they were using so many ballet dancers, who probably couldn't sing in tune. I cheated and sang away on stage whenever I knew the song. I was so green that I said, "Good luck," to my partner just before we went on stage for the first time. "You take that back, this minute." "What? Why?" " You never say, 'good luck' to a performer because it brings bad luck. You say, '*merde*.'"

The first show was *The Great Waltz*, based on the life and music of Johann Strauss, starring Giorgio Tozzi, the great Metropolitan Opera basso, whom I knew from childhood because he dubbed the voice of Rossano Brazzi in the movie of *South Pacific*. I stood in the wings warming up for one of the dances, and Mr. Tozzi stood next to me waiting for his entrance. "You know, I always wanted to be able to do what you're doing," he said to me. "That's strange because I'd love to be able to do what you're doing," I responded.

In the next show, *The Desert Song*, my costume was a *djellaba*, the full-length tunic worn by North African men. The problem with mine was that it was very tight below the waist. We were expected to climb over a fence, with a rifle in hand. In the dress rehearsal, I couldn't get my legs apart to vault the fence, so I simply had to lift my skirt to get over it, completely dissipating the threatening macho illusion that was required.

The ballet in *Oklahoma* was one of the hardest dances all summer. There was a section for the boys that was particularly challenging. My friend Philip Arsenault, who was a good dancer, was having a lot of difficulty learning it. Tony Nelle said, "Philip, I can't take any more time with you. Try it once more. If you can't do it, I have to take you out of the ballet." Philip tried again in vain and out he went. It was my first lesson in how harsh this business can be, especially when everyone is under pressure.

Susan Watson, the original Kim in *Bye, Bye Birdie*, played Laurie. She had been selected by Richard Rodgers personally to play the role at New York's City Center production and was wonderful in the part. Because she was a trained dancer she assumed she had been contracted to dance the role in the ballet, as well. However, a ballerina from the Chicago Opera Ballet had been engaged to dance it. Susan was very disappointed but, never a diva, she didn't create a scene at all. She would play a larger role in my life three years later.

During the "shivaree" scene, we were told to bang on pots and pans and make a terrible ruckus under the just-married couple's bedroom window. Tony' Nelle's Russian interpretation of the scene: "They goin' to make leettle beet foeking."

Several of the male dancers became friendly with Tom Bate, the production stage manager. He was a wonderful character actor from New York, with a deep voice and a somewhat affected English accent, who spent his summers in Pittsburgh. After the show, he entertained us at his apartment with wonderful stories. He informed us that Joan Crawford, herself, had called to say that she was making Pepsi Colas available free of charge to all performers for the season. Years later, I wondered if this giveaway was in any way related to her warning the Pepsi board of directors, "Don't fuck with me, fellas."

Nancy Walker (Bounty's quicker-picker-upper woman) had played Ruth in *Wonderful Town* at Civic Light Opera three seasons earlier. During an on-stage costume call with the entire company she yelled out, "If you think I'm wearing these rags, baby, you're nuts," and she stormed off. A few minutes later she returned. "Since you refuse to provide a decent costume, I'll just wear this." She was completely naked. Aghast, Tom said, "Miss Walker! RRReally, Miss Walker, I simply must insist," and before he could finish she said, "Oh shut up you old fruit basket."

The Civic Arena was renowned for its movable dome. On pleasant evenings the dome was opened for the second act. I detested working outdoors because it meant, sirens, loud planes overhead, heat, humidity, and nasty bug bites. Tom, however, made a major production of the event as he dramatically announced, "Ladies and gentlemen (extended pause), the movable dome of the Civic Arena will now be opened." This feat would take at least ten minutes to accomplish. "Ladies and Gentlemen (extended pause), behold the stars."

Following the first three shows, Bob Tucker came to choreograph the final four productions. He began with *The Most Happy Fella*. His dance for the "Big D" number was one of the most exciting to perform all summer. He included a step right out of Fosse's *Sweet Charity*, which when I saw that show I thought, "I could never do that." But I did. It involved running several steps, then kicking the left leg up, while sliding across the stage on the top of the right foot and landing on one knee.

Barbara Meister, who had been a replacement for Mary Martin in *The Sound of the Music* on Broadway and was rumored to be Frank Loesser's mistress, played the lead role. I stood in the wings every night to hear her sing the beautiful ballad, "Somebody, Somewhere," which took on poignant significance for me.

I wrote to Hal every few days and called him occasionally. In my letters, to keep him reassured that I was not seeing any other men, I told him about my new friendships, with Don Douthit, who had danced with San Francisco Ballet, and especially about Philip Arsenault. I phoned him after he received that letter, and he sounded drunk and very angry. When I asked him what was wrong, he said, "What's wrong? You know very well what's wrong."

"No, I don't."

"Well, I spoke to Bob about your new 'friend' Philip, and he said, 'If he's hanging around with Philip Arsenault, you can bet that he's sleeping with him because Philip is never just friends with any guy.'"

"That's a lie. I'm not the least bit interested in Philip in that way, and he's never so much as made a pass at me. We're just buddies. I've never even gone to a gay bar, not alone or with him."

"You expect me to believe that?"

"I certainly do expect you to believe me over Bob."

"Well, I don't. We're through and I want you to send your keys back to me because I don't trust you coming into my apartment any more."

"Don't trust me?"

"Who knows what you might do in my home?"

"What? Are you kidding me?"

"I'm not kidding. Send me the keys!"

I don't think I had ever been angrier in my life and said, "You know what? You can take your damned keys and shove them up your ass."

I heard the most deranged laugh on the other end, and it made my skin crawl. "I knew you'd finally say something like that to me," as he continued to laugh maniacally.

"You and your evil friend Bob are two very sick men," and I hung up. What an appalling end to a relationship.

When I heard Barbara sing, "Somebody somewhere wants me and needs me. That's very wonderful to know," all I could think was "nobody needs me and probably never did." The need was only in my imagination. No, he didn't need me, at least not for love and support, but perhaps as a tool to justify his self-destructive quest. Was he so pathological that he had been egging me on, just waiting and hoping that I would denounce him all along? Had our whole relationship been some kind of psychological sadomasochistic ritual?

The intoxicating drug of feeling needed had seriously clouded my reasoning. I realized that people who are as troubled and addicted as he is are not really helped by a caring person. Rather, they drag that person down to their debased level to feel better about themselves. I was crushed by the whole affair.

The season in Pittsburgh closed with *Showboat,* which starred Andy Devine as Captain Andy and the magnificent Terry Saunders, who played Lady Thiang in the movie of *The King and I,* as Julie. My parents came to the see that show but had little to say. I couldn't tell whether they were still embarrassed by me or proud. I felt as though I had performed fairly well considering that all the other dancers had been studying since they were children and were far more experienced. My partnering was adequate, though not exemplary.

I was involved in only one stage mishap, which wasn't my fault, involving one of my partners, who was not a ballet dancer and whom Tony Nelle referred to as "my deesee blonde" because she was a bit scatterbrained. We were doing a series of turns that ended in a lift. At one performance, I intuitively sensed that she was miscounting the number of turns and was preparing to jump for the lift too early. Under my breath, I kept saying, "Don't jump, don't jump." She jumped eight beats too soon. I didn't catch her and she ended up on her ass." I was mortified by the whole thing.

At least, I was now a member of Actor's Equity, the union that represents actors, singers, and dancers in the theater. This entitled me to good health insurance, free tickets to certain shows, and best of all, allowed me to go to Equity auditions, rather than the open cattle calls I had been forced to attend, giving a slightly better chance of getting hired.

The Wrong Side of the Room

I RETURNED TO NEW YORK with little money in my pocket. Never the type to impose upon friends and crash in their apartments, I took a room at the 63rd Street Y, which was made only slightly less depressing because it was just off Central Park. I needed to get my things from Hal's apartment. Setting up a time with him turned out to be an unanticipated hassle. If I had harbored any delusions that he might have regrets about what he had done, they were quickly dispelled. Only Amy, the dog, was glad to see me.

Hal argued with me as I packed away some of my cherished show records. He claimed that I was stealing some of his, though I knew definitely that they were mine. When I made mention of all the money I had put into furniture and redecorating, he said, "I certainly don't owe you a cent for that. If anything, you owe me money." "How is that?" I questioned. "You moved into a fully furnished apartment. You should have been paying more than half the rent, but you didn't." Hadn't he virtually begged me to give up my apartment with its few sticks of furniture and move in with him? I was twenty-one years old at the time; he was nearly ten years older, earning substantially more than I did. This is what I deserved after the three years I devoted to him? I left his place so utterly defeated and despondent at the execrable ending that I cried in the cab all the way to the Y.

I needed to resume dance classes but didn't have the extra money. I saw an audition for ballet dancers for a new production at the New York City Opera. It was the first time I'd ever been in those enormous rehearsal studios at the New York State Theatre. Thomas Andrew, the opera's resident choreographer, gave the audition, and I made the cut for the finals. A few days later I was chosen as one of the corps de ballet, and asked to return on Saturday for a costume fitting and to sign the contract. I could hardly believe this. I've just gone from the best summer-stock job to a ballet dancer at Lincoln Center, all with less than three years of dance training. The opera was a new production of Handel's *Julius Caesar*, with Beverly Sills as Cleopatra. As it turned out, this was the role that made her into a major opera star.

I filed for unemployment compensation just after I was told I had the job because there would be a few weeks lag time before we began rehearsals. Unemployment is the lifeline for performers who otherwise would probably not survive between engagements. To my amazement, the official told me that I was not eligible because I had worked only nine weeks as a dancer, while I worked more weeks as an office temp, so technically I was not a dancer in their eyes. I explained that I had just been hired for a dance job at Lincoln Center and was signing my contract at the end of the week. "Fine, we'll okay the compensation beginning this week, but you need to bring in your signed contract as proof. If you don't do so, your unemployment checks will be terminated immediately." No reason to be concerned about that, I thought.

The contract-signing day was September 12, my twenty-fourth birthday, and what better present could I ask for than this job? A dancer friend, Gary Dutton, arranged to meet me after the signing. He wanted to ride me on his Vespa to Coney Island for a day of celebration, because I had never been there. I confidently went into the rehearsal studio ready to sign my first New York contract. Thomas Andrew announced, "Will those standing on the right side of the room, step over farther to the right, and those standing on the left side of the room, step to the left." I happened to be directly in the center of the room and was uncertain which way to move. "Okay, I'll just step to the left."

"I'm sorry to report that the budget for this production has just been cut in half, which means we can only hire half as many dancers as we had planned. Those who are on the right side of the room, please remain to sign your contracts. Those on the left side, I'm sorry to say, I will not be able to use you, but thank you for auditioning for me."

No, no, this is not possible. How could it be? Why couldn't he at least have asked us to dance again and chosen the best dancers out of the group. That would have been the fair way to handle this. But no, I'm out because I stepped the wrong way? And not only am I out, but I lose my unemployment compensation and have to go back to work as a temp. Happy birthday, Norman. The Coney Island of my mind turned into a house of horrors.

I thought I had a reprieve from office work when I was given a scholarship to study at a struggling, fledgling ballet company, the Manhattan

Festival Ballet, directed by Ron Sequoio, who had been a lead dancer with the Metropolitan Opera Ballet. My classes were all paid for and I was to become a member of the company, though there seemed to be no performances scheduled at that point. They offered me some administrative work at a very minimal salary to keep me financially afloat.

Paul Taylor, whom I worshipped, and his leading dancer, Dan Wagoner, were in the class, my first time positioned next to major dance stars. Paul also began dancing late in life so it was fascinating to watch him in this setting. His large frame was ill-suited to ballet, and he always looked out of his element and awkward to me. The little money I had saved in Pittsburgh, plus my two unemployment checks, ran out quickly, and I needed to get a job that paid a living wage. I went back to temping and was forced to give up the scholarship because all the classes were during the day while I would be working.

Luckily, in the evening classes at the American Ballet Theatre School, I found the best ballet teacher I had had since Joy O'Neill: Leon Danielian, who had been a leading dancer with the Ballets Russes de Monte Carlo. Danielian was extremely helpful to me in class. However, he took a personal interest in me beyond the dancing, and I politely discouraged this, saying I never got involved with my teachers.

While studying with him, I auditioned at the Palace Theatre for the Las Vegas company of *Sweet Charity,* which was to star Juliet Prowse. This was the first time I had danced on a Broadway stage and the fact that it was such a famed theater brought forth memories of all the greats that had played the Palace. I had already learned Bob Fosse's combination— an amalgam of ballet and jazz set to "Tea for Two"—from Bob Tucker at the Pittsburgh Civic Light Opera audition. Fosse seemed to like me, and I was invited to the finals. He also had given sections from two numbers in the show, "Rich Man's Frug" and "I'm a Brass Band."

Everyday after Danielian's class, I remained in the empty studio to practice the combinations over and over until I had every nuance polished. I survived all the eliminations until the end. At one point, he said, "All you dancers who have worked with me before, if you don't start dancing full-out, you're not getting hired." After Fosse called out the dancers he was hiring, he uttered the four most dreaded words in the English language, "Thank you very much." He preceded these words with "When I say 'thank you very much' to the rest of you, I don't mean anything personal by it, I simply mean thank you so much for coming. I'm sorry I can't hire you." This speech was given I was sure because of a story I had heard about a previous audition. A girl angrily approached him, "What do you mean, thank you very much, after thirteen years of ballet school?"

and she proceeded to clobber him with her dance bag. I understood the impulse behind that rage.

As I forlornly picked up my bag to depart, he singled me out, put his arm around me, and said, "I loved watching you dance very much, but I just can't use you in this show. Please come and audition for me again next time." I was somewhat soothed by this kind gesture but still felt as though I had been punched in the stomach for not getting hired. As I left the stage door, I broke down and started crying, which I had never done after an audition. Rejection is so much a part of this business that you had better learn to take it or find another field. This time was particularly painful because I needed the job so badly and longed for the opportunity to work with Fosse.

The fall season was marred by a series of morale-grinding close calls. The audition for the Pennsylvania Ballet was my first for a major company. Unlike musical-theater auditions, ballet auditions always consist of taking a class. During the *barre*, I noticed the directors were constantly watching me, and especially my feet. When we came to the center, I was also dancing very well, and it was clear that they were interested in me. We were given a combination of fast *jetés*, which I executed easily. Then the ballet master said, "Add beats to the *jetés*." I had no idea what he was talking about. I had never done or even seen this. How could I have missed this step in all my training? I desperately tried to figure it out from the two guys who went ahead of me, but never good at faking it, I looked bewildered when my turn came and didn't get the job.

My strengths in ballet were that I had very good line (meaning that the arms, legs, pointed feet, head and body all form pleasing contours to the eye), exceptional feet, excellent musicality, and well-stretched achilles tendons, which gave me a good jump. My double air turns and my *entratchat six* (straight up-and-down jumps with the feet switching back and forth three times in the air) were quite decent. Where I fell short, because I began so late in life, was doing the fancy tricks such as the double saut de basque, a traveling step in which the dancer does two turns in the air with one foot drawn up to the knee of the other leg.

The Harkness Ballet, which the philanthropist Rebekah Harkness formed by stealing the major talent away from the Joffrey Ballet, was auditioning "young dancers." I went to the Harkness House for Ballet Arts, a mansion at 4 E. 75th Street on the day I was scheduled to fly to Rockford for Christmas, and I could scarcely believe my eyes: crystal chandeliers and wall sconces and beautiful period furniture pieces with sweaty dancers unattractively sprawled over them. We had to fill out an application specifying our age. I wasn't sure what they meant by "young."

Though I was twenty-four, I looked very young so I nervously wrote that I was twenty. The full-salaried program consisted of performing with their "B" company, a troupe of dancers who played in minor venues, while receiving free training in ballet, modern, jazz, Spanish dance, and acrobatics. This would solve all my financial and work problems.

The class was given by former New York City ballerina, Patricia Wilde. I sensed immediately that there was no other boy in the group who was dancing at my level, giving me the impression I would be a shoo-in. After the class Madame Wilde called me into her office. "You were unquestionably the best dancer in the room, but I'm afraid I can't hire you because you're too old." "Too old?" "Yes, because it'll be at least a couple years of training before you're ready for the major company, and by then you'll be twenty-two, which I'm sorry to say is just too old for us." Twenty-four and already over the hill. Not great news to take home to my family.

I'd been trying to find an apartment so I could get out of the Y, but I could never scrape together enough money for a month's rent, plus a security deposit. I wasn't about to ask my parents for help. In the gym at the Y, I met a man named Duncan Steck, who lived on West End Avenue and worked at a prestigious public relations firm. We had a brief affair, and he made me an offer: "When you come back from the holidays, stay with me until you can put away enough money to get a place of your own." This was a godsend. Duncan, who had studied theater at Carnegie Tech, was also a first-rate photographer, and he took good publicity photos of me (I had always photographed deplorably, my forced smiles making me look like a doofus), which I used throughout my dance career. As we examined the proofs to select the best shot, he said, "Such a handsome face. Too bad it's just slightly flawed by a weak jaw." I had never thought about my jaw before, but I began spending a lot of time in the mirror analyzing bone-structure deficiencies I couldn't fix.

When it became evident that I was not making enough money temping to afford my own apartment, I bit the bullet and began looking for a roommate. I saw this as a reversion to adolescence, because I had either lived alone or in a relationship for so many years. A dancer in one of my ballet classes, Jerry Bell, was searching for a roommate. He lived in a small apartment in a townhouse on West 91st Street, just off West End Avenue. It had two narrow rooms, one a living room, which Jerry slept in and became our common room during the day; the other a bedroom, which I would inhabit. It also had the most cramped, inconvenient kitchen I had ever encountered, and a roof terrace off the common room.

Jerry was from Birmingham, Alabama, and was the most fervent musical-theater fanatic I had ever met. His knowledge of the subject was encyclopedic. He lived, ate, and took every breath of his being in relationship to it. He had lost his Southern accent completely, but he couldn't rid himself of certain regional colloquialisms, such as, "you might could" or "dry as cornbread." He was also the most aggressive chaser of men conceivable. When he found prey that piqued his libido, he stalked them, hounded them, and in some cases charmed them unmercifully until they submitted to him. I was astounded at how successful he was at this, given his average looks and build. His approach, totally in contrast to my own reticence and shyness, made me look hopelessly inept. Once he conquered these hapless creatures, he lost interest in them almost immediately and moved on to his next victim.

We got along very well, but there were times when I got home late and just wanted to retire to a quiet night alone in my room. If I suspected he was asleep, I'd enter the apartment silently, try to sneak into my room, and shut the door. It never worked. The minute I closed the apartment door, he'd snap on the lights and harangue me mercilessly for hours about the latest news on the Broadway theater. I'd end up going to bed drained and exhausted. I thought I was beyond the roommate stage, and I was right.

Just downstairs from us lived Steve, a Ph.D. candidate in psychology at Columbia University. Steve and I had so much in common, from our Italian heritage, to our backgrounds in psychology, and our interests in the performing arts. We could talk for hours on end. I asked his recommendations for psychology texts that would help me better understand myself. His response was, "Don't read psychology, read the great works of literature. You'll learn much more about human behavior." Reading had already become a salvation for me in the many lonely nights I spent in the Y. Now I was determined to move from novelists such as Somerset Maugham, who classified himself as a "first-rate, second-rate writer," to genuinely great writers such as Thomas Mann and Thomas Hardy .

Somehow Steve had managed to get opening-night tickets for Marlene Dietrich at the Lunt-Fontanne Theatre on Broadway. When something came up and he was unable to attend, he loaned me his tux and asked me to go in his place. I had never been to an opening night, and this one was about as star-studded as they get. As I entered the theater lobby, Joan Fontaine and Tallulah Bankhead were directly in front of me. Someone yelled out, "Oh my god, look, look, it's Joan Fontaine. It looks just like her." Who else? Another person began pawing at Tallulah, who in her most sinister voice said, "Don't touch me." "But, Tallulah, these are your fans. They love you." "Well, I love you, too, dahlings, but

DON'T TOUCH ME!" The evening was smashing, but I remember being most impressed by Burt Bachrach and his perfect arrangements, which made Marlene sound even better than she was. Dietrich had once recommended Bachrach to Frank Sinatra, who turned him down. When Bachrach became famous, she gloated to Sinatra, "I told you so."

In the winter, I was sent to the American Bankers Association to work. It was a good match, so I remained there throughout the spring, making my work life easier. My boss was a handsome married man with three children, whose photos he kept on his desk. He was very accommodating in allowing me to take off for auditions. I worked at a desk just outside his office. Every time I looked up, I caught him staring at me.

One weekend, the organization held a prescient conference at the Americana Hotel devoted to the emergence of a cashless society. Bank credit cards had been offered nationally, only six months earlier. During the conference, my boss invited me up to his room to do some work. He appeared at the door in his undershirt and offered me a drink, though it was ten AM on a Sunday morning. He sat pressed against me on the couch and discussed some reports, which had no bearing whatsoever on what I was working on. I realized he wanted to hit on me, but by turning down the drink I didn't give him an opening, and he couldn't bring himself to it.

To me, married men were off limits, but I found him very attractive and wasn't sure how I would have responded if he had made a move. When I left his room, I sensed the pain this man must be in, almost wishing I had kissed him. How sad these closeted married guys were, and how lucky I was not to find myself in the same unenviable position.

The Metropolitan Opera Ballet was hiring four male dancers for the following season. Hundreds showed up for the call. I survived from one round to the next, until it came down to just five of us. Sadly, I was the one rejected. After that audition, I said to myself, "Self, you have got to face the facts. You are never going to be hired as a ballet dancer."

Spring came and with it were all the auditions for summer stock. I noticed that dancers who were either muscular, a rarity in those days, or could do acrobatics got hired, no matter the quality of their dancing. Foolishly, I did nothing to rectify my deficiencies in these areas. At last, I was hired by Jacques d'Amboise, a leading New York City Ballet dancer, to perform the role of Simon Legree in a stock production of *The King and I*. A few days later I was offered another job at the St. Louis Municipal Opera, a job analogous to the one I had at Pittsburgh. I signed that contract, rather than *The King and I* offer. Don Douthit also got the job, so we would be working together again. *Funny Girl*, which required tap dancing, was scheduled for the season. I did not tap so I took one quick tap lesson to learn some basic time steps.

Then I learned about a summer tour of *West Side Story* that was being choreographed by Michael Bennett. His assistant, Leland Palmer, gave the preliminary auditions without Bennett. I did so well that she said, "I want to be certain you show up for the finals because I know that Michael is going to love you." Naturally, I showed up. We did the "America" combination in a group of three, but I noticed immediately that Michael was completely focused on the cute little blond boy to my right, who was not mastering the steps at all. Michael stopped and worked personally with this boy to get him up to speed. I knew I was doing the combination perfectly, but he never once looked at me. I was eliminated and the blond boy got the job. Leland called me over and said, "I'm so sorry, Norman. I can't explain it." Despite the rejection, I learned that I would be dancing in this same *West Side Story* production because the tour of the show was scheduled to play St. Louis, and we were to be incorporated into their company to help fill the Muny's enormous stage.

I kept on auditioning to see whether any better offers would come. One did, in the form of a summer tour of *Half A Sixpence,* which was to begin in the Poconos, then play East Hampton, Denver's Elitch Gardens, and some delightful Maine resorts. I asked Don Douthit what I should do. His advice, "Don't be a fool. Sign the *Sixpence* contract. Since it doesn't begin until six weeks after St. Louis, you can just give two weeks' notice to the Muny. You're within your Equity rights." As it turned out, he also had another offer, so we would both give notice and leave St. Louis.

Jerry Bell was to be away all summer at a different summer stock job, so the apartment was sublet for the period, and we didn't have to continue to pay rent while we were gone. My college roommate, Barry Booth, lived in St. Louis, where he had found a job as a librarian at Southern Illinois University, just across the river from the city. "Why don't you stay with me while you're in town?" he suggested. "I don't think I can because I've already agreed to room with my dancer friend, Don Douthit." "I have a three-bedroom apartment. He can stay, too, and it will help me out financially, as well." Barry's place was within walking distance of the Muny and the rent was much less than what we would have paid to rent an apartment, so it was a win-win-win situation for the three of us.

The end of my relationship with Hal left a large hole in my life. In the Y, I often dreamt that we were still blissfully together, only to awaken with a jolt to the reality that I was completely alone in a claustrophobic, grim room, my life spiraling downward. I made desultory attempts at meeting other men, but I always hated the chase, which often made me even more despondent. In the spring, I met a wealthy Dutch businessman who offered some promise of hope. We dated for several weeks, and Joe, who lived on Gramercy Park, but also retained a residence in Amsterdam, enticed me with tales about how as both a homosexual and a performing artist, the Dutch government would welcome and assist me.

A few weeks before I left for St. Louis, Joe invited me to join him in opening his Fire Island house, named *Beyond the Forest,* after the Bette Davis movie. Never having been to the Pines, I saw this as a pleasant respite. It was very early in the season, with only a few homeowners in residence. Joe took me to the house of some friends who were top executives at Tiffany's. Though they were fully aware of my background, they began their whining lament, "Fire Island just isn't what it used to be. There were always interesting people, people with class. Now it's mostly just a lot of chorus boys."

I looked over at Joe to see if he would defend me, but instead he simply nodded in assent. Perhaps he was merely trying to avoid a disagreement with his friends and would apologize for their rudeness after we left their house. Not a bit of it. He said not a word. I absolutely cannot tolerate being condescended to in that way, and I thought to myself, "Who do these people, born with silver spoons in their mouths, think they are. I'm proud of how hard I've worked to achieve my small successes." I didn't want to risk lowering myself even further by confronting Joe, but when I returned to New York, I told Jerry to answer the phone for the week, "If Joe calls, just tell him I'm not home." He must have called me a dozen times in the next few days, but I never returned his calls.

St. Louis was altogether a different story. I was never so popular in my life. I met several hunky men, which became an ego reinforcer after my nine months of no dance jobs and a miserable love life. To my astonishment, Barry was known to everyone in the gay bars as "The Baroness," and he relished the role of the grande dame. What a change I thought to myself, "Barry, you're not in Denver anymore." Because he knew everyone, he introduced me to a man named Al, whom I was especially fond of. We saw each other three times a week. Don Douthit began to be concerned for me, "Nor Man (which was what he called me), you are not going to give up dancing and settle down as a St. Louis house frau, do you hear me?" I did hear him, though I was tempted.

The Muny was a much larger venue than Pittsburgh. The outdoor arena seated 11,000, had a treacherously raked stage, and rehearsals were held outdoors in open pavilions because they had no indoor studios in 1967. The running joke was, "When you pass out from the heat, they just throw you a salt tablet and order you to get up and dance." With a generous two weeks of rehearsals before performances, we began with *Wish You Were Here,* a silly musical about a Catskill's resort, with James Darren in the lead role. The only thing memorable about the show is that it features an onstage swimming pool. Once again, I faced a different choreographer from the one who gave the audition. Bob Haddad was a very sweet man, who called me "the wussy." I think he meant it as a compliment.

On the second week of rehearsals, Michael Bennett arrived with his *West Side Story* cast from Houston, where the show had opened. The production starred Anna Maria Alberghetti (it soon became obvious why she had won a Tony Award for *Carnival*), David Holliday, and an incredible dancer, Carolyn Morris, as Anita, who tragically died in a motorcycle accident a couple years later. In the chorus was Margo Sappington, an ex-Joffrey ballerina, who went on to become a choreographer, most notably of *Oh, Calcutta.* We began with "The Dance at the Gym." About twenty minutes into rehearsal, Michael came over to me and in his most snarling voice said, "Could you please try to look a little less like a ballet dancer?" "What am I doing wrong, Michael?" "Well, you might try turning in." Because of my ballet training, I had a habit of turning my feet out. The problem was so easily corrected that I couldn't believe he had made such a scene over it.

Bennet's personality was on full display during the first rehearsal of the "America" number. For some reason I could not understand, he took a passionate dislike to the actor playing Bernardo, who was said to have performed the role in London's West End.

"Carmine, get out of the number," he demanded.

"What?'

"You heard me. Get out of the number."

"But why?"

"Why? Because I can't stand to watch you dance another minute."

"Michael, just tell me what you want me to fix, and I'll fix it."

"You've already had several weeks in Houston to fix it, and you never will. You look terrible in the number. Now, get out!"

"Michael, I've signed a contract to play this role, and I will play the entire role."

"You will play exactly what I tell you to play and not one thing more. Do you understand?"

"Then I'm walking out of my contract," as he picked up his dance bag to depart.

Laughing sinisterly, Michael responds, "Oh, no, you won't. You are not walking out of any contract with me. If you want out, you'll have to buy your way out. Now go sit over on the side so the rest of us can rehearse."

Carmine, completely defeated, acquiesces and Michael screams, "All right, get back to work everybody."

All of us stood watching this dreadful confrontation, in which Michael obviously relished inflicting the maximum humiliation on this man, with our mouths gaping wide holes. We weren't in an enclosed room, and still Michael managed to suck all the air out of the place. Try going back to a rehearsal after a scene like this. In my years in the theater, I never witnessed anything comparable to it, and despite Michael's enormous talent, I found it difficult to have any respect for him.

West Side Story ran for two weeks, and at the end of the second week I had to give my two-week notice. "You know the rules, Norman. If we can find a dancer locally you're free and clear. If not, you'll have to pay your replacement's airfare from New York." Surprise! I had to pay. When my replacement arrived, he told me he had an idea for a musical he wanted to write. I rolled my eyes, thinking how many of us had ideas for musicals that would never even get written, much less produced. How wrong I was. My replacement was none other than Nicholas Dante, who in a few years would write *A Chorus Line* and serve as the inspiration for the character of Paul, whose dramatic monologue details the humiliation of having his father see him in a drag show. Thus I had to pay nearly $300 in airfare out of my pitiful salary for someone soon to be a millionaire.

After opening night of *Wish You Were Here,* the producers were unhappy with Bob Haddad's choreography, so they fired him on the spot. They brought in Mavis Ray, who had been Agnes de Mille's assistant choreographer on many shows. A wonderful person and choreographer, she began with *Do I Hear a Waltz?* starring Dorothy Collins, Enzo Stuarti, and Monique van Vooren. My partner and I seemed to be Mavis's favorite dancers, and she gave us lovely things and beautiful lifts to do. My parents came to the show because they planned to drive me to the Poconos for *Half A Sixpence.* Mother, who never liked Dorothy Collins when she was on "Your Hit Parade," loved her in this piece, and dad was so excited to get a picture of her. They were finally beginning to respect my dance career. I realized I was now a certified "gypsy," the dancers and singers who migrate from one show to another.

My friend Philip Arsenault, who was also in *Sixpence*, and I shared a large room in a rooming house right near the barn of the theatre. Mountainhome, Pennsylvania, was a very pleasant but isolated little place where there was absolutely nothing to do at night, and without a car we were stranded. We ate excellent cheap dinners in a bar that transported me nostalgically to those roadhouses in the '40s Hollywood movies.

I was given a flashy ballet solo, which concluded with *tours à la seconde* (turns on a bent leg with the other leg fully extended out to the side). The talented cast had no big stars, but one of my dance partners in the show was Adrienne Barbeau, who later found fame on Broadway, television, and more prominently as a sex symbol. On the day we were departing for East Hampton, I hopped a fence outside the rooming house and landed in a hole in the ground, spraining my ankle. At first it didn't seem like much, but by the time we got to the Hamptons, it had swollen to the size of a grapefruit, and I could barely walk. Dancing was out of the question, so I returned to New York. Jerry's apartment was still sublet, so my friend Steve let me stay with him. The next day I went to the doctor, who gave me crutches and told me to keep off the leg for the next six weeks, meaning I would miss all the desirable resorts on the tour. I rejoined for the last week in Paramus, New Jersey, unable to perform my solo because the pain was still rather intense.

Joe Yanello, a new dancer friend from St. Louis, and I often walked around Riverside Park near my apartment at night. It was a heavy gay cruising area at the time, and Joe termed the Soldiers' and Sailors' Monument, "The Wedding Cake." When I asked him why, he said, "Because it looks just like the ornament on top of a wedding cake and because so many unions take place before it." We began attending auditions together, one of which was for the national tour of *Cabaret*. Shirley Rich, who was Hal Prince's casting agent, supervised the audition and though neither Joe nor I got the job, I noticed that Shirley was watching me very closely and taking copious notes. Joe and I joked endlessly that one day "Shirl baby" would call us and beg us to come work for Hal Prince.

Dorothy Lamour on the Road to...

VERNON LUSBY, another Agnes de Mille assistant, gave the audition for the national company of *Hello, Dolly!* starring Dorothy Lamour, who was replacing Carol Channing on the tour. Is there any actress who is more perfect to star in a road show? I was hired, giving me at least nine months of solid work at a decent salary. At the audition, I met a dancer, Frank Newell, who was to become my best friend. Frank was a tall, handsome blond, a very animated performer who had also done some modeling.

A few weeks before rehearsals for the tour, I got a call from Vernon saying someone was leaving the Broadway company of *Dolly*, which at the time was starring Betty Grable. "Would you be interested in filling in for a few weeks?" "Of course, I would." As it turned out, Frank had begun rehearsing several days earlier to replace another dancer. Replacements in a show are generally required to be about the same size as the person they're replacing, to avoid having to make a whole new costume. Frank had replaced a tall boy, and I was to replace a shorter dancer.

I went to the St. James Theater on a Thursday to rehearse and we were both expected to know the show for Monday night, a harrowing amount of dancing to learn in just a couple days. What I didn't realize until I started rehearsals was that the dancer I was replacing did all the acrobatic stunts in the show, something I had no ability to do. This was baptism by fire.

I rehearsed during the day and watched the show at night to learn exactly where my place on stage was in relation to the other performers. On Saturday morning, Frank and I had our put-in rehearsal, where the entire company, sans Betty Grable, goes through the numbers very quickly and sketchily with the replacements. Vernon thought I needed a couple more days of rehearsal. I agreed. Sunday was a day off, but I was to rehearse Monday and Tuesday, then go into the show Tuesday night.

I knew the dance numbers and the songs, but the acrobatics were another matter entirely. One stunt during the "Hello, Dolly," number involved jumping over the orchestra pit, which was covered by a net, and landing on the narrow ramp, which encircled the pit. This was a scary but manageable move. The two other feats, which occurred during "The Waiter's Gallop," were of a different order. One involved running and jumping onto another dancer, with both legs straddling his chest, sliding down his body, and rolling backward into a handstand. I could do it but the handstand looked pathetic.

The most difficult trick involved running halfway across the stage, diving head first onto a tabletop and doing a hand spring over the table, and landing feet first, arms outstretched. The stage hands' union does not allow the use of props during rehearsals without union people present, which David Merrick, the producer, refused to pay for. Vernon surreptitiously brought out the table, and I got only one try to do it right. It was nearly a disaster. During the put-in rehearsal, we couldn't use the table so I didn't get another chance to try it out.

On Sunday, Joe Yanello, who had trained in acrobatics, tried to teach me the handstand and the hand spring in Riverside Park. The results were not pretty. That night was one of the worst I had ever spent. I couldn't sleep at all and broke out into a terrible sweat, envisioning how on a Broadway stage I would end up falling on my ass going over that table.

Mornings have always been difficult for me, but after a night of agonizing angst they become excruciating. I found myself unable to stir from my bed, my guts roiled by constrictions. The longer I hid under the covers the worse the torment. It became painfully obvious that I couldn't do this. The thought of humiliating myself in my first Broadway show and being responsible for completely ruining the most exciting dance number in *Dolly* was more than I could bear. I've always been about competence, and with these stunts I knew I was not competent.

I called Vernon and used the excuse that my ankle, which hadn't yet completely healed, was reaggravated after practicing the tricks. Consequently, I could not do the show. This was a self-protective lie and one of the most painful things I'd ever had to do, considering that I'd been dreaming of Broadway for years. I was afraid I was endangering my job with the touring company as well, but I assured him I would be fine by the time rehearsals began. I've replayed this decision in my mind dozens of times but feel it was probably the right choice, considering how unlikely it was that I would look reasonably professional doing those stunts.

About a week before the tour rehearsals began, they still needed two more dancers. I quickly told Joe about it, hoping we might be able to room together on tour. I went to meet him after the audition, but before I got there I saw him running toward me on Eighth Avenue. "You'll never guess who got hired instead of me." "Who?" "Jerry Bell." This meant Jerry would want to room with me, and I knew I couldn't handle that much closeness to him. He was not pleased when I told him I needed a room of my own.

Back at the St. James Theater for rehearsals, I discovered that Vernon would not be involved. Now there was a Terry D to add to the A. B. and C. Terrys in my life. This time he wasn't Swedish, but an Italian. Terry served as both dance captain and swing dancer on the tour. As dance captain, he was responsible for staging the dances, running clean-up rehearsals to maintain the integrity of the choreography, and rehearsing any replacements. As swing dancer he covered every male dance role, ready to go on in case anyone was out of the show. Most of the dancers already knew the choreography, having been either in the Carol Channing part of the tour or in the Broadway company. Three of us were new to it. I assumed I had already learned much of the material but discovered the sections I would be doing were completely different from those I had learned for the Betty Grable company.

Terry started with the "Hello, Dolly" number and a storm began brewing for the three newcomers when we got to the famous applause-getting ramp step, in which the male dancers parade around the ramp in a tribute to Dolly. The step, though not at all technically difficult, had so many complicated arm, leg, and hand movements to it that I assumed Gower Champion must have cunningly devised it to confound his dancers. When the three of us did not master the step immediately, Terry became enraged.

Knowing that I learned better if I went off by myself to work out the problems, I said, "I promise I'll have it for you by tomorrow," and, of course, I did. Tomorrow wasn't good enough, though we had two weeks of rehearsals. Later that first day, he staged the "Dancing" number, several sections of which I had already learned in the Broadway rehearsals. The three of us were left out of the number completely, and I felt crushed because that dance was the most balletic and therefore my favorite. I was, however, chosen to be the first dancer on stage to begin the flashy jumps at the end of "The Waiters' Gallup," which meant I was the only one to perform the entire set.

We opened at the University of Indiana in Bloomington, and the show was a joy to perform because audiences loved it and Dorothy Lamour so much. When I heard the waves of applause after the "Dolly" number, I couldn't help but smile at what Hal Prince had told Jerry Herman when he first played the show for him: "Whatever you do, please cut that dreadful title song." I was a bit taken aback that Dorothy gave a lengthy curtain speech at the end of the show, which the former sarong girl ended with, "and to each and everyone of you out there, aloha," followed by blowing a big kiss with both hands. I'd never heard anyone do this before, but she continued it at almost every performance thereafter, to the chagrin of the cast, which had to stand there and endure it night after night. Dorothy was wonderful in the role, which she learned directly from Carol Channing herself. Her singing was first-rate. I wasn't aware that she had been a big-band singer before she became a movie star.

That night after the opening performance some of the gay boys on campus threw a party for the male dancers. I had just met a trumpeter in our orchestra, whom I found very appealing and was dancing with him when quite unexpectedly Jess Richards, who was playing Barnaby, cut in and swooped me away from the horn player. Jess was very cute, but not in the least my type. Everyone else in the company seemed to be interested in him but me. He was very persuasive and persistent, and he coaxed me into going to his room. The next day when I insisted that I could not get involved with him, he would not hear of it. Still feeling vulnerable from having been overlooked by Terry D. and somewhat flattered that Jess chose me over everyone else in the cast, I reluctantly gave into him, and we were together throughout the tour.

It was common in those days to send a congratulatory telegram to friends on opening night. I received one, which read, "Can you come to New York to audition for dancer and understudy to the Joel Grey role in Broadway *Cabaret*? Shirley Rich." This had to be a joke. How would she know where to find me? How could she even remember me from that single audition weeks ago? No, it must be Joe Yanello playing his "Shirl baby" trick. The next morning, I called him, "Joe, I didn't find that telegram you sent me funny at all." "What telegram?" "Come on, Joe, the one you sent claiming Shirley Rich wants me for *Cabaret*." "I didn't send you any telegram." "You didn't?"

I didn't know what to do. Two days earlier, I had signed a six-month rider to my contract with the David Merrick office for *Dolly*. The rider gives a performer extra pay for committing to a period of six months and agreeing not to leave the show. One can break the contract if offered a principal role, but not an understudy. I called Shirley Rich to explain, and she said, "Well, perhaps, another time then." When I asked her how she found me, she said, "I heard you were in the tour, so I called the Merrick office to get your address." I could hardly believe she went to such trouble. The emcee in Cabaret was a role I always wanted to play. I knew all the songs, had the German accent down pat, and was confident I could have done the part well.

The *Dolly* tour covered ninety cities in every one of the continental states except Washington and Oregon. It was a bus-and-truck tour, in which the cast and crew traveled by two buses, and the sets traveled by truck. Dorothy and her husband motored in her private car. The dancers managed to put all the "fun people" on one bus, consigning the musicians, stage hands, and duller principals to the "other bus." In 1967, Actors' Equity allowed only five hours of travel time on performance days. Anything beyond those hours required overtime pay.

Our company manager was Boris Bernardi (brother of the Broadway star Herschel Bernardi), and we were convinced that he bribed the bus driver to speed to avoid paying overtime. One of the singers on our bus, Jim Bovaird, began to sing Gregorian-chant style every time he suspected we were speeding. "Sweee-tah Jeeezus in heaven, protect us in this our hour of neeeed," which drove Boris completely bonkers. It was clear that our suspicions were justified when our driver was cited for speeding more than once. If, perchance the driver slowed down, Jim said, "Thanking you-ooo." Jim's boyfriend, Tony Stevens, whom he called, "Coocher," was the best dancer in the company and later went on to be a Broadway choreographer and a favorite of Chita Rivera. The duo of Jim and Tony, led the rest of us in a chorus to plague Boris every chance we got.

One night three male dancers were out sick. Terry D. shifted some parts around but had to cover much of the absenteeism himself. "The Waiters' Gallup" is timed within a split second and even one beat off can cause a train wreck on stage. At one point offstage, I handed Terry a skewer, waiting eight counts before making our entrance together. Terry grabbed the skewer and went straight toward the stage without waiting. "Terry, stop," I shouted and tried to restrain him, but he slipped out of my grasp. The result: four dancers, including Terry, crashed into each other mid-stage and fell on their asses. I heard Terry yell, "Oh, shit!" There's so much chaos in the number, I believe the audience thought it was part of the act. I couldn't help feeling a certain comeuppance, considering how nasty he had been to me in rehearsals.

Shortly after, Terry and a couple other dancers left the show. The day he left he said to me, "I'm so sorry I completely underestimated your talents." There was that underestimation once again. What exactly was I doing to contribute to it? Don Lawrence, who had been with the show since the beginning of the Channing tour, took over as dance captain. Jess Richards went immediately into action on my behalf. He went straight to the stage manager and Don and virtually demanded that I be given all the prime spots that had been vacated. I inherited two of the most visible spots in the "Dancing" number, including a solo of turns across the whole stage and a soft shoe down front with the principals. I would never have had the nerve to do what Jess did for me. Perhaps, that's my problem.

Jess was extraordinarily talented. He had a great voice and though he never trained as a dancer, he moved so fluently that it appeared he was trained. He was also an exceptional actor, who performed Shakespeare as easily as musical theatre. Later he had a Broadway starring role written specifically for him in a musical called, *Blood, Red Roses*. Though the show ran for only one night, John Simon, the hard-to-please critic of *New York Magazine,* cited his performance as the most exceptional he had seen all season. In 1971, Jess received a Theatre World Award for his performance in *On The Town*, with Bernadette Peters.

Jess would never eat before a show, believing it made him too slug-gish for the performance, so Frank, who loved good food as much as I did, went out to dinner with me every night. After the show, I'd go with Jess to have a snack. He was a nonpracticing Mormon, but he refused to take even a sip of alcohol. I found this refreshing after my ordeal with Hal. Unfortunately, he and Frank had a run-in over an entrance, and they refused to speak to each other, which made things uncomfortable for me. We had good times together. I liked Jess very much and was in awe of his talents, but I didn't love him. I was never interested in a relationship with another performer because it engendered too much competitiveness. Men were always waiting at the stage door for him, and often they would call our room to invite him on a date. The worst of it was that there was sim-ply no chemistry on my part toward him. He, on the other hand, was head over heels with me.

When we played Dayton, Ohio, the local critic savaged Dorothy cruelly and unfairly, complaining that he could see the bags under her eyes from the back row. The next night in her curtain speech she said, "I just want a certain critic to know that I have had these bags under my eyes since I was twelve years old."

She was a tough cookie and was very proud of the work she was doing in the show and had done previously in the movies—especially the stunts she performed herself. She vividly described how she was lashed to a tree, wearing the sarong that was her signature, during a ter-rifying storm in *The Hurricane*. In *The Greatest Show on Earth*, she actu-ally learned to hang by her mouth and spin in the air, high above the big top. But don't get her started on the "Road" movies. She had absolutely no fondness for either Bob Hope or Bing Crosby, whom she claimed, "screwed me out of millions."

She loved when I relayed stories people told us relating to her. One waitress who learned I was in *Dolly* said, "Oh, that Loretta Young. I always loved her show." New Orleans was Dorothy's hometown, and when we played there, a woman on the street said to me, "Dorothy Lamour? I've loved her ever since I saw her in *The Wizard of Oz*." A very slow "ha, ha, ha," would emanate from deep in Dorothy's chest, a laugh that always sounded as if she'd just told a dirty joke.

Dorothy's son was in the Marines, and she made a special point of it during her curtain speech each night, perhaps to counter all the antiwar demonstrations sweeping the country. During World War II, she had raised a fortune for war bonds and often entertained soldiers at the Hollywood Canteen. It seemed appropriate then that she requested that we perform for the troops at Ft. Leonard Wood, Missouri. We played in a large hall that bore no resemblance to a theater. It was impossible to use any sets, only the furniture and props. There was, in fact, no stage, but rather large pieces of board set up on sawhorses. One could quite literally apply that old showbiz saying, "treading the boards," in this case. Our stage crew was ingenious at adapting the show to any environment. There was no air conditioning and the space was stifling. Dorothy used her usual device to remain cool and diminish sweating, a small ice pack on her wrists.

During the first act, we gave it everything we had, but there was virtually no reaction from the soldiers in the audience—no laughs and very little applause. The commander came backstage to speak to Dorothy during intermission. "What's going on out there?" she asked him in a very upset state. "Do they hate the show that much?" The commander said, "Oh, not at all, Miss Lamour. They were all warned that they had to behave themselves, remain quiet, and act respectfully to the performers." "Well, you go out there and tell them to loosen up, have a good time, and enjoy themselves, because we're dying up here."

Never has an audience changed so radically mid-performance. During the second act, they began shouting, laughing, and applauding riotously at everything we did. The jumps at the end of "The Waiters' Gallup" provided unheard of thrills. I noticed at my first jump that I rose higher than I thought possible, and with each successive jump, we soared higher and higher. This was because the boards resting on sawhorses were acting as a sort of trampoline. The orchestra had to adjust the tempo constantly because there was no consistency in the length of time between jumps. We were literally flying by the end of the number. The experience turned out to be one of the more satisfying performances on the tour. Often, we found that when we were constrained in our use of sets and paraphernalia, we got the most enthusiastic audience reception.

My parents came to see the show twice when we played anywhere within driving distance of Rockford. They had obviously come around to accepting my dancing career, and dad was especially the proud father. Mary Giovingo, true to herself, had to interject an ill-informed criticism. In talking about the "Waiters' Gallop" she said to me, "The least you could do is smile." Of course, we were specifically ordered not to smile during the number. We were scheduled to play Rockford in March for a couple performances at the Coronado Theatre, a beautiful old movie palace. Dad convinced the relatives, coworkers at the shop, and everyone he knew to buy tickets.

Sally Riggs, one of the dancers, was from Little Rock, Arkansas. When we played there, she was feted in all the papers and was given a key to the city by the mayor. Every time she made an entrance, the audience applauded her. Dorothy showed extraordinary generosity to her at the curtain call. "There's a girl in this show who seems to be beloved here in Little Rock, so I think Sally Riggs deserves a solo bow of her own." The audience, of course, went wild. I thought, perhaps, I would get similar treatment in Rockford.

We received our revised itineraries a month in advance, and to my dismay I noticed that the dates initially booked for Rockford were now scheduled for Buffalo, New York. I called dad to tell him. He said, "That can't be because they just announced on TV that the show is coming and where to buy tickets." I checked with the stage manager, who said the Rockford date had been canceled because of some problem. Dad called the TV station, telling them to stop the announcements. It appeared that the local promoter didn't have the necessary funding to bring in the show, and he absconded with all the money he had received in advance ticket sales. For years, my relatives asked me, "Did you ever hear anything about how we could get our money back for those tickets?" Once again, Rockford thwarts me.

Though he was not at all effeminate, everyone would kiddingly say, "Frank, you're such a tall girl." When his birthday came round, some of the girl dancers noticed a shop in the town we were playing called, "The Tall Girl Shop." They went in looking for a dress to buy for him, but nothing seemed large enough. The clerk said, "Well, just how tall is she?" "Oh, about six foot three." "Wow, that *is* a tall girl." Finally they found a lime-green chiffon number and they bought it. That night after the show we had a party for Frank. He laughed and was very good natured about the dress. Everyone wanted him to try it on so he did. Just as he was modeling it, Dorothy walked into the party, "Frank Newell, if your dad could see you right now, he would die of a heart attack, and I'm telling him. I'm telling him." Frank's father was the district attorney of Baltimore and Dorothy, who lived in Baltimore, knew his father very well.

It was the era of facial hair, and several of the boys, including Frank, grew mustaches, which actually fit the period of the show. Dorothy was unhappy with the look and complained to the stage manager. Word came down that she thought we were a particularly handsome company, and she believed the mustaches were detracting from that. She wanted them shaved off, causing much grumbling by those who were sporting them.

She was a genius for issuing oblique complaints during a performance, too. The dancer who played Stanley, a waiter, was visibly expanding in the butt, and his pants needed to be let out several times. In the "Dolly" number the lyric reads, "You're looking great, Stanley. Lose some weight, Stanley?" One night during the number, she sang the lyric with a somewhat different inflection: "You're looking great, Stanley. LOSE SOME WEIGHT, Stanley!"

We played the South during the height of the civil rights marches and looking different than the locals, we were not always the most popular tourists in town. In Jackson, Mississippi, we had some interesting encounters. Frank and I were shopping for ties in a small men's shop, when a young clerk approached us in a decidedly hostile tone:

"Y'all with the show?"

"Yes," we said cautiously.

"What d'y'all do in that show?" he said with disgust in his voice.

"Dance."

"Huh! Dancin'. What kind of dancin' you call that."

"Modern jazz. Musical-theater dancing."

"Yeah? I think I seen that once. My aunt took me to Atlanta, and we had to put on them glasses to watch the show."

Frank and I looked at each other quizzically, wondering "Is he confusing this with 3D movies?"

A new replacement dancer was joining the show in Nashville. Don Lawrence, who had a beard and was wearing sandals, took him to the stage door and addressed the guard. "Hello, sir, I'm the dance captain for *Hello, Dolly!* and I need to have this guy admitted so he can watch the show tonight."

"I ain't admittin' no one to this here theeAter."

"No, I'm afraid you don't understand, sir. He's a new replacement in the show, and he needs to see it so he can learn where he belongs on stage. Obviously, he doesn't pay for a ticket because it's part of his job."

"I understand fine, but I ain't admittin' nobody."

"Sir, please, I need to have him in the theater."

"You get the hell outta here. I don't like the looks of you, and we don't want your kind 'round here."

Don was livid. He went back to his hotel, put on a suit, tie, and good pair of shoes, and finally got the dancer admitted.

I had never had encounters with the police, but three times during the tour, always while I was out with Jess, we ran into trouble. The worst incident was in Jackson, Mississippi . We were going to get burgers after the show, and we were about to cross the street to a diner when a cop car nearly ran us down. Two cops jumped out, grabbed us, and threw us violently over the hood, roughing us up.

"What are you two doin' in town."

"We're here with the show."

"What show?"

"With *Hello, Dolly!* starring Dorothy Lamour."

After presenting our IDs, they finally let us go, but we were very shaken up by the incident.

In San Diego, we went out for a walk. For some unfathomable reason we left without our wallets and IDs. We crossed the street against a red light, something New Yorkers do instinctively. Two cops spotted us and pushed us up against the building. When they asked for ID, we had none to produce. They wanted to take us in because we had apparently committed a crime, but Jess was very good at apologizing and explaining how we were ignorant of California laws.

The most amusing incident occurred in Providence, Rhode Island, while we were in a department store. We passed a group of three women, who were in their sixties. Jess, whose ego could be expansive, indeed, thought they had recognized him from the show and smiled broadly, acknowledging them as if they were his fans. We moved onto another department, when a policeman accosted us. The women complained to the officer, that Jess had been leering at them in a sexually threatening way—wishful thinking on their part. Again, *Hello, Dolly!* saved us from arrest.

Also, in the South, we heard that the "other bus" had been stopped for speeding and everyone had been taken to the local police station for questioning and not released until a steep fine had been paid. This incident made national news, because my parents questioned whether I had been arrested.

In Pensacola, Florida, the theater was right next to a navy destroyer, and our dressing room overlooked the deck of the ship. Jerry Bell spotted a sailor on watch that he liked. He wrote out his hotel and room number and folded it into a paper airplane. We warned him about the dangers of soliciting on-duty military personnel, but he was undaunted. Surprisingly, the sailor showed up at his room, and Jerry couldn't get done telling us what a great time he had had. A life lesson I sadly failed to learn: aggressiveness pays results.

Dorothy knew that *Hello, Dolly!* was one of former President Johnson's favorite musicals. She called him personally, "Mr. President, since I know that you've seen every other woman who has played the role of Dolly, I truly hope that you will not miss my performance when we play Austin." Sure enough, the President, Lady Bird, Lucy Baines and her husband drove in from their ranch to see the show. Back stage was a mass of Secret Service members, and Jerry Bell took a fancy to one of them. I had to warn him that if he didn't want to end up in prison, he'd better back off and let this one go. When the show was over, we were asked to line up on the stage because the first family wanted to come back and congratulate us. They were so generous and enthusiastic about the performance as we chatted and laughed with them. Lady Bird seemed particularly enchanted with the male dancers when she unwittingly said to us, "Y'all so gay."

Our tour criss-crossed the country along with Ginger Rogers's touring company of *Dolly*. Rumors had it that Miss Rogers, who tackily added high kicks as she descended the staircase in her red dress into the Harmonia Gardens set, fell on her ass one night. She was so disliked by the cast that not one of the boys who stood on either side of the stairs bothered to help her get up.

Initially, we were to be given a week off between Christmas and New Year's because of low theater attendance during that period, but someone in the Merrick office decided they had no intention of paying us for doing nothing. It was no easy matter to arrange last-minute bookings, but the office scoured every Podunk town in the country to keep us busy, working, and out of trouble.

As a result it was Christmas in Chanute and New Year's in Del Rio. Chanute, Kansas, provided the Merrick office with nearly an empty house, probably costing more than if we had been given the time off. The producers were also too cheap to give us a Christmas party, so Dorothy arranged and paid for one, herself. Kansas was a dry state and it was hard to find liquor, especially on a holiday, but somehow she managed to spike the punch for us.

Del Rio, Texas, was a deadly place to spend New Year's Eve. We ate in an incredibly dreary restaurant, with abysmal food, and Jim Bovaird asked, "Do you have anything at all for dessert?"

"Just ice cream."

"What flavors?"

"Vanilla."

"Well, I won't let it throw me."

Our cast got along famously with the stage hands who traveled with the show. Every night as I warmed up with a series of *pliés* before "The Waiters' Gallup," one of them would say to me, "Doing your clichés again?" One day I overheard a group of them in conversation:

"You know, these gay boys in the company? They're okay."

"Yeah, they don't come after us at all."

We had a good laugh over this later, considering that they were all fifty and over and were very unattractive. Just one more fine example of wishful thinking among straight men, who believe that all gay men are dying to get in their pants.

In our company was a wonderful mature dancer named Arnot Mader, who years earlier had danced with England's Royal Ballet. He had once danced with Moira Shearer, star of the *The Red Shoes*. Arnot took me under his wing and advised me in much the same way, I learned later from Donna McKechnie's autobiography, that he had done for her when she was young. I found it disturbing that after months Arnot and other cast members still did not know my last name was Cancelose. They called me Congrillos, Congolese, and even Cantaloupes, though on this last one I believe Arnot was referring to a part of my body he particularly admired. "This is a business where it is very important for people to remember your name," I concluded. I had tried out the name Norman Allan when I was in Pittsburgh, but there was a well-known British actor with that name so I had to drop it. Well, I've made you "hold your horses" long enough. Here then is the convoluted explanation for my various names.

My grandfather, Ignazio, immigrated to America with the name Cangialosi, though our family mistakenly believed it was spelled Cangelosi. Somewhere along the line, it got bastardized to Cancelose. We were never certain whether this was done by my Uncle Tom, who clearly preferred not being Italian, or whether immigration officials somehow messed up the spelling, as was common in those days.

The name always caused trouble. On a family vacation my father made a motel reservation, and he called the day before to confirm. When we arrived, there were no rooms. Dad said, "But I called and verified that we had two rooms." "No, our records state you called and said 'cancel those.'" Because the ugly name, Cancelose, did not even indicate an ethnicity and was certainly not working for me, I needed to find a new name. Jess Richards, who was born Richard Sederholm, suggested that I take my father's first name and make it my last. I envisioned that Mathews would look better on a marquee with one "t" rather than two, and thus Norman Mathews was born, following the tour of *Hello, Dolly!*

In Utica, New York, I got quite sick. We were leaving town the next day, and I knew I couldn't travel on a bus for several hours in my condition. In the middle of the night, I told Jess I needed to go to the hospital. They admitted me and administered intravenous antibiotics and hydration. It was eerie being left all alone in a hospital where nobody knew me. I spent three days, mostly out cold, recuperating from whatever undefined disease I had contracted. On the third day, nurses offered massages, but I had noticed that an extremely handsome orderly was doing the same for other patients, so I turned down the nurses. Finally, the orderly made his offer to me. It was as though I woke up in heaven out of a three-day stupor.

I rejoined the tour in Grand Rapids, Michigan, and was very glad to be back in the show. Those three days were the only ones I missed during the entire tour, which tends to be grueling on everyone's health because we played many one-night stands and never spent more than one week in any town.

In Los Angeles, we stayed at the lovely Hollywood Roosevelt Hotel and spent our days lounging by the poolside. Dorothy arranged for the cast to have a free, specially escorted tour through Universal Studios. We had a wonderful time performing the "Dancing" number on various movie sets for our own amusement. It gave the illusion of dancing in an MGM musical. While in Hollywood, 20th Century Fox Studios called Jess to do a screen test for the role of Barnaby in the upcoming film version. He didn't get the part, which was given to someone named Danny Lockins. I always felt the studio made a big casting mistake.

A most surprising letter arrived for me from Hal Shaw, who tracked me down through my parents. They most reluctantly gave him my address. He wrote that he wanted us to get together again and suggested that he was willing to join me somewhere on the tour. I wrote back saying that I was involved with someone else and that he was under no circumstances to visit me. "Would you meet me when you return to New York?" he responded. I told him I didn't know when I would be back, but we could discuss it at that time. This turn of events threw me for a loop and forced me to reassess my affairs with men. What was I looking for? What did I expect from these guys?

I knew that I had to do something about my relationship with Jess, because I was certain he was not the person I needed. The physicality of our affair was becoming more and more problematic for me. It reached the point that I had to close my eyes and envision other men, such as the orderly, when we were making love. Painfully aware of what a terrible betrayal this was, I thought to myself, "Please let no one ever do this to me."

I finally insisted that we had to separate and that I needed my own room. This lasted for only one night. Jess came to my room the next day and pleaded with me in tears to come back to him. I knew how desperate he was because he said he would not be able to go on that night. Jerry Bell was his understudy, and Jess had earlier vowed to me that he would have to be nearly dead before he allowed him to go on in his place. I felt so dreadful about the whole thing that I relented, and Jess did perform that night.

Once the six-month rider was up, the Merrick office wanted us to sign another rider or lose the extra pay we were getting. Three of us, Frank, Ron Sukenick, and I were reluctant to sign because the remainder of the tour was very uncertain. There were rumors that we would go to Hawaii, London, or possibly even play New York, but nothing was definite. The three of us asked to continue at the same pay without signing, but of course they balked at this. We then threatened to leave the company, costing the producer more to replace us than giving us the extra pay. We won our case, and when I returned to New York, I learned that we had earned the reputation of being rebels, who stood up to the powerful David Merrick, certainly a dubious distinction in the theater community. I was motivated as much by the need to separate from Jess as I was by the money.

About six weeks later when the itinerary was finalized, the show was booked into the Lambertville, New Jersey, Music Circus for late May to early June. This was a summer-stock theater just across the stateline from Bucks County, Pennsylvania, and a huge letdown, not only from the glamorous rumors we'd been hearing, but also from the kind of theaters we'd been playing. Lambertville was theater in the round, which meant a whole week of rehearsals to restage the show. This was asking more than we were willing to give, so the three of us proffered our two-week notice.

I realized that as long as I remained with the show there was no chance of separating from Jess. Both Jerry and Jess decided to remain with the company. Jerry's apartment was still sublet, so once again I had no place to live in New York. Before the tour began, Jess had been rooming with a conductor named Milton Setzer in a spacious two-bedroom apartment on West End Avenue. He asked Milton whether he would consider me as a roommate. Milton was glad to have the extra money, and besides he would be gone for most of the summer, conducting summer stock. I realized that Jess was using this ploy to keep me in his life, but it seemed to be the best solution.

The apartment was wonderful and Milton had a Steinway grand piano, which was an added plus. Because he was away so much, I had the luxury of the place to myself most of the time. The day after I arrived in New York, I learned about an audition for *Fiddler on the Roof,* which was being conducted by Shirley Rich. I should never have gone to this audition because I was seriously out of shape. When you're on the road with a show, your body learns to do what's needed for each performance, but because I hadn't taken class in nine months, it couldn't do much of anything else.

The audition was at ten AM at the Imperial Theater. I'm always at my worst in these morning hours, whether being born or auditioning. I overslept and got there just in time, so I had no chance to warm up. The first combination given was the Kazotsky squats and kicks in a circle around the stage. This Russian Cossack step requires moving from one knee to the other, with the opposite leg extended forward. I had no trouble doing these, but half way around the stage both thighs cramped up so badly that I looked like a cripple. Miss Rich gave me a most disappointed look that read, "What on earth happened to this guy? I thought he could dance." I'd just screwed myself with Shirl baby.

A few days later, I was cooking dinner for Frank when he called. "I just heard that they're auditioning dancers for the *Dolly* movie in one hour. Get yourself together, sistah and let's go." "I can't go now. I'm in the middle of cooking dinner." "Never mind dinner. They're only looking at people who have done the show already. I'll meet you there," and he hung up before I could respond.

Frank, Ron Sukenick, and I showed up, and we were all hired. If I had signed that second six-month rider, this good fortune never would have happened. Those dancers who stayed with the show in Lambertville were green with envy.

169

At age four

Mary Giovingo Cancelose and Matt Cancelose

Francesca Spera Cancelose, Ignazio Cancelose, and daughter, Jennie, at St. Joseph's altar

Second from left in WEST SIDE STORY, St. Louis Municipal Opera

Far left in HELLO, DOLLY! "Waiters' Gallop" (*Friedman-Abeles*)

In CELEBRATION: Left to Right, Norman Mathews, Gary Wales,
Ted Thurston, Frank Newell, Stephan de Ghelder (*Robert Alan Gold*)

Todd Lehman

The groom and family at Larry Cancelose's wedding

In rehearsal with Sarah Renberg

Karen Mason as Dorothy Parker
(R. W. Cabell)

John Dossett and Michele Pawk

Becky Fisher as Dorothy Parker

With Tracy Bidleman at Stuart Shapiro and
Janice Lee's CD-release party *(John Sutera)*

Eustaquio Limon and Tony Lin

At our marriage ceremony in 2014

Hello, Barbra!

THE MORNING AFTER the audition we were told to report to Grand Central Station at five AM. Five AM? Are they kidding me? As the details about the film became clearer, we learned that most of it had already been filmed in Hollywood. Two numbers were left: "Put on Your Sunday Clothes" was to be shot in Garrison, New York, and the finale was to be shot at West Point. They hired forty New York dancers to add to the Hollywood dancers already on the set. At Grand Central, we discovered that an entire train, called "The Dolly Express" was devoted to us, as well as the three thousand extras who were being transported each day.

When we arrived in Garrison, dozens of buses were waiting, already air-conditioned, to transport us to the large tents that housed the various units. Our first grueling chore was to have a sumptuous breakfast in the dining tent. Then we were taken to the wardrobe tent to be fitted for costumes. New costumes were not being made for the New York contingent. Rather, we were given costumes from 20th Century Fox's wardrobe collection. Next it was time for a big lunch back in the tent. By then we were completely exhausted, so we needed a long afternoon rest. Never have I been so coddled in any job I had ever done.

One could see the marked disparity between Hollywood dancers and Broadway dancers immediately because the Hollywood dancers were busy checking their stock portfolios in the *Wall Street Journal*, while the Broadway dancers were squabbling for a measly ten-dollar-a-week pay increase through Actors' Equity. I was earning nearly ten times as much on the film as I made on the tour for doing one-tenth the amount of work.

The setting for the "Sunday Clothes" number was the actual Garrison railroad station, which, along with the houses behind it, had been re-furbished. Is that the right word when something is made to look old, in this case turn of the century? The street in front of the station was painted to look as if it were brick. This was so realistic one had to reach down and touch it to be sure it wasn't the real thing. Any filming had to be stopped when a regularly scheduled train went through. Howard Jeffrey, one of Michael Kidd's assistants, began teaching us the choreography, in which we ran onto the vintage railroad car as it pulled into the station, took our seats, and began a series of movements, using handkerchiefs, hand gestures, and much rocking and swaying—certainly nothing challenging. Never-theless, I was so pleased that I finally was working alongside the "big boys." Many of the New York gypsies were Bob Fosse's best dancers.

The Hollywood dancers kept telling us how when we saw Michael Kidd's choreography it would make Gower Champion's work for the stage look dull and pathetic. I, along with most of the show dancers, completely disagreed with that assessment. Kidd's choreography lacked all the style and sophistication that Champion had achieved. In its place was gratu-itous athleticism, with no distinctive quality whatever. Like the rest of the film, it was too much of everything—too many people, too many cos-tumes, too many sets—trappings that overwhelmed the story completely. Its $25-million budget made it the most expensive film ever produced to that point. Watching Gene Kelly direct was also uninspiring and some-what dispiriting because I had so worshipped him in the movies. Here, he seemed out of his element and completely over his head. There was not a moment of subtlety in anything he did.

And don't get me started on the casting. As much as I love Barbra Streisand, having a 26-year-old playing a woman who should be in her fifties was ludicrous. She covered up some of the anomalousness by doing unfortunate Mae West imitations and singing the role, perhaps, better than it had ever been sung. Whenever I mention being in this film, every-one wants to know, "Was she difficult? Was she impossible? Was she a diva?" In the six weeks that I worked with her, I never saw even a hint of her creating a scene or any behavior that was less than professional. How she behaved in the Hollywood segment I can't answer. When she wasn't rehearsing with us or shooting a scene, she was cradling Jason Gould, her nine-month-old son.

By dusk we were back on the train to New York. We returned to the city about seven-thirty P.M., which left little time for anything but a quick dinner before an unseemly early bedtime. It didn't matter to us how late we got back because we were paid from the moment we boarded the train in the morning until we disembarked at Grand Central in the evening. As a result, we accrued enormous amounts of overtime pay, which made our salaries higher than those of the Hollywood dancers, who were housed near the location site and who were doing most of the work.

When the Lamour *Dolly* company completed its run in Lambertville, Jess Richards decided to stay on for the next show, *Finian's Rainbow,* playing Og, the leprechaun. On our Sunday off, I went down to see him perform, and he was exceptional, as usual. His staying on for the extra production gave me more time alone in the New York apartment, though he always came to visit me on his day off. The visits were more strained than either of us would have liked because I had begun to separate from him, both physically and emotionally. I was seeing other men, though I never brought it up with him.

Busy with summer-stock conducting jobs, Milton Setzer came home to his apartment in the city only rarely and only for a day or two at a time, which was a godsend for me. He was a talented pianist-conductor. One evening he invited his friend David Baker, the composer of the Broadway musical *Come Summer,* who had also written the dance arrangements for *Cabaret.* The two sat at the piano and played through Schubert four-hand pieces (two pianists at one piano) for most of the evening. I had never heard these pieces and knew nothing about the four-hand literature, but I was enthralled with what I heard. I couldn't have imagined the major role this music would play in my later life.

Milton had an obvious alcohol problem, and I suspect it diminished his career, though he did conduct two Broadway shows. In the 1990s, I was shocked to hear about the brutal and grisly end that came to Milton. He and a young lover had their throats slit in the very apartment where I had lived. The newspapers claimed that he had placed an ad to sell a grand piano—the same one I had been listening to, no doubt—and two prospective buyers came to the apartment and murdered them.

My source, a New York City medical examiner who worked on the case and a student of mine at the time, claimed that actually the two murderers had been invited to the apartment for kinky sex and then slashed Milton's and the young man's throats. According to newspaper accounts, the murderers were a twenty-four-year-old man and a fifty-seven-year-old man, who claimed he loved the younger man so much that he became his slave, doing whatever nefarious deed he commanded. Both were given life sentences for four murders. Two months before Milton's murder, they had also killed Chitresh Kehdker, an Indian prince, and his Paraguayan-born wife, Nenenscha, in their Park Avenue apartment, robbing them of all their jewelry.

On the train in the morning, Frank Newell and I began referring to the extras as the "exotic extras," because several had eccentric manners and wardrobes to match. This moniker eventually got abbreviated to the "exotics." One of the extras, who was neither eccentric nor exotic, sat with us on each trip. His name was John Lightfoot, a gorgeous, tall blond model and aspiring actor, who claimed that he was part Cherokee. So much time in moviemaking, and particular in filming out of doors, involves just sitting around waiting for something to happen. The weather isn't just right or there isn't a "match," which means the light isn't precisely the same as in the previous take. During this downtime, I often took naps on the back seat of one of the buses. The five AM call at Grand Central was killing me.

One day, as I was sound asleep, John Lightfoot, joined me and said, "Do you mind if I sleep with you on that seat?" Oh, no, I absolutely did not mind a bit since, owing to the narrowness of the seat, he would be sleeping virtually on top of me. He slept. I was wide awake with arousal. When he was through napping he kissed me, without saying a word. I took this gesture as a sign that he was interested in me and began plotting how I might ask him for a date. On one of our train trips, I learned that he was a ballet fan. American Ballet Theater was performing at the time, so I suggested to him that we take in a performance. I got a very tentative, "yes." It gave me guarded hope. A couple days later, Frank said, "Guess who I have a date with this weekend?" "Who?" "John Lightfoot." I was devastated.

I now knew precisely how my friend Joe Yanello felt when we were in St. Louis. Whenever we went to the bars together, we were inevitably attracted to the same men. "Why do you always get them, and I never do?" he complained, Of course, I had no consoling answer to why life can be so monstrously unfair,

My movie costume was a heavy tweed suit of wool that felt as though it were three inches thick. The summer was brutally hot, and with the addition of huge overhead lights the temperature was well in excess of one hundred degrees. This required that makeup people had to attend to us every few minutes, so we didn't look like sweaty laborers. My seat was near the front end of the train car, and when Barbra made her entrance onto the car, she paused for a moment right next to me. She was as calm and collected about the heat and the constant redoing of makeup as the rest of us.

Michael Kidd walked up the aisle of the car explaining exactly what he wanted from us in the scene. At one point, he unwittingly placed his hand on Ron Sukenick's head, stopped short, gave a very confused look, then patted the hair several more times to be certain he wasn't hallucinating. Ron's hair, piled rather bouffant-like on his head, was held in place with so much hair spray that it felt like plaster.

The scene took days and days to film. There were complicated helicopter shots as the train entered and departed the station, Gene Kelly constantly calling for retakes. Many times we had to stop to let a regularly scheduled train go through. Because the music in films must be prerecorded in a studio, I was fortunate to hear Barbra's final rendition of "Sunday Clothes" dozens of times before the release of the film and of the LP recording. We, of course, just sang along, stupidly lip-synching with the prerecorded music.

Once "Sunday Clothes" was completed, we moved on to the finale, which meant piling thousands of people into buses and driving us across the Hudson River to West Point every day. I could scarcely believe what I saw when we arrived. They had flown in by helicopter the frame of a full-sized New England-style white wooden church and placed it strategically at the tip of the point. The scene involved a wedding procession, beginning at the top of the hill and ending as Barbra and Walter Matthau entered the church.

I was assigned a partner, and we began learning our little dance steps, which once again required no remarkable technique. I was excited when I learned that we would be positioned in the front row just before the entrance to the church, and therefore very visible to the camera as Barbara and Walter passed us on their procession. The three thousand "exotics" literally cloaked the hill overlooking the point,

The music began to play, Gene Kelley called "take one, action," the cameras started to roll, and Barbra and Walter made their way slowly down the hill to the church. Just as they passed in front of my partner and me, I heard a screaming voice from up on the hill. "Stop the cameras. Stop the movie this instant." All action ceased. Everyone was frozen in place as the woman whose voice we heard came storming down from the top of the hill. Who is she? What does she want? Why is she so angry? Everyone looked puzzled. This particular "she" was famed Hollywood costume designer Irene Sharaff.

As we watched her approach the church, she seemed to be heading straight for me and my partner? Is that possible? Yes, she was definitely glaring at us. What could we possibly have done wrong? When she reached us, she gave immediate and irrevocable orders to Gene Kelly, who came to see what the problem was. Pointing accusingly at my partner, she screamed, "Get that ugly dress out of my movie and get it out now. It's hideous." My partner had been fitted in a dress worn by Judy Garland in the *Harvey Girls*, at least according to the label inside the dress. Admittedly, it was one of the most unsightly dresses I had ever seen—a nauseatingly colored brown crepe, covered with turquoise chenille balls. My partner and I were swiftly exiled to what was the equivalent of Siberia—the far reaches of the hill, behind even "the exotics," where no camera would catch the slightest glimpse of us. Photographs of the finale were soon to be seen in *Life Magazine*, but I couldn't find myself in the picture. The couple who took our place in the original prime spot, naturally, were quite prominent.

My ex, Hal Shaw, phoned me and pleaded with me to have dinner with him. The fact that he was virtually on his knees to get me back gave me a perverse satisfaction. In any case, I wanted to see what this was all about. He admitted that he had made a terrible mistake in breaking up with me. I was staggered, however, when he casually informed me that he had come to Pittsburgh to watch me dance and never even bothered to let me know he was in town. I told him that I was no longer that naive little boy he had known two years earlier, that I was a very different person. "Why," I asked, "would I want to go back to someone who, not only threw me out of his apartment, knowing I had no money, but also couldn't even trust me with the keys to his place?" He denied he had ever done such things to me, and at that moment all became clear. I knew he had no ability for self-reflection.

He had not in any way matured or improved as a human being, and there was no possible way I was returning to such an unhealthy relationship. He seemed very sad as we parted, but he never stopped calling me, always when drunk (which I could instantly discern even over the phone), up until a year before he died at age eighty-one. As I grew older, his calls rankled more and more, because they made me confront the hard reality of just how stupid I had been in allowing myself to be treated so badly. As a result, I became quite rude to him, in the hope that he would stop calling. He was not dissuaded.

I found myself noodling around on Milton's grand piano, though never with any serious intent. One day I came up with a simplistic but typical Broadway ballad, really quite by accident. Though I never played for anyone, Jess. who was home on in his day off, overheard me from the next room and wanted to know what it was. When I told him he said, "I really like that tune. Why don't you write it out for me?" I didn't have the skills to do this, so he asked to hear it a few more times, then promised he would write it for me.

There was no lull in my career after the movie. I was cast in a production of *Irma La Douce,* playing two major theaters in Canada, the O'-Keefe Center in Toronto (now the Sony Center), and Place des Arts, which is the major opera house in Montreal. Frank Newell was also in the show, but he backed out at the last minute when he was cast for the role of Riff in *West Side Story* at a summer theater in Maine. I made a few fast calls and managed to get Don Douthit hired in his place. The entire cast is male, except for the character of Irma. There were only four male dancers in the show: Don Douthit, Eric Paynter, who had been in *Mame* on Broadway, Rodney Griffin, who was a leading dancer with the Donald McKayle Company, and I. A couple of the principals danced, as well.

Pat Suzuki, who starred in the original *Flower Drum Song,* played Irma. Sweet and personable, as well as a wonderful singer, whose voice was perfect for the role, Pat was a bit addleheaded about the other elements of theater. Through no fault of her own, she was dressed in a particularly unflattering costume. In the dress rehearsal, as she appeared in the unsightly black dress, Rodney whispered a highly inappropriate remark to me, "She looks like a Thalidomide baby up there." After the rehearsal, she asked us what color pancake and other makeup items we used because she wanted to use the same ones. Of course, our pancake shade was specifically designed for men and was far too dark for her complexion. When it came to the dance numbers, she was lost, admitting, "I can't dance at all." I asked her how she was able to get through *Flower Drum Song,* with all those big dance numbers. "What dance numbers? I didn't do any dancing in that show," which was directed by Gene Kelly. "You didn't? When I saw the national company in Denver, the character had serious dance numbers." "Oh, that's because Elaine Dunn was a dancer. We didn't do any of that on Broadway."

The choreographer for our show was another dancing Charisse family member, Rita Charisse. She choreographed a series of jetés in a circle, which she explained, "You do two plain, and two wit de tweest." At one point, she couldn't think of anything to do so she said, "Juust do some frug, freestyle." I had never in my life spoken up to a choreographer, but I said quite emphatically, "Rita, you need to choreograph something. This is a period piece. It's set in the 1950s. They did not do the frug in those days." "Oh, no?" "No." The frug was a popular dance craze of the mid-'60s, She invented some lackluster steps to fill the void.

The cast was extremely talented, but rehearsals moved at a snail's pace. The director, who had been a top Broadway stage manager, seemed in over his head. When we got to Toronto, we had never run through the entire show even once. The day of the dress rehearsal the pathetically amateurish sets were still being painted and some pieces had not yet arrived. Again, we didn't get through the whole show.

In the Clive Revill part was the marvelous British-Canadian actor, Barry Morse, who was best known for his role as Lt. Philip Gerard in the long-running television series "The Fugitive." Barry, who was a first-rate Shakespearean actor, was the soul and the anchor for this haphazard production. At the end of the rehearsal, he gave a speech, directed to the producer, in his wonderfully mellifluous Shakespearean voice. "Sir, I humbly entreat you to cancel tonight's performance for the sake of the actors, as well as the audience. You have a grave responsibility, indeed, as a producer to uphold the highest standards for our magnificent art—the theater. It is unconscionable that you would put forth a production, particularly in this highly esteemed O'Keefe Center, that is unfit to be seen by the public. In the end, it will do you and all of us a tremendous disservice and prove to be an embarrassment to us all." It was everything I could do to keep from applauding both the content and the delivery of this speech.

The producer, who was a young, inexperienced charlatan said, "Oh, you'll see. It'll all go fine tonight. Bad dress rehearsals always mean a great performance." I hadn't heard that fatuous cliché in many years, and eyes rolled at the hollowness of it. We opened to utterly disastrous reviews. One critic wrote, "Irma, you can take yourself and your finky friends and get out of town as fast as possible." When we went to the gay bars after the show, I was too embarrassed to tell anyone I met that I was in the production, so I simply said, "Oh, I'm here on business."

Rita Charisse departed after the opening. With the blessing of the director, one of the principals, who also danced, decided that the problem was the choreography and by god, he would fix it if it killed him and the rest of us. He completely redid the big dance number in one day, and while the muse, Terpsichore, touched him (in the wrong part of his body, I fear), he cut out a section of the dance music, as well. He discussed the cuts with the conductor, so we assumed everyone was on the same page for the second performance. The number "Dis-Donc" ends with the dancing boys lifting Irma above their heads, her hands outstretched. Unfortunately, the conductor misunderstood the cuts, and when Irma flew into the air for her big finish, the orchestra kept right on playing. Looking totally confused, the conductor, completely defeated, simply dropped his arms and the music came to a thudding halt. We all stood on stage with egg on our faces. The perplexed audience didn't know what to make of it, and consequently there was no applause. Moving on folks.

The choreography was the least of the problems with this show. At one performance, Pat came on stage in her pregnant costume two scenes earlier than her pregnancy was supposed to have occurred. Her big title-song number was sung mostly from off-stage one night because she forgot to make her entrance. Both incidents were surely as much the fault of the negligent stage manager, who was not on top of things.

The director seemed not to have a single clue as to how to bring out the humor, which is so essential to the piece. It was the first show in which I played some small parts, for which I got to use my French accent. He wanted me to do something funny in one spot but had no ideas or suggestions for me. I tried several different things, but none worked, which may have been because the audiences hated the show so much that they weren't about to grace us with a laugh. The sets were highly criticized as being sub-level summer-stock quality, totally inappropriate for the major venues we were playing. The score by Edith Piaf's composer, Marguerite Monot, is quite wonderful, but the book is convoluted and very difficult to bring off.

If things were bad in Toronto, they got worse when we moved to Montreal. Our hapless producer assumed that a show set in Paris would be very popular in the city. What he didn't know was that les Canadiennes at that time would simply not attend a production in English. It was so bad that one night we had twelve people in a two-thousand seat opera house, and the show, scheduled to run two weeks, was cut to one.

Rodney Griffin was a dancer who had performed at St. Louis Municipal Opera a couple years before me, and while I was there everyone who knew him said that we looked exactly alike. When I told him this, we compared ourselves in the mirror and couldn't understand what they were thinking. Except that we were the same height and had the same dark hair, there seemed to be no resemblance whatever.

Rodney kidded me that in our curtain calls, which the two of us took together, I looked like someone out of a roller derby, racing to get to center stage on time. We both began exaggerating the movements, so that they were unmistakably derbyesque. At one point in the show Eric Paynter, dressed as a priest, rode across the stage on a bicycle. Rodney decided to shake up the cast by dressing him in one of the long black robes used in a judges' scene, and turning Eric into a nun. These were the sort of inanities we indulged in just to keep our sanity and survive these humiliating performances.

The best memories I have of that show were having dinner in some great restaurants, and especially the French ones in Montreal, with Eric, who loved good food as much as I did. When the tour ended and we were saying our goodbyes, Barry Morse said to me, "Strange how one meets the finest and most talented people in the most dreadful productions."

When I returned to New York, Jess had completed his run at Lambertville and was back living at Milton's apartment. By this point, I had become so distanced from him I couldn't imagine our living together. I had to end the relationship, which of course meant that I had to leave the nicest apartment I'd ever lived in. Jerry Bell was also back in town, so on a moment's notice the easiest solution was to move back with him. Convincing Jess that we were finished as a couple was one of the more difficult things I had to do. He took it very poorly. I was overwhelmed with feelings of guilt, thinking that what I had just done to him was nearly as bad as what Hal had done to me.

One day I happened to pass two facing mirrors. I stopped short. Both hands involuntarily covered my mouth. What did I just see? Were my eyes deceiving me? I walked back to have another look and to my horror discovered that I was losing hair at the back of my head. Oh, no, I have the dreaded curse, Spera male-pattern baldness. It was barely noticeable at that point, but I went into immediate action. I had to do something. How could I possibly work as a Broadway dancer as a baldy? I went to see a dermatologist, who suggested injections of female hormones to the scalp. He sprayed my head with some ice-cold anesthetic so the eight injections would be less painful. Ow! They hurt like hell, period. After four sessions of these shots, he suggested transplants, but I was skeptical about this procedure, not to mention its exorbitant cost. When he left the room, I peeked at his notes and saw, "good candidate for transplants." In other words, sucker for a scam. Then I learned that one could develop breasts from these female hormones. Somehow I couldn't see how big tits would in any way boost my chances for a Broadway career.

Love and Celebration

VERNON LUSBY ASKED THREE OF THE BOYS and two girls from the *Dolly* tour to audition for a new show he was choreographing. We were told we didn't have to dance for him because he knew our work, but it was important that we prepare something impressive to sing, something that would show off our voices. The show was called *Celebration* and was written by Tom Jones and Harvey Schmidt, authors of *The Fantasticks,* the longest-running musical ever. I worshipped them ever since Barbra Streisand on her first album sang "Soon It's Gonna Rain" and "Much More" from that show. We were told to come to Portfolio Studios on West 47th Street, which was not really a studio at all, but an old town house that Tom and Harvey had converted into a small theater space and costume shop.

Vernon sat silently while Tom and Harvey were very cordial and put me at my ease, by letting me talk about my background and hopes. I sang a ballad called "If I Gave You" from the Hugh Martin musical *High Spirits.* I had been singing this song for auditions because few people knew it, and consequently it caught their attention. When I finished, Tom and Harvey both asked, "What is that beautiful song?" Once I explained, Tom said, "Well, you sang it beautifully and you've got the role."

The authors intended to workshop the show at Portfolio Studios, rather than face the grind of out-of-town tryouts. *A Chorus Line* is considered the first Broadway musical to be workshopped because the performers, many of whom contributed material to the show, were paid under Equity's rules. *Celebration*, on the other hand, was workshopped without any Equity contract, nearly seven years earlier. They were unable to pay us during the rehearsal period, which is why they were interested only in performers who were collecting unemployment compensation. I began collecting checks directly after the *Irma La Douce* fiasco. The hope was that the show would go to Broadway after the workshop performances.

The whole cast was invited to Tom Jones's apartment just off Central Park to hear the musical. With Harvey at the piano, the two of them performed the entire piece for us. I could hardly contain my excitement that I was hearing the authors performing a new work that I would soon be appearing in. This is what I had wanted and worked for my whole life. Tom's wife, Ellie, who was also a playwright, prepared some lovely foods for us, which we took out onto their large terrace, overlooking the park. Wasn't this precisely why I came to New York?

We began rehearsals at the end of August, and every moment was sheer joy. The chorus, which was billed as "The Revelers," consisted of five singers and seven dancer-singers. For many of us this was our first chance at being in the original cast of a Broadway show. Besides me, the other male dancers from *Dolly* were Frank Newell, and Stephen de Ghelder, who was made dance captain; the two female dancers were Sally Riggs, who had understudied Mrs. Molloy on the *Dolly* tour, and Cindi Bulak, a self-declared white witch with a very ample bosom. There was already a close bond between the five of us, which was soon extended to the other Revelers.

Never had I known a group of people so dedicated to making a theater piece work. Because we weren't under Equity rules, no one ever asked for a break in rehearsals, or to cut down the number of rehearsal hours. We probably would have worked through the night if we'd been asked. People were working for no pay harder than I had ever witnessed, even among well-paid performers. The creators were humanitarian enough never to abuse their position.

While we were rehearsing, three contiguous wooden platforms, one high, the two on either side low, were being constructed for the set. Tom and Harvey are big believers that no elaborate scenery can equal what the human mind can imagine. Therefore, they preferred shows that were small, simple to put together, and used minimal set pieces. I very much agreed with their philosophy. Give me two actors with a great script on a bare stage and I'm in heaven. Harvey, who had also been a top graphic artist, was constructing a series of tribal masks for us to wear, which were based on those he had studied at The American Museum of Natural History.

Set on New Year's Eve, the ritualized allegorical plot was a sort of battle between the young and the old, the rich and the poor, mechanization and the environment, love and ambition—many of the same issues we are struggling with today. Besides the twelve revelers, there were only four principals: Potemkin, a cynical narrator; Orphan, a young, innocent idealist; Mr. Rich, an unscrupulous businessman; and Angel, a young girl, an entertainer who's torn between Orphan and the material success Mr. Rich can provide.

Ted Thurston, who was playing Mr. Rich, one day asked Harvey if he could please take a song down lower because he was struggling.

Harvey said, "No, I can't do that."

"Why not?"

"Because I can only play it in whatever key I wrote it in. I can't read music."

"What? Then why do you have the score on the music stand?"

"That's not the score. I'm just reading the lyrics." I was quite surprised at this revelation because Harvey was so fluent at the piano. It was even more shocking when at a Christmas party he played carols in the style of Debussy and Mozart. I never understood this because learning to read music is not one of the more challenging aspects of the art. It seemed to me that with his obvious good ear and natural ability to play, he would have learned the skill in a month. Because he couldn't read, he was completely dependent on the musical director, Rod Derefinko, to write out the score for him.

On the upper floors of the building was the makeshift costume shop. One day passing through the shop, I noticed a man I found especially attractive. He was wearing a sweat shirt with cutoff sleeves, and the first thing that caught my eye was a pair of very good biceps, unusual in 1968, when gym bodies were rare among gay men. There he was with those biceps, incongruously sewing sequins on a woman's red bikini-type bottom. He was good looking with slightly thinning hair, but wearing studious glasses, which gave him two contrasting or, perhaps, contradictory traits—both rather hunky and intellectual, a combination I've always found irresistible.

I did some inquiring and found out that his name was Todd Lehman. He was an out-of-work journalist, who had been lured into working on the show by his friend John Scheffler, the assistant to set designer Ed Wittstein. Though he was a big fan of Jones and Schmidt, Todd was also drawn to the project by the prospect of meeting some cute boys.

The revelers' costumes consisted of black ballet slippers, black tights, long-sleeved black turtlenecks, and black hoods. We wore white makeup, giving us a unearthly appearance when our faces were not covered with bright-colored masks. Rehearsals progressed so smoothly and without incident up until three days before the first performance when Pamela Hall, who was playing Angel, announced that she had just won a major role in the Jerry Herman musical, *Dear World,* starring Angela Lansbury. The producers of that show would not allow her the time to do the four work-shop performances. We were in a serious crisis because major Broadway producers and investors had been invited to see *Celebration* in Portfolio's one-hundred seat theater.

Susan Watson, angel to the rescue. She had been involved with Tom and Harvey from the beginning of her career when she did the lead in *The Fantasticks* in its initial one-act version at Barnard College. She had been slated for the off-Broadway opening when she was cast as Kim in *Bye, Bye Birdie,* and had to bow out. She did, however, later perform the role on television with John Davidson. Also, she was married to Ellie Jones's brother, Norton Wright, so she was in actuality part of the family. She managed to learn the entire role, which is significant, in two days and give flawless performances. Never did I note a moment of panic or anxiety, either in those rehearsals or at any of the performances. Painfully aware that I probably would have had a nervous breakdown under such pressure, I had the deepest admiration for her.

Being a Reveler was very unlike being in the chorus. Because the show was small, we were all very visible. In fact, almost all of us were given special moments to make us stand out. In the "Winter and Summer" number, a ritualized battle symbolizing youth and age, I did a slow-motion ballet atop the highest platform, portraying Summer, while Gary Wales portrayed Winter. For "Where Did It Go?" the show-stopping number, four of us—Frank, Stephen, Gary, and I, backed up Ted Thurston in a hat and cane song and dance, wearing crushed hats and weird puffed-cheek, translucent masks. Still, the conductor, Rod Dere-finko, told me he felt my talents were underestimated. Once again, that enigmatic word, "underestimation."

I invited all my friends to the workshop, including Ric from Denver. He said, "I loved everything about it, the book the music, the lyrics, and the choreography." I learned from him that he had been cast to play Riff in the same Michael Bennett *West Side Story* I had done, but somehow Michael dumped him before rehearsals had even begun. It seemed ironic to me that despite his years of training my career was outpacing his.

The response to the show was extremely enthusiastic. David Merrick, who had produced both Jones and Schmidt's Broadway shows, *110 in the Shade* and *I Do! I Do!,* was interested in producing it until he discovered that Tom insisted on directing the Broadway production himself, as he had done for the workshop. Tom told me he believed that both of those shows had been over-produced and that the respective directors, Joseph Anthony, for *110* and Gower Champion for *I Do! I Do!,* had distorted their original intentions. He was not about to let that happen again. Despite his criticisms, it should be noted that both those shows were quite successful.

Further, he implied that Agnes de Mille had over-choreographed *110*, though I was certain that he must have met Vernon Lusby through Agnes because he was her assistant on that show. I was somewhat relieved that Merrick turned it down because I was afraid his office would remember that Frank and I had been paycheck rebels on the *Dolly* tour and Merrick might have taken his revenge.

The producer who came through was the renowned Cheryl Crawford, one of the founders of the famed Group Theatre and The Actor's Studio, who had produced *Brigadoon*, the first revival of *Porgy and Bess*, and four Tennessee Williams plays, including *Sweet Bird of Youth* and *The Rose Tattoo*. Tom wanted the show to open on New Year's Eve because that was when the play was set.

During the workshop performances, Todd was recruited to run the lights, which seemed more suited to him than sewing sequins. Months later in a taxi he told Tom, "You know, I had never run lights before in my life." Tom said, "I'm really glad that I didn't know that at the time," and then gave him a check for $100. Throughout rehearsals, I found myself shamelessly flirting with Todd, doing such things as feeling his biceps. Either he didn't pick up on my efforts or he just wasn't interested. I subscribed to the latter theory. Perhaps I was simply inept. I was used to being the one pursued and at best could only indicate to someone that I was interested and open to any advances.

Surprisingly, one day he invited me to dinner at his apartment on our evening off. I was delighted until I discovered that he had also invited Stephen de Ghelder. We both showed up at his place on West 89th Street unaware the other had been invited, wondering what was up. Was he interested in one or the other of us, both of us, or was this just a friendly gesture? Neither of us could decide. I took note that here was someone who could cook, which piqued my interest even further. The apartment was a pleasant two-bedroom with a dining room and a double living room, which he shared with a man named Patrick Shannon, an aspiring playwright who was working for Delta Airlines.

The incredible excitement and anticipation of knowing that the show was headed for Broadway was enhanced when Tom and Harvey presented each cast member with $500 for our participation in the workshop. Taken together with our unemployment checks, this gave us more money than we would have earned under an Equity contract. Rehearsals for the Broadway production were to begin after Thanksgiving.

I went home to Rockford for the holiday—my first Thanksgiving home in nine years—in a mood so elated that my feet rarely touched the ground. The leading newspaper in town interviewed me about my career and my upcoming Broadway bow. I so hoped that my old high-school drama teacher took note of the article, with a tinge of regret for having always cast me in invisible roles.

Mary Giovingo had settled into having *Nonna* as a permanent house member, and it seemed to be working out, as my grandmother was really no trouble. Larry had replaced me as the problem child. There were several incidents with the police when he was caught with a group of friends in underage drinking in the public parks, but no big deal. After graduation, dad got him a job at Nylint, which he had been handling apparently very well. Unfortunately, he began chafing at the bit, almost literally. Because of his small size, friends tried to convince him that he would make a perfect jockey. One small problem: he's scared to death of horses. When we vacationed in Yellowstone National Park, he and I were allowed to go horseback riding. I loved every minute of riding up and down some of the narrow mountain trails, at a very safe trot and under supervision of a guide. Larry, however, began to tremble the minute he mounted his horse and couldn't wait until the short ride was over.

After visiting a stable and talking to some jockeys, Larry learned that he would have to start by caring for the horses and cleaning stables. We never heard another word about the horse-racing business after that visit. Instead, he went to a bartending school in Chicago, where he aced the course, another indication that both he and my father could handle schoolwork if only they had put forth the effort.

Working at a bar in a local bowling alley, he met an underage cocktail waitress who was potentially a bit unbalanced mentally. He kept trying to break up with her, and she threatened suicide if he did. At one point this led to a fight between them, and she called the police on him. The policeman who came to my parents' house knew Larry very well, and convinced the girl to drop the charges. Mom and dad, who had never had any incidents with the police, were horrified by these events. A couple years later, she talked Larry into marrying her. I was the best man for the wedding, but we all knew this was a disaster in the making. I hardly recognized the Larry who had been so lighthearted and fun throughout my childhood. He became somber and somewhat morose. I couldn't help but equate this change in him with the one I had heard about my Uncle Paul when he married Rose.

Rehearsals for our Broadway opening began early in December. Cheryl Crawford had selected the Ambassador Theater on West 49th Street, just off Broadway for the show. It was not her first choice, but the only suitable theater available. The Ambassador, which has housed the years-long running revival of *Chicago*, was far too large for such a small show. The theater is very wide, which further detracted from the intimacy that *Celebration* required. A New Year's Eve opening proved impossible. In fact, previews did not to begin until January 9.

Harvey and Tom were supposed to have been rewriting sections of the show during the interval. This was, after all, why they set up the workshop process. The downtime afforded them a relaxed period to think deeply about what improvements needed to be made. By contrast, during out-of-town tryouts writers have to make nearly instantaneous changes late at night in hotel rooms, then get those changes incorporated in a frantic rehearsal process.

I was somewhat astounded that almost no changes had been made. In fact the only change was an eight-bar addition to the song, "Under the Tree," which didn't add anything significant to the piece. One of the problems I detected early on was that the book lacked dramatic intensity. The love affair between Angel and Orphan was never developed sufficiently to create any real tension or crisis when Mr. Rich bought her off with material success. There were many wonderful and magical moments as well as some lovely music in the show, which was addressing so many contemporary issues, but would they coalesce into something moving and meaningful?

My fears that I would lose sight of Todd after the workshop were unfounded—I hadn't completely given up on him. He was hired to be an assistant to Cheryl Crawford and her associate producer Richard Chandler. The job was a perfect fit for him. Though his Master's Degree from Penn State was in journalism and English literature, he wrote his thesis on the famed English theater critic Kenneth Tynan. He had also taken many courses in theater history and had done some performing in community theater. In addition to the usual tasks of a producer's assistant, he read and evaluated incoming script submissions for Miss Crawford.

Just after Christmas we moved the rehearsals from Portfolio Studios into the Ambassador. The contract gave The Revelers $175 per week, a $25 increase over the usual chorus contract. This was not an insignificant amount of money in 1969, and was meant to compensate us for all the special bits we did on stage.

Harvey created one of his beautifully simple, signature posters, using a rendering of the eclipse of the sun, an important visual element in the musical, and under it just the word "Celebration" in his unmistakable jagged handwriting. It was both classy and memorable. The first day I saw the marquee, the posters, my picture outside the theater, and my name in the cast list in the lobby, I recalled that time eleven years earlier, when I stood in childish awe in Shubert Alley at the Broadway theater world. Could I have imagined this would ever happen?

Again the rehearsal process moved along very smoothly—perhaps too smoothly. In my estimation, there needed to be some angst, some drive to make things better. Instead, we saw no changes in the script, the choreography, the costumes, or the set. All we needed to do was expand our movements to fill the larger space. Perhaps changes would be demanded when we put it before audiences.

I remember feeling a bit of agoraphobia in the slow-motion ballet, which required a lot of tricky balancing on one leg. There had been no raised stage at Portfolio Studios. In the darkness of the theater, the small platform felt as though it were floating high in the air, and I couldn't see any ground below me. Fortunately, this sensation subsided after the second performance. Audience response at the first previews seemed rather tentative. I expect they had no idea what to make of this unusual show.

The orchestra was not in the pit, but rather behind us on the stage. It was also very small for the period, when large ensembles were the norm. It had only nine pieces: three keyboards, three percussion, a harp, a guitar, and a bass.

Cheryl Crawford clearly saw the need for more work to be done, because she kept sending Todd to the theater with written suggestions to Tom Jones for changes she wanted made. Todd said that Tom simply threw them in the wastebasket. Unfortunately, Todd had such integrity that he never peeked to see what changes she was requesting. One change we know she was insisting on was plain to all of us, however.

Tom had an unfortunate penchant for tasteless gimmicks, which seemed to amuse him enormously. Whenever Mr. Rich sat down, one of the female revelers would sneak a fart cushion under him. It was bad enough when it got no more than a few snickers on its first use, but when it was repeated several more times it became a disheartening embarrassment for everyone on the stage. It was never cut. Here was an obvious problem when a creator is directing his own work. It obviates the possibility of analyzing the show with any critical distance, offering no opportunity for different insights.

New Year's Eve was conflated with the winter solstice right at the beginning of piece. The implication was that primitive man saw the shortening days in apocalyptic terms. "Look, they said, 'the day is being eaten by the night.' Look, they said, 'the darkness is devouring the light.'" In Scandinavian countries, in particular, where the winter solstice is a major event, the musical became extremely popular. Symbolism infused the entire work, including the sets and props, where decorated umbrellas served as trees, and a stained-glass window served as the eye of god. Was it more symbolism than an American audience could process?

At one point, it was rumored that Cheryl Crawford convinced Jerome Robbins to look at the work and that he agreed to become the "show doctor," which would necessitate pushing back the opening night, set for January 22. I was both excited about the prospect of working with this great man of the theater and frightened because I knew how hard Robbins could be on his dancers, fearing that firings might be in the offing. Not to worry. Tom threatened to shut down the show rather than have another director interfere with his vision. Because Harvey and Tom were also investors in the musical, they had been granted total artistic control by Miss Crawford. Opening night would not be delayed, period.

After a few previews, audiences began to warm to the show. Perhaps, word got out that they should expect something unusual, something fascinatingly new and different. In any case, the response turned so positive that it looked as though this was a big hit in the making. I told my parents I would arrange free tickets, so they must come for the opening and be a part of what promised to be an exciting event.

One night in our dressing room, a letter arrived for Stephen de Ghelder from Todd. The assistant company manager, Alan Schnurmacher, who was very wealthy, was giving a party at his East Side apartment for the company. In the beautifully written letter, Todd invited Stephen to be his date for the party. Stephen had the incredibly poor taste to read the letter aloud in the dressing room because he was not interested. He had always been partial to tall blonds. I felt hurt and envious that such a touching letter hadn't been directed to me.

Both Alan and Todd's friend, John Scheffler, made it clear that they had designs on me. I hated being rude or crushing their hopes, but I hadn't the least interest in either of them. The intrigue created a tangled web of disappointments and unfulfilled longings among all of us. I decided to kill two birds with one stone. I made it known in no uncertain terms to both John and Alan that I was infatuated with Todd. This got the two of them off my back, while I was certain they would pass the word on to Todd. I waited in tense anticipation to see what reaction I might get.

Two nights later, the stage doorman handed me a note. It was from Todd. I opened it with expectant but trembling hands. It simply stated, "I'm picking you up after the show tomorrow night." He didn't ask; he just assumed I was available. To say that I was more than a little titillated by his forcefulness would be an understatement. To me, it read, "I'm giving you no choice. Just be ready for me." Yes, sir! I loved it. On January 15, 1969, exactly one week prior to opening night, he was at the stage door, and he took me to Joe Allen's, a favorite after-the-show rendezvous for the theater crowd. Throughout our meal, I kept wondering, is this it, just a late-night snack and then each to our respective homes, or would there be more? There was more.

He invited me to his apartment. His roommate was mercifully absent. I had waited four long months to see him naked, and I was not disappointed. His pecs and flat, washboard abs were impressive, and even his thin, slightly bowed legs I found appealing. I expect I had a wide-eyed, open-mouthed, foolish look of lust on my face. That night I experienced an explosive physical passion, a volcanic release I had not known for years. I couldn't tell whether the sensation was reciprocal. Positive development—he made another date for the weekend.

Frank Newell had planned out his particular vision for opening night for both of us. His parents were coming from Baltimore. Both families were to have an early dinner together at Downey's, a Broadway steakhouse, before the show. After the show, we would make an appearance at Sardi's before we ventured to the opening night party, where I would introduce my parents to Todd.

My parents arrived early in the day, and I took them to the theater, showed them my photos outside, then guided them backstage and onto the set. I wanted them to see each of the masks that I would be wearing so that they could always identify me on stage. I wasn't really hungry when we dined, not out of nervousness but the sheer excitement over what was about to take place.

The performance went astoundingly well. We all seemed to be performing at a level we had never achieved throughout the previews. The audience was ecstatic and the applause was thunderous after every number. It felt as though waves of love were enrapturing us. In the finale, we all carried wooden placards mounted on long poles. On one side of the placard was the, by now, well-known eclipse symbol. On the final chord, called "the button," we spun the placards around. The reverse side was covered in copper-colored mylar, and when the lights caught the reflection, it appeared that the sun was shining everywhere, a *coup de théâtre*. The audience went wild. There was no question: we were a hit!

Dressed in our best, we followed Frank's plan and went to Sardi's. As Frank and I entered, everyone in the place stood and began applauding. Mary Giovingo said, "Who are they clapping for?" I turned around to see whether some star had entered behind us, but there was no one. "I guess they're clapping for us." It was one of those magical moments, never to be repeated in life.

From Sardi's we went to the restaurant at the top of the Allied Chemical Building, formerly the New York Times tower and the reason the square is known as Times Square. We were surprised and dismayed to see that the party was already winding down. What could be wrong? What was wrong was that the reviews began coming out and everyone was depressed. The most important critic was Clive Barnes of the *New York Times*, that same Clive Barnes that I used to edit and who once asked me personally how good my "double tours" were. His review was not entirely negative but definitely not written to sell tickets:

> At its worst it seemed like a Madison Avenue apology for art, and all the simplicity, magic, and uplift that had been lavished on the show came out as chic and heartless. . . At its best, and it very definitely has a best, there is a campy style of originality here, some nice lines from Mr. Jones, some sweet percussive melodies from Mr. Schmidt, some pretty performances, all adding up to a musical decently above the admittedly flagging average.

Richard Watts, the *New York Post* critic, was seen coming into the theater very inebriated and upon leaving remarked, "I was in no mood for that kind of show tonight."

We were given a sort of pep talk and told by Jones and Schmidt to hang on tight. *The Fantasticks* received similar kinds of reviews, until word-of-mouth made it into a hit. They also had put aside $100,000 to keep *Celebration* running until it clicked. It was difficult to keep our spirits up, however, when we faced the second-night audience. Never had I realized just how powerful the New York critics were. The audiences, which had been so enthusiastic through the final previews and opening night, suddenly became sullen, silent, or surly. By the end of the week, they began yelling things out to us, "You tell him, honey." "You're a real nut job up there, mister."

For the entr'acte, The Revelers had been given toy instruments on which we played the musical interlude. I had a toy trumpet. This played very well in the small space of Portfolio Studios before a lot of friends, but on a Broadway stage it became a travesty. I darted offstage as quickly as possible when we finished the number, in fear for my life. My parents loved the show so much that they insisted on buying tickets for another night. They, too, were completely puzzled by the change in the audience response.

On Sunday morning, the day that Capitol Records was to record the show, I woke up with a nasty sore throat. I had no intention of letting this interfere with making my first original-cast recording, and I happily sang full out all day. As we listened to the playback after recording each number, it all sounded so exciting that we couldn't understand how the critics had responded so coolly. Although I had no solos to sing, I loved being in the recording studio and being a part of the whole process. To me it was only incidental, that we were being paid the equivalent of two weeks' salary for the day.

Tom and Harvey wanted the recording out as fast as possible to help promote the show. This turned out to be another error in judgment on their part. Proofreading must have been nonexistent because the original jacket cover failed to mention Tom Jones and Harvey Schmidt. Worse, the LP sounded a pale imitation of what we had heard on the playbacks. Rushing through the process meant that the crucial mixing and mastering elements were given short shrift, obliterating the presence and excitement the recording should have had. It wasn't until years later when a remastered CD was issued that the recording came to life.

On Monday, when I awoke I couldn't make a sound. What was I to do about that night's performance? I decided that since I had no solos, I would simply mouth the lyrics and hopefully no one would notice. I loved doing the show and I was not about to miss a single performance.

When the weekly magazine reviews came out we had a renewed burst of hopefulness. *The New Yorker,* and *Time* each raved about the inventiveness of the show. *Life* was so enchanted that it decided to run a four-page pictorial spread, celebrating the fact that the show was introducing audiences to a refreshing new kind of theater. There were the inevitable and erroneous comparisons with *Hair,* which was running concurrently. My favorite was from Edward Albee's producer, Richard Barr, who hoped to take our show to London, "*Celebration* makes *Hair* look like a toupee." The two full pages in *Life,* on which my picture appeared, dad proudly displayed in their house, next to his baseball idols. I was now in the gallery of the gods.

Todd and I were dating at least three times a week. After two failed relationships, I wasn't ready for another full-time lover. What I needed was someone I really liked, someone I could do things with, and sleep with several times a week—someone who could keep me out of the gay-bar scene and the awful chase of looking for men, which was something I despised having to do. He didn't seem to be seeking anything more than that, so we were a perfect fit.

In fact, for the first time ever, my life seemed perfect. During the day I had the money and time to pursue dance classes and voice lessons. At night I had the show, which I adored doing so much that I probably would have performed for no money. And in the evenings and Sundays off, I had Todd.

Frank and I took joint voice lessons with a seasoned Broadway soprano, Marian Haraldson, and a favorite of Jule Styne and conductor-arranger Buster Davis. We also took a jazz class, my first serious study of the kind dancing I was being paid to perform, with Betsy Haug, who was Michael Bennett's dance captain in the hit, *Promises, Promises.* She taught a whole new contemporary style of jazz I had never before encountered. For ballet, I studied with Patricia Wilde, who had rejected me for the Harkness Ballet. She was now teaching the professional class at the American Ballet Theater School, and in the class was prima ballerina Cynthia Gregory. I always stood behind Cynthia because I found that dancing behind a major talent was the ultimate learning experience.

Another ballet class I loved was taught by Elizabeth Hodes, who had never been a major dancer but was an extraordinarily fine teacher. In her class was Robert Blankshine, the former star of the Joffrey Ballet, who proudly told me, "You know that I can do things that Rudolf Nureyev could never hope to do." And he was right. Elizabeth often asked the two of us to do combinations across the floor together, and though Robert could dance rings around me, I kept up and learned so much from watching him. Also in this class were many Broadway dancers including Graciela Daniele, who was soon to become a major director-choreographer. Frank would say to her, "Grazie, you look terrific." She would answer, "But my de-ah, I cahn't even find feefth posseetion."

Also in the class was a wonderful dancer named Pamela Blair, with whom I often lunched. She was so terrific but so mousey-looking and plain. I could hardly believe my eyes when a few years later I saw her as the sexy blond bombshell in the original *A Chorus Line,* performing the "Tits and Ass" number.

The four dancers who did "Where Did It Go?" the showstopper in *Celebration,* got a call from Buster Davis. He wanted to audition us personally at his apartment for a new project and requested that we prepare a '30s-period song. We all showed up together and learned that he was planning to put together a musical version of the Katherine Hepburn classic, *Holiday,* using mostly unknown music by Cole Porter.

He took us each into his studio individually, and I sang "Thou

Swell" from Rodgers and Hart's *Connecticut Yankee.* He liked what he heard and asked me to sight read an obscure and difficult jazz piece. Again, I had to admit that I couldn't sight read, but if he played it for me, I could sing it back to him, which I did very easily. Marian Haraldson, who was one of his favorite singers, told Frank and me that we were the two who impressed him and he was seriously considering us for roles. A few months later I went to a dance audition for the show and was also singled out. Was I about to move out of the chorus and into featured roles? Not on your life. They couldn't raise the money for the production. Years later it was eventually produced as *Happy New Year,* but ran only a few performances.

The good publicity from the weekly magazines did nothing for business, and *Celebration* struggled to find an audience. An unfortunate ad ran in the *Times,* "If you liked *The Fantasticks,* you'll love *Celebration.*" Hardly a winning slogan. Papering the house to put butts in the seats was becoming the norm. Our about-to-retire dresser, who loved us and the show because it required so little work for her and her poor tired feet, would peek out front each night with sadly misplaced hope, "It's awll cash out they-ah tonight, dee-ahs. No paypah at awl." But in fact, there was very little cash and reams of paper. I was able to get all my friends, Helen Wicks Reid, who was reunited with her husband, and even the Brooklyn Speras in for free.

Despite the dwindling audiences, we still had a wonderful time doing the show each night. Keith Charles, who played Potemkin and received the strongest reviews of anyone in the show, lived on the upper West Side, so we were generally on the subway together. We got off at 50th Street and just around the corner was a wild old man who stood there night after night blowing raspberries at passersby and shouting, "Sex pervert!" One night just as I made my entrance in a frightening feathered mask, Keith turned upstage, blew a raspberry, and said, "Sex pervert." Facing downstage, my poor cheeks were puffed out to bursting, as it took everything I had to keep from breaking up.

In my estimation, the show had attempted to deal with too many pressing contemporary issues, but always on a superficial level, never with the commitment and point of view that would have packed a wallop. Vernon Lusby later told me that Tom felt he had over-choreographed the show. I believed exactly the opposite. The opening number, "Celebration," with its ancient primitive dance motif, should have been far more demanding and exciting to get the show off to a more rousing start.

Todd's roommate, Patrick, hinted that he thought I was being very cool, aloof, and noncommittal in my relationship with Todd. I wasn't sure whether this resulted from Todd's having complained about me or just something Patrick intuited. Admittedly, because of past experiences, I was afraid of turning our affair into something deeper, and I got no sense from Todd that he wanted to either. Then unexpectedly, Todd got an unsightly lump on his neck. It was first diagnosed as the mumps.

May Muth, our production stage manager, was near hysteria when she learned about this. She was afraid that I was going to infect the entire company, even though I assured her I was immune because I had had the mumps as a child. May was an old-time stage manager, having worked for David Merrick for years, and had many tales to tell. Her favorite concerned Lauren Bacall, whom she knew when she stage managed *Cactus Flower* on Broadway.

Apparently Miss Bacall was extremely tightfisted. She gave a party for the cast, and as it was winding down she asked if everyone was through eating, because she had an agreement with the caterer that she could get a refund on any uneaten food. May's line in the sand was crossed over toilet paper. Lauren was always asking for more paper for her dressing room. The numerous rolls disappeared within a few days, and Lauren would request more. Finally, May had her watched, only to discover that she was stealing them in a shopping bag. A nasty confrontation ensued.

Because of my relationship with Todd, I had direct access to all the rumors emanating from the Cheryl Crawford office. Very strange things began to occur. Soon after the opening of *Celebration*, her associate producer, Richard Chandler, went into Cheryl's office and closed the door, which he never did. Cheryl was sitting at her desk, and he walked behind her. Moments later, a large poster of *One Touch of Venus*, which had hung on her wall for years, suddenly fell and struck her on the head, causing a lot of bleeding. She was taken to the emergency room where she required ten stitches.

Then Richard's aunt from Peoria died. He claimed that she was leaving him a large fortune, and from it he intended to set up a significant annuity for Cheryl, who was grateful because she had been having financial difficulties. They were to meet the aunt's lawyer in a restaurant to work out the details. The lawyer never showed up, but Cheryl began to feel sick after drinking a cocktail. She asked Richard to take her home and call her doctor. The doctor never showed up. Richard probably never called him. Her maid, however, managed to obtain medications for her. Cheryl quipped at the time that she felt as though she had been slipped a Mickey Finn, a term for a drugged drink.

One night Cheryl got a call that her beloved house in Connecticut was burning. The next morning when Todd came into the office, Richard told him to book a rental car because he and Cheryl were driving to the house to assess the damage. Virtually nothing remained. Even the piano on which Gershwin wrote some of *Porgy and Bess* had been destroyed.

Cheryl's suspicions were aroused, and she began asking Todd to have the building's super bring up all her records from the basement. Each time she did, Richard told Todd that it wasn't necessary. He would bring them up when they were required. Todd, as instructed by Richard, deposited the royalty checks from all of Cheryl's past productions into two different bank accounts, one at Chase Manhattan, the other at Bank Leumi.

In the meantime Todd's "mumps" burst and Patrick rushed him to the hospital. Tests showed that it wasn't the mumps but rather an infected lymph gland, which needed to be drained, and treated with antibiotics. He remained in the hospital for several days. During that period, we got the announcement that *Celebration* would be closing on April 26, after 13 previews and 109 performances. Todd was aware that his job would be terminated along with the show, so he decided to leave New York and return to his home in Pennsylvania. I was more than a little taken aback because he had not even mentioned to me that he was considering such a move. It said to me that our relationship meant nothing to him, and I was thankful that I hadn't let myself get too emotionally involved.

The last performance of the show was extremely painful. Most of us were in tears all night. Despite its problems, we had loved it so and dreaded the unhappy ending. Another blow was dealt when we learned that the show had not been nominated for a single Tony Award. Todd had left town before the closing, so he missed out on the end of the Richard Chandler saga, which we learned about later.

Richard had been embezzling Cheryl for years. Todd was unwittingly assisting him by depositing the checks in the two accounts, one of which was a shell account. Richard had been diverting royalty payments from *Brigadoon* and other hit shows into his own account by forging Cheryl's signature. He had wormed his way into her office twelve years earlier by offering to work for no pay. He did very good work for some time before she took him on as a paid employee. He then assumed all her bookkeeping duties. She even produced a Broadway play that he wrote, which was a disastrous failure. *Celebration* was the first and only show that they produced together.

She came into the office one day and found no Richard, only a note saying, "I've left town forever. Please forgive me." She phoned the lawyer in Peoria who had failed to show up for several scheduled meetings, only to find out he had never intended to come to New York. The "wealthy" aunt, it seemed, lived in a poor, lower-class house and had no fortune. The boxes were finally brought up from the basement, and Cheryl had to face that she had been betrayed by someone she had trusted, someone to whom she had given a singular opportunity. She seemed such a tough, savvy woman, that I found it hard to believe she had been taken in so easily.

About two weeks after the show closed, I got a letter from Todd, saying that he had made a big mistake and that he was very unhappy at home in Pennsylvania. "I'm coming back to New York and we're going to live together." Once again, no asking, just pronouncing. I pondered this for awhile and decided it was worth a try. I was eager to get out of Jerry Bell's apartment and despite the fact that I had saved some money, living on unemployment insurance, there was no way I could afford my own place. Bob Schear, the stage manager under May Muth, told me that he and his boyfriend were taking the summer off to go to Europe. Did we want to sublet their apartment while they were gone? This seemed a perfect opportunity. Todd and I could try living together and see if it worked. If not, we could go our separate ways.

Bob's apartment was in the enormous complex called London Terrace, which takes up the entire city block between 23rd and 24th Streets and Ninth to Tenth Avenues. My expectations were very low. I doubted that we'd even make it through the whole summer together. How wrong I was. Everything seemed to change once we were living together.

I had not fully appreciated just how much we had in common— virtually everything. We both loved food and cooking. Todd had studied classical piano for ten years. He was a far better pianist than I. In fact he had pipe dreams of becoming a concert pianist as a child, and he knew the symphonic literature far better, as well. We had already established our mutual love of theater. We were both avid readers of good literature. We both wanted to travel to Europe some day. Perhaps, most importantly, we were both basically home bodies, who were not terribly social. We loved just being home together. He brought new interests into my life: his love of foreign films, which quickly infected me, and a passion for hiking, which revived my love for nature.

Todd and I generally swam outside the mainstream of American life, but we also swam outside the mainstream of gay life. We didn't go to bars. In fact, we both hated them. We didn't go to Fire Island, and we weren't party animals. We almost never went out dancing because Todd was not fond of it. So when the Stonewall Riots occurred that summer in June 1969, we were very proud that those queens had the courage of their convictions and glad to witness the beginning of a gay rights movement, but we were somehow removed from the events.

Within weeks the enormous physical attraction I felt for him turned to love, my first experience of it in years, and I was certain that it was mutual. Perhaps it had been there from the beginning, but I was just closed to experiencing it. The strange way we had come together often made me smile. For a romantic like me, it seemed pitifully unromantic. I was reminded of the lyric, "Love is lovelier the second time around. Just as wonderful with both feet on the ground." And, indeed, it was. It renewed a conviction I had held from my first relationship, but had lost. The physical aspect of sex can be wonderful in itself, but it is nothing compared to the transcendent phenomenon it engenders when coupled with love.

During the summer, Todd got a call from his mother, Ellie, saying that she would be visiting New York with a younger man, named John. She wanted us to have dinner together. She was a very attractive woman at age forty-nine, and I thought she seemed very nice, but I was somewhat befuddled by the arrangement. I could not even begin to picture Mary Giovingo in such an intrigue. Ellie had been happily married, or so we thought, to Todd's father, Ralph, for nearly thirty years, but something must have gone wrong. While she was in the city, Todd's father called, "Is your mother in New York?"

"Yes."

"And is she alone?"

"Well, uh…not exactly…no."

His father began to cry on the phone. I felt dreadful about the whole situation, but Todd seemed to take it as a matter of course. It appeared that Ellie had felt neglected, Ralph having been away on business so much, so she was assuaging herself with attentions from a man at least fifteen years younger. The affair ended abruptly when Ellie discovered, to her astonishment, a stash of gay porn in John's apartment. Ah, life in the burbs.

One afternoon, Todd and I ran into Jess Richards on the street. I could tell that he was distraught to see that I was with someone else. A week later I received an envelope from him.

He had notated the piece he had heard me compose when I was living at Milton's, and he set it to lyrics he wrote, titled "Are You Singing?" The opening lyric read, "I wrote a song for you. Are you singing?"

Todd found work in publishing. He was hired as an editor at Harcourt on a trade magazine called *Flooring*. As the summer came to an end we had to find our own place. There was no question as to whether we would remain together. Todd and I were both unsophisticated and utter dolts when it came to New York real estate. We found a lovely newly renovated one-bedroom apartment, with a brick wall, a fireplace and a skylight in a brownstone on West 83rd Street, steps from Central Park. The location was perfect, but the apartment was a fifth-floor walkup at $362 per month, a steep rent in those days. If we had been the least bit knowledgeable, we would have found ourselves a fully rent-controlled apartment, which still existed in 1969 for apartments built before 1947. Because our building had been gutted and totally renovated, it did not qualify.

Don Lawrence, the dance captain from *Dolly*, said, "The two of you make the most delightful couple I've seen," and he gave us an old Louis Quinze table that needed refinishing for our new apartment. The place had a small, but brand-new kitchen, so we began to cook in earnest. We had been watching Julia Child's "French Chef" series and decided to buy the two-volume *Mastering the Art of French Cooking*. And we did master it. Between the two of us we made every recipe that interested us. We were so impressed that by learning her basics such as, how to deglaze a pan, how to make stocks, how to degrease, concentrate, and enrich a sauce, how to beat and properly fold egg whites, we could apply these techniques to every recipe we knew, bringing them up to a higher level.

Two doors down from us a series of brownstones had been renovated into cooperative apartments, which were on view in an open house. We stood in line for nearly half an hour, just out of curiosity. We had no intention of buying. The couple ahead of us was admitted, but when it came our turn the attendant said, "I'm sorry were closing the open house for the day." "But you just let in that couple." "I'm sorry, sir, we are closed." We left the line only to watch those behind us admitted. It was the first time I had ever experienced blatant antigay discrimination, and it rankled deeply.

Auditioning was not going well. Vernon was slated to choreograph a new Jule Styne musical, *Look to the Lilies*. Naturally, Vernon kept me throughout the audition, after which I was asked to sing for Jule Styne, the composer of *Bells Are Ringing, Gypsy* and *Funny Girl*. I sang my usual song, "If I Gave You." Styne let me sing the whole piece, which often doesn't happen, then said, "That was just lovely, but that's not how I want to hear you sing it." He then yelled out to the pianist, who happened to be Paulette Haupt, one of the three pianists in *Celebration*. "Paulette take the piece up a third. This kid's got a good voice and I want to hear it again." I suddenly got a bit nervous because I wasn't sure I could hit the top notes with it being so much higher, but I did. "Now that's exactly how you should sing that song in the future."

Coming from the great master, this was the compliment I most treasured throughout my dance career. The finals were to be held in a couple weeks, and I was quite certain I would be hired. Unfortunately, during those two weeks, Vernon was replaced as choreographer by Joyce Trisler, who had her own dance company. Not surprisingly, she hired her own people and I was eliminated. The show turned out to be a flop.

Betsy Haug told me there was soon to be a replacement audition for *Promises, Promises,* and she wanted me in the show. Frank was already in another show and wasn't in class at the time. To give me an edge, she taught me the audition step from "Turkey Lurkey," a truly stupid song that resulted in a triumphant and exciting dance number. I learned it thoroughly. Frank showed up at the audition because his show, *Jimmy,* was closing. Betsy gave the audition, but Michael Bennett was sitting in the house at the Shubert. I knew that I was dancing better than I ever had. Several old gypsies came up to me and said, "Why are we even here because it's obvious you're going to get the job?"

We performed the number in groups of three, with Frank on my right. Again, I noticed Michael was not watching me, but rather Frank, who was struggling with the steps. He then came up on the stage and began working personally with Frank. Does he have a thing for blonds? Was this going to be a dispiriting replay of my *West Side Story* audition for Michael? Yes, indeed, it was.

I was eliminated immediately. The next day Betsy asked, "Do you want to know what Michael said about you?" "Yes." "He said that you are just so ordinary looking." Wow! This set me back more than a few steps. I went home and began examining my face in the mirror, convinced I had to be the dullest looking dancer on Broadway.

Offers came but they were always for long out-of-town runs. I knew I would have to be away from Todd for several weeks, even with a Broadway tryout, but months were another matter. The Harold Prince office called and offered me a chorus job in the national company of *Fiddler on the Roof,* as well as the understudy to the role of Perchik, who sings the beautiful song "Now I Have Everything." It meant being away at least six months. I turned it down. I'll wait for a New York job.

Many auditions came and went, but no New York jobs. My self-confidence began to sink precipitously, and when that went my dancing declined with it. Betsy came to me with an offer. She had been hired to restage Michael's choreography for the Rome company of *Promises, Promises,* which was expected to run a year. She asked if I wanted to be her assistant, then remain in Rome as dance captain. Unfortunately, the pay was so minimal I would just barely earn enough to exist in Italy. I thought about it seriously but realized how much it would jeopardize our still fledgling relationship.

Todd said, "Take the job if you want it. We'll find a way to work things out." With the low salary, I wouldn't have enough income to continue to pay my share of the rent on the New York apartment, and I knew he couldn't afford it on his own. Once again, I was confronted with that terrible choice: love or career. Once again, I chose love. Years later, I learned that Betsy also restaged the London company, the Tokyo company, and others. I probably would have assisted her on each of these productions, as well, which then would have qualified me to restage summer-stock companies of the show myself. Despite wondering about all the might-have-beens, I have never once regretted the choice I made in this case.

My parents, who had met Todd only briefly during the opening of *Celebration*, visited us and to my delight they loved him, though the five flights nearly killed them. I no longer needed to worry that they would despise any man in my life. In fact, they loved Todd, in a way they could never extend to my brother's wife or future girlfriends.

In 1970, Todd's father died unexpectedly of a heart attack at age fifty-seven. Todd's mother took it very badly, but some months later we convinced her to come visit us. We took her to see *Company*. Though I had always admired Stephen Sondheim, I came to realize that the musical theater now had found a new genius. Ellie was particularly taken with Donna McKechnie's performance. Frank Newell, who was dancing in *Promises, Promises,* had much to my surprise begun an affair with Donna. To my knowledge, Frank had never been interested in women before. The five of us had dinner at Joe Allen's. Donna appeared in a theatrically glamorous black cape, and Ellie was so impressed with her hair that she wanted to know who her stylist was. Donna gave her the name of the man at Henri Bendel's, and Ellie made an appointment with him the next. day.

Years later I was very surprised that Donna made no mention of Frank in her autobiography. Though their relationship lasted only a short while before Frank found a boyfriend and Donna married Michael Bennett, they remained close friends. When Frank moved to California and became an interior designer, he told me that he and Donna shared a house at Laguna Beach.

My unemployment checks had run out, and I was living on my savings and becoming more and more despondent. I needed to take some time and reassess my career choices. I stopped taking classes altogether. I even called Cheryl Crawford to ask her if she had any ideas about how I might begin to work for a producer. She had no suggestions, but it's possible she suspected me of being another conniving Richard Chandler, though Todd told me she spoke very highly of me in the show. At the time she was pressing charges against Chandler, who received only probation for his extortion, with the stipulation that most of whatever he might earn in the future be returned to Cheryl.

I hit upon an idea. I had heard that every German city maintained an opera and a ballet company and that any competent dancer could find work there. Also, I learned that Germany was looking for people who could teach American musical theater dance. I thought between the two skills I would have no problem finding work. Todd, who is of German and English extraction, was bored with his position at Harcourt and was eager to see Europe and discover what work he might be able to do there. Why we didn't think of this solution when I was offered the dance captain position in Rome remains a mystery to both of us.

To put this plan into effect, I needed to get a job so I would have money to go back to ballet classes and to build a decent savings reserve in case I didn't find work in Europe immediately. While I began searching for work, I woke up one morning with a strange pain in my back and running down my right leg. In a few days, it got much worse, and I began limping. Someone recommended a top orthopedic surgeon, who had treated many well-known dancers. He told me I needed to rest in bed for several days. The bed rest seemed to make it worse, and I was now experiencing serious pain.

I was sent to the hospital, diagnosed with a ruptured lumbar disk, and placed in traction for two weeks. A canvas belt was fastened around my waist. Attached to the belt were straps with bags of weights on the ends, which were hung over the foot of the bed. For about two hours I had the first relief from pain in several weekss. After those hours, the pain returned with a force so virulent that I could hardly bear it. Pain killers and hot packs applied to my back were administered every hour to get me through this two-week period of medieval torture. "That's fine," I thought to myself, "I'll endure anything if it gets rid of this."

At the end of the two weeks, I was placed on my back on a canvas strap that ran vertically along my body. While balanced on this six-inch-wide strap, they wrapped me in plaster-soaked gauze from my chest to the bottom of my hips. Before the plaster dried, the canvas strip was pulled out. Once the cast dried, an electric circular-blade saw was run down the front of my body to open the cast and make it removable. I was so tense during this process, in utter terror that the saw would cut through my abdomen and pubis, that I had to be given sedatives to stop the debilitating cramps I developed. The cast was then lined with a soft felt-like material and fitted with Velcro® straps that held it shut. I was ordered to wear this one-plus-inch-thick cast for nearly a year, whenever I was out of bed. I could sleep and shower without it.

Playing the role of the model patient, I did exactly as I was told. I had to buy pants and shirts that were much larger to fit over this contraption, all of which gave me the most bizarre tank-like body shape. I loved watching people's faces as they examined me on the subway, wondering, "Is this guy really built like that?"

Every two weeks I visited the surgeon and explained that I saw no improvement, in fact, I was much worse. "Will I ever be able to dance, again, doctor?"

"We'll see. Just keep wearing the cast and come back in two weeks."

"But I haven't done any exercise at all in nearly three months, and my legs and feet are beginning to cramp up on me. Can't I at least do a few *relevés* (rising up on the toes)?"

"No, I don't want you doing anything at all, No exercises of any kind." he ordered adamantly. Doctor knows best. I followed his advice to precision.

During this terrible period, I had to find work. In desperation I went back to my office temp agency and was assigned to an organization called The National Commission on Resources for Youth, headed by a former family court judge, Mary Conway Kohler. Am I really to be relegated to a typing job again after my career in movies and Broadway? Not for long. Within a few weeks, Lorraine Kavanagh, who was second in command at this office, saw potential in me. Despite my lack of a college degree, she created a position for me under the rubric education researcher and provided me with a private office.

The Commission ran a wonderful program called Youth Tutoring Youth, in which high-school underachievers were trained to tutor grade-school underachievers in reading and math. The results showed that both the younger and older students benefitted enormously, but particularly the older ones, and the program is still available today. My job was to study, assess, and write critical reports on other youth enhancement programs throughout the country.

Lorraine became very close friends with Todd and me. She knew of our desire to go to Europe and encouraged us. Every day the pain I experienced made it more obvious that I would never be able to dance again. I didn't dislike my work, but both Todd and I were confined, restricted, and mind-deadened in any sort of office job. We both could excel in these settings, but we were not cut out for such a life. Lorraine had taught at the American School in Lugano, Switzerland, and her loving description of the place made it sound like one of the most beautiful locales on earth.

She felt certain that we could find some way to make a living there. This became our new goal, as soon as I could save up enough money.

One starkly faces the extent to which someone loves you during the bad times. When I didn't get hired for dance jobs that I really wanted, Todd took the news as hard, and often harder, than I did, sometimes being reduced to tears. And when the back problems began, I marveled at the million and one ways that he found to comfort me or to make things easier for me. Though I had no doubts about his love before, these acts of kindness and caring were proof that this was the real thing.

My disheartening visits to the surgeon continued with no sense of relief. He suggested disk-removal surgery and vertebral fusion as the only possible remedy for my condition. Two nurses lived above us, and when they learned I was considering surgery, one said, "Before you decide to do this, we suggest you read this book." They handed me the text book on lumbar surgery, and I was horrified by the time I finished reading it.

The first thing I learned was that the whole rationale for putting a patient in traction was a systemic fraud. "You tell the patient that the traction is to stretch the spine to relieve the pressure on the disk. In fact, the only goal is to keep the patient fully immobilized." Then I discovered how much medical science purported to know and how little, in fact, it actually knew about lumbar pain. The final blow came upon learning that the surgery posed a fifty percent risk of paralysis. When I told the surgeon I had read the textbook, he angrily asked, "Where did you get that book?" "Some nurses I know gave it to me." "Well, you shouldn't be reading such things. They're not meant for patients. Just come back in two weeks." I never went back.

In *Time* magazine I read an article about James Reston's having an appendectomy in China without anesthesia, but rather under acupuncture. In the same article, there was mention of an acupuncturist in London who had success treating back pain. I wrote to him and asked whether he could help me. Acupuncture, though probably practiced in back rooms in Chinatown, was essentially illegal in New York at the time. He said I should come to London, and he would see me. He estimated that treatments would take about three weeks. We planned our Europe trip around that.

The Grand Tour and the Momentous Decision

ON THE EVENING OF OCTOBER 11, 1971, Todd and I, trembling with excitement and anticipation, boarded the Icelandic jet for Europe. The flight, after a layover in Reykjavik, landed in Luxembourg, where we spent our first evening. The weather was the typical cold, damp, and fog of the northern European autumn. I suffered an initial stab of disappointment as the bus took us from the airport to the city. The very first sight I saw was an Esso gas station. I wasn't sure why this threw me, but I expected quaint and got trashy modern American instead. That was my last serious disappointment of the tour. Our first dinner of blanquette de veau, and buying delectable pastries the next morning reassured me. We purchased train tickets to Ostend, Belgium. We didn't want to begin using the Eurail Pass until we left England so we wouldn't waste three valuable weeks on it. From Ostend, we took the ferry across the English Channel, gasping in wide-mouthed wonder as the majestic beauty of the white cliffs of Dover came into view.

We arrived at London's Victoria Station about nine PM and were immediately accosted by a man who called himself Frank Haggis, saying he was from the British Tourist Authority, the office of which had already closed for the night. "How long is your stay in London?" "Three weeks." He grabbed two of our bags and began leading us to a bed and breakfast, called the Allison House on Ebury Street. He quoted us a very reasonable rate for our stay. Being typical New Yorkers, we were very suspicious of him and kept a close eye on our bags.

The Allison House was only a few blocks from the station, but when we reached Ebury Street, the beauty of it simply took my breath away. Most of the townhouses were enameled a glossy white, and in the faint mist of that London night they glistened like a spectacular set out of *My*

Fair Lady. Allison House was a brick structure but was just as lovely. Only a couple doors away at 180 Ebury Street was the house the eight-year-old Mozart lived in while in London, where he composed some of his earliest symphonies. We could also see Rex Harrison's garden from our room. Frank and his wife turned out to be the most gracious and charming hosts imaginable. We kept in touch with them for years until they retired to Spain. I was a bit thrown when Frank said, "I'll knock you up at eight in the morning for breakfast, gentlemen." Either he was as ignorant of the meaning of that phrase as I was in Dr. P's office, or it had a completely different connotation in England.

Breakfast, which of course I never really enjoyed anyway, was not exactly my cup of tea. There were fried eggs, which were swimming in the liquid from stewed tomatoes, and a sort of bacon that I couldn't equate with having come from a pig. It was served in broad slabs that seemed to be covered in warts. I believe the British refer to it as Irish bacon. We began offering excuses for why we couldn't get up for breakfast, trying desperately not to offend our hosts. With my penchant for British accents, though not British breakfasts, it didn't take long before I started sounding like a Brit.

We headed for the acupuncturist's office in Harley Street, and this turned out to be a startling revelation. The first thing he asked me to do was remove the plaster cast. "Now bend over." I bent forward about an inch or two.

"No, no, bend over."

"For me, this is bend over." That was as far as I could go.

"Let me look at your back." He began carefully examining the muscles of my spine. "We're throwing away this cast immediately."

"But why?"

"Why? Because the muscles in your back have atrophied to such a degree that I can guarantee if you wear it another few months, you will be a cripple for the rest of your life."

He began treating me with the needles on my back and down the sciatic nerve on my right leg. Always having been a bit squeamish about needles, I happily found it relatively painless. Todd also received a treatment for his digestive problems, but whether it was watching the needles inserted in me or when one was stuck between his eyebrows, he nearly passed out on the table. So much for my big butch boyfriend.

Before the treatment was complete, the doctor said. "I want you to begin exercising several times a week. Start with swimming," and he recommended a public pool we could visit. "But my orthopedist forbid me from doing any kind of exercise." "And that was the worst possible advice he could have given you. Start going to the pool and come back three times a week for the next three weeks." At the time, I had no idea that serious improvement in my condition would take several years. Acupuncture is an extremely helpful treatment, not a miracle cure. I needed to participate more fully in my own recuperation, not just leave it up to doctors.

That night we went to the theater, and the excruciating proof of what he told me made itself evident. I was unable to hold myself erect in the chair without placing my hands on the armrests and propping myself up. Because the muscles were so weakened, I experienced the most severe pain. The theater, which we luxuriated in while in London helped me take my mind off my pains. We were fortunate enough to see so many of the greats, including Ralph Richardson, John Gielgud, Alec Guinness, and Glenda Jackson, and at prices so far below Broadway's. We were both struck by the high quality of the actors even in minor roles.

We returned to the Continent, using our Eurail pass for the first time, as we went from Brussels to Amsterdam. Though we adored the city and especially staying in a lovely canal house, what most affected me was the music. We attended concerts at the Royal Concertgebouw in both the main hall and the smaller chamber-music salons. A concert of Brahms chamber music, and especially the Piano Quartet in C Minor and the Piano Quintet in F Minor, had a visceral and lasting impact on me. I first became aware of just how attracted I was to Brahms at a performance of Elliot Feld Ballet's *Intermezzo*, choreographed to his piano pieces, before we left New York. In vain, I longed to be a good enough pianist to play these works.

My fanaticism for trains accelerated with the European railroads. We both loved the idea of the separate compartment and the old-world romanticism it conjured up for us. Often, we made long train trips overnight because off-season we could frequently have the whole compartment to ourselves, allowing us to stretch out on the opposing seats, thus saving the cost of a hotel room. From Amsterdam we traveled to Copenhagen and then to Berlin. The compartment was crowded and sitting across from us was an attractive young blond boy, flamboyantly dressed, who we assumed was gay.

We reached the East German border in the middle of the night, where very threatening and gruff guards entered our compartment, ordering each of us in turn to open our luggage for inspection. They carefully went through everything we had. The guard who inspected my bag spotted a copy of Thomas Mann's *Buddenbrooks*. He picked it up with a look of disgust, and I thought he was about to confiscate it when he flung it aside as if it were some subversive capitalist propaganda tract.

As they came to the blond boy, he balked at opening his bag because it was elaborately tied shut with ropes. The guard was incensed and began yelling at him that the inspection was mandatory and that he must comply. Another man in the compartment translated the German for us so that we knew what was happening. The guard took out a pocket knife and began cutting the many ropes. When he opened the bag, he discovered a cache of elaborate and highly decorated knives of various sizes and shapes. The other five of us were ordered out of the compartment into the corridor. We were able to observe what was happening but couldn't really hear what was being said. It appeared at first that the boy might be taken off the train, but the knives were replaced in the case and he was allowed to bind it up again with the ropes.

We were permitted back into the compartment, thinking the matter settled when the guard discovered that the pocket knife he used to cut the ropes was missing. He seemed to be implying that the boy had stolen the knife, so he ordered him to untie the ropes and reopen the bag. Sure enough, the knife was found in the bag, though we suspected that the guard had inadvertently left it there, not that the boy had stolen it. After another thorough examination of his papers and much discussion, he was allowed to retie the bag, and we were permitted to proceed on our journey, much to our relief.

In Berlin we found an old pensione on Güntzelstrasse, and quite a spooky establishment it was. As we entered, about fifteen old people were seated in a salon that looked as though it had not been redecorated since the turn of the century. The musty septuagenarians, who were permanent residents not tourists, glared at us as we passed through, completely disconcerted that we had the audacity to interrupt their afternoon newspaper reading. Our bedroom was enormous and over the bed hung a monstrously large and terrifying painting of a saber-toothed tiger. Quite the artwork to ensure a night of peaceful rest. The place reeked of Fräulein Schneider's establishment in Christopher Ishwerwood's *Berlin Stories,* except that it housed dour senior citizen's, not fascinating young ex-pats.

In the misty and foggy evening, we walked toward the Kurfuerstendamm, the main shopping street, when we were pulled up short by an eerie blue light straight ahead of us. The light emanated from the site of the Kaiser Wilhelm Memorial Church, of which only the shell of a tower remains after the devastating bombing by the British in 1943. Termed "the hollow tooth," the structure was preserved in its bombed-out state as a stark warning against the atrocities of war. A modern hexagonal church tower of concrete, steel, and glass, with honeycomb walls containing thousands of stained-glass inlays, was constructed adjacent to the old church.

In the dense fog, the refracted blue light from the new structure was diffused and bathed the whole site, giving it its other-worldly appearance.

Two days later at the sinister-looking Checkpoint Charlie, where we were forced to change a specific amount into East German Marks that must either be spent or relinquished, we crossed the wall into East Berlin. The shocking change from West to East was jolting, from the garish commercialism of West Berlin to the rubble of East Berlin, as though the war had just ended yesterday. The clichéd old adage "moving from technicolor to black-and-white" seemed utterly appropriate. The drabness of the eastern sector was belied, only by the red banners that draped all the government buildings, declaring something to the effect of "25 Years of Communism; 25 Years of Prosperity." Nowhere was such prosperity visible.

We were unable to find a thing in the dreary understocked stores that we would have been interested in buying. Eventually, we had a dreadful lunch in the opera-house cafe, where even the beer was remarkably insipid. How do Germans manage to brew bad beer? When our waitress learned that we were from New York, she pumped us for information on what it was like to live in a free and exciting city, and the comparison with her own bleak life elicited regret that was palpably evident in her face. The opera company was doing a production of *Porgy and Bess* that evening, which neither of us had seen, but our train departed before the performance would have ended. As we left East Berlin, we had to relinquish most of the money we had exchanged at the border.

Though our journey through Germany and Austria was delightful, we encountered such frightful blizzards in Vienna, which made sightseeing so impossible that we decided to head for more hospitable climates. In late November, Lugano was warm and subtropical, anomalously displaying itself with both palm trees and snow-capped mountains. It was as lovely as Lorraine Kavanaugh had described it to us. Boat trips on the lake to the small old-world towns of Gandria and Morcote were charming. We were in the land of Hermann Hesse, whom we were both avidly reading at the time. We made a half-hearted attempt to inquire about working in the city, but neither of us was ready to give up our freedom and our wanderlust just yet.

We were delighted with Venice, Rome and Florence, but our arrival in Sorrento revealed a town abandoned. Late December is not the season for this gateway to the Amalfi Coast. Many hotels were shuttered, but we found one, The Carlton, a first-class hotel, generally beyond our means, which was open and offered affordable off-season rates. The desk clerk asked us if we wanted full pensione. As usual, we refused this option because we wanted to be able to try various restaurants in a town, not be limited to the same hotel food. A search for a place to have lunch told us in no uncertain terms that we had made a mistake. Nothing was open. We returned to the Carlton and changed our minds.

By this time it was after three in the afternoon, and we assumed we had missed *pranzo*. But no. We were ushered into the dining room, which was the size of a large ballroom. "Would you care for some pasta, *signori*?" No menu was offered and we were the only diners so we said, "Yes." After the pasta, the waiter asked, "Would you care for some *arance*?" "Well, yes." We watched as the waiter went into the garden and picked two ripe oranges from the tree. "I guess because we came in so late we're the only ones having lunch," I said to Todd.

About seven, the telephone rang in our room. "Would you care to have dinner now, *signori*?" This seemed strangely early, but okay, we quickly dressed to go down. When the elevator reached the main floor, the doors opened onto total darkness. Someone at the desk heard the elevator doors open and immediately switched on all the lobby lights. We entered the enormous and eerily empty dining room. "We must be the first down for dinner," I whispered. "Would you care for some *zuppa di verdure* and some *pesce*?" "Si, si." It was clear that this is what they had cooked for the day, thus no menus. The exquisite soup arrived. We finished it. Still no other diners. "Todd, do you realize we are the only two guests in this grand hotel?" The staff outnumbered the guests ten to one. What fascinated us about this episode was the incredibly nonchalant and elegantly sophisticated manner that the staff handled the situation. No one would have been so gauche as to mention that there was anything untoward about having only two guests in a one-hundred-room hotel. In fact, it was not to be mentioned, or even hinted at, in the least.

Palermo, the city of my grandparents. We were a bit at sea here because our Frommer's *Europe on $5 a Day* (ah, the nostalgia of those prices) hardly mentioned the city, and we had not been diligent enough to do our research. As we walked about—and especially in the area of the beautiful opera house, Teatro Massimo, and symphony hall, Teatro Politeama—all I could say was, "My grandparents left this magnificent place to move to Rockford, Illinois?"

In one street, we noted a large and very official looking 19th-century building. Chiseled in stone along the top of the building was the name Cangelosi. Was there a renowned branch of my family I didn't know about? We spent only two days in Palermo, and because we had failed to do our research, we missed nearly all of the important sights. Not until nearly forty years later would we return and discover just how special the city is. We never again were able to locate the Cangelosi building on our return trips. Despite our brief stay, what struck me most was, "How could I possibly have been made to feel inferior in high school for my family's coming from such an incredibly rich and beautiful heritage?"

Christmas was spent in Taormina. Goethe was right. This is surely one of the most beautiful places on earth. Sitting and eating our lunch in the ancient Greek theater, looking straight out past the open stage at the Mediterranean and slightly to the right watching Mt. Etna sending up plumes of smoke is indescribable splendor. Anyone not moved by this panorama is undoubtedly a non-sentient being. When 19th-century Prussian Otto Geleng exhibited his paintings of Taormina in Berlin and Paris, critics accused him of having an overworked imagination, exaggerating its beauty beyond the confines of reality. Geleng offered a challenge: He would pay his critics' expenses to Taormina if they could prove that his paintings were figments of his imagination. Geleng won the bet. He paid not a cent.

We were startled that in front of the many souvenir shops were old photographs of naked young boys on postcards. What was this all about? They were turn-of-the-century photographs by the German Baron Wilhelm von Gloeden, a painter who came to Sicily for his health. Von Gloeden's work was exhibited in all the major capitals to high acclaim. The photos were considered art and never pornography. In fact, Oscar Wilde helped von Gloeden arrange the settings and head ornaments for many of the shots, with their an ancient Greek motifs. After the photographer's death in 1931, Mussolini destroyed as many as 1,000 of the negatives and arrested Pancrazio Bucini, van Gloeden's model, assistant, and lover, for creating and distributing pornography. Mussolini was overrruled by the courts. Interestingly, when we returned to Taormina many years later, the postcards were no longer to be seen outside the shops. One had to go inside to a secluded corner to find them. Apparently, the huge increase in tourists, many of which found the postcards offensive, relegated them to the back of the shops.

On Christmas eve, Taorminans gather in the main town piazzas, where twenty-feet-high bonfires are set ablaze to commemorate the warming of Jesus in the stable. One group began singing, children were dancing, some just watching in celebration. Todd unfortunately was laid up in bed with a cold and missed this charming festivity. During the holiday, we felt the encroaching pressure to face reality and try to find employment. Following New Years in Geneva, we decided that perhaps Paris would be the best place for some inscrutable reason.

The tiny Hôtel de Vieux Paris at 9 Git-Le-Coeur, on the Left Bank, a half block from the Seine and about two blocks from Notre Dame was perfect for our extended stay. The four-franc-a day room (about $1 a day) with private bath was a good buy even in 1972. Only years later, did we learn that in the late 1950s and in a more ramshackle state, it had been a favorite of Allen Ginsberg, William S. Burroughs, and Gregory Corso, who nicknamed it the Beat Hotel. Today it is an expensive, four-star boutique "relais." The only disadvantage was that the late-night desk clerk had offensively smelly feet that nearly knocked you on your ass as you entered. It seemed entirely fitting that the most momentous decisions about the rest of our lives were made in this hotel given notoriety by artists.

We immediately enrolled in a French conversation course at the Alliance Française. Because I hadn't studied French in thirteen years and because I wanted to be with Todd, I enrolled in the beginner class with him. I had never taken a course where only the language studied is spoken. This not only forced one to learn more quickly, but also was essential because the students, who came from all over the world, spoke different languages.

There was Mademoiselle Couscoun, who never had any idea as to what was going on. When the teacher, whose slovenly attire was completely covered in chalk dust, asked her a question, she would frantically start flipping through all her notes in a desperate attempt to unearth some hidden clue that might spare her embarrassment. She never did. There was the Japanese boy who could not pronounce "g's" or "j's," something that becomes physically impossible if not learned in childhood. Through tightly clenched teeth and with herculean effort, he would issue forth from the back of the throat a "dzheee." Then there was the Spanish woman who brutalized her conjugating of the verb *marcher*. She pronounced the "ch" as in church, rather than as the French do as in shout. As she progressed through the pronouns from "I" through "you" and "she," her voice rose precipitously in pitch, so by the time she arrived at "they" it was a virtual hysterical scream.

I was horrified by how much French I had lost in thirteen years. My pronunciation was perfect. In a restaurant, the couple at the table next to ours mistook me for a Parisian when they heard me ordering and were shocked to find I was an American. My grammar, my vocabulary, and my comprehension, however, were positively abysmal. When I decided to change my Citibank account from Lugano, I went into their branch in Paris, resolved to do the transaction in English to avoid any misunderstandings. As I began to explain, the tall, severe woman rose from her desk and with flashing eyes and in great indignation pointed at me and said, "Monsieur, parlez français s'il vous plaît!" I was shocked at this treatment in an American bank.

One evening on the way to dinner, we heard an enormous roar behind us from a crowd of people running in our direction. To avoid being trampled, Todd and I ducked in between parked cars. The next thing I knew a gendarme grabbed me roughly by the arm, with his baton about to strike me over the head. "Je suis un touriste," I yelled, sparing myself the blow. We were caught up in one of the famed student riots of the era.

Our free time was spent in museums, concerts, the ballet, and the opera. Everything was so cheap it barely made a dent in our savings, which suddenly and happily increased when I received an unexpected check for $1,800 from my health insurance in compensation for my two weeks of traction torture at the Hospital for Special Surgery.

Foolishly, I did not continue my swimming and exercise regimen, as I had been instructed by the London acupuncturist. I wasn't suffering, but I had many bad and painful days. I had yet to learn to take responsibility for managing my back problem, and I would pay for this negligence later. Todd was very sensitive in recognizing when I was in pain, without my mentioning it, and he generously did the lifting and carrying for me at those times. Bending was still problematic, so if I dropped something he invariably rushed to pick it up for me.

In the sixth week of our stay, it was reality-check time. We had to figure out what we wanted to do with the rest of our lives. We sat in our four-franc-a-day room at the Beat Hotel and made our momentous decisions in a matter of minutes. Todd said, "Sitting in the *Water Lilies* room of the Musée Marmottan Monet, I knew what I want to do, be a painter. I'd like to go back to school and study art." That museum, dedicated primarily to the works of Claude Monet, had a circular room lined with his *Water Lilies* and *Wisteria* paintings. "Sitting on that round divan. looking at those beautiful paintings was as peaceful as sitting in a garden."

"And I've been considering two ideas. One, that I would enroll at Le Cordon Bleu cooking school and become a chef. I love to cook, but then I thought about cooking ten to twelve hours a day, and I don't think I could do that. The second idea I like better. The more we attend concerts, the more I love classical music, and I miss the piano so. I'd like to study music seriously. I think I might become a good enough pianist— certainly not to perform—but to teach little children."

How those few minutes of thought would change our lives we could not have imagined. So what was the plan? Because neither of us had any real mastery of the French language, Paris did not seem to be a good choice. "What about Amsterdam? Almost everyone speaks English," Todd suggested. Amsterdam it was. On our return, I was laid up in bed with a sore throat, but Todd went directly into action. He made an appointment at the Rijksakademie, Holland's great art school, to inquire about enrolling. "They'll accept me as a student, but unfortunately, the classes are taught in Dutch, even though the professors all speak English," he reported, disappointingly. Amsterdam was a worse idea than Paris.

We came to another decision, one which we've questioned throughout the rest of our lives. We loved Europe and wanted to live there, but it seemed more efficacious to return the United States for our reeducation. We could always return to Europe to live once we completed our studies. Ha! Because we hadn't visited several countries on our itinerary yet, we decided to give ourselves two more months of touring. But we were inhibited. Our Eurail Pass had expired. Owing to Todd's ingenuity, it became a nonissue. He wasn't about to let it stand in our way.

I was still sick in bed when he announced a solution. He found an office-supply store just down the street from our canal house, and he purchased a date-adjustable stamp, an ink pad, a lettering pen, and ink eradicator. Very meticulously he removed the previous start and expiration dates. Miraculously, the eradicator did not blur or remove the printed patterns on the cards. Then he stamped new dates on the cards and *voilà*, a forgery became his first work of art. This was the only time I ever knew him to skirt the law.

We were off to Spain and Portugal, and when Spanish border guards entered our compartment, I experienced waves of terror in fear that we'd end up in one of Generalissimo Franco's prisons for life. Not to worry. The forgery was so imperceptible that we breezed through without incident. Eventually, we worked our way up to Scandinavia, passing through Munich. The incredible freedom afforded by the Eurail Pass allowed us to disembark the train there simply because we wanted to have a special pastry that we had sampled our first time through Munich. Once we indulged ourselves, we simply boarded a later train without any added expense.

In Oslo, while we were visiting the Viking Ship Museum, Todd began complaining that he did not feel well. By the time we got back to our hotel, there was obviously something very wrong. The hotel arranged for a taxi to take us to a hospital, several miles away. It was about seven o'clock at night, and I was the only person left in the waiting room after they admitted him. For five agonizing hours I sat alone becoming more and more agitated, wondering what on earth could be wrong. There was no attendant around to ask. About midnight, a nurse came into the waiting room and said, "Are you the friend of the American?"

"Yes."

"I am so, so sorry," she said with the most somber look on her face.

My, god, he died. What'll I do? What do I do with the body. She must have seen the blood drain from my face.

"I am afraid your friend had an emergency appendectomy, but he's doing fine."

Never had I ever experienced such a sense of relief. The Norwegians did an excellent job. Todd remained in the hospital for a day and half. Under Norway's socialized medicine program, the surgery and the hospital stay were fully covered. They did present him with a bill for $110 to cover the food and the medications, only because we were foreign nationals. When he offered to pay the bill, he was told, "No, we will send the bill to the American Embassy, and they will get in touch with you to arrange for your insurance to pay it." We never heard a word from our embassy. Even in 1972, it was an obvious indictment of the American health-care system. Such fine treatment would never be offered to a foreign visitor in the United States. We spent another day in Oslo, eating fresh-caught shrimp from a boat at the wharf. The next day Todd felt well enough to resume our travels.

Easter arrived and before returning home, we decided to pay one last visit to Lugano, our original intended place to settle. After visiting thirteen countries, we left Europe and flew home with very heavy hearts. Those seven months, which cost us only $6,000, were among the most memorable of our lives. I came up with the preposterous notion that we should not pursue our studies in New York because of the high cost of living. We settled, quite without foundation, on Phoenix because we believed it would be cheap and there were decent universities. Upon landing in New York, Todd went home to visit his mother in Pennsylvania, and I left for Rockford. The plan was that he would join me in Rockford a week later and we would travel to Phoenix by bus.

At home, my brother Larry had departed with his cocktail waitress wife for Lake Tahoe, where they were hired at Harrah's Casino. It marked the beginning of a startling transformation and long decline for him. As an excellent bartender, he made a very good living, but he was unable to resist the lure of the gambling tables. He explained to the family how the casino helped grease his slide into addiction. "They made sure that any competition—dancing, entertainment, sports—was shut down. There was no place else to go to have a good time. When the staff got off work, everyone was so wound up that no one was ready to just go home. The casino gave free drinks so we would stay after work. It was easy to take the big tips and try our luck at the gambling tables." Mary Giovingo offered one of her pithy metaphors, "Just because your friends go jump in the river, you have to do it, too?" It didn't take long before he was hooked. I couldn't resist asking, "Why, coming from a family that's never had any luck, do you think you can beat the odds?"

Most surprisingly, the incredibly tightfisted little boy, who refused to spend a dime on a Coke, turned into the big-spending show off. Years later when I visited him in Napa, we went to a restaurant and had a drink at the bar before going to our table. The bar was packed and Larry ostentatiously announced, "Drinks for everyone." I was stunned and distressed when I realized he was buying drinks for more than forty people. Was he trying to impress me? Matters got worse a year after he arrived in Tahoe. His young wife, who had threatened suicide if he ditched her, left him for another man. This led to a series of women, many of whom had their own psychological and addiction issues. He never remarried, adding to Mary Giovingo's woes—she would never have grandchildren.

When Todd arrived in Rockford, he got to meet both of my grandmothers, and both seemed to take to him very warmly. Though our relationship was never discussed openly in the family, it was wonderful to see how accepting of it everyone was. I so admired my strict Roman Catholic parents, who in 1962, (ten years before the famous poster, "Parents of Gays Unite in Support for our Children" appeared at a New York City Pride Parade) gave me their loving support. They did insist on keeping it quiet, however. Once Mary Giovingo's mother, referring to Todd said, "I don't know if it's his husband or his wife." My mother went over the edge, "Don't you ever say anything like that again." "I didn't mean anything by it," her mother cowered, as she often did as the victim of her daughter's sharp tongue.

Off we went by Greyhound to Phoenix. I thought it would be a bit of reliving my bus-and-truck days with Dorothy Lamour and *Dolly*. It wasn't. We both experienced profound culture shock, after seven months in Europe. Well, it was the '70s for god's sake, and America wasn't looking so great. The food was abysmal. Center cities had deteriorated precipitously in the ten years since I had been out West. American culture seemed so crude when compared with what we experienced in Europe. Phoenix was hot, brutally hot, considering it was only April. We had a fascination for the Italian-American architect, Paolo Soleri, a protogée of Frank Lloyd Wright, who under his concept of arcology (the combination of architecture and ecology) was just beginning to build his city in the desert, Arcosanti. We visited his workshop and purchased one of his beautiful bronze wind bells, made to help finance the project.

Other than Arcosanti, the Phoenix area seemed dull, duller, and dullest. I couldn't imagine living there, so I had my second "bright" idea. "Let's go to Denver instead. The weather is much milder. The town is more interesting. The university has an excellent music school, and I'm certain they must have a good art program." Another Greyhound bus, another serious mistake. Denver was no longer the town of my college years. Downtown was dreary and unrecognizable from the vibrant center I had remembered. The public transportation system had seriously deteriorated, which meant we would have to buy a car, something that was anathema to me.

We stayed in the YMCA, and Todd had an encouraging interview with a publishing company. That night I had a panic attack in the Y. "There's no way I could live here now," I frantically announced to Todd. "Let's just go back to New York." Three days and two nights on a Greyhound bus. Further culture shock when we returned to New York: In the seven months we had been away, the subway cars were completely covered in graffiti. How did this happen?

We had no place to stay in the city so I did something I am generally loath to do. I imposed on Lorraine Kavanaugh, who lived in London Terrace Towers, the same building where we had sublet an apartment from Bob Schear. The four corner towers of the complex were under different management than the rest of the building, and the apartments were rented furnished. We tried desperately to be good house guests, making ourselves unobtrusive, staying out of the small apartment as much as possible, helping wherever we could, and presenting her with a beautiful Waterford crystal jam jar as a thank-you gift. Nevertheless, Lorraine, who was a very private person, had had it with us by the end of our week's stay. and our relationship never recovered, something I found very upsetting. Lesson learned. I never made this mistake again. Fortunately, Lorraine put in a good word with London Terrace's management, and we were able to rent a decent-sized furnished studio apartment in one of the towers at the opposite end of the building from hers.

Music, Music, Music

FIRST THINGS FIRST. TIME TO BUY A PIANO. We scoured the used piano stores and in Hell's Kitchen found just the one for us. I sat down at a small non-brand-name grand and began to play. It was only $600, about what I hoped to spend, and seemed to be just about right for me. Across the room was an ebony Steinway Model A, a six-foot-one grand. Todd began to play it, and with its incredibly rich bass, there was clearly no comparison between the two.

"How much is it?" I cautiously asked the salesman.

"It's $1,300.

"Why is it so cheap? Is there something wrong with it?" Though it was out of my range, I knew that this was an unusually good price for one of the finest pianos.

"It's old. It was built in 1896, and with the battered case and those fat fluted legs, no one seems to want it."

Todd and I conferred. It was so superior to the other smaller piano, so he offered to contribute to the cost. The Steinway was ours. This was one of those rare instances when a material purchase gave me more than momentary, in fact enormous, pleasure, every time I looked at it.

Next up, we had to find jobs. Todd was hired by the public relations department at Blue Cross Blue Shield, where he also edited their monthly in-house magazine. Interestingly the founder of the organization had some radical ideas in 1972: first, that no one was worth more than $25,000 a year in salary (including himself); and second, that the government should take over the health-care industry, with Blue Cross handling only the administrative work for the program. Today we are still arguing over this obvious fix to our broken health-care system.

I wanted a job with no commitments beyond nine-to-five because I knew my extra time needed to be spent practicing the piano. I had a lot of catching up to do before I could consider music school. I found such a job as an administrative assistant in the Education Department at The American Museum of Natural History. I met some interesting people there, including Edna Lewis, who later become the head chef at Gage and Tollner's Restaurant in Brooklyn and whose cookbook, *The Taste of Country Cooking,* based on her African-American Southern heritage, became a staple in my kitchen. C. Bruce Hunter, an older scholar and an expert in Meso-American archaelogy, became a very close friend of ours, and I was asked to copyedit his book, *Guide to Ancient Maya Ruins.*

My Korean piano tuner, who was a Juilliard graduate and a sensational pianist, gave me advice that I try to live by, even today. "You must set as your goal to be as good as Vladimir Horowitz, though you will never achieve it. You can't set your goal to be Abby Simon (an acclaimed, but not top-tier pianist) because when you fall short of that you won't be good enough for much of anything." The tuner's four-year-old daughter was less inspiring, however. As she sat on our floor, she pointed down accusingly, "Eww! This carpet is yucky." "What did you just say? Don't ever say things like that again," scolded her father. "If she'd been born in Korea, she'd never dare to be so rude." Unfortunately, she was absolutely correct. The black, white, and gray nap was appalling.

Then it was time to find a piano teacher. I contacted the Juilliard School of Music, which provided me with a list of recommended teachers. I chose one just a block from the museum, because it gave me quick access after work. Her name was Delores Modrell, and a steely woman she was. I had studied the audition requirements for the conservatories, which included a Bach Prelude and Fugue, a Beethoven Sonata, a Romantic-era piece, and a piano concerto. With my ambitions far beyond my capabilities, I spent a week or two prior to my going to Delores working on the Brahms Intermezzo in B-flat Minor and the Schumann Piano Concerto. When I began the Brahms at my first lesson, Delores frowned and said, with more than a hint of disdain in her voice, "I think we'll just put these away for now. Let's try the Schumann *Kinderscenen* (Scenes from Childhood) instead." I, of course, didn't have the nerve to tell her I was considering majoring in music. I simply presented myself as an adult amateur.

I quickly began learning all the scales and arpeggios, which I had neglected as a child. Once she showed me a tricky exercise that I couldn't execute immediately. She screamed, "That is just so stupid that you can't do it. Now just play it, for god's sake!" I couldn't, but I had it down for her by the next lesson. The first time I attempted to play a Bach Fugue, she sharply criticized, "It's obvious that you don't have the slightest clue what a fugue is, much less how to play one." She was absolutely right. Wasn't I paying her to teach me these things?

I spent three hours a night practicing, desperately trying to learn the things I should have learned with Irene Glasford. During my lunch hours, I studied a very basic music theory text, and slowly began to grasp the topic that made me appear to be a dimwit in my younger days. I kept pushing Delores to let me play difficult pieces because starting so late in life, I foolishly felt I had no time to spend on intermediate repertoire. "What do you want play, the Liszt B-Minor Sonata?" she asked snidely. I'd never heard that piece, but I decided if it was considered one of the most difficult pieces in the literature, I would have to play it one day. At the end of nine months, I'd learned the Bach Prelude and Fugue in E-Major, a Scarlatti Sonata, the entire *Kindserscenen*, the Opus 2, No 1, Beethoven Piano Sonata, two Brahms *Intermezzi*, including the one we initially had to "put away," plus his G-Minor Rhapsody. I thought, all in all, it was a major accomplishment, so I got up the nerve to tell her about my aspirations for majoring in music.

"Do you have any idea at all what it takes to be a music major? It's a great deal more, you know, than being able to play a few pieces." Behind those dismissive words was the implication that I was too old even to consider such a thing. I wasn't kidding myself, after all, that I would ever be a performer, but her attitude scared me. Then I thought to myself, "Are you going to allow her to dissuade you from doing this the way you let people talk you out of an acting career? Are you going to let someone tell you that you're too old, as many tried to do when you started dancing?" You're damned right I'm not. I'm forging ahead. Period. I quit on the spot.

Todd at the same time enrolled at the Art Students League, at first studying drawing then moving on to a painting class, both of which were taught by Edward Laning, the highly regarded WPA muralist who had done a piece for the New York Public Library Main Branch. Within a short time Todd was so proficient, he became Laning's monitor, essentially an assistant to the teacher. One of his jobs as a monitor was to set the poses the model would take.

On one occasion, a particularly beautiful male model appeared. He undressed, assumed his pose, and proceeded to get a full erection. Being stared at and scrutinized was apparently a turn-on for him. Todd told everyone to take a break for a few minutes, in the hope of cooling things down and bringing equanimity back to the class. Next pose. Fresh erection. Todd, beside himself, called for a long break. He pulled the model aside, "You know, I think we could fix this if you'd just take a moment, go into the bathroom and jerk off." Hard problem solved.

Todd's easel was set up right next to my piano in our studio apartment. Evenings were spent with him painting away as I was pounding at the keyboard, an arrangement not conducive to concentration for either of us. A truer test of a relationship's durability cannot be envisioned. We continued in this way in these close quarters for three years without killing each other—in fact, without fighting about it.

When my *Nonna* died in her nineties, the three surviving brothers gathered together to discuss the terms of the will. My Uncle Paul, who was not yet severely debilitated by dementia, told my dad, "I'll be giving my share to your two sons. I don't need her money." Dad had for years tried to get Paul to write a will, but the gruff response was always, "Don't worry about me. I know what to do with my money." The will was never written, and when he died a few years later everything in his estate, including that money from *Nonna*, naturally reverted to his wife, Rose.

She remained friendly with my parents even after Paul's death, because she had virtually no friends of her own. How could she possibly with her irascible personality? Determined that Larry and I should inherit Paul's money as he had promised, my parents indulged her in order to achieve their uncharacteristic mercenary scheme. Here was the final twisted irony to the tale. Paul could not stand his wife and despised her family so much he forbade her even from visiting them. When Rose died a few years after him, she left no will, and all of Paul's estate went to Rose's niece, a particularly despicable individual. Paul did horizontal pirouettes in his grave. So much for mercenary schemes.

At the end of a year, I left my job at the museum and enrolled at Queen's College because it had an excellent music department and required no further liberal-arts courses. I could concentrate strictly on music. This was a great idea until I took my first trip out to Queens for a theory-placement exam. It took me over an hour and a half by subway and bus to reach the campus from our Chelsea apartment. Three hours a day traveling? I don't think so, especially when I should be spending that time practicing.

The whole plan needed rethinking. I decided to enroll at Hunter College for the winter term. The school also had an excellent music program, but did require a few more non-music courses. Both Queens and Hunter were part of the City University of New York and at that time both were tuition-free. Fortunately, neither required an audition, as did all the conservatories, and which I believed I was not yet ready to attempt. We have the temerity these days to be debating whether or not free-college tuition is feasible. It was in 1972, and it still is, if only we had the will.

This meant I had five long months before my term began. What to do? I took a freelance job with an office sponsored by the New York State Council on the Arts, which was doing feasibility studies on how New York should engage in the country's bicentennial in 1976. At the same time, I enrolled in evening classes in basic music theory and ear training in the adult extension division at the Mannes School of Music, a fortuitous choice on several levels.

I spoke to the dean of the school to get a recommendation for a new piano teacher. "I have just the person for you. His name is John Ranck. He's a wonderful man, a top-rate pianist, and an excellent and patient teacher." When I called John, he said that I would have to audition for him. This made me very anxious, indeed. Would he expect a concert-level performance from me? He quickly made me feel at ease, as I played a few of the pieces I had learned with Delores. I was stunned when I heard his response, "Of course, I will take you as a student. I'll have you playing in public within two years." I could hardly believe my ears. This was nearly the inverse of what Delores said to me. Was it just a sales pitch? He can't be serious. He was, and he became close friends with Todd and me.

John had been a wunderkind, performing concertos on the radio by age eight or nine. His critically praised Town Hall recital debut began a promising concert career in New York. His recording of famed French composer Francis Poulenc's *Les Soirées de Nazelles* was highly acclaimed. In fact, Poulenc (another member of *Les Six*) sent John a postcard of the chateau where he composed the work and said, "I never thought very highly of this piece until I heard your recording of it." Why his career had languished was always a mystery to me. My own assessment was that he was a very shy man, who never really promoted himself assiduously. Also, he was wealthy and therefore had no need to make a fortune or even a living, thus lacking a crucial impetus. He lived in a beautiful apartment on East 9th Street, where stars such as Oliver Platt resided. Once I ran into Richard Gere, who also lived in the building, in the elevator.

Mannes was renowned for its excellent theory department, and I got a very good basic introduction there. Teaching the ear-training class was a young woman named Judy Meites. Still a student in the school, she was recruited to teach this adult beginner class because of her stellar abilities. I was most fearful of ear training because I don't have perfect pitch, and I knew it would be extremely challenging for me. Judy had the most wonderfully relaxed, but beautifully methodical, approach for teaching a subject that strikes fear in many music students. She removed all the tension and made the class a joy. We became close friends, often cooking dinners together.

In January I took my theory-placement examination at Hunter College. It was given by Louis Martin, a top-level music theorist who was to become my first harmony professor. The test was difficult and one of the students complained about it. Louis quickly put him in his place. "You know, when I was young I wanted to be a geologist, but when I took my first college courses in the subject, I realized that I was just a person who loved rocks. I was not meant for a career in that field. You may discover something similar here—that you're just a person who loves music but has no aptitude for it."

I knew immediately that I was in a very different environment from the warm supportive classes at Mannes. I did well on the placement exam and was exempted from Hunter's basic theory course. Still afraid of the ear training, I did not attempt to place out of the initial class. The professor for that course was a thin, mean-looking man, who entered the classroom on the first day with an intimidating scowl. He violently grabbed the chalk, turned to the blackboard, and with a force that looked as though he was about to engrave the board wrote, "Myron Fink," then vehemently underlined it. He turned back to the class and said, "Yes, my name is Myron Fink. Laugh about it now, because I can assure you it will be the last time you ever laugh in this class." And he was right, we never did. What a change from the Judy Meites approach.

Myron taught through intimidation. I learned immediately that I needed to be over-prepared before entering his classroom. Those who were not endured a man who became so red-faced that the veins in his forehead appeared about to explode. His verbal assaults on anyone who made a mistake were enough to make even the most stoic individual wither before his eyes. I don't believe I ever left his class without a severe headache. Yet, he was brilliant. Blessed with absolute pitch, he was an excellent pianist and a very fine composer. He once gave a lecture-demonstration in which he asked students to call out random notes. On the spot, he improvised a complete formally correct fugue (one of the most complex musical structures), based on the shouted-out notes.

Ear training consists of learning to recognize and sing any given musical interval, with the goal of being able to sight sing. The real bugbear of the course, however, is dictation, where one is expected to be able to notate correctly any rhythmic pattern or musical phrase, simply by hearing it. Once when I did particularly well in the class, Myron said, "I hope that the rest of you now see what your competition in the world of professional music is going to be like." Though I was flattered by the compliment, I had so wished he had voiced it privately. Everyone in the class now resented me.

Almost every music class at Hunter was superior. The music history professors were truly inspiring. Recalling how the music majors at Denver University grumbled about the difficulties of counterpoint and having no clue what it actually was, I had an irrational dread of this course. In the most simplistic terms, it is the setting of one melody against another. This is taught by a series of exercises called species counterpoint, beginning with setting a single note against another single note, and progressing through very complex tasks. The species are regulated by virtually hundreds of inviolable rules. I often spent hours on a simple line, fixing one mistake only to find that it created another, much like moving a wrinkle from one end of the fabric to the other.

Much to my surprise, the boy who was too dense to understand music theory discovered it was his strongest subject. I had done so well in my courses that my advisor arranged to get me a cash scholarship to attend graduate school. When I finally got my Bachelor's Degree from Hunter, I could not afford to go straight to graduate school, so I had to take another job for a year, though I continued to study piano with John Ranck.

I was hired as office manager for an organization that excited me very much. It had an international component seeking a better world, and had on its board such illustrious members as Buckminster Fuller and Margaret Meade, both of whom I highly admired. However, the organization's main function was a large treatment facility for troubled youth, who were offered services in drug rehabilitation, medical care, and legal counseling, as well as educational and vocational training.

I supervised a small staff of people. The office staff was never allowed in the treatment facility. One day as I was waxing ecstatic about the good this organization was doing, a woman who had worked there for several years, stopped me. "Before you get any more stars in your eyes about this place, let me tell you what's really going on here. Are you aware that the people running this are a cult?"

"What? You're kidding."

"No, I'm not kidding. They all live together in a loft in the Village."

"But there are nearly twenty-five of them."

"Yes, and they all share the same space. They were brought together by a wealthy Swedish industrialist. Most of them were drugged-out hippies from the '60s. This guy got them cleaned up and back to school to become doctors, psychiatrists, lawyers, and social workers. Oh, and they also have a mountain retreat in the Catskills."

As Mary Giovingo. would have said, "I was fiberglassted." I had a difficult time reconciling what I heard with the obvious good work that they were doing. In fact, I wondered if this was just office gossip. I got my answer when an older woman named Alice, who had not worked at the facility for several years, died suddenly. My immediate supervisor approached me, "Norman, I feel that you are sympathetic to the work we do and that you understand us. I would like you to come this evening to a small funeral service we are having for Alice." I was the only person from my staff who was asked to attend.

I showed up at a given Greenwich Village address and went up to a third-floor apartment. My supervisor answered the door in a flowing white floor-length robe. "Bizarre," I thought. As I entered, I realized that the entire supervisory staff was dressed in identical robes. Creepy. To my left, I saw a long hallway with possibly ten doors on either side. Was this the dormitory? Turning to my right, I was warmly welcomed by everyone and ushered into a large stark-white circular, amphitheater-like room, with three rows of tiered seating, covered in a purple carpeting. On a purple-carpeted pedestal in the middle of the room was Alice in her coffin, also dressed in the same white robe. Around the outer walls of the amphitheater, large, brightly lighted niches had been constructed. In each niche was some sort of deity, apparently representing ancient religions from around the world.

We all took our seats in the tiered seating, I being the only person in the room in normal street attire. The room began to slowly fill with incense. The lights were dimmed. Candles were lit. Everyone grabbed hands, including my sweaty palms, and began swaying back and forth. Drone-like chanting reverberated throughout the space. I hate this. Will they drug me and turn me into one of their zombies before this is over? Is there an emergency exit for my escape?

The ceremony continued with chanting, singing, speeches, and what looked like a lot of hocus-pocus over Alice's body. Will she rise from the dead? My eyes shifted wildly from left to right and back again. I tried to concentrate on the niches in order to hang onto my sanity. I couldn't make any sense of them, and the more I stared the more sinister they became. Even in kindergarten I didn't feel this uncomfortable. I was being prodded into participating in the chanting, the singing, the swaying. Why me? I hardly knew Alice. Oh, the swaying—back and forth. The whole room seemed to spin. The chanting lapped over me liked waves of swill. The sickening smell of the incense mingled with the smell of bodies in their unified tribal gyrations.

These are professional people. for god's sake—doctors, lawyers, psychiatrists receiving hundreds of thousands of dollars in government funding—I work with everyday, and here they are swept up in a dizzying frenzy. I was nauseated and beginning to feel faint with terror. Would there be a human sacrifice next? Would I be the victim?

My mind went completely blank when I was jolted back to reality. Was I hallucinating? The ceremony was over. How I don't remember. My boss approached me and said, "Norman, we are all very fond of you, and we would like to extend an invitation to you to take supper with us this evening and learn a little more about our life here." "Oh, thank you so very much, but I already have a dinner engagement tonight," I blurted out a bit too hysterically, so eager was I to escape this den before I slipped any farther down the rabbit hole. What about me, exactly, made me appear to be a good candidate for this coven of wackos?

I could hardly wait to get home to tell Todd. I have a mortal aversion to this sort of group think, communal behavior. That night I had some of the worst nightmares of my life, as though I were being besieged by a band of mad, drooling maniacs. I woke up in a sweat. How was I going to go back to the office and act as if everything were normal after this episode?

I did manage it, but my antennae were on perpetual alert to any unusual behavior, and everything I saw became suspect to me. One day I noticed on the seat of the chair in one of the social worker's office, a pair of forks crossed with the tines facing upward. What could this mean? Some sort of evil curse? I eventually got the nerve to ask my boss, but she just laughed it off with an "Oh, it's nothing." For an office Christmas party we were all asked to contribute food. Some of my staff brought in pans of fried chicken and collard greens, I baked some pastries, and many others contributed homemade succulent dishes. My boss said to me, in tones that implied she was about to bestow a great gift, "And we (meaning all twenty-five of the sect) will contribute an eggnog." My staff became apoplectic when they heard this. Twenty-five people with tons of money; one eggnog?

One woman, part of their cult, who seemed particularly intelligent to me, acted as a secretary, to one of the sect's older men (later I learned he was her lover and a raging alcoholic), who never seemed to actually do anything that I could ascertain. She came into my office and I presumptuously asked her how it happened that with her very bright mind, she hadn't gone to college. "Oh, the group decided that I could best serve in the capacity of secretary, and I'm just happy to be of use in whatever small way I can." I was horrified.

To keep things light in the office, I would sometimes pretend to be the boss from hell to my own staff. They all knew it was an act and laughed about it. The cult had no sense of humor whatever. One of the psychiatrists must have overheard my banter. She drew me aside and said, "Norman, you are one of the most frightening persons I have ever met." Me, the wussycat? My staff had a big laugh over that one. While we were talking about it, we all independently stopped abruptly and looked about the room. Each knew what the other was thinking. Was there a microphone listening into our conversation? We never knew.

The true horror of the group made itself known when two of the psychiatrists, who were married, had a child. I learned surreptitiously that the cult began demonizing the couple because they were becoming too independent of the group, spending too much time with their newborn. After I left the organization, I found out that they had finally been excised from the group. I made it through the year by telling myself, "At least they're doing great things for the kids." I so hoped this was true, as I tried to imagine what kind of counseling they actually provided to these vulnerable children.

Todd and I decided we probably had lived in a furnished studio long enough. He found a lovely one-bedroom, full-floor apartment in a brownstone on Stuyvesant Street, across from St. Mark's Church. It was on the third-floor, and I was concerned about getting my grand piano up the stairs, so I measured them, as well as the turns. I called the piano movers and gave them the measurements to determine if this was possible. "Oh, certainly, that'll be no problem at all," the man assured me. We signed the lease. When the movers got the piano in the front door of the building and took one look at the steps. "There's no way in hell that piano is going up those stairs, bud." I'm now in state of total panic. "What'll I do? Todd, can we break the lease?" "Call a hoister and get it in through the window," the movers advised.

I measured the depth of the piano case and the width of the windows to see if it would work. The legs of a grand are removable. I had not calculated the thick padding that movers wrap around a piano. First the entire window and its wood frame had to be removed. Then a hoist was rigged up on the roof. The piano was attached to the ropes, and it slowly and precipitously began to rise. "My, that padding looks awfully thick. Todd, is it going to get through?" "We'll see," he said, not reassuringly.

By the time the piano reached the second floor it began swaying over the sidewalk, and a crowd assembled on the street to watch. They watched my beloved Steinway in mid-air. I had to look away in terror. Finally, it reached the third floor, and it was hanging outside the window. "That's never going to fit through that opening," I yelled. One of the movers inside the apartment started guiding it. It squeezed through the window without even a fraction of an inch to spare. I gasped for air after not breathing for the last three minutes.

Todd and I wanted desperately to hear Vladimir Horowitz live, so when we heard he was making one of his many comebacks, we joined an endless line that circled Carnegie Hall more than once. It was snowing and bitter cold, but we were determined to wait, something neither of us would have dreamed of doing for any other performer. As we neared the box office almost three hours later, an announcement was made that the concert was sold out. The sense of disappointment was overwhelming.

Suddenly, his manager appeared and said, "Maestro Horowitz has agreed to give a second performance. All who are waiting in line will be given a slip entitling you to buy a ticket for that concert." His recital was every bit as breathtaking and inspiring to me as I had imagined. Once I read that when young pianists played for Horowitz they always performed the most fiercely difficult pieces to impress him. "Well, that was fine, but can you play the *Träumerei*?" he would say. This gorgeously melodic and easy piece from the *Kinderscenen* Horowitz played with exquisite simplicity and beauty on the program we heard.

A few years later, I purchased an LP recording of Julius Katchen playing Brahms solo piano works at Tower Records. From there we crossed the street near Lincoln Center to see a German film about neo-Nazis. Once we were seated, I handed Todd the LP and said, "I'm going to the bathroom."

"Stay here. I'll get the popcorn."

"No. I don't want popcorn. I'm going to the bathroom."

"Just sit. I'll go get it for us."

"What is wrong with you? I'm going to the bathroom," I said in exasperation. When I returned, I saw Todd speaking to someone in the row behind him. I got closer. Why am I here and Todd's there talking to Vladimir Horowitz? The whole exciting world is happening and where am I? Pissing life away in the bathroom. By the time I reached my seat, the conversation had ended, and Horowitz was talking to his companion, a nice looking young man.

The credits for the movie began. "Music by Gustav Mahler" flashed across the scene. "Gustav Mahler?" Horowitz nearly shouted, loud enough for the whole theater to hear. "Oh, god, I hope he isn't going to talk through the film because someone's bound to shush him." Shortly after the movie began, we heard him snoring softly.

When we left the theater, Todd explained the whole scene. "I tried to stop you from going to the bathroom because I knew Horowitz was behind us, and you hadn't seen him. Once you were gone I took out the Katchen LP, held it up, and started reading. I felt a tap on my shoulder. I turned around and he said, 'That's the one to have, Katchen.'" I was reminded of a radio interview I heard Horowitz give in which he said, "Yes, we talk about the three B's of music: Bach, Beethoven, but Brahms? Already a leetle bit Brooklyn."

Todd, who abhorred being chained to a desk, decided after a stint as an editor at McGraw-Hill that he'd take a substantial pay cut and work as a sales clerk in a highly respected art-supply store a block from our new apartment. He rationalized the cut by saying, "At least I'll get a fifteen percent discount on my art supplies."

I got a call from home. It was the late 1970s and life at Nylint Toys took an unwelcome twist. Management efficiency experts with business degrees were taking over. Dad was not being supplanted but rather shoved to the side at the factory to make room for one of these bottom-liners. He was unhappy and complained that the new man was making a mess of things that he handled perfectly well. It was affecting him both physically and emotionally. An opportunity presented itself. One of his Chicago Cubs heroes, Ron Santo, whom he had engaged for a Senior Holy Name breakfast, had started a franchise of pizzerias and wondered if dad was interested in owning one.

He and Phil Giovingo, my mother's cousin and a banker, went in together for the purchase. It was a great success almost immediately. Santo made appearances to help give the pizzeria a boost. Dad loved the place and especially because he was aligned with one of his ballplayer idols. He could hardly wait until I came home to show off his new business. Unfortunately, neither he nor Phil had the courage to leave their jobs; they worked only in the evenings and weekends. This, of course, meant they hired managers to run the place. One turned out to be worse than the next. Mother suggested that he leave Nylint and run it full time himself since he had become so unhappy with the situation at work. He was afraid the pizzeria wouldn't provide an adequate income. As a result, the business deteriorated and they ended up selling it.

Back in the city, I decided to do my Master's Degree at New York University, which gave me a departmental scholarship in addition to the one I had been awarded from Hunter. When I had a personal interview with my advisor, he asked, "What was your grade-point average while you were at Hunter?"

"It was four-point."

Oh, dear, you may be too smart for us. We don't have any four-pointers at our school."

Oh, I'm sure that I'm in no way too smart." I had pretty much dismissed my stellar average as a function of the grade inflation that had crept in during the years I had been away from school. And besides, though I had done so well, it wasn't as though I breezed through the undergraduate program. I had had to work my butt off, just as I had done in high school.

After my first semester of classes, I began to suspect that he was right. What I hadn't realized was that the Master's Degree program at NYU was set up primarily for New York public-school music teachers, who were required to obtain the degree to retain their positions. Thus the program was made rather easy. Nothing here was going to be as challenging as what I had been given at Hunter. Should I transfer out? I was already deep into the program so I decided to stick with it and just get the degree. I resolved, however, to make every class a part of my thesis research. My motto became, "Student, teach thyself."

In my classes was a young, very bright woman named Sarah Renberg, who just happened to be a Swede from an Illinois town less than seventy miles from Rockford. Several times we caught each other rolling our eyes when some particularly questionable concept was spouted by a professor. We hit it off immediately. Sarah was also a pianist. She had been a philosophy major in undergraduate school and read classical Greek.

Sarah and I were pretty much on the same level in our piano playing. I can't recall which of us suggested we should try playing some four-hand piano music together just for fun. I was immediately transported back in time to the days when I was living in Milton Setzer's apartment, and he and composer David Baker played through Schubert's four-hand pieces. Neither Sarah nor I could have imagined how transformative this decision was. We quickly gravitated toward one of the greatest pieces written for piano four hands, Schubert's Fantasy in F-Minor, a sonata-length work ending with a magnificent fugue. In a few weeks, when it started sounding rather good to our ears, Sarah said, "Let's take it into my teacher. I think he can give us some good pointers." Her teacher, Roger Boardman, was a fine pianist, and I ended up taking a few lessons from him because he gave some excellent technical advice, though I never stopped studying with John Ranck.

Upon hearing us play the Schubert, he said, "I would like you to perform this piece on the department's spring concert program." Perform? Oh, my god, no. I never considered being a performer at the piano. I had achieved a degree of success as a dancer, and I knew what performing at a professional level required. Surely, I fell short of that level of ability in music. Despite all my protestations, Sarah talked me into it. I was nearly paralyzed with anxiety, fearing that my fingers would refuse to move and I would collapse off the piano bench in a pathetic heap on the floor. Todd gave me one of his beta-blockers to ease the nervousness (which helped only minimally), and the performance was a success.

Sarah and I soon began adding other works to our repertoire: Debussy's *Petite Suite*, the Poulenc Sonata, Ravel's *Mother Goose Suite*, the Brahms Waltzes, and the Mozart Sonata in F-Major—more than enough for a full-length program. At that point neither of us had a plan as to what we should do with out new repertory.

In my first term, I decided on my thesis subject. I would take a very technical idea from Charles Rosen's award-winning book, *The Classical Style, Haydn, Mozart, Beethoven*, and try to prove a point that Rosen was making. He hypothesized that Beethoven's successful use of alternate tonalities for the dominant in the second themes of some of his sonatas was achieved by making the alternatives function as though they were, in fact, dominates. Phew! That was quite a mouthful of theory jargon—this from the thirteen-year-old boy who didn't even know what a dominant was in Irene Glasford's class.

To the extent possible, I tailored each of my classes so that any papers or analyses would complement and supplement the work of my thesis. As a result I produced a rather massive paper. My advisor said, "I believe this is good enough to be published in the music journals. Would you mind if we kept an extra copy of your thesis on file to show other students what a professional work should look like?" "Not at all." I knew that this praise was blown completely out of proportion. There were many holes and questions to be addressed in my writing. Unfortunately, there was no one on the faculty I felt I could turn to for assistance and criticism.

I eventually sent the thesis to Rosen himself, but sadly I never got a response. At first, I was convinced that this was proof that I had concocted a very amateurish piece of analysis, not worthy of comment. Rosen was a genius, a performing pianist who appeared at Carnegie Hall, a top music historian and theorist, as well as a Ph.D. in French literature. When I attended a lecture he gave on the relationship between landscape painting and the art song, I came to a different conclusion. He probably misplaced my thesis in a morass of scribbled notes, old treatises, books, and forgotten manuscripts in his hopelessly cluttered office. The ideas presented in his talk were brilliant, but unlike his lucid and precise writing, his lecture was disorganized and somewhat incoherent. He appeared befuddled, riffling through a pile of haphazard notes. I didn't have the nerve to submit my thesis to the journals without his input, and it was never published.

Once I earned my degree, I thought perhaps I should embark on a Ph.D. program, with the possibility of teaching college. I met with Louis Martin, my former harmony professor. "Norman, I remember your harmony exercises so well. You always wrote the most interesting turns of phrase and found the most elegant solutions to each problem. But as for getting a Ph.D., I don't advise it. Take a look at this stack of resumes." The pile was four-feet high. "We got these in response to a call for a single opening for an instructor. What I will be looking for is not just a good resume. I will be looking for someone with a major name, who will attract better students to our department, someone who's written an acclaimed book or has a distinguished career. You wouldn't stand a chance against such competition. If you want to teach, just hang up your shingle and begin teaching piano and theory."

And that's what I did, naive as I was about how difficult that would be in New York, a city awash in piano teachers. I was already at a serious disadvantage because I had run out of money. which forced me to take a part-time editing job at a small legal newsletter firm called Business Research Publications.

Bruce Hunter, even before I received my Master's Degree, talked me into giving him piano lessons. He had studied the harpsichord but had exchanged that instrument for a Steinway. "But I'm not at all ready to teach yet. I don't even have my degree." "I've heard you play. We're friends, and I would feel comfortable studying with you." By this time he had retired from the Museum of Natural History and moved to his house in Northport, Long Island, where we spent many delightful weekends. He was my first student. Bruce introduced us to a friend of his, David Hemphill, who became one of our dearest friends and certainly the most ardent fan of both our careers. David was a pianist who had studied with Menahem Pressler of the Beaux Arts Trio and taught the children of Haile Selassie, emperor of Ethiopia. He had settled in as a public-school music teacher on Long Island, and was one of the most culturally sophisticated and wonderful human beings we'd known.

When I graduated, I posted some fliers around the Village and ran a couple of ads in neighborhood papers, managing to get a few students. Most were adult beginners, but there was one child whose father was a surgeon. When the boy made a mistake, he always stopped playing. "Try to keep going, even if you hit a wrong note," I coaxed. The father interjected to his son, "Yes, it's just like in the operating room. If you cut the wrong thing, you never say, 'oops.' You just keep cutting." I involuntarily flung my hands to my abdomen, in an attempt to protect my vital organs. Is this what surgeons really do?

After graduation Sarah and I took our expanded repertoire into John Ranck for criticism. Sarah was so taken with his sophisticated interpretive ideas that she switched to him as her teacher. John was impressed by what he heard and arranged for us to appear on our first non-school concert program, a Sunday afternoon series at the Wellington Hotel, near Carnegie Hall. Then he arranged for us to do a full-length program on a series at the Webster Apartments, where he had given several solo recitals.

I said to Sarah, we need to make something of this, even if all it does is promote our teaching careers. She also had a few students and was earning a living as a waitress. I got the idea that we should play at senior-citizen centers and churches just to give us more performance experience. When these went very well, I learned about Hospital Audiences and the Jewish Association Serving the Aging.. We made a demo tape and began submitting it. Both organizations hired us to play, and these were our first paying jobs as a piano-duo.

On the way to one of our recitals Sarah said, "Something really terrible happened to me last night. Jack (her boyfriend) and I were in bed sound asleep when I was startled by man with a knife standing over me."

"No. How did he get in?"

"It was so hot last night that we left the window open, and he came in through the fire escape. Norman, he raped me, and Jack did nothing."

"Why not?"

"I guess he was afraid."

"And we're blithely going to play a recital after all this?"

"Well, I have to just keep going, as though nothing happened."

I was extremely skeptical about it, but amazingly the concert went off very well. I was afraid to ask any more questions about the incident for fear of stirring up any emotional traumas, but in my mind a lot of things needed explaining, particularly about what Jack was doing during the rape. The damage and the scars to Sarah manifested themselves gradually and only after time elapsed.

John Ranck then told us about some concerts he had done for the American Landmarks Festivals and arranged for us to audition for its director. "That was really lovely," he said as we played sections of the Schubert *Fantasy*. "Most of the duos who audition for me are not true duos at all. They're soloists who are just playing at the duo game. The two of you truly play as one person, so though I generally offer only one recital, I've decided to give you three engagements." The performances were at Federal Hall, where George Washington was inaugurated, and at the Theodore Roosevelt Birthplace on East 20th Street, which had a lovely small concert hall.

I got the idea that we should form a chamber group and establish our own programs for senior citizens. We engaged a board of directors and applied for not-for-profit status so that we could qualify for grants. The National Endowment for the Arts was interested enough in the idea that they phoned me personally to help us apply. In the meantime, Ronald Reagan was elected, and though he didn't succeed, his goal to end the Endowment changed everything. Months later they called again and said. "I'm afraid your project just doesn't meet our criteria because you're focusing on the aged, and there is no audience-development potential in that." "So you're saying that the elderly are not worth the bother of support, simply because they're old?" "Well, I certainly wouldn't put it that way." But I certainly would.

I told Sarah that I thought it essential that we expand to the two-piano literature if we were to make a success of our duo. I learned Mozart's Piano Concerto for Two Pianos in E-flat Major and the fiendishly difficult Brahms Two-Piano Sonata in F-Minor, which at Clara Schumann's advice he later turned into the magnificent Piano Quintet that we had heard at the Concertgebouw in Amsterdam. What a joy it was to be playing this music I never imagined would be within my grasp. I started scouting around for small orchestras that my be interested in our playing the Mozart concerto and for venues that had two pianos available.

Sarah appeared strangely ambivalent about learning this music, which I thought was unfortunate because John Ranck was approaching some wealthy friends to try to obtain funding for our Carnegie Recital Hall debut. We would need to add some two-piano pieces for such a venture. Carnegie Hall? Could this be happening to me? It made me more and more nervous to think about it. I could no longer pass Carnegie Hall without a sneaking fear invading me, and whenever we attended a piano recital there, I was anxiety-ridden just looking at that big black box on the stage before the pianist made an entrance.

At Business Research Publications a full-time position was created, and they wanted me to accept it. I declined because it would mean the end of my music career. Between the teaching, the paid concerts, which were about four to five a month, and the part-time editorial job, I was at least making a small living. I mentioned the position to Todd, who was growing weary of waiting on famous pampered artists. He applied and got the job. Within a few weeks after he started, they fired our editorial supervisor and Todd was promoted to that position. Oh, no! Todd's now my boss. I had never counted on this at all. What would this do to our relationship?

Around the same time, Todd was given his first one-person show at the Caravan House Gallery. The entire show consisted of paintings he had done from sketches and photos taken during a trip we had made to Courmayeur, the beautiful alpine town located at the foot of Mount Blanc in northern Italy. We had great hopes that this exhibit was the first step toward a major career. Unfortunately, the gallery closed months after the show ended.

Sarah and I were getting better concerts, including the Donnell Library, which had a magnificent auditorium, Trinity Church Wall Street Concert Series, and the Performing Arts Library at Lincoln Center. The Trinity Church gig was the most prestigious because it paid very well and some prominent names in the music world performed on that series. We also performed at some of the major synagogues. Sarah, who was about ten years younger than I, was particularly beautiful, and we noticed that people assumed we were a husband-and-wife team. It seemed to make them like us even more. We never confirmed their suspicions, but we also found it to our benefit not to disabuse their belief that we were a couple. We continued to perform at senior-citizen centers, and these were often the most emotionally fulfilling programs. Invariably, the older people would approach us after the concert to say such things as, "Thank you for bringing some joy into my life." "I was moved to tears by your playing."

After one of our concerts at Federal Hall, my wrist was so sore that I was unable to hold even a pencil in my hand for the next week. I had been practicing the Liszt B-Minor Sonata (the one Delores Modrell implied I would never be able to play, though one day I would teach it) and the Scriabin D-sharp Minor Etude, both wrist punishers. I saw a doctor, and he said, "My best advice to you is to stop playing the piano. It's causing severe tendinitis." "Oh, no you don't, mister," I thought. "I went through this once before with dancing, and it's definitely not going to happen again."

I first saw a biomechanics therapist who videotaped my playing and made suggestions on how to reduce the strain. On top of his piano, I noticed one videocassette marked Vladimir Horowitz.

"Is Horowitz a patient of yours?"

"I can't discuss my patients, but since you noticed the tape, yes."

"I'll bet his problem is the result of playing with flat fingers and low wrists," I ventured. I had always noticed this eccentricity and wondered how he could play that way.

"Yes, but that's only a fraction of the damaging habits he has." He refused to elaborate further.

Of more use to me was a physical therapist, who gave me exercises using small weights to strengthen my wrists. They seemed to work very well. I was still having intermittent bouts of back problems, and I wondered if maybe some light weight training would help that as well. I bought a set of dumbbells and barbells and began tentatively working out. My body was beginning to take on a hint of a middle-aged appearance, and I didn't want Todd to have to look at that and grow bored with me. The weight training, as long as I was careful, also seemed beneficial to my back, and as I gradually increased the amount of weight, my body began to take on a more vigorous appearance. Friends who hadn't seen me in awhile were amazed at the change. Working out was one more factor in helping me with my back problems, but others were yet to be learned.

Terry Anderson, my friend from grade school whom I had not seen or spoken to in twenty-five years, phoned. "Norman, I'm in town on business. Could we have dinner?" I met him in a restaurant in Little Italy. Through the *primo* and the *secondo*, he told me about his business (he had invented a combination smoke- and carbon-monoxide detector), his wife, his two high-school-age children, and his home in San Diego. I thought to myself, "Well, we certainly don't have much in common any longer," when he said, "Now let me tell you why I really asked you to have dinner." Uh-oh. "I've been married for twenty years, I love my wife and my children, but I think I'm gay. I really need someone to talk to about it."

"And how do you happen to come all the way across the country and choose me as your confidant?"

"Well, you know our mothers speak all the time." A "mother's study group," which began in grade school was still meeting all these years later so these women can keep in touch and discuss their adult children. "My mother told me that you were not married and that you've been in the theater. When I called your number, a man's voice answered the phone so I just assumed you were probably gay."

"Even though San Diego has a large gay population and I'm sure many gay counseling services, you choose me?"

"I really don't know anyone I can talk to there."

"And have you had any homosexual experiences?"

"No, I have gone to some gay bars and just observed."

"And you're just realizing these attractions now?"

"I guess I was just not aware of it." Having been aware of which sex attracted me from the time I was a little boy, I find it difficult to relate to this line of thinking, though I expect it's my own personal bias. In my mind, I hear the crude questions being asked: What gave you an erection? When you had a wet dream, which sex were you dreaming about? I couldn't bring myself to ask Terry these questions.

"Norman, what do you think I should do?"

How do I answer this? I'm thinking, "You're in your forties, you're basically happily married, gay culture is so heavily focused on youth, you don't exude the 'daddy' image that some boys might find attractive." With this swirling about my mind, I gave a very poor response that I still regret, "I think you should stay with your wife."

"I can't do that. You know, it would help me so much if you and Todd would ask me to your house so I could see how a gay couple lives."

My first reaction, not verbalized of course, was, "What are we, animals in a zoo to be observed?" Instead I said, "Why don't you come over for dinner on Friday night." I invited David Hemphill to join us. Now how do we act to look like an average gay couple? Obviously just as we always do. Terry seemed perfectly comfortable with the scene and seamlessly fit right in. He returned to San Diego, and its was a few years before we saw him again. When David retired out West, he and Terry became friends, and Terry told David that he had had a crush on me all through school. Oh, those unrequited high-school longings.

Our landlord, a City College professor, informed us that he had decided to turn the building into cooperative apartments. He set it up as an eviction plan, which meant we either had the choice to buy the apartment or we had to vacate. He was asking only $75,000, but with our constrained economic situation that was an astronomical amount of money for us.

We began to look at other apartments in the Village and were shocked by how much rents had increased. We had been paying $450 a month on Stuyvesant, and were willing to go as high as $700. Agents said, "Surely, you can spend at least $1,000." No, surely we couldn't. When it became obvious we could no longer afford to live in the Village, we began looking elsewhere.

I saw an ad for a seven-room prewar apartment in Washington Heights for $408 a month. Washington Heights? Where the hell is that? We took the long subway ride uptown to see it. The neighborhood seemed to be a totally different world. This is Manhattan? The apartment had a formal dining room, French doors in the living room, and a seventy-foot-long L-shaped hallway, which became a perfect gallery for Todd's paintings. The place was a total mess. The walls were all painted a shit-brown, semi-gloss enamel. All the wood floors were covered in hideous linoleum, and the kitchen seemed out of the previous century.

The landlord said, "You have to take the apartment as is. In fact, I need to know how you will renovate it. I'm giving it to whoever has the best plan." This was completely illegal on his part, but we didn't challenge him. We realized that one of the bedrooms could be Todd's studio. He had been sharing pricey studio space with Robin Sherin, a fellow clerk and artist he met working in the art-supply store. Another bedroom could be made into my studio, and there would be fifty feet of space between the studios, giving us a more quiet environment.

We did as much of the renovation as possible ourselves, which took six weeks before we could move in. Sixty gallons of paint and three coats were needed to get the walls white. We tore up the linoleum to reveal beautiful parquet floors, which we had refinished. We put in a whole new kitchen and did some remodeling in the bathroom. Despite the fact that we turned the apartment into very attractive living quarters, I was in tears as we left Stuyvesant Street. I couldn't believe that Manhattan was forcing me out, exiling me after my having loved it all my life and having lived there for twenty years. It was cruel and unfair. The city had turned against the artists who gave it vibrancy and distinction, in favor of bureaucrats and financiers. Yes, technically we were still in Manhattan, but Washington Heights seemed like the outer boroughs to me. Well, we would live there only until we earned enough money to move back downtown. Uh-huh, sure.

Todd's first show after our move was a group exhibit sponsored by the Westside Arts Association. The show was held in a building that used to house the restrooms at the 96th Street subway stop. The exhibit and the space were actually quite nice. Although Todd was pleased to be in the show, he felt it was a big letdown after his one-person show at the Caravan House Gallery. "Look at it this way. After 'Art in the Toilet,' things can only improve," I chided.

My father called to tell me that he had interested Uncle Tom in presenting Sarah and me in concert in Rockford. Tom had added more performance sponsoring to his sports promoting. We flew to Rockford together. Sarah was terrified of flying and had to fortify herself with several drinks. On the afternoon of the concert, dad drove us to the Rockford Theater (a lovely Broadway-sized house) so that we could rehearse.

Our many concerts at senior centers had served us well. Pianists, unlike other musicians, are disadvantaged by having to play on different instruments at every performance. Pianos differ radically: the touch, the heaviness of the keyboard action, the sound, the pedal. Having played on a huge variety of pianos, often with no chance to try them out in rehearsal, made us impervious to the problem.

Stage hands and other workers at the theater told us how beautifully we played. In the car on the way home, dad said not a word about the rehearsal. I felt Sarah's anxiety rising throughout the trip, and she finally blurted out to my father, "Well, did you like it?" "It was all right."

When we got home Sarah said to me, "I don't think I can do this."
"Do what?"
"The concert tonight."
"What? What are you saying?"
"Well, even your own father doesn't think we're any good."
"No, Sarah, you don't understand. When my father says, 'It's all right,' that means he liked it very much. He's completely incapable of expressing himself more effusively."

As we were about to leave for the theater, Mary Giovingo, asks me, "Are you nervous?"
"Yes. Playing in front of all these people I've known since I was a kid is a little scary."
"Well, I sure hope you're not going to make a fool of us in front of all our relatives."

Thanks, mom, for that encouraging note just before we go on. I warned Sarah that we could expect my mother to find some little something that bothered her about the performance.

The house was packed and the concert was a big success. We got a standing ovation at the end. In the midst of all the adulation, Mary Giovingo says to me, "That was very good, but what was that funny thing you do with your head when you're playing." I nodded to Sarah with a "See what I mean?" look.

My old piano teacher, Irene Glasford, was in the audience, and I overheard her proudly telling everyone she knew, "He was my student when he was a child." I thought to myself, "That is literally true, Irene, but I don't think you can take much credit for this."

I found it interesting that a lot of the tired gender issues from childhood were still in play. All the women from my extended family were in attendance, but many of the men chose to skip it and play cards instead. "Men do only the things that men do," was still the rule, apparently.

When we left Rockford, Sarah said, "I don't know how you survived with parents who are so unsupportive." "They're really not in the least unsupportive. They just have bizarre ways of showing it." I began thinking back to my childhood and how they often found something to criticize about everything I did, even when I well knew they were completely behind me. What was the reason for this? I knew there was no malice behind it. They were trying to be helpful. As an adult I spoke to them about it in an attempt to understand, but they seemed completely unaware that they had ever been the least bit critical. We recognize only what we choose to recognize about ourselves.

I had read about anthropologists who studied hunter-gatherer groups and how when a person killed big game or performed some astounding feat, the group, rather than praising him, would belittle him mercilessly. This was their method for preventing anyone from gaining too much power, trying to become the leader of the group, becoming a boorish bully, or just "getting a big head." Could it be that there is some genetic reason for my parents' hypercriticism, some atavistic, and perhaps beneficial, trait that had never been dampened throughout the eons? I often thought when I heard blowhards who had precious little to blow hard about, "I'll bet their parents constantly told them how wonderful, how special, how extraordinary they are. They could have used a little of the Mary Giovingo treatment to bring them back to earth."

I knew my parents hated the idea of my "getting a big head." One of Mary Giovingo's favorite sayings about people who came from humble backgrounds and grew rich, well known, or powerful was, "She forgot where she came from." She didn't want me to forget. As a not very self-assured child, however, a little more verbal support would have been welcome. One lasting detriment of their criticism is that I've never been able to shake the feeling that no matter how well I do something, it is never quite good enough for those who matter, not to mention not even good enough for me.

My music career began to disintegrate when we returned to New York. I had already lost all my students by moving so far uptown. No one was willing to make that trip. Then Sarah became more apathetic about our career. She had hardly learned the Mozart concerto, and hadn't even looked at the Brahms. I finally just played both pieces with John Ranck at one of his Sunday home soirées, which gave his students performing opportunities. Then I observed that Sarah seemed unwilling to spend the necessary time practicing for our concerts. We had in the past practiced together two to four hours a day, and another three hours separately. Because we both suffered from performance anxiety, we surmounted the problem only by being incredibly over-prepared, and by performing frequently enough so that we wouldn't face long dry spells, which might overwhelm us.

This issue came to a head when a performance we gave on Long Island seemed particularly sloppy to me. It wasn't a disaster, but I was becoming very concerned about the direction we were taking and needed to confront her. "Sarah, since I've been the one doing all the leg work to get every engagement for us, I believe that it's time you share some of that work." I was staggered by her response, "I don't think I want to continue with the duo. I've been thinking about my career, and I would really rather be a soloist." How could this be? After all the effort, after all the progress and success we've had, and just when John is trying to arrange a Carnegie Recital Hall debut, we're just going to throw it all away? I was completely devastated by this turn of events, having poured nearly six years of my life into building this little career of ours.

Her solo career went basically nowhere. She auditioned for the Landmarks Festival director, who told John Ranck, "Frankly, I heard nothing special in her solo playing." John arranged one small concert for her, but she became so nervous at the prospect that he had to step in at the last minute and take her place.

The whole fiasco did severe damage to our friendship, and I was heartsick over it. Our relationship went far beyond music and extended to literature, art, philosophy, and theater. We both loved Proust's seven-volume novel *In Search of Lost Time,* especially the way it delineated the redemptive and transformative attributes of art. Sarah and I lived by this idea. Proust confirmed for me what my psychologist friend, Steve, now a professor at a major college, advised me years ago: "Don't read psychology, read the great works of literature. You'll learn much more about human behavior." From Proust, I learned more about what motivates people than from any other source, though I lamented that I could never be as perceptive as he was, and thus I never truly comprehended Sarah's reason for abandoning the duo.

With my very limited understanding, I suspected that the rape, combined with other emotional problems stemming from Sarah's childhood, had a great deal to do with the abrupt end to our duo. She broke up with Jack, began therapy, and eventually moved to Chicago, where she taught at a community music school, did a few solo concerts, and performed four-hand concerts with another faculty member.

I was painfully aware that my piano playing was not good enough to command a solo career. We were special as a duo, not individually. In addition, my mortal fear of having memory lapses was an enormous impediment. Though I had no problem memorizing pieces, my irrational fear triggered the dreaded result. I had had a couple of lapses, playing solo at John's soirées and wasn't about to chance it in a public forum. Four-hand pianists always use the music. Damn Clara Schumann for starting the tradition of playing from memory. So where was my music career now? Evaporated without a trace.

In Rockford, the deterioration was far more serious. My mother's eyesight had become progressively worse and especially at night. One evening, they went shopping for new furniture. On the way out of the store, she fell down some steps, which she hadn't seen, and broke her hip. The store had failed to put a handrail or any lighting on the steps. Dad, honest to a fault, made many fatal mistakes. He failed to call his lawyer immediately. Rather, he called the store's insurance company and told them because my mother's eyesight was poor he had no intention of suing. He just wanted my mother's medical expenses covered. The call sealed the case: the possibility of a suit was precluded, and the store's insurance company refused to pay any medical bills. In desperation, dad then called the lawyer who told him in no uncertain terms what a fool he had been because he could have easily filed a negligence lawsuit against the store.

Poor Mary Giovingo lay in a hospital room for two days in pain because most of the staff happened to be on strike. When hip-replacement surgery was finally performed a few days later, the doctors failed to take the necessary and standard precautions for avoiding infection. She suffered in pain for months, finally having to go to a hospital in Chicago, where she spent six weeks on intensive antibiotics before they could redo the hip replacement. Again, dad failed to seek legal advice about the obvious malpractice in the Rockford hospital.

At the same time, dad was diagnosed with diabetes and a heart condition, which required missing a lot of work. His beloved Nylint employers, the Klint brothers, after more than forty years of dedicated service, gave him not even a single sick day with pay. The workers, instead, took up a collection to help him, which I found embarrassing and pathetic. And how my father years earlier had bragged that no one ever voted to unionize the shop because the Klints treated everyone so well. Right.

In 1983, mother phoned in the middle of night to tell me that she called 911 to take dad to the hospital, and she didn't know whether he'd survive. I booked the next flight home and went straight to the hospital in the hopes of at least seeing him one last time. The hospital staff told me they had no patient named Matt Cancelose and could give me no further information. I knew this meant he had died. I went to our house to find my mother and the rest of the family grieving. There were so many things I wanted to say to him, so many issues that I felt were unresolved, and now it was too late. When I returned to New York, I found a letter from the dead. He had written it the night he died, telling me about a party they had attended earlier that evening. I turned ashen.

Mother, whose quality of life deteriorated after the hip surgery, had had to give up her sales job at Stewarts three years before dad's death and was left in a rather vulnerable position. We learned that dad had made another fatal mistake. His pension plan had offered two alternatives: he could take half the amount, which would allow my mother to continue to collect a monthly check should he die before her; or he could take the full amount, which would leave her with nothing. At the time, he was very healthy, so he chose the second alternative, assuming that being the healthier one, he would outlive her.

Dad retired only a year before his death and was so happy to be relieved of the workaday world. He died in the middle of March, and I was told I had to return that month's pension check to Nylint. Of course his beloved employers did not even offer a small payment in recompense to my mother, though they knew her very well and had even socialized with her. A year later, she was forced to sell her house and move into a nice apartment building, the Versailles, which naturally she pronounced Versales.

I asked her to come spend the first Christmas after dad's death with us. I was amazed how much her eyesight deteriorated and how that was affecting her walking, already impaired after two hip surgeries. As her Christmas gift, I took her to Lord & Taylor's and told her to pick out whatever she wanted. I always kept her on my arm because of her vision, but for some reason I made the mistake of letting go for a moment to look at some item on the main floor. When I turned back around, I couldn't believe what I was seeing. There she was in the middle of the aisle with her palms on some man's chest, feeling him up and down. The man just stood there, his mouth gaping. "What are you doing?" I yelled. "Oh, I'm so sorry," she said to the gentleman," I don't see very well." The man had an "Oh, right, lady," look on his face. Because she couldn't see the fabrics clearly, she judged everything by touch, and she mistook him for a mannequin.

We had a lovely Christmas together, despite the sadness that dad was no longer with us. I realized, however, that this was probably the last time Mary Giovingo would be able to travel on her own. She made a few more visits accompanied by my cousin Jo, whom I hadn't seen in years. I took them to the theater and it brought back the memory of my Friday-night "dates" with Jo when I was a child, and how she had instilled in me the love for theater. But mother's health continued to deteriorate. She moved to a senior-living facility. Whenever I visited I did a thorough cleaning of the apartment, as well as cooked and froze dinners for her that she could just pop in a microwave. The last time I visited that facility I noticed the dinners I had made the previous time were sitting, untouched, in the freezer.

Encroaching dementia and frequent broken bones from osteoporosis necessitated that she be placed in a nursing home, a very painful decision that produced overwhelming guilt. I was grateful to her sister Lena who visited her nearly every day. There were no more stinging criticisms of me, no malapropisms, and no more pithy sayings from Mary Giovingo. How I missed them. Wistfully, I recalled the time when a cousin of hers was lamenting that her daughter had just come out as gay. "Well, you need to do what I did when I first learned about Norman," Mary Giovingo instructed. "I loved him twice as much."

Whenever I visited, I fed her because she could no longer eat on her own, something her sister and the caring attendants did when I was not there. How heartrending to see her reduced to this deplorable state, the dignity she spent her life cultivating torn to shreds. Mercifully, her stay lasted only a little over a year, and she died peacefully at age eighty-one. Her unique mannerisms were not completely obliterated, however. They were about to find a new life in a person I came to know shortly before her death.

A Slip on a Banana Peel

COMPLETELY DEMORALIZED by the decline of my music career, I decided to spend an afternoon in Central Park sunbathing and contemplating my future. It was a perfect late spring day. The sky was clear, the sun was shining, and I had a vast field of grass all to myself. I spread out my blanket and the *New York Times*. I began formulating a plan. If I worked for ten years in publishing, saving and investing as much of my salary as possible, I would be able to retire, perhaps in Europe, and return to music without the need to earn a living from it. I knew Todd was unhappy with his publishing job, as well. Perhaps I could convince him that we could live on one salary, save the other, so we could both retire.

My eyes closed and lost in my future formulations, I was startled by a loud explosion. Something hit me. The noise came from something striking the open pages of the *Times*. I opened my eyes to discover that both the *Times* and I were covered in shit. What could this be? I looked up and saw a flock of geese flying hundreds of feet overhead. The whole of Central Park and they had to aim their oversized turds directly at me? Was this some sort of ominous omen?

Todd and I discussed my plan, and he agreed we should give it a try. Though having him as my boss hadn't caused any problems while I was working part-time, I decided it would be best to find a full-time job, at better pay, elsewhere. I was hired as a production editor at a start-up magazine, which was already claiming to be the largest-circulation magazine in the world. *New Connections* was a joint project of the Reuben H. Donnelley Corporation, the publisher of telephone directories, and Dun & Bradstreet.

Anyone who connected with the telephone company, automatically received a copy of the magazine, which provided all pertinent information about the geographic area they lived in: maps, shopping, restaurants, culture, services, and history. Each edition was specifically tailored to nearly every major city in the country. The work was heavily detailed, with so many different editions published simultaneously.

Because I no longer had the need to practice the piano for hours a day, I found time to give elaborate dinner parties and expand my culinary skills. Also, I had outgrown my home gym and decided to join the 63rd Street Y, where I had lived for five miserable months after breaking up with Hal. I enjoyed the gym environment, but I became uncomfortable when a group of straight bodybuilders, who had been very friendly to me, would use the most horrible homophobic slurs among themselves. When Rock Hudson died from AIDS, I overheard such despicable comments as, "That faggot deserved to die." I knew I had to get out of there. I joined the Chelsea Gym, a gay establishment for men only, and felt much more at home.

Todd and I had been spared the AIDS epidemic because our relationship kept us cloistered from sexual encounters during its onset. However, we both began to be hit by the dreadful loss of friends, particularly those in the theater. Frank Newell had died in California, and I was particularly surprised to read of Jess Richards' death in the newspapers. I had lost touch with so many of the other dancers I worked with, so when I couldn't locate them to reconnect, I suspected the worst.

At the end of a year, Dun & Bradstreet startlingly decided to pull the plug on *New Connections*. The company, somewhat of a magazine novice, did not comprehend that new periodicals take time to establish themselves, so when the magazine did not make money in its first year, they lost their nerve. Bruce Hunter arranged an interview for me with a major publishing executive. The interview went extremely well, and I was surprised when I never heard back from him. Bruce eventually confessed to Todd, "He was very impressed with Norman, but could not recommend him for any position because he has not achieved an executive-level position commensurate with someone his age." Oh, my god, I'm too old even for a publishing career? From now on my age is nobody's business.

The next week I was hired as a production editor at *Sylvia Porter's Personal Finance Magazine.* I knew virtually nothing about the financial world but saw this as an opportunity to learn how to make some money. The magazine was another start-up, which traded on the name of the famed syndicated financial-advice columnist, though she had little to do with the publication. Within a few months, I was promoted to managing editor when the man in that position was bumped up to executive editor. The staff was young, bright, and very personable. Patty Seyburn, a young Master's Degree graduate from Northwestern, was hired as an editorial assistant, and our mutual love of theater quickly brought us close together. Patty had been in a high-school production of *Celebration* and was excited to have met an original cast member.

Except for the editor, Pat Estess, who had worked with Sylvia Porter, almost no one on the staff had a financial background, but we were fast learners. In its first year, the publication was nominated for Best New Magazine at the National Magazine Awards, though it didn't win. I used to tease my staff that I understood how deeply they wanted to be in publishing, getting their advanced journalism degrees and dreaming about becoming the Dorothy Parker of the '80s, while I, on the other hand, just wanted to be a department-store announcer who simply fell willy-nilly into the field.

I imagined myself becoming more sophisticated about investing as I put most of my salary into blue-chips and established mutual funds. However, when we ran a story about penny stocks, which we had researched and fact-checked very thoroughly, I was tempted by a company that was developing a larger storage disk for computers and invested a few thousand dollars. This was the age of the soon-to-be obsolete floppy disk. The company was run by former top researchers for Bell Laboratories. This was a hot new field, where the demand was very high. How could it possibly fail? I don't know, but it went belly-up within a few months.

I mailed Mary Giovingo, prior to her decline, a copy of the magazine when I became managing editor. Never one to disappoint, her response was, "For such an important job, your name is sure way down on the list." This was, of course, because the publishers and ad staff were listed in the masthead above the editorial staff. Instructing one of my fact-checkers, I suddenly stopped on a dime and thought, "Norman, do you actually hear yourself? You sound completely ridiculous. You're an artist, and here you are explaining the intricacies of zero-coupon bonds to this young woman. Who do you think you are?"

Hoping to reach my ten-year retirement goal a little faster, I thought to myself, "As long as I have to work this hard at doing something I don't enjoy, I might as well go to Wall Street, where I can earn some real money." I began sending out resumes. One day at the office I received a phone call from a Faith Hart, a woman with a girlish, high-pitched voice.

"Mr. Mathews?"

"Yes.

"Hello, this is Faith Hart from Merrill Lynch."

"Oh, hello."

"Now, why did I call you?"

"I don't know. Why?"

"Uhmm. (Embarrassing pause.) Oh, yes. You sent us your resume."

"Yes, I did." (The eyes rolled.)

"Well, I think I would be interested in interviewing you."

"Really, that's wonderful." She thinks?

This conversation was a real tipoff of what was to come. At the interview, she began with the usual approach. "I see your background has until recently been in theater and music. What makes you think that you would be the right person to work in a financial firm."

"Well, as you know, I've just been working as managing editor of a financial publication." Then I launched into my generic bullshit spiel to this line of questioning, which inevitably won them over. "Both theater and music require a level of discipline and excellence that I find unmatched in the publishing and corporate worlds. Naturally, I carry that same degree of discipline with me always, and I adapt it to fit every job I've ever done since leaving the world of the arts." She was impressed.

I was hired at nearly double my previous salary. Pat Estess congratulated me, but warned me that I would not be happy with the sort of people I would be working with on Wall Street, especially after the very bright staff at *Sylvia Porter's*. How right she was.

Wall Street was a whole new world to me. I was amazed, and even cowed, by the aggressiveness and rudeness of many of the employees, though my staff was very sweet and welcoming. For the life of me, I couldn't figure out what the fiftyish Faith Hart ever did in her office. I sensed that she delegated nearly everything to me. My job was to produce a whole series of weekly newsletters designed to give the company's employees, and particularly its brokers all over the world—excuse me, financial consultants or FCs as they were reverently called, as though they were deities—the information they needed to do their jobs more effectively. Most of the stories we ran came from the various marketing departments: bonds, funds, options, capital management, and so forth.

These marketing geniuses, many of whom could not write a simple comprehensible sentence, were the most belligerent. Redeeming their execrable prose led to exchanges such as, "You will run the article exactly as I wrote it, or I'll be taking up the issue at a level much higher than you." My staff referred to this woman as "the pit bull."

On Monday morning, October 19, 1987, five months after I began at Merrill Lynch, I walked into my office to learn the market had crashed. The Dow Jones Industrial average lost almost twenty-three percent. Goodby retirement savings; goodby ten-year plan. Faith Hart came to me and said, "Well, Norman, you'd better close yourself in your office and write an article on what Merrill's position is on the crash."

What? I'm going to speak for all 47,000 employees on this? Does she delude herself into thinking I'm some kind of financial expert?

When she saw the concerned, and somewhat terrified, look on my face, she said, "Just call Chuck Clough, he'll tell you what to say." Clough was the chief investment strategist, the one who appeared on CNN each week, offering his advice..

"Hello, Mr. Clough, I need to get a statement from you on the company's position regarding this crash."

"Are you kidding? I don't have time to do that. Just write something yourself, and I'll look it over."

Phew! Okay, if he's going to rewrite it, then I don't have to worry, right? Nevertheless, I was sweating profusely as I banged out some drivel. "Stop worrying. It's not a problem, Norman. Clough will rewrite the whole piece," was the mantra I repeated to myself.

When I finished it, I needed a break so I went out to lunch, ruminating not only about Chuck Clough and the article, but also about how much of Todd's and my retirement savings had just gone down the drain. Lost in these concerns, I was not terribly aware of my surroundings when "bam," I was on my ass on a Wall Street sidewalk, my suit pants torn. "What the hell?" I looked down, "Damn, I just slipped on a banana peel. What am I the third banana in some tired burlesque routine? Next up, my pants fall down as I get a cream pie in the face?" My brilliant ten-year retirement plan began with geese shitting on me and ended with my slipping on a banana peel.

Having lost my appetite, I returned to my office to hear my phone ringing. It's Chuck Clough. "Norman, it's fine. Run it just as it is." "What?" I yelled after he hung up the phone. "How could it be fine? What the hell do I know about any of this?" The article ran. The next week there was a huge purge of staff. Life-long employees were told to pack up their things and, under security escort, were forced to depart the company immediately. I survived and was promoted to editorial director and made a vice president.

One marketing head, with whom I had a good relationship, was a very rough-hewn, loud-voiced Italian from Staten Island. Whenever Bob called me, it was always "Norman, how the hell are you today?" I would respond with parallel banter. A couple weeks before Christmas, the phone rings, "Norman, how the hell are you today?" in the loudest voice I've ever heard. I answered, "Why in the hell are you yelling in my ear?" Absolute silence on the other end. Was he offended? I always responded in that way. What's happening? "Norman, this is Launny Steffens." What? No! Launny Steffens, the president and CEO, and I just swore at him on the phone. I was mortified and couldn't even find the words to apologize. I had never heard his voice before. Who knew he sounded just like Bob? He continued with some request as though nothing had happened. Later, I called his secretary, "Please tell Mr. Steffens that I apologize for the way I answered the phone. I thought he was someone else." Will I be fired, blackballed? Will he call Faith and tell her what happened? Chalk this up to the most embarrassing incident of my life.

As Christmas approached, Faith said, "Tomorrow, I want you to wear your very best suit. You'll be meeting with the president." Oh, no, I'm about to be fired. I've never been fired in my life. I don't know if I can handle it. The next day, I was told to report to a particular room. I cautiously entered and was stunned to see a throng of people and long tables with elaborate food presentations. We were asked to be seated and Steffens made his announcement: "All one hundred of you assembled in this room have been selected, out of Merrill Lynch's 47,000 employees, as the top employees in the company for 1987." After lunching at the buffet, we were presented with an envelope. Inside, I found a check for $10,000. What show am in, *How to Succeed in Business Without Really Trying?* So much for being too old for the corporate world. It didn't make up for all the money I lost in the crash, but it was a big help. In a world where mediocrity—and I include my own— is rewarded so freely, is it any wonder that egos explode through the walls of a room? What would these same pampered people do if they faced, even for one day, the constant rejection and criticism one gets in the arts?

With the promotion came more responsibilities. We moved into new offices in the World Financial Center, and my office commanded a lovely view of the plaza and the harbor. Faith told me that we would now both be expected to spend one day a week in Princeton, New Jersey, where Merrill had its corporate campus. This added an extra hour-and-a-half train trip each way to my already long commute from Washington Heights. Neither of us had an office in Princeton, but rather adjoining cubicles separated by a partition. Busy working on a project, I heard, "Okay, Faith, good for you. That's quite a job you've done here. You've come in well under budget. Great work, Faith." I peeked over the partition. There was no one there but Faith sitting at her desk, giving herself a pat. This is even worse than I thought. Dorothy Parker once said, "The one dependable law of life—everything is always worse than you thought it was going to be."

I was responsible for computerizing our department, eliminating typesetting equipment and typesetters in favor of the latest publishing software. It required that I fire several people, which was extremely painful, and hire more computer-literate staff. I brought in a very accomplished and experienced editor. Two weeks after she began she came into my office and closed the door. "I'm really annoyed with you, Norman." "Why is that?" "I just left a job because I was working for a crazy woman, who made my life hell. Then a few minutes ago I was in the restroom, when I overheard some psycho in another stall ranting to herself in the most bizarre fashion. I couldn't imagine who it could be, but as I was leaving I saw that it was Faith Hart. And you never said a word about her in my interview." "I know. I know. Don't worry. Everything you do will go through me. You'll have next to no contact with her."

One of our newsletters, "Derivative Products Alert" (known as DPA), dealt with options and futures. The exotic products that caused the 2008 crash were not yet in use. I suspected that Faith understood nothing whatever about this publication, but I wanted to test it out. Before a department meeting, I asked my staff to bring up DPA continually to see what reaction we would get. Everyone complied, asking intermittent inane questions about it. Suddenly, two heavily jeweled fists pounded on the table, "What the hell is DPA, anyway?" Faith screamed.

She really had no idea what the department was up to, depending entirely on her staff to keep everything afloat. How she advanced to this very high-paying position was a mystery to me. I deduced that it had to do with the way she was able to play the political game in the company, and then, of course, there were her miraculously low budgets. Good for you, Faith.

I had not given much consideration to the morality of working on Wall Street when I was told to run an article instructing the FCs to press senior citizens to buy bonds on margin (borrowing money to invest). The company claimed that interest rates would go down, increasing the value of bonds. We're seriously asking seniors to incur debt on a mere guess about interest rates? As everyone in finance knows, any person who could consistently and correctly predict interest rates would be the richest person on earth. Not surprisingly, interest rates when up, rather than down, in the next six months. I wondered how many seniors were burned by that specious advice. I felt sick. Do I really want to be a facilitator to such devious practices?

As the workload expanded, the workdays got longer and longer. Oh, sure, I was always provided with a limousine to take me home, ironically to my dowdy, down-scale neighborhood, when I worked late, but I had next to no life. Music was mostly gone, and even the gym was slipping away. It's not as though the work was challenging or interesting, just voluminous. It had the unique and dispiriting quality of being both stressful and boring. I was a miserable, complaining wretch at home. Todd said, "You're job is killing me, and I wish you would quit." I was having more severe problems with my back. I needed to get away, so I arranged to spend a week with my brother in Napa.

Larry was living with a new and temporary girlfriend, and working as a chauffeur for some wealthy Italians, who owned a tomato cannery. I suspected they were mafia-connected (Mary Giovingo would have died had she known), though I never met them. By the time I arrived, I was in very serious pain. We went out to dinner, and when we returned to Larry's apartment I could hardly move. That night was one of the worst I've ever spent. The pain was excruciating, the bed was a torture rack, and I was on my hands and knees moaning on the floor most of the night.

The next morning I told Larry I had to return to New York. Getting into his car took me nearly fifteen agonizing minutes. I took the subway from JFK into the city because I couldn't bear the agony of getting into a cab. When I came out of the train station, I must have looked so pathetic that some guy offered to carry my bag the three blocks to get me home. I spent the rest of the week on my back in bed, trying not to move any muscle whatever. Something had to give.

My spine was so twisted out of shape that I was bent over and listing to the right side. I started seeing both an acupuncturist and a physical therapist. The acupuncturist said to me, "Your problem is not your back. Your problem is your life, and if you don't do something about it soon, you'll be facing far worse than back problems." The physical therapist gave me a series of exercises, "You must do these religiously the very first thing when you get out of bed in the morning because that's when you experience the most severe problems." Oh, no, that means I have to get up a half-hour earlier. Then I learned about Dr. John Sarno and his book *Mind Over Back Pain*, which postulates that most back pain is caused by stress and repressed emotions, such as anger. Merrill Lynch, anyone? My posture gradually normalized as the combination of these three treatment modalities put me on the road to healing, or at least minimizing and managing pain.

My job had put a severe strain on my relationship with Todd, the first time I ever feared it might be in jeopardy. In addition, a very talented artist friend of his whom he had met years earlier at the Art Students League added to our problems. This woman, though always supportive of me to my face, harbored some grievance against me that I could never define. It seemed to center on my inhibiting Todd's creativity, which was nonsensical because I was his biggest supporter and fervently admired his work. She was continually trying to interfere in our relationship by introducing Todd to attractive young men, in the hope of weaning him away from me. To my knowledge, Todd never took the bait. He did, however, take a trip to Amsterdam and Paris with her, which put a further pressure on our relationship. However, the trip dealt a blow to their friendship, because she was drunk most of the time, turning a vacation into an ordeal. I became very concerned about what was happening to us. Something had to be done, and Todd's out-of-left-field suggestion startled me.

"Why don't you just quit Merrill Lynch and start composing?"

"Composing? Me? What makes you think I have any talent for composing. I've never written anything but one little tune and some school exercises. I've never been a creative artist. I don't even have a creative mind. I've always been about recreating others' work."

"Just give it a try. I think it will help you, and it certainly will help me and our relationship, not to hear you constantly complaining about your job."

This seemed a ridiculous idea, but I was so unhappy with my life at that point that I began giving it serious consideration. Our ten-year plan was pretty much kaput. It would now have to be a fifteen- or twenty-year plan, which essentially defeats the purpose of freeing us so that we could return to music and art full-time.

What would I compose? It would have to be musical theater and cabaret songs, I guess. The idea of my writing classical music was ludicrous. Todd was on a mission and learned about a course in songwriting at the 92nd Street Y, taught by Richard Adler, who had written *The Pajama Game* and *Damn Yankees*. I took the weekly course in the evenings, while still at Merrill. To prepare for it, I borrowed songs by Richard Rodgers and Stephen Sondheim and used them as models, maintaining the form and the harmonies but writing whole new melodies and arrangements. Many classical composers teach themselves in the same way, using Mozart and Beethoven works as models.

The tunes I wrote did not play well in the class because they had no lyrics. Adler then gave us the assignment to write a piece to a lyric he had written for a show about a boy committing suicide by throwing himself under a bus, which was inspired by Adler's son's death. One woman in the class asked, incredulously, "Is this supposed to be a musical comedy?" Adler hated the way I set his lyric, although several classmates disagreed with him. I learned next to nothing in the class because Adler had no musical training and could play no instrument. He simply sang a melody into a tape recorder and his pianist turned it into a harmonized song. His two major musicals were written with his collaborator, Jerry

255

Ross, who died very young. I began to wonder if Ross was the real talent in this team.

Certainly this class did nothing to encourage me that I had any talent in composing or in being creative, but I found that I enjoyed the writing so much that I simply had to continue. Dare I leave a well-paying job for such a hare-brained scheme? How would I earn a living? Perhaps I could go back to teaching piano and theory. I had saved enough to live on for two to three years, and unlike my earlier attempt at teaching, funds were now available to advertise myself.

When I finally mustered up the courage to give my resignation to Faith's boss, she said. "You're resigning to do what? To be a composer? You know you're on the fast track to bigger things here, and you're willing to toss that aside?" My explanation was lame, simply because what I was doing made no sense in the practical world. On parting, she admitted, "You know, I'll have to say I admire you for having the courage to make such a move. There is, after all, more to life than Merrill Lynch." Well, I should hope so.

One of my editors told me that her roommate, Laura, who had studied piano for several years, was interested in taking lessons. And the art director of our department connected me with her neighbor, who had a young daughter, Harper, interested in studying. What was most amazing to me was that these colleagues recommended me without having any idea about my abilities in playing, much less teaching piano. They assumed that since I was good at my job, I would be a good teacher. So Merrill Lynch relaunched my piano-teaching career.

It had been several years since I had to demonstrate my skills at the piano, and I became significantly insecure. Laura turned out to be a very advanced pianist, who eventually began teaching piano herself. This added to my insecurity because I had never taught anyone at that level before. I took a course for pianists who were debilitated by performance anxiety. Interestingly, everyone in the class was a piano teacher. Each week we were expected to play for each other.

My goal was to overcome my fear of playing without music. At the same time, I began seeing a therapist who specialized in treating performance anxiety. I told her that I wasn't sure that I was even competent to be teaching piano. She asked me for a recording of my solo playing, so I supplied her with a tape I had made of Beethoven's, Opus 110, Piano Sonata. At my next session, she asked me, "Do you know who Ruth Laredo is?"

"Of course, I know. She's one of the finest concert pianists."

"Well, Ruth is my neighbor, and I asked her to listen to your tape and tell me what she thought."

Suddenly, I'm feeling very nervous.

"Do you know what she said?"

"No." I responded warily.

"She said, 'Is this guy crazy?' Now I'm in total panic mode. Here goes the end of my teaching career before it's even started. "Anyone who can play Opus 110 like that, should not be questioning whether he's good enough to teach. He should be demanding that students audition for him before he accepts them." Phew!

The performance class did not go as well. The memory lapses continued. I believed that if I kept at it, I would eventually overcome the problem, but it would take a herculean effort and a good stretch of time. Why was I expending so much energy on this when I would never be playing solo concerts? The plan was to compose and teach. That's what I must do. Both Laura and the little girl, Harper, who was a beginner, needed to be taught at their own apartments. It had not really occurred to me before that I could be an itinerant piano teacher, simply charging a higher rate for making house calls. This solved the problem that almost no one was willing to come to Washington Heights for lessons.

I took out a year's worth of ads and posted fliers at strategic locations, stating that I could teach beginners through advanced students in their own homes. I put together my own lesson plans and a syllabus of piano pieces tailored to all levels. I also created a step-by-step text in music theory for those who had never been exposed to it. I modeled my teaching after Judy Meites's approach, obliterating the fear and tension levels that so many music teachers inflict upon their students.

Hammerstein's lyric comes to mind, "If you become a teacher, by your pupils you'll be taught." I found myself having to invent methods for helping students overcome difficulties, a process that improved my own skills. The old adage is: "Those who can, do; those who can't, teach." But this is twisted logic. Often those who can do, can't teach. Those performers who are natural talents, often have no idea how they do things. They never had to work at it and therefore can offer no help to students. The first couple years of teaching brought in only enough students to cover my living expenses, but at least I wasn't depleting my savings. I was back in music.

A Composer Is Born

I HAD NEVER TAKEN a composition lesson, so it seemed imperative that I get some training. But where to turn at my age? I know, I'll write to Stephen Sondheim for advice. I explained my background, that I wanted to write for musical theater, and asked if he could recommend a teacher for me. Within a week I received a letter.

> Dear Mr. Mathews,
>
> I wish I could help, but even Jonathan Tunick (Sondheim's orchestrator) didn't know who to study with privately (he eventually asked Leonard Bernstein, who gave him a couple of lessons). I have what may seem an obvious suggestion, however. Composers of "serious" (i.e. concert music—and you should only study with such, I think) support themselves through teaching. Why not write one that you admire? Almost all, even those who deal exclusively in "contemporary" sounds, have had thorough classical training in both theory and composition. (That's why my college got in touch with Milton Babbitt, and why he took me on, even though he was teaching at Princeton at the same time.)
>
> Yours sincerely.
>
> Stephen Sondheim

I wrote to Ned Rorem, a composer I admired, "The only teaching I do is three handpicked geniuses at Curtis...I take a dim view of schools. . . imitation is the only way to learn anything, and it's cheaper than tuition." This was actually better advice than I realized at the time, when I was adamant I needed a teacher to guide me. Mark Bennett, a fine composer and a top Broadway sound designer, whom I met at the Chelsea

Gym, recommended that I call John Corigliano. John recommended a teacher named Charles Turner.

I had no concert music to show him, so I needed to write something in a hurry. I decided that an art song (serious music set to poetry) would be a good place to start, and I chose Elinor Wylie's *Velvet Shoes,* about the silence of walking in the snow, to set. "Where do I even begin?" I wondered. I took each line of the poem and notated it rhythmically. Then I created a melody to fit my rhythmic notation and found harmonies and accompanimental figures to underscore the melody.

Fortuitously, Turner had been a pupil (and most likely a lover) of Samuel Barber, one of my most admired 20th-Century composers. Co-incidences piled one on top of another. Charles was introduced to Barber by Ned Rorem, and Barber's four-hand piano piece, *Souvenirs,* which Sarah and I performed, was actually written for Charles Turner. He said to me, "I'm going to teach you exactly the way Sam taught me." He looked over my *Velvet Shoes* piece, "This is good. Very good. It should be published." I dismissed this as flattery to build my confidence.

For each lesson, I was assigned to study a Bach Two-Part or Three-Part *Invention,* then write a comparable piece modeled precisely on Bach's. I wrote four of them, and his critiques were always the same, "These are fine, just fine as they are." By the fourth *Invention,* I countered, "But you can hear that this phrase is dull and awkward." "No, no. It's fine. Just leave it."

Charles had some wonderful tales to tell about his life with Sam. A well-known singer programmed Barber's *A Nun Takes the Veil,* but she wanted to make numerous changes to the piece. Barber said to her, "Great, by all means make all the changes you want, only you must retitle the piece A Veil Takes the Nun." Once Leonard Bernstein came to Barber's house to play a new piece. Barber stopped him shortly after he began playing and said, "Lenny, you can't write that." "Why not?" "Because Debussy already wrote it."

After the *Inventions,* Turner asked me to write a contemporary piece based on the octatonic scale (the eight-note, alternating half step-whole-step scale). Todd suggested to me a beautiful passage from Virginia Wolf's, *A Room of One's Own,* about a student rowing through willow trees. Again, I set the text to music, and again all I heard was, "It's fine." When I pressed for criticism, he suggested changing a B-natural to a B-flat. Why am I paying this guy if everything I write is just fine? After six lessons I quit.

At the same time, I began studying jazz piano with Harold Danko, who had performed with Gerry Mulligan and Chet Baker. Though I loved jazz, I didn't really know much about it, and I definitely was no jazz whiz. Danko was patient with me and tried to get me over my fear of improvising. I never got really good at it, but I did learn my way around the chord changes and did a facsimile of improvisation. That ability, as well as putting my theory to practical use at the keyboard, turned out to be more valuable than any composition lessons. My accompaniment writing grew much more sophisticated as a result.

Danko convinced me to write a few jazz pieces, one of which was for soprano sax and piano, called *Anders' Theme* and dedicated to Anders Paulsson. a brilliant sax-player friend from Sweden. When we got to the blues, Danko said, "You play the blues like such a white boy. You really need to spend some time in Harlem." "But, Harold, I live a couple blocks from Harlem. I guess it just didn't take with me."

Because I was writing art songs, Mark Bennett suggested that I take them to a well-known art-song composer for evaluation, as he had done a few years earlier. This composer, Richard Hundley said to me. "I don't know how to teach, but I'll give you my opinions." When I showed him my work, he said, "And why have you waited until this late in life to begin composing?" Was this simply a nice way of saying you're too old for this field? I was forty-nine, and I really had no good answer for this. "I guess because it never occurred to me that I had any ability in this direction," I mumbled.

My five sessions with him were quite strange. He became defensive for some reason as he played through my material. "I know you're going to become famous before me." "Richard, how can you say that when your work is being performed by some of the greatest singers in the world?" He especially liked a song I had written to the Walt Whitman poem, "Sometimes With One I Love." "You know, Ned Rorem has already set this poem. Let's compare the two versions." I didn't know the Rorem song, but I was struck by how different it was from mine, in tone and intent. Rorem treated Whitman's unrequited love as resignation, while I read the poem as a passionate plea for love, even when it is unreturned. "If Ned had heard your version, he would have taken you as a student in a minute," Hundley claimed.

"I want you to write a couple different songs. First, a little ditty." He chose an anonymous children's verse for me to set. "Then how about some Shakespeare?" He selected "Fancy" from *The Merchant of Venice*. Carefully going over my newly composed pieces, he said. "Are you even aware of what a wonderful phrase you've written here? I'm warning you now I can't promise that I won't steal it from you." "Richard, if you like it that much, help yourself."

He thought I needed a demo tape of my songs, so he put me in touch with a mezzo-soprano, Mary Ann Hart, who with a fantastic pianist, Dennis Helmrich, recorded five of my songs. Dennis complained that he had to spend more time practicing the piano part for my little ditty, than for all the other pieces combined.

With the encouragement I had received from these various sources, I decided, "No more lessons. I'm just going to compose." Because the Whitman song seemed to be my best, I decided to write a song cycle based on his poetry. I read through his entire works and selected six more poems that I thought would make a nice musical and dramatic arc. The seven-song cycle, which I began with "Sometimes With One I Love," I entitled, *Songs of the Poet*.

I engaged soprano Theresa Snyder and her pianist David Rebhun, to make a demo recording of the cycle at Town Hall, which they later performed at a tiny venue in New York. This was the first-ever public performance of my compositions, which led to my first royalty checks from ASCAP, the performing rights organization. Despite the fact that the venue was rather disheartening, I experienced sheer joy at hearing my work performed by professional musicians. The heart pounds. The adrenaline surges. The high is equal to or even greater than giving a good performance, and it became the driving force for me to write. I was hooked.

Richard Hundley generously introduced me to Paul Sperry, a highly respected tenor, a champion of art songs, and a teacher at Juilliard. Sperry admired my Whitman song cycle and convinced a young soprano, Rebekah Wilshire, who was giving a joint concert in New York with another soprano, Tracy Bidleman, to program it. I attended a rehearsal and was very excited by how good she made my work sound. Just weeks before the concert, Rebekah was thrown from a horse while riding in Central Park. She didn't appear to be injured, but a week later she complained to her husband that she didn't feel well. They went to the emergency room, where she died shortly after from a blood clot caused by the fall.

Gregory Wiest, an American tenor who sings with the Munich Opera, informed me that he planned to program *Songs of the Poet* for a concert at Amerikahaus in Munich and later to do a commercial recording of the whole program. My career was going international. Todd and I went to Germany, and I was the only composer on the program to appear at the concert, so Gregory presented me to the audience for a bow after singing my piece. Was my work really going to be preserved on CDs? When I began this composing journey, I couldn't imagine that anything would come of it, and certainly not with classical music. It was all castles in the sky.

The trip proved fruitful for both Todd and me. Gregory programmed other songs of mine on future concerts, which he also recorded. Todd spent time canvassing the galleries in Munich, and though it took a couple of years and more trips, he managed to have two successful exhibits—a one-person and a two-person show—at the Otto-Galerie. before the owners retired. A beautiful catalog, which he was able to use as a promotional tool, was printed for the one-person exhibit. Dr. Baranov, the gallery owner, provided us with an apartment above the gallery.

We were accompanied to the Munich opening, by my brother, Todd's brother, Jon, and his wife, Dee, and David Hemphill. I had never before seen how my brother, Larry, could work his charms. In restaurants, he won over the waiters and bartenders to the point they seemed ready to hire him, out of hand. Though he spoke not a word of German, they were so taken with him that free drinks were served to all of us.

I had heard that Dalton Baldwin, one of the world's leading accompanists, who had performed with Gerard Souzay, Elie Ameling, and Jessye Norman, was now teaching at the Westminster Choir College in New Jersey. I was a big fan of his since my student days. I sent him my Whitman cycle in the hope that he would simply pass the score on to vocal students. The response I received astounded me.

> You have chosen poems that interconnect effectively. You have set them with striking sensitivity and emotional depth. If I am late in responding, it is that I need time to get to know your songs—to take them to heart. I am so moved by Tears and "Set ope the doors O soul. Tenderly" etc. There are many marvelous moments for the pianist as well. I am sailing through That Music Always Round Me with such joy!

Even better, he suggested that if I was willing to transpose some of the higher pieces into lower keys, he would show them to David Arnold, a baritone with whom he planned to do a concert of Whitman songs by various composers. David Arnold's agent contacted me a few days later, requesting that I FedEx the score immediately to Boston, where Arnold was singing with the Boston Symphony.

Is this real? I'm actually a classical composer, and major artists are considering performing my music? Is this the way it works, how careers are born? If it hadn't been for Stephen Sondheim's advice, I would never have ventured into the world of serious music. I believed I had finally found what I was meant to do in life.

Todd and I went to hear David Arnold at Carnegie Hall, where he was a soloist in Bach's *St. John's Passion*. I was a bit taken aback when I heard him sing because his beautiful deep voice was more of bass-baritone than a true baritone. We went backstage to his dressing room after the performance. "Ah, you're the composer who wrote those beautiful Whitman songs. You know, they are awfully high for my voice." This was precisely my concern when I heard him sing. I had transposed the songs, originally written for soprano or tenor, down as low as possible without having the piano part fall off the bass end of the keyboard.

The concert didn't happen, whether because the pieces were too high or because, as Dalton explained, they couldn't coordinate their schedules, I never knew. It was my first harsh lesson that nothing in this business is certain until the contracts are signed. There would be many such disappointments in the future. Dalton Baldwin's letter, however, provided reassurance in those depressing times when I questioned whether I had any talent whatever.

My teaching career took a sudden turn for the better, and I had Merrill Lynch to thank for it. Noreen, whose daughter Harper I had been teaching after a recommendation from a fellow employee at Merrill, was a director at a preschool. She recommended me to Janice Lee, one of the children's mothers who was looking for a piano teacher for her daughter. Janice and her husband Stuart Shapiro owned a stunning Italianate Greek Revival townhouse on Morton Street in Greenwich Village. Stuart had his own law firm, which was housed in the former Finnish consulate on Madison Avenue. Janice, who had also been a successful attorney, was now devoting herself to her four children, Lily, Sam, and fraternal twins, Kenny and Mark.

I began teaching Lily, a bright and talented five-year-old, on a digital keyboard. Within a year, Sam began studying, followed by the twins, and the Shapiros purchased a Steinway grand. All four children were students at the Village Community School, a private academy. Janice and Stu recommended me to the parents of other students at the school, and within no time I had a large class of pupils. As Stu said, "We can fill your dance card every day of the week." At its peak, I had thirty-five students. Because I was now earning a good living, I decided to limit the class to that amount so that I kept time open for composing. These new students all lived in the Village, which helped cut down my travel time between lessons.

I loved writing the serious art songs and continued to do so, but I didn't want to toss aside my initial idea of writing for musical theater or cabaret. Enter Dorothy Parker. It occurred to me that her acerbic verses might serve well for some jazzy settings. I chose about ten poems from her collections and put my nine months of jazz piano lessons to good use. I wasn't certain what to do with these songs, but I had a vague idea that they might make a cabaret act. One of my adult students suggested that I send them to Mary Cleere Haran, who was a rising cabaret star. She wrote, "Where were you when I needed you?" She had been asked to do a tribute to Mrs. Parker on the centennial of her birth but didn't like any of the Parker settings she had been sent, so she simply sang songs of the period. She liked my songs very much but was now booked up for the next couple years with her own club act. Tragically, she died, hit by a car while bicycling.

Todd then introduced me to the celebrated jazz singer, Susannah McCorkle, with whom he had performed *Bye Bye Birdie* in community theater in Pennsylvania. She had returned from living in Europe, and after engagements at Michael's Pub she was about to begin a long run of appearances at the Algonquin Hotel's Oak Room, where of course, Mrs. Parker was a member of the famed Round Table. Susannah especially admired two of the songs and was considering including them in her act. I waited patiently for this to happen but began to realize that there was a real fear among cabaret performers of presenting new work. Their audiences came to hear the great old standards, and moving away from that repertoire was risky.

Susannah was a very intelligent and literate singer. She knew exactly what she was singing about and made the most of every word. One of the things I admired about her was that despite the lack of a superior vocal instrument, she took the small voice she was given and made it into something glorious. I was completely incapable of such a feat as a performer. Every deficiency I owned loomed large before me and proved an insurmountable obstacle.

On a Saturday afternoon, when Todd was visiting his family in Pennsylvania, I heard a news report that a well-known cabaret singer had just committed suicide. I listened carefully and learned to my horror that it was Susannah. She threw herself from her sixteenth-floor apartment, leaving a will on her desk and a note, pleading that someone take care of her cats. I called Todd to warn him. What could have caused this? We learned that her record contract had been canceled and that her appearances at the Algonquin were being terminated. The cabaret world had been dying a slow death for years, and coupled with her years of depression it became too much for her.

Cabaret seemed the wrong route for my songs. Mrs. Parker's life was so fascinating, and the poems were so personal that a theater piece seemed a better choice. In the '70s, I saw my first one-person play, *Gertrude Stein, Gertrude, Stein, Gertrude Stein,* and fell in the love with the form. What about a one-person musical? This seemed the perfect way to tell Dorothy's story. I would need more songs, but who would write the script? I made a tape of my singing and playing the songs I had written thus far and sent it to Andre Bishop, director of Lincoln Center Theaters, asking if he could recommend a playwright who might be interested in working with me.

He responded, "As I've never admired Miss Parker or her verse I don't think I'm the one to ask!" Well, now I know it will never be done at Lincoln Center. He did, however, turn my tape over to his musical theater department. A week later I received another letter from him, "Our musical theater dept. greatly admired your songs but felt that they were cabaret songs and should remain as such. They felt strongly that your music gave the verse some dimension and that the songs support themselves and don't need anything else…though they like your work a lot," the last word underlined several times. I had already run out of leads in the cabaret world so I ignored their advice. The problem of where exactly the material fit, however, caused disagreement and plagued me endlessly.

A Broadway conductor friend, Jack Lee, recommended an actor who was doing some playwriting, so I met with her. The actor was June Squibb, who played one of the strippers in the original production of *Gypsy* and some years after I met her was nominated for an Academy Award for her role in *Nebraska*. I went to her apartment, but sadly we could not come to any agreement on a concept for the piece.

I know, I'll just write a draft of it myself, then a real playwright can see what I have in mind and rework it into something professional. I read everything Mrs. Parker, born Dorothy Rothschild, ever wrote and every book written about her. Many of her early poems at that time had been published only in magazines, so I spent months in the New York Public Library, going through old microfiche copies. The undertaking became as mammoth as writing a biography. I needed to get the rights to her material, and I learned that, strangely enough, they were held by the NAACP. Dorothy had deeply deplored racism and left her entire estate to Martin Luther King. She died in 1967 and when King was killed in 1968, her estate was turned over to the NAACP.

I knew nothing about the art of playwriting, but it didn't matter since a real playwright would rewrite whatever drivel I concocted. I used scenes from her short stories and even musicalized one of them, *The Waltz*, into a ten-minute piece that took me two months to write. I tried to give the songs context by fitting them into episodes in her life. The more I came to know Mrs. Parker, the more I loved her. We had so many traits in common: her insecurity about her work, her pessimism about life, her desperation for love, her suicide attempts, and her political views. I was becoming proprietary over what I had written, believing that I knew and understood her as well as anyone did.

My old roommate, Jerry Bell, suggested that I show what I had written to Douglas, a young director he knew. Douglas seemed taken by the project and told me that in college he tried to work on a Dorothy Parker musical with a composer classmate of his. I later learned that this composer was Stephen Flaherty. Douglas said that they couldn't seem to make Dorothy sing, and they abandoned the project. He thought I was well on my way to something that could work. So I can do what Stephen Flaherty couldn't?

"You need a demo recording, and then we'll do a reading. I know it's casting against type, but how do you feel about Karen Mason in the role." Karen was a tall blonde; Dorothy Parker was a small, dark-haired woman. I didn't know Karen's work so I bought a recording and loved what I heard. She was the standby for both Glenn Close and Betty Buckley in *Sunset Boulevard* on Broadway. It just so happened that she was performing the role, while Betty Buckley was on vacation, so I went to see it. Never have I been an admirer of Andrew Lloyd Webber and *Sunset Boulevard* did nothing to change my opinion. However, Karen did an excellent job in the role, and I engaged her for the project.

Two days before we were to go into the recording studio I insisted on hearing a rehearsal, and I was dumbstruck. She was still in the process of learning the songs. Later I phoned Barry Levitt, the jazz pianist, who was playing for her, "Should I postpone the recording date? I've spent a lot of money on the studio, and she doesn't seem prepared." "Don't worry, she'll know it in two days. By the way, you've written some true jazz, not the pseudo stuff that most theater composers do."

Todd and I went to Manhattan Beach Studios together. I was a nervous wreck worrying about what I might hear. This was the first time I'd been in a major recording studio with a top sound engineer since the *Celebration* cast recording. Barry was right. Karen was wonderful on the recording. Because I always need to be prepared well ahead of a performance, I had not yet understood that some performers work best only when they are at deadline. Todd and I were so excited to hear her magnificent voice performing my work that we could barely contain ourselves. When we listened to the playbacks and Karen didn't like something she had done, she'd scream at the speakers, "Just shoot her, please."

The piano part, like almost all my writing for that instrument, was extremely difficult to play. When I began composing, I believed my weakest point was simplistic and insipid accompaniments. Beginning with the frightfully difficult Whitman cycle, I overcompensated for this perceived weakness in a monumental way.

Barry had a bit of trouble with one of the songs near the end of the session, and they had to start over several times. "I'm just trying to find my groove," he apologized. Karen sharply retorted, "Well, find it now, Barry, because my voice won't hold out much longer." He did, on the next take. I wanted to experience performing at the piano in a recording studio, so I played *Dorothy's Theme*, the opening piano solo, myself.

The high from the recording session lasted only a few days. Karen called to tell me that she was overwhelmed with work and had to bow out of doing the reading. I felt crushed at the time. What I didn't realize was that she was going through a period of vocal-cord problems, and she had to save her voice for *Sunset Boulevard*. We recorded nine of the twenty songs from the show on the demo, and they were universally praised. Even Mary Giovingo was impressed. And no criticism. I've been able to use that CD to promote the musical ever since.

I had recently seen a production of Michael John La Chiusa's *Hello Again* at Lincoln Center. Here was another musical I did not appreciate. However, there was a woman in the extraordinarily talented cast who made a large impression on me, Michele Pawk. I phoned Douglas, and asked him what he thought about her in the role. "If you can get her, she would be terrific." Her agent told me that she was now in Hollywood, auditioning for pilot season and that I should send her a script. She immediately agreed to do the reading. Michele had had a starring role in the Broadway production of *Crazy for You* and had played the role of Gussie in the York Theater's production of Sondheim's *Merrily We Roll Along*. She was incredibly beautiful and could do everything brilliantly: act, sing, and dance.

She came to my apartment to run through the score with me, and my hands were shaking at the piano, though she managed to calm me down. Rehearsals for the reading were helter-skelter to say the least. It was my first experience in trying to coordinate schedules for several busy people, and it was a nightmare. Most disconcerting was the fact that Douglas would at the last minute fail to show up for rehearsals on several occasions. This angered Michele, who is a consummate professional, and it didn't endear him to me.

The first of three titles for the show was *Wit's End*. The reading was done in a large studio and nearly one hundred people attended. I was confident about the music, but when I heard the script being read and the unenthusiastic audience response, I wanted to crawl under my chair. I was the one at wit's end. This was no reflection on Michele, who did a bang-up job on some pretty inferior material. "Whatever gave you the idea that you could write the book for a musical?" I thought. Maybe they were right at Lincoln Center about not expanding this. I apologized to Douglas, "Well, I guess I've written a big old bomb." "Not at all. You just need to work on it. We'll meet in a few days to discuss it."

I had adopted my Korean piano tuner's motto: I set as my goal the impossible task of being as good as Stephen Sondheim, and I came up miserably short. One of Mrs. Parker's lines, which I used in the show, kept echoing in my head: "If you're going to write, it has to be the best that you can do. And it's the fact, that it *is* the best that you can do that kills you. It just kills you." I wasn't sure I had the courage to face another audience with this tripe, but I met with Douglas to see what his thoughts were.

He gave me two ideas: the first was to have Dorothy putting together a collection of her works, which would give context to her reciting the poems; the second was to turn her short story, *Big Blonde*, into a mini-musical within the musical. The first I did and it provided more weight to the piece. The second, I found impossible because all her poems were so obviously about herself that I couldn't fit them into the character of an unsophisticated floozy. I did turn it into a ten-minute monologue, underscored by a set of variations based on "Dorothy's Theme." Michele did the story brilliantly—almost a *coup de théâtre*.

We did readings on two consecutive nights at the Dramatists Guild. Just before the first performance, Douglas and I approached Michele with a suggestion. Although Dorothy was drinking most of the time, she never appeared drunk, and we both felt Michele was overdoing the besotted characteristics. If ever there was wrong time and place, this was it. Michele became very upset with us, "In order for me to have the courage to do this, I need to feel as though I'm a talented performer, and you two have undermined me just before I have to go on." We suddenly turned into the damage-control squad. We had in no way meant to impugn her prodigious talent. I learned right then that even the most competent and self-assured actors are extremely vulnerable and need to be treated sensitively. We managed to restore her confidence, and she gave two splendid performances. I was back in the theater at last.

The piece, now with its second title, *Life of the Party*, was significantly improved, though far from finished. I made the mistake of inviting many producers and artistic directors to these readings before the piece was ready. I learned the hard way that once these professionals have seen a work, you will never get them back again, no matter how much you've rewritten it. I had also noticed a change among critics regarding one-person shows, which had proliferated in this era. I saw and read every one of them, carefully studying their structure and their critical reception. The reviews had become increasingly more negative and took on a definable pattern. Who is the character talking to, the audience, himself, herself? The context is contrived. Where is the drama with no other person on the stage? How many one-person pieces about celebrities do we need? Are these plays simply an excuse to string together a lot of one-line jokes?

These were issues that did not resonate with me, because as an audience member I felt as though I had been invited into the person's living room, privileged to hear them telling the wonderful stories about their lives, much as I had enjoyed hearing my own family's stories. I did take these concerns seriously, however. My piece was not just a series of *bon mots*. I tried very hard to find a logical context for each quip I used. I didn't try to depict Dorothy as simply a clever jokester. To me, she was a serious writer who fought her whole life to be taken seriously. She had strong political beliefs, and she took many career risks to stand up for them. This was the complex and enigmatic Dorothy Parker I wanted to portray.

Michele called me and said, "I don't want to tell you what to do with your piece, but I don't think Douglas is the right director for it. He's not helping me at all to find the character, and as far as I can tell he's not helping you much, either." I sympathized with what she was saying, but I was torn. I was so grateful that any director would take an interest in my writing and always blamed myself for its shortcomings. However, I managed to secure a more prominent reading engagement at the York Theater, a company devoted to the development of new musicals. Jim Morgan, its director, knew Michele from the production of *Merrily We Roll Along* at York, and was eager to have us at his theater. I worried that a conflict between the actor and director would undermine everything. I hesitantly approached Douglas, "Michele and I feel that the piece needs to have a fresh point of view from another director." I would dearly regret this move later.

Mark Bennett thought enough of the Dorothy Parker play to recommend me to his agent, Helen Merrill, one of the most important for creative artists. She called to tell me how much she admired my music and surprisingly compared me to Samuel Barber. Though I couldn't understand how the jazzy Parker songs related to Barber's genre, I took this as a great compliment. She was at that point unconvinced that I had brought Dorothy to life in my script, as was I. She promised to come to my next reading but as luck would have it she died before it happened.

Through all the hubbub related to Dorothy Parker, my classical career was still on track. Tracy Bidleman, who was to have done the joint recital with Rebekah before the tragic accident, had heard my Whitman songs and was programming them for a concert on the Music in Chelsea series. She sang my cycle brilliantly and with overwhelming dramatic intensity. Fortunately, the performance was recorded, so I began using her version to promote the piece. Tracy, who is a very versatile performer, became my go-to soprano on all different genres of my music.

I had Paul Sperry to thank, indirectly, for connecting me with Tracy, but he also convinced the American Composers Orchestra to include some of my songs in a program they presented called Walt Whitman and Music. Well-known composers, such as William Bolcom, were represented in this concert, and we all participated in a panel discussion moderated by the cultural historian and *New York Times* contributor, Joseph Horowitz.

Rehearsals for the York Theater reading of *You Might as Well Live*, the final title of the Dorothy Parker musical, began under Don, Director No. 2. Don was scheduled to direct a new Broadway musical later in the year, and he never missed a rehearsal. Michele, who was concurrently performing as Fraulein Kost in the Broadway revival of *Cabaret* had, along with her second husband, actor John Dossett, become a close friend. I was now privy to some of her backstage stories. She and John met when they played opposite each other in *Hello Again* and soon after they played the leads in the Philadelphia Orchestra's concert version of *A Little Night Music*.

When she performed in *Crazy for You*, she was married to Kevin McCollum, the producer of *Rent*. After one matinee, without removing her stage makeup, she and Kevin went out to dinner. As they were leaving the restaurant, their waiter rushed up to her and said, "Thank you so much, and good evening, sir."

"That's mam," Michele responded most firmly.

"Right. Well, whatever."

"No, not whatever. It's mam!" and she proceeded to lift her shirt to prove it, before Kevin stopped her and pulled her out the door. The waiter apparently was convinced that she was a drag queen. How he could have made such a mistake is unfathomable.

On opening night of *Cabaret*, Whoopi Goldberg came to her dressing room to congratulate her, saying, "Girl, I could fuck you right here." "Well, too bad, I don't have my own dressing room," Michele responded sardonically, uncertain whether the comment was meant metaphorically.

Rehearsals for the York reading went smoothly, and Don's major contribution to the piece was to get me to be more specific in my writing and heighten the drama. We were practically rolling on the floor laughing as Michele assumed the various characters from Mrs. Parker's short stories. Jennifer Jason Leigh, who had played Dorothy Parker in the film *Mrs. Parker and the Vicious Circle*, had replaced Natasha Richardson in *Cabaret*, so Don asked Michele to talk to her about the role. Michele said, "I totally disagreed with her interpretation in that movie, so I don't want to get into a thing about it with her."

I learned that the reading was completely sold out, with a long waiting list. I couldn't even get in some people I had promised. The day before the performance I received a letter from an arts foundation saying that I had been given a substantial cash grant for excellence in playwriting. The postscript to the letter read, "Mrs. Parker would have been so pleased with what you have written." This made me feel that at least I was on the right track. I never considered myself funny, but many of my own lines were getting big laughs, and I found that euphoric.

Some of my students' parents attended, and the performance gave me added credibility among them. Janice Lee and Stu Shapiro were especially taken with the show, and it set them on the path to becoming patrons and close friends to both Todd and me. Also in attendance was a man called Brady, whom I had met at the Chelsea Gym. Brady was an intermediary who advised a wealthy man about investing in theater. Brady simply adored Michele and said he was interested in helping promote my piece, "But what you need is a direcTOR," always with an affected accent on the last syllable. He was not impressed with Don's work on the show.

The day after the reading, Michele, Don, and I met in a diner to discuss the future of the musical. Though we knew it still needed more revisions, Michele and I were both very positive about the reading. Strangely, Don threw cold water on the whole thing, suggesting that maybe it needed to be totally rewritten, perhaps with another writer. Michele said, "I was really up about the show until I met with you."

I was never sure what prompted Don's reaction because the audience response was very positive. The producer of his Broadway show had just pulled out, a few weeks before it was to go into rehearsal, and I thought perhaps this had soured him on my piece as well. In any case, if I was to move forward with Brady and his investor, Don had to go.

Brady told me he had spoken with David Van Asselt, the artistic director of Rattlestick, a small off-Broadway theater in Greenwich Village. David was interested in doing a workshop of *You Might as Well Live* and if it went well to do a production at his theater, though they had never done a musical. I believe this was made possible when Brady agreed to put up the money through his mysterious investor. The first order of business was to find the right direcTOR.

Interestingly, Brady suggested Douglas as a possibility, not knowing he had directed the initial readings. I had to explain that Douglas wouldn't even speak to me any longer, and in any case Michele would not have him again. Any production needed to be done within a few months because Michele was pregnant.

An actor at my gym suggested his friend, Greg, who he believed was a very talented upcoming director. I sent him the video of the York reading, and we had lunch. He had the strongest ideas of the several candidates I interviewed. He insisted that he would not take the job unless I cut out the *Big Blonde* story. Though the twelve-minute set piece beautifully synthesized the story, he felt that it stopped the show in the wrong ways at a crucial moment, making it difficult to return to the thread of Dorothy's narrative. I had spent so many weeks writing this that it was painful to cut, but I had to admit he was right. Greg became Director No. 3. Independently, I cut all the other nonmusical dramatizations of her short stories, which seemed so hilarious on the page and in rehearsals but laid a big egg on the stage.

We seemed to be in agreement on so many issues about the show. Greg had been a musical-theater performer before becoming a director, and he had very good instincts about weaving text and music together. He helped me turn the poem, "A Pig's-Eye View of Literature," in which Dorothy gives succinct and humorous opinions on various poets, into a show-stopper.

Michele was also a big help. She suggested that I see the musical *Hedwig* for ways that I might give more urgency to the through-line. It occurred to me that if in addition to putting together her collected works, Dorothy was also required by her contract to write a new poem, one she was stymied by until the end of the play, that would add a whole new through-line, as well as increase the level of tension. I had never written any lyrics before, but I took the poem "A Little Old Lady in Lavender Silk," which had been the closing number from the first reading, and devised a series of bad and aborted lines, slowly developing the poem, as well as the underlying music, until she finally gets it right at the end. I wasn't too concerned about the quality of my lyrics since they were all purposely bad.

Then I faced the fact that my opening number, in which I combined three different poems into one song was not really working. It needed another verse to tie the poems together and end the song. Nothing in Dorothy's writing would work here so I had to come up with something myself. Surely, this was the height of folly for me to try to imitate Dorothy Parker. I had no choice. The song was about how she should be working to produce a fine piece of writing, but "I just don't give a damn," her closing line. I struggled to come up with a single verse that would end with that same line:

If I could curb the glib bons mots,
Perhaps I'd write some worthy prose.
But I'm a slave to epigram.
I devour with joke
All the dearest folk
Because I just don't give a damn.

I was terrified at how this would be received. No one even noticed. Perhaps it was that innocuous.

During rehearsals everyone seemed so excited about the project, even Brady, who was a bigger worrywart than I am. "That Michele Pawk is quite something," he said to me almost every day on the phone. It was clear from the performance that the play was finally shaping up into a piece of theater. The audience was very enthusiastic. Jim Morgan was so impressed with how it had grown since the York reading. But where was the investor? Did he even attend the performance? No one knew.

The next day Brady phoned Greg to meet with him. He was very concerned about the project. "What if the critics don't like it?" Greg told him, "Brady, that's the chance you take with every show." Brady handed him a copy of *The Belle of Amherst,* the one-person play about Emily Dickinson that Julie Harris made famous. Greg called me, "Our meeting was so depressing. Brady couldn't even define one specific problem he had with the show. And what the hell am I supposed to do with *The Belle of Amherst?*" It bore little relation to a Dorothy Parker musical and didn't provide any insight, despite being a wonderful play in its own right. The daily phone calls from Brady suddenly stopped. David Van Asselt told me that Brady could not summon up the nerve to invite the mysterious investor and didn't want to proceed with the show.

Michele was furious when she learned this. She felt that Brady had been untruthful and that he wasted weeks of her valuable time. I grew angrier myself for fear that Brady had, perhaps, undermined my relationship with Michele. How could I have put my trust in a diffident, dithering dilettante, when the theater demanded nerves of steel? It was clear from our conversations that Brady knew no more about what a direcTOR does, than I did as a child.

His superficiality became evident when all he talked about was Mrs. Parker's toy poodle. "Ah, Cliché, Cliché." He spoke of the dog so lovingly that it rated more concern than Michele or Dorothy. I spoke to David and told him I was considering writing a strong letter to Brady about the problems he had caused all of us. David said nothing to dissuade me.

The more I thought about the situation the angrier I became, and a few days later, I mailed the letter to Brady, saying that he should adopt the Hippocratic oath of the medical community when involving himself with a play, "First do no harm."

Just a few hours after I mailed the letter, I got a call from David, "Brady changed his mind and convinced his investor to provide the money for Rattlestick to produce the show."

"Oh, no, I just mailed a very nasty letter to him."

"I thought you were going to wait to send it."

"When you didn't warn me against it, I just went ahead."

Needless to say, Brady never spoke to me again, and the production was off. Of all the dumb, self-serving things I've ever done in my life, this was by far the dumbest, and I've never stopped beating myself up over it. If only I'd waited another few hours. My lawyer had forbid me to sign a contract Brady had offered because he believed the terms were unfavorable to me. I was supposed to have received a check for my part of the workshop. Naturally, Brady paid everyone but me.

I was in a serious state of depression over this incident and decided to return to my classical music career. One of the things I noted about being a serious composer is that people respect your work, you're treated as an artist not a hack, and they almost never tell you what you should have written.

In the theater everyone has an opinion, and no one is shy about flinging it in your face. One influential person, who should have known better, actually suggested, "Have you ever considered backing her up with four boys?" My real teeth nearly dropped out of my mouth as I envisioned, "Dorothy Parker Plays The Sands in Vegas." "No, you know, the thought has never ever crossed my mind," I responded dumbfoundedly.

Others wanted her to be played by three actors, young, middle-aged, and old. Brady had brought a highly derided, two-bit direcTOR to see the workshop, who suggested that Dorothy should sing the entire show. "You mean she's going to sing for two hours straight? Eight times a week?" I asked incredulously. Seriously, does this guy even know the limitations of the human voice? "Write your own damned play if you know so much," I wanted to yell at these people. During my period of depression, *You Might as Well Live* was a finalist for two best-play competitions (not musicals, but plays).

A Playwright Is Born

I DIDN'T WANT TO BE JUST a song composer so I approached Richard Danielpour to give me some lessons in orchestration, which I had never studied. I hoped to take my Whitman cycle and rearrange it for soloist and chamber orchestra. In six months, I turned out a score. Danielpour convinced me to write another work for full orchestra. Though he admired my music, he said, "If you want to be taken seriously as a composer, your music will have to become much more dissonant." I could do that, as I had done in the large orchestral work and in my twelve-tone string quartet, but my strong point is my melodic writing and when I stifle that the music is not really me.

Orchestrating is probably the most demanding role for a composer. Knowing what each instrument is capable of doing and how those instruments blend together when you don't play any of them is daunting. Danielpour reaffirmed this for me. He had been commissioned to write a cello concerto for Yo Yo Ma and the Pittsburgh Symphony. He rehearsed his score with only the orchestra the day before the performance. When he heard his orchestrations, he panicked because some of the orchestral sections were so loud they would completely have drowned out the cello. He and his manager spent that whole night reworking the orchestrations. Please let this never happen to me, I thought to myself.

Chelsea Gym, where I had made so many new friends and contacts, closed suddenly, and the members were allowed to transfer to a nearby gym called American Fitness Center. At the new gym was a young, extremely handsome Asian who never spoke to anyone, looked terribly serious. and went from one exercise to the next with hardly a breath between sets. He was a man on a mission, that was clear. One day, he was working right next to me, so I said, "You certainly do work out very hard." I was anticipating a nasty response since he seemed so unfriendly but was surprised by his amiability. He mentioned that he traveled quite a distance to work-out at this gym because he lived in a terrible neighborhood called Wash-ington Heights. "But I live in Washington Heights, too," I said. He explained that he was a second-year medical student at Columbia Pres-byterian Hospital, just a few blocks from our apartment.

I sensed that he needed someone to talk to and that what appeared to be unfriendliness was actually shyness and insecurity. As a child he claimed he was fat so he worked especially hard to transform—and trans-form he did—his body. Shockingly, one day he referred to himself as "fugly."

"You're what?"

"Fucking ugly."

"Surely you're joking."

"No, just look at my eye." He had one lazy eye that didn't appear to look straight ahead. I had never even noticed this until he pointed it out. In his opinion, it was a grotesque flaw. He was some sort of cyclops in his own mind. Also, he still saw himself as fat because he didn't have a defined six pack. He would pinch the skin on his sides, "See how fat I am?" Fat? He had a perfect, slim muscular physique. This boy had prob-lems. Then I learned that he was gay but wasn't yet socially and emotion-ally prepared to come out. This statement, of course, had a familiar ring to it, and I put on my counseling hat.

Good food was his passion. He cooked but was for the present in-hibited by living in the dorm with only a hot plate and a rice cooker to work with. He seemed to have no gay friends at school, and when I told him that Todd and I were avid cooks, he hinted that he would be happy to get an invitation for dinner. I thought it best that we first dine together at a restaurant to see whether Todd would like him. We went out for pizza and later to the Carnegie Deli for gargantuan slices of cheesecake. Todd grew as fond of him as I was. Thus Tony Lin entered our lives and added a whole new dimension to our relationship. Neither Todd nor I ever wanted children, but within a year it was clear that Tony was now unof-ficially our adopted child.

Michele Pawk fortunately remained a friend after the Brady incident. She was cast in *Hollywood Arms*, a new autobiographical Broadway play by Carol Burnett, directed by Harold Prince. Michele played Miss Burnett's mother, during the comedian's teenage years. She was especially admiring of Prince's assistant director, Brad Rouse, and she asked me to send him the Dorothy Parker script and recording from the workshop. He wrote back, saying, "I think *You Might as Well Live* is smart and delicious…

Michele is her usual genius on the workshop recording. And with any luck *Hollywood Arms* will turn her into the star we all know she is. Then you'll have your production in no time." From his mouth to god's ear.

Michele's husband, John Dossett, asked us to accompany him to the final run-through. The play was incredibly moving and Michele gave a brilliant performance in a role that demanded stark changes of mood. We went to her dressing room after the performance, and there was Carol Burnett, whom I thanked for having written such a beautiful part for Michele. Sadly, the critics didn't find the play as engaging as I did, though Michele got rave reviews. What I learned from this is that material that thwarts expectations can be risky. The reviewers were anticipating a side-splitting comedy, and though there were several comic scenes, the play was dark and tragic, leaving them confounded and disappointed. It ran only two months, and the play didn't confer on Michele the star power to get *You Might as Well Live* produced.

When the 2003 Tony-Award nominations were announced, Todd and I were elated. Michele was nominated for *Hollywood Arms* and John Dossett was nominated for playing opposite Bernadette Peters in *Gypsy*. I've been unable to locate another occasion where husband and wife were nominated in the same year. We watched the telecast, sitting on the edge of our seats. When Michele was announced the winner, and for a play that closed so quickly, we began screaming as though we were possessed.

I had never lost touch with Patty Seyburn, whom I worked with at *Sylvia Porter's Personal Finance Magazine.* She had given up journalism to get a Ph.D. in poetry. She was living and teaching college in California, when she won a major award, for which a volume of her poetry was published to much acclaim. Although I enjoyed her enigmatic poems very much, they never suggested the need to be set to music. "Would you be interested in trying your hand at some lyric writing? I thought, perhaps, we might try some cabaret-type songs together," Coast-to-coast collaboration was not easy. She emailed me a lyric, I set it to music, then played it for her over the telephone. When we had written about twenty songs, we put together a revue, comprised of twelve of the best ones and titled, *Somebody Write Me a Song.*

I was able to convince John Znidarsic, who hosted a series called Arts and Artists at the Donnell Library, to book our revue for a program. I lined up Debbie Gravitte, a Tony-Award winner, Emily Skinner, a Tony nominee, and John Dossett. Both Emily and John were rehearsing Lincoln Center Theater's production of *Dinner at Eight,* and the director refused to let them out for a few hours to do the performance. At the last minute,

I was able to replace Emily with Liz Callaway, also a Tony nominee, and John with Peter Samuel, who had previously sung my work, all great voices. I got Patty to write a song called "No, Kidding, I Love Being Famous," and engaged Steven Brinberg, the popular Streisand impersonator, to sing it as Barbra. Dick Gallagher, Patty LuPone's top-drawer accompanist, was the pianist.

Patty flew in from California with her husband, Eric Little. The auditorium was packed. John Znidarsic interviewed Patty and me about our collaboration and how we came to write the songs. Liz Callaway gave a stunning performance, especially on a funny patter song about people who talk too much, and Debbie Gravitte, with her big-belt voice, pulled out all her showbiz pizzazz to win over the audience. We got encouraging feedback from John, saying that it was one of the best programs he had presented. Fortunately, I hired a recording engineer to preserve the performance for us.

Buoyed by this success, we decided to try writing a musical, but we couldn't find the right subject. My friend, David Hemphill, to the rescue. He introduced us to a novel by J. B. Priestley called, *Lost Empires.* Set at the beginning of World War I, it was about a twenty-year-old boy, Richard, who wants to be an artist but joins his uncle Nick's magic act on the English musical-hall circuit. The novel had been serialized by the BBC and then shown in the U.S. on *Masterpiece Theater*, starring Colin Firth and Laurence Olivier. I didn't think I could handle the book writing on my own, so I asked Todd to work with me.

We needed to purchase the rights, so we traveled to London, where we had a very amiable meeting with the literary agent. She informed us that Priestley had a son, Tom, a film editor, who was in charge of his father's estate. We signed the contract, but foolishly, did not spell out what rights Tom had, if any, over our creation because it never occurred to us that it would be an issue. I had had no problems with the Dorothy Parker estate and assumed this would be a similar arrangement.

Collaborating with Todd on this project was an exhilarating and inspiring experience. As a creative team, we worked as beautifully together as we did in our personal relationship. One of the binding forces in our relationship was our never-ending struggle with our separate careers. Now we were struggling for recognition on the same project. Every night we discussed the plot, what to keep what to discard from the novel, what dialog to use, and we studied the TV production, other works about the English musical hall, and dictionaries of English slang to get the tone just right. Bringing characters to life on stage was such a joy. We came to know them and love them as though they were dear friends. As much as I enjoyed writing songs, working theatrically provided a much deeper satisfaction, a melding of my childhood love of good drama, my experience in musical theater, and my passion for composing.

We emailed Patty scenes we had written, with suggestions for where the action demanded a song. She emailed us a lyric, which I set to music and sang to her over the phone. On two numbers, the opening and a patriotic march, I had tunes already in my head so I wrote those before any lyric was provided. Patty found this process much more difficult than the reverse, and yet those two numbers were among the better songs we wrote. I made the decision early on that period-specific musical-hall-type music would not play with modern audiences. So I used an approach that Sondheim used in *Follies* and Kander and Ebb used in *Cabaret*. Whenever we were depicting a music-hall act or "turn" as the English call it, I wrote period music. The book songs, those that moved the plot forward, were in a more Sondheimesque style.

I decided to involve a director from the beginning of the process, so I asked Greg, my Dorothy Parker director, to work with us as we developed the piece. We put together a starry cast for the demo recording: John Dossett, as the magician uncle, Michele Pawk, as a 35-year-old actress who has a torrid affair with the young Richard. In that role, I chose the golden-voiced Danny Gurwin, who had played Henrik in both the New York City Opera and Kennedy Center productions of *A Little Night Music*. For the role of Nancy, Richard's true love, Danny recommended a young performer, Brynn O'Malley, who had just come to New York. I auditioned Brynn at my apartment and loved her voice immediately. A few years later she starred in Jason Robert Brown's *Honeymoon in Vegas* on Broadway. Tracy Bidleman sang the operatic march, and even Greg sang one number.

Watching Michele and John work together was interesting. They never bickered. Yet, at one point Michele suggested a different way for John to approach his song. "Who's singing this number, girl, you or me?" Happily, all reverted to affability, and they each gave superb performances.

We were overwhelmed by the tremendous response we got to the demo recording, from Jack Lee and other Broadway conductors, to Michael Kerker at ASCAP, to Sondheim himself. We sent the demo and script to Tom Priestley with a confidence that he'd be overjoyed by how good it was. He liked our script, but he complained that Patty's lyrics did not scan well. Then he began carping that he expected to hear something like "I Could Have Danced All Night" or "Send in the Clowns," and instead got what he called "recitative," a term I was certain he did not understand in the least. My music was so heavily melodic it was the antithesis of recitative, a term that comes from opera and refers to the rhythmically free, sung dialog. as opposed to the melodically driven arias.

How is it possible that these top Broadway professionals loved it, and Tom Priestley was so disappointed? I wrote to Sondheim, who tried to console me with a similar incident that happened to him with regard to the Jean Anouilh play *Ring Round the Moon.* I was not to be consoled. Tom didn't threaten to pull the rights, but he implied that he wanted a rewrite. Stu Shapiro drafted a strong legal letter, delineating that Priestley's right to creative decisions had not been spelled out, and he was therefore exceeding the contract's terms. Tom backed down, but he had flung a pall over the musical from which it never recovered. Never again would I work on a project not in the public domain.

In 2004, Greg connected us with two women who were fledgling producers. They were interested in sponsoring a full reading, after Uncle Nick's song "That's Always Champagne" caused excitement at a showcase of various works they were considering. People were intrigued enough by the song that they wanted to know what the rest of the show was about. Then the most enigmatic thing happened, which I never understood. Greg asked to meet with Todd and me in a restaurant.

"I've been thinking about the show. I believe the score is stylistically wrong for the period. You need to rethink it," he said, shocking us both.

"Greg, what are you saying? That I need to rewrite the music after spending more than a year composing it? And we just spent a fortune producing this demo, which almost everyone loves?" I asked, incredulously.

"Yes."

"Greg, we must have that reading to determine how an audience reacts to the material."

"Not with that score, you won't."

Wow, I really pick the winners as collaborators. Brady now this. Greg brought the piece to these two women, without my asking. They were excited about the show and wanted to move forward, but now he was preventing us. Furious with his presumptuous attitude that he now decided the musical's fate, I angrily responded, "You've been working with us for over a year. You sang on the demo yourself, and you even coached the other singers on their interpretations. And now you discover that I wrote the wrong music? Why didn't you bring this up before?"

We got no answer. I had never told Greg about Tom Priestley's objections, so that was not the issue. I was certain that somebody he respected must have criticized the music after hearing the demo. Where are the people who have the courage of their own convictions? Todd and I were demoralized by this turn of events. We saw it as an enormous betrayal. Greg and his boyfriend had become friends. Greg was the director and a performer in a noted star's concert act for which Jack Lee was the conductor. He and Greg were close friends, and Jack who went through the whole piece with me, said he believed that *Lost Empires* was one of the best scores he had heard in years. I suspected that this sort of erratic behavior was a major reason Greg was not more successful, despite his talents.

Jim Morgan at York Theater was a big supporter of the piece. He wanted us to do a reading at his theater, and he recommended me to Susan Schulman, a director who had helmed Jim's revival of *Sweeney Todd* on Broadway. Susan was very intrigued by the musical and agreed to direct the reading. Suddenly, after much back and forth, I heard nothing from her. I learned that she had accepted a position as head of the directing program at Penn State. By then the rights to the work expired, and the literary agent wanted a substantial amount of money to renew them. Todd and I were aware that if we ever went into rehearsal, Patty would need to be with us in person because changes have to be made minute-by-minute. That can't be done over the phone. She was now a full professor with two young children, making this impossible for her, so we made the difficult decision not to extend the rights.

Janice and Stu Shapiro, both ardent supporters of our work, became the modern-day version of the Medicis for us. They bought numerous paintings from Todd, many of which were hung in Stu's offices. The others were hung in the Morton Street townhouse. One large painting, "Dorothy Parker's Red Dress," inspired by her poem, hung over the mantelpiece in the living room and could be seen from the street. One day Stu was outside when a woman approached him, "I see that you have a de Kooning in your living room that I don't know, even though I'm a curator at the Museum of Modern Art."

"Would you care to come in and take a look?"

"Yes, thank you."

The curator was admiring the work when Stu said, "Actually, the painting is not a de Kooning, but a Lehman." It was an earlier work from Todd's transitional period, during which he moved from representational to abstract painting, just prior to finding his own personal architectural style.

Stu had previously worked with an attorney who became a produced playwright. When Stu sought his advice on how to move my Dorothy Parker show forward, the former attorney agreed to show the piece to Martin Markinsen, his producer and the owner of the Helen Hayes Theater on Broadway. Marty had been an insurance executive before turning his efforts to show business. Stu arranged a luncheon meeting for the four of us at Sardi's. I looked around the room, remembering the applause Frank Newell and I got there after opening night of *Celebration*. Now here I am again, discussing my own show. Is this how these deals are made? Marty seemed to love the script and asked, "Who do you see playing this role."

"I'm very fond of Michele Pawk, who's been workshopping it from the beginning of its development."

"She won't sell a dime's worth of tickets. I thought we'd get Sigourney Weaver or Susan Sarandon."

"Do they sing?"

"What does it matter? We're going to cut the music anyway. It's not any good, and it doesn't add anything to the play."

"But I'm a composer more than I am a playwright." My mind is reeling at the insulting abruptness of this man. It goes without saying that this guy, who found his true calling peddling insurance, is a more expert judge of my score than Lincoln Center's musical theater department or any of the musical directors I'd worked with on this piece This was clearly not going to be a reprise of my Sardi reception on *Celebration's* opening night.

"So are you suggesting that she just recite the poems in the piece?"

I get no clear answer to this, so I'm thinking to myself, "Yes, this worked with Julie Harris's playing Emily Dickinson in 1976. But Mrs. Parker is not Dickinson, and this is 2002, when I doubt you can get an audience to sit through a poetry reading. I say nothing.

"Well, what major musical-theater star do you feel is right for the part?" he asks.

"Patty LuPone?" I venture.

"All right, I'll see if I can get her to look at a script."

Whether he sent it to her, I don't know, but I spoke to Dick Gallagher, her pianist, "Oh, if she ever got it, I doubt she would read it. She's got a stack of scripts, and she never looks at any of them." Nothing more was heard from Mr. Markinsen.

I saw an announcement that the Dramatists Guild was holding a symposium for people who have written one-person shows. Participants were asked to present a short scene before directors who worked in this genre, who would then give their opinions. I decided to perform a monologue that did not involve music. It gave me the chance to play three different characters, all with different accents. In the scene, Dorothy Parker has just married her second husband, Alan Campbell, who has talked her into going to Hollywood, a place she loathes, to write screenplays together.

> I loved the money—swimming pools, Valentino gowns, hundred-dollar bras—but I hated the movies. And Hollywood!

All those palm trees—the ugliest vegetable God created. Even my pets didn't feel at home there. Once I took my toy poodle, Cliché, with me to the Beverly Hills Hotel. I was walking her across the lobby when this officious manager rushes up to me and says, "Miss Parker, Miss Parker! Look what your dog did." I made myself as tall as possible and gave him a look that shriveled his—ego and said,"I did that."

Oh. And those script meetings. Priceless. We were working on a picture called *You Can Be Beautiful* at Metro-Goldwyn-Merde. It was about a Helena Rubinstein-type. Sam Goldwyn asked me for a new plot twist. "What about making her into a plain sort—a completely contented ugly duckling who's transformed into a tragically unhappy beauty?'"

"Got tem it, Dottie! You and your Got tem zopheesticated chokes. You're a great writer. You're a great vit. You're a great vooman, but you haven't got a great ohdience and you know vy?" I simply held my breath. "Becausse you don't vant to geef people vat dey vant, dat's vy."

"But Mr. Goldwyn, people don't know what they want until you give it to them."

"You see dot? You chust deet it again. Vicecrecks. I tell you there's no money in vicecrecks. People vant a happy endingk."

"I know this will come as a shock to you, Mr. Goldwyn, but in all history, which has held billions and billions of human beings, not a single one ever had a happy ending," and as I was making my exit, I heard him say, "Duss anybody in here know vat da hell dot vooman vas tokink about?"

Why, he didn't have enough sense to bore assholes in wooden hobby horses. What the hell was I doing out there with those people? The country was in a depression. "People vant a happy endingk." People couldn't afford a happy ending! And there we were agonizing over mascara. In my younger days that would have been my cue to change at Jamaica and get the hell out. But it was the '30s, and a few of us thought we were going to make the world a better place. And what better place to start than with Hollywood.

The monologue got the same laughs it got in performance, but the comments startled me. "You should play the role yourself." "Yes, she's right, no one could do it better than you." Well, they hadn't seen Michele Pawk perform it. Was I supposed to do it in drag? I don't think so. Is this why Mary Giovingo was always dressing me up? In any case, that was the beginning and end of my stint as an actor. Maybe my high school dream of acting was really the right career choice, after all.

Despite Brady, *You Might as Well Live* was not yet kaput. It was selected as one of the musicals to be presented at Theater Building Chicago's Stages 2003: a Festival of New Musicals, along with works by Wally Harper, Barbara Cook's musical director, and playwright Arthur Kopit. I, of course, wanted Michele Pawk to play the role, but she was at the same time performing in Sondheim's new musical, *Bounce*, at Chicago's Goodman Theater. Because Karen Mason was a Chicago native and a Windy City celebrity, John Sparks, the artistic director of the theater, insisted that she play the role in a gala benefit for the company. After all these years since the demo recording, Karen was back as Mrs. Parker. The fascination for me was seeing two very different actors portray the role. Greg directed the piece (this was prior to our falling out over *Lost Empires*).

Karen's voice reminded me of the women I heard sing at Wrigley Field when I was a kid. Though she was too young to have heard of bands and singers at the ballpark, I asked her, "Did you ever sing at Wrigley Field?" "I sang the national anthem there once, and I forgot the words in the middle of it. My dad told me to write them on my hand next time." Here I was, back in the city I prayed my father would get lost in when I was kid, and now my musical was being performed by a celebrity.

Michael Kerker from ASCAP attended one of the two performances, "I guess you must be pretty pleased that your piece is the hit of the festival. You know, a lot of people have tried to write the Dorothy Parker story, and you're the first to get it right." A well-known Chicago critic, Albert Williams, wrote a review of my music:

> With its bouncy rhythms and cleverly rhymed couplets, this material is well suited to the classic American show-tune style, as composer Norman Mathews proves in *You Might as Well Live*. . .Mathews's jazzy settings highlight the mix of urbane wit, anxious yearning, and satiric gallows humor that makes Parker's ruminations on sexual folly and emotional dependency as fresh today as when they were written in the 1920s and '30s . . . the score is packed with delicious new numbers in the sassy, sophisticated vein of Porter, Sondheim, and Rodgers and Hart.

Take that, Mr. Marty Smarty Insurance Markinsen with your, "The music's not any good, and it doesn't add anything to the play."

Sitting next to me at the second performance was a woman named Eileen Mackevich, who was the producer of the Chicago Humanities Festival. She liked the show so much that she invited us to present it at the next festival. When I learned that the play would be seen in Chicago's new 1,500-seat opera house, the Harris Theater for Music and Dance, I was beside myself. An even greater surprise was that the performance was sold out. Sarah Renberg, with whom I had reconnected, came to see the show, and loyal David Hemphill flew in from his new home in Tucson. The performance was a success, but my tiny one-person play, meant to be seen in intimate settings, looked lost on that enormous stage.

An even more prestigious venue, the Kennedy Center in Washington, D.C., seemed completely out of my grasp. Yet, three of my Whitman songs were performed on the Center's Millenium Stage. The Other Side of Broadway, a program directed by Barbara Irvine, presented classical music by theater composers. Was I really on a program that featured art songs by such Broadway luminaries as John Kander, Charles Strouse, and Galt MacDermot?

I had not yet pursued any publishing opportunities when two unexpectedly presented themselves. My Whitman song, "When the Time Draws Nigh" was published in an anthology called *American Art Song for the Sacred Service,* because it had vaguely religious undertones. Next, a new online vocal-music firm called Graphite Publishing, run by two married composers, Jocelyn Hagen and Tim Takach, published several of my songs. "Velvet Shoes," my first piece—the one Charles Turner said should be published—was now finally in print. They also published both the piano and the orchestral versions of *Songs of the Poet.* I expect that I am the only composer in the history of the world to have an orchestral score published but never performed, though several conductors including JoAnn Falletta, conductor of the Buffalo Philharmonic have expressed interest.

Dorothy Parker rose from the dead once a year. When I entered the piece in the 2005 New York Musical Theater Festival, I hardly knew what I was getting into. The festival provided the venue, the publicity, the ticketing, and box office, but I was now a producer, and David Merrick I was not. This meant I had to hire the cast, the musicians, director, designer, stage manager, stage crew, and rehearsal space, among a million other things. I had only a few months to put the production together. I called Michele and asked if she would play Mrs. Parker, with Brad Rouse directing. Unfortunately, both had made other commitments. Under pressure, I thought, "I'd better go with what I already know." Karen Mason agreed to do it. It pained me to have to call Greg, after our rift, but it seemed the most expedient course.

This was not to be a full production, but rather an Equity Showcase, with minimal sets and costumes. Still it was almost more than I could handle and certainly more expense than I anticipated. The Shapiros, parents of another piano student, and the Speras, made generous contributions to help me out. John Scheffler, from *Celebration*, had become a highly respected set designer, so I engaged him to select some set pieces and a graphic-artist friend, Jean Carbain, to design the program and postcards.

In rehearsal, Greg and I were amiable, with no mention of the *Lost Empires* dustup. I brought in Denis Jones, an upcoming Broadway choreographer, to stage "The Waltz," one of Dorothy's funniest stories, and the only short story remaining in the play. The long number had never really worked, and I thought it was because the actual dancing was missing. Greg took umbrage because he believed this was his terrain.

Rehearsals moved slowly, too slowly for the short rehearsal period we had. Karen seemed to retain very little of what she performed only a year earlier, so much time was wasted on relearning. Three days before the first performance she was still struggling with her lines. In a one-person show, that task is monumental. Both Greg and I were becoming frantic. Karen hired someone to rehearse her. I remembered how on the demo, she didn't learn the music until the last minute so I hoped for a reprise. When actors are unprepared and insecure, they become testy and start lashing out. Two days before the opening, Greg had a concert engagement and had to miss rehearsal, which meant I had to take over the directing chores for that day. I became the victim of her wrath.

I was so dispirited by this point, because everything was going wrong. The festival's ticketing site indicated that all six performances of my show were sold out, so I stopped trying to promote it. At the last minute, I learned that they had inexplicably held back almost half the tickets, and when people called to buy they were told none were available. In true friendship, Stu Shapiro bought up a block of tickets and tried pressing all his friends to come. Nevertheless, only one performance sold out because of the snafu.

During that final frantic week of rehearsals, Todd's old roommate, Patrick Shannon and his live-in boyfriend, who were displaced when Katrina struck New Orleans, asked if they could stay with us for one week and with John Scheffler for a second week. Who could deny them after the terrible devastation? The boyfriend, who made himself a nuisance the entire week, was a bit of a flake and managed to wipe out all the emails on my computer, hundreds of which were essential to the production.

Patrick and John were friends from Louisiana. John maintained his family house in New Orleans. and was so distraught about the damage it sustained that he couldn't concentrate on my show. As a result the few set pieces he picked out were inappropriate and in some cases didn't work with the staging. Greg was furious.

Being a true professional, Karen knew her part by opening night. The Dorothy Parker Society bought a block of tickets for one performance, showing up in 1920s garb. Reviews for the piece were decidedly mixed. Greg convinced me not to use mikes because the theater was small, but the resulting lack of presence was pointed out in some reviews. I felt waves of guilt that people had invested money in me, and the results were so modest.

David Hemphill, loyal as ever, flew in from Tucson to see the show. Also my old school friend, Terry Anderson, showed up with his new boyfriend. How wrong I had been about his coming out. Shortly, after he came to dinner at our apartment to "observe gay life," he met David Ponser, a young State Department employee, whom he later married. They were very compatible and happy together, and visited us each time they came through town. Despite my initial concerns, when Terry informed his wife and children that he was gay, they were not at all surprised and took the news with equanimity.

Jim Morgan, who always wanted my show for York Theater. said to me after the festival ended, "I wish you had spent your money at my theater instead. We could have given you a much better production." York unfortunately could no longer fully fund its own productions. Jim was right, but a production there would have cost at least three times what the New York Musical Theater Festival cost.

What I learned from the festival was that the show was too long. Audiences teach you a great deal about what works in a production. This was the first time I had a chance to see it before six different audiences. I had read that Michael Stewart, the book writer of *Hello, Dolly!*, had a simple rule: "If it doesn't advance the plot, develop the character, or get a laugh, cut it." I cut "The Waltz," which didn't work, even with the choreography. Elaine Stritch had been trying to do a dramatization of it for years, finally giving up. If Stritch can't make it work, it's certain that I can't. By trimming a few other unnecessary moments as well as the intermission, I was able to turn it into a tight ninety-minute piece.

Just prior to the festival production, Jack Lee recommended that his agent, Bret Adams, one of the best on Broadway, take me as a client. Bret was very encouraging about all my work, but he came to see *You Might as Well Live*, and he told me he was very displeased with the show's director, even though Greg was his friend. He didn't understand why Greg constantly had Dorothy rise from her desk and pour herself another drink. I explained, "I believe Greg resorted to this stage business, which also bothered me, because Karen had trouble with some of the abrupt changes of mood. It was an easy, if inelegant, solution to the problem. Take a drink and the mood changes." When I relayed this to Greg his response was, "Oh, Bret doesn't know anything," which I found very unfair. Sadly, several months after Bret took me as a client, he died. I seemed to be the kiss of death for agents and singers. Astoundingly, five people seriously interested in my work died within a span of ten years.

I had made so many mistakes, so many bad choices, especially with directors. I needed to take cognizance of them. Several of the directors I had interviewed and rejected had developed impressive careers. Worse, Douglas, whom I had fired, had become the artistic director of a major regional theater that developed musicals for Broadway, a position whereby he could easily have helped promote my work. Greg's career, on the other hand, seemed to languish in limbo.

I needed a break from the world of showbiz, and Todd's art career provided it, with two trips to Europe. First, he had his second show in Munich, followed by an idyllic artist-in-residence program in a Tuscany villa, called Atelier d'Artista. At the end of the residency, Tony Lin joined us for a trip to Cinque Terre, the five villages perched on the rugged coastline of the Italian Riviera. We spent our days on the Sentiero Azzurro, the hiking trail that connects the villages and offers spectacular sweeping vistas of the sea. Tony, who by now was truly a member of our family, dined with us every week on Saturday nights, and it reminded me of my own weekly dinners with the Brooklyn Speras when I first came to New York.

Born in Taiwan, Tony's father was a well-known, wealthy Taipei pediatrician. Inexplicably, his mother moved Tony, his sister Sunny, and his two brothers, Alex and Kenny, to San Marino, California, when Tony was six years old. He never questioned this move, but Todd and I thought it curious that his mother would do this, considering that the Taiwanese schools were excellent. Though his parents did not officially separate, we suspected some problem with the marriage. All his siblings are doctors, and both his brothers are gay. Tony was a brilliant student at Stanford, graduating number one in chemistry, and was the editor of the yearbook, which was named the best in North America, in his senior year.

He had to keep his homosexuality and his friendship with us secret, "How could I explain to my parents that I have two geriatric gay friends?" His older brother is the only one to come out to the family and his father's reaction was, "I'd rather be dead than have a gay son." This did not encourage Tony to follow suit. Whatever would daddy do if he knew he had three gay sons?

Todd and I had to guide Tony through the gay dating process and provide moral support through two disastrous relationships: one with a male nurse whom he met during his residency at Mt. Sinai Hospital and who once threatened him with a knife; the other with a selfish and self-absorbed Hungarian chemist.

One day I foolishly ventured that Tony reminded me of my mother with her little sayings such as: "Here, make yourself useful," if I was in the kitchen while he was cooking; "That hit the spot," something I'd not heard since I left the Midwest; or answering the phone with an anxious, "What happened?" a response I always got if I called either of them unexpectedly. Tony was always "putting his foot down," something Mary Giovingo always did when she asserted herself. This little untoward comment of mine was sufficient to trigger his vivid imagination into maintaining that he was, in fact, Mary Giovingo reincarnated—unlikely in that she died when he was twenty-five. Anyway, how did this work? My adopted son was now actually my mother? Tony explained, "She died of a broken heart because of her disappointment in her two sons. Then she channeled herself into me because she knew her work here was not yet done," meaning she still needed to keep me on track. He loved my stories about Mary Giovingo, and he internalized them all as his own. She was reborn.

If I made fun of her malapropisms, he chided "She's been in her grave for years and you still make fun of the poor woman. You'll burn in hell someday." When I insisted that I didn't do it maliciously but rather to keep her memory alive because I missed her so, he'd say, "You don't have to miss her. I'm right here." "Tony, you're a real piece of work," I countered. It was uncanny how he'd toss out criticisms of me and Todd that sounded just like her. If I mentioned something about my Italian heritage, he'd say, "Oh, please, I'm much more Italian than you could ever be." Tony brought much laughter into our house from his "I Love Lucy" imitation of the Vitameatavegamin routine, to his ability to quote every line from *Strictly Ballroom,* but especially his embodiment of Mary Giovingo's persona. She would have loved him.

In 2007, *You Might as Well Live* was selected for PlayFest, The Annual Festival of New Plays at the Orlando Shakespeare Theater. The theater was honoring playwrights, not musical theater composers, and my piece was chosen along with three Pulitzer-Prize finalists. The theater put Todd and me up in a lovely hotel with a pool for two weeks. There we were surrounded by "god's ugliest vegetable." I was a bit concerned that a local actor was playing the role because it requires a true virtuoso performer to bring it off. I needn't have worried because Becky Fisher was excellent. Though the performances were considered workshops and didn't need to be memorized, she had the whole piece from memory before I arrived. With extraordinary dedication, she made every effort to assume Dorothy's persona and look. The director was a bit inexperienced, and I found myself doing most of the directing myself. "Norman, remember how in high school you told people you wanted to be a director, though you didn't understand what the job was?"

The first of the three performances was smashing and played to a full house. The theater's associate director, Patrick Flick, said, "Your piece is marvelous, and I know we're going to want to produce it." Finally, after thirty-two drafts I've become a playwright. The old axiom is "musicals are not written, they are rewritten." Admittedly I had carried this to absurdity. Never had I felt more like a celebrity. Because of a talkback after the performance, which was completely positive, people recognized me and stopped me on the street to tell me how much they enjoyed the show. Even a waiter in our hotel, gave us a free breakfast. All the performances went extremely well, with encouraging talkbacks after each.

After the final performance, one of the other playwrights, who wrote the only bad piece at PlayFest, an unfunny piece about China, stayed for the talkback. Todd and I were certain that his embarrassing travesty was selected only because he was a good friend of the artistic director. His play was so dreadful and so racially demeaning that Todd walked out of the performance. I endured to the bitter end and had the decency not to make any comments at his talkback. At mine, the stage manager announced that there was time for one more question.

This playwright, who was seated next to the artistic director piped up, "I felt in watching your show that I had been invited to a party where I knew none of the guests, and no one bothered to introduce me." Before I could respond, the stage manager said, "I'm afraid we're out of time."

This was the first time I'd ever witnessed a competitor brazenly try to undermine me. As Todd's mother might have said, "He's as mean as cat shit." His comment was unfair and inaccurate because I defined all the characters I introduced in the play, with perhaps the exception of Edna Ferber. "Do you have the nerve to tell me, Mr. No-Talent, that as a playwright you never heard of Edna Ferber? For shame." My director complained that the playwrights should not be allowed to comment publicly on each other's work. This playwright's uncalled for remark may not have carried any weight, but Patrick Flick had already warned me that the artistic director disliked musicals and had a strong bias against producing them.

Except for this incident, the whole experience had been so positive. When I got back to New York, the final blow came. The critic for the *Orlando Sentinel* had attended the first performance and talkback without my being aware of it, and though critics were not supposed to review workshops, she published an online critique. "What do you do if you're a member of the PlayFest audience and the reading or workshop you're seeing seems to have what you might call a serious flaw?" She went on to say that my play's premise was that Mrs. Parker was putting together a collection of her writing. "So why is she trying to write a new poem?" she asked. Well, the reason was simple, the contract with her publisher demanded it.

Becky, who was understandably very nervous on opening night, forgot the line that explained this, and the critic spent the rest of the evening obsessing over why she was writing a poem. Then she went on to complain that it appeared from the talkback that I was not interested in hearing criticism but only praise from my "friends." First of all, I knew absolutely no one in Orlando, and I didn't control the questions and comments in the talkback. Why she did not express her concern in the talkback, so that I might have explained it, was incomprehensible. The damage was done. The theater was not going to produce a play already panned by the local critic. Breaking into the world of theater began to feel as daunting as trying to be part of the clique in high school. To paraphrase Sondheim, I should have gone to a cooking school, that seems clear.

How to assess this roller-coaster career of mine? Was I a no-talent hack, a lauded creator of high-quality work, or something in between? It was impossible to determine from all the yeasayers and naysayers, all the ups and downs I'd experienced. The one word that best sums up my career is "almost." I almost became a ballet dancer. I almost had a featured role on Broadway. I almost had my classical music performed by leading figures. I almost had a major success with my musical theater works. Why didn't "almost" ever become "definitely?"

Is it insufficient talent? Perhaps. Luck and its sister, timing, obviously, played a major role. Even the most talented will admit that without the "big break," they might still be struggling. Was I undermining myself? Certainly, with Brady I did, but if there are other examples, they were inadvertent. Age? Though it can't be used as an excuse, the young simply have more doors open to them. Eighty percent of all advertised opportunities to submit one's work come with an age limit of thirty-five.

Critics and artistic directors are continually on the lookout for cutting-edge work, which mine is definitely not. They all too often focus on the "new" (if, indeed, there is anything in any art that hasn't already be done) at the expense of the "good."

Not being a man of my own times is clearly a factor, something I sensed even as a child. My love for popular music spanned the decades from the '20s through the early '60s. Even Sondheim admits his success came in just under the wire. John Kander pinpoints the change to 1967. In 1966, songs from *Cabaret* were frequently broadcast on the radio. At the end of 1967, with *The Happy Time,* they were unable to get any airplay, despite the fact that Robert Goulet sang many of its best songs.

Time had simply passed me by. My musical-theater compositions would have fit nicely into those earlier decades. When I began composing, I mistakenly thought, "With so many wonderful revivals, wouldn't people love to hear new versions of the same type music?" In a word, no. If they want to hear the sound of the American Songbook's standards, with rare exceptions, they want the originals, not some modern-day facsimile.

Broadway demands pop, rap, rock, or country today. Many have suggested that I write in those styles. The fact is I have no feeling for those types of music and would get no enjoyment from writing it. My highly melodic music, with moments of strong dissonance to express angst, anger, or despair, precisely expresses what I have to say. Melody is almost necessarily imbued with beauty, but melody and beauty have little currency today. I've always been a hopeless romantic by nature, but in our era, which is decidedly unromantic, romanticism is seen as nothing more than banal sentimentality.

In my classical compositions, I'm neither an atonalist nor a minimalist. Fortunately, in classical music, no one style dominates to the exclusion of all others. so there are still half-open windows of opportunity for me. And that's where I decided to put my efforts.

The Right Side of the Room:
Sicily and an Opera

PATTY SEYBURN SUGGESTED that I look at Christina Rossetti's poetry because she thought her lyricism lended itself to music. I read through her entire work and chose five songs to set as a cycle I called *Rossetti Songs,* for mezzo-soprano, piano, flute, and cello. In order not to limit performance opportunities, I did a second version for just voice and piano.

Parma Records was planning a CD of new art songs under its Navona label and invited composers to submit works. *Rossetti Songs* was accepted and scheduled for recording in Boston in a former Masonic lodge that had been turned into a first-rate recording studio by members of the Boston Symphony. Just before Todd and I departed for Boston, I had a Richard Danielpour panic attack about the score. I was suddenly terrified that I had overwritten the flute part so that it might drown out the voice. I conferred with the musicians by phone, who assured me that it would not be a problem.

Though five of the composers on the compilation, which was titled *Rapport*, were relatively unknown, I was glad to learn that one work was by Pulitzer-Prize-winner David del Tredici, who had been composer-in-residence at the New York Philharmonic. The recording session gave me my first opportunity to hear my writing for instruments other than voice and piano, and I was relieved to discover that they blended very nicely. The performers said, "We hope you can tell what we think of your piece by the love we've poured into it." Bob Lord, Parma's owner, took us to dinner after the recording session. He had not yet chosen the cover art for the CD, and when he learned that Todd was a painter, he asked to see samples of his work. Bob chose a painting, entitled "Drums and Banners," which hung in Janice Lee and Stu Shapiro's dining room.

My work received good reviews, and Janice and Stu gave an elaborately catered CD-release party at their house for nearly one hundred people. Tracy Bidleman and I performed two of the songs in the piano/vocal version. I spoke about the genesis of the cycle, why I dedicated the work to the Shapiros, and pointed out Todd's painting.

A few years later, the piano/vocal version was performed by an excellent mezzo-soprano, Sara Fanucchi, at the Source Song Festival in Minneapolis. With famed composer Libby Larsen as mentor, it was one of the most inspiring music festivals I'd ever attended. The performance was recorded live, so I now had recordings of each version. The Navona version was recently broadcast on Hawaii Public Radio, giving a nice boost to my ASCAP royalties. One ASCAP statement I received gave me $100 royalty for airplay of a piece, called "I Like the Way She Do It." Strange, I thought, that certainly doesn't sound like any piece in my repertoire. On closer examination, I determined it was by rapper 50 Cent. How did this happen? ASCAP couldn't explain. I returned the royalty.

Shortly before the CD release, I returned home one evening to find Todd in tears. "What happened?" "Your brother died." "What? How can that be? I just spoke to him yesterday." Larry, who never took good care of himself and smoked three packs of cigarettes every day, was found dead of a heart attack on his living room floor, a lighted cigarette still in his hand, and the TV blaring. I couldn't believe this. He was only sixty-one years old, and he sounded just fine on the phone the day before. He was found by his girlfriend, Lois Johnson, a name Larry mysteriously had never mentioned to me, despite the fact that this had been a serious relationship. Lois, who was devastated by his death, told me about their enduring relationship and that they were planning to be married.

Todd and I flew out to Napa. We were escorted into his apartment by Lois, a friend, and a man called Gabby, who ran an online gambling site. As a sideline to his bartending job, Larry had been Gabby's "bagman" or money collector for several years. I worried that he would end up in jail if Gabby ever got caught. Todd and I had met Gabby when the two of them came to New York. Gabby insisted on going into Larry's apartment first because he knew Larry was holding a large amount of the gambling proceeds in a safe. He went into the bedroom, where the safe was kept, opened it, and found it empty. "What happened to the money?" Gabby questioned Lois and me, somewhat accusingly. Neither of us knew anything about it. Nor was the money in Larry's bank account. Had he lost it gambling? Had he loaned it to friends? We learned that friends owed Larry a great deal of money. I didn't know what to think because except for his gambling addiction, Larry was scrupulously honest. I was so grateful that Mary Giovingo and my father weren't around to know about this. It would have devastated them.

A memorial celebration was held in the bar and restaurant where Larry had been a bartender for several years. Again, I was struck by my brother's popularity. Hundreds attended the celebration, and their sense of loss was touching. Many of us gave eulogies in his remembrance. Dozens upon dozens of his customers talked to me about what a wonderful person and friend he had been, how he had sympathetically listened to their woes at the bar. Many continued the commemoration every year on the anniversary of his death. I was impressed and moved by this outpouring of love.

It helps to have a doctor "in the family." A routine colonoscopy detected that I had a villous polyp, the flat type that can't be easily removed and is highly likely to become cancerous. I consulted with several doctors, and it was determined that I must have twelve inches of my colon removed as a safeguard. I made an appointment for the surgery. Tony Lin said, "Before you decide on surgery, send your results to Stephanie Santos," a woman he had befriended during his residency. She was now a fellow in gastroenterology at Mt. Sinai Hospital and was an assistant to a doctor who had developed a special technique for villous polyp removal without colon surgery. All the other physicians advised against this. Once again, bad advice from many doctors.

I decided to go with Stephanie because I knew her and trusted her judgment. The procedure, performed like a colonoscopy, is very tricky and involves dying the polyp a bright blue, providing visual clues to help prevent the accidental perforation of the bowel. At least forty residents observed the procedure, which Stephanie performed herself, under the guidance of her mentor. I had Tony and Stephanie to thank for keeping my colon intact.

Tony by this time had become a hospitalist at Montefiore Hospital. Todd and I were the proud "parents" when he described his treatment protocol. We knew that he was both extremely competent and extremely caring. Patients gave him gifts, old women insisted on kissing him, and one called him her "guardian angel." Once he even paid for a poor patient's room television service because the man had no family to visit him. Tony was constantly checking up on his patients, even when he was off duty, providing personal care, so rare in today's highly impersonal medical environment. If he lost a patient, he was consumed with self-reproach. He was also on top of any symptoms Todd and I might develop, always providing excellent advice.

I had written my own choral arrangements for *Lost Empires,* but had never composed a serious choral work. I took Shakespeare's "Sonnet No. 61" and set it for mixed choir, piano, and oboe. The piece was a winner of the prestigious American Composers Forum 2011 VocalEssence Award. Todd and I were flown to Minneapolis, where my work was rehearsed by the highly acclaimed thirty-two-voice VocalEssence professional choir, under the direction of Philip Brunelle, one of the world's major choral conductors. They also engaged a first-rate oboist.

We were feted, dined, taken to a symphony concert, and on the final day my work was performed and recorded. Because of its success I added two more sonnets, plus a flute to make up a cycle, entitled *Love's Not Time's Fool.* The work has been selected by internationally known conductors for ProjectEncore's catalog of recommended choral music. Things were looking up career-wise.

Jocelyn Hagen, my publisher, recommended me for an artist-in-residence at Shorter University in Rome, Georgia, which is thought to have the finest college vocal program in the Southeast. Jocelyn held the position a year earlier, and they asked her if she knew someone who could write both classical vocal music and musical theater. The less-than-a week residency offered a commission to write a work for faculty to perform on a whole-evening program devoted to my compositions. In addition, I was required to supervise rehearsals, give a lecture on my career, and answer students' questions about the music business.

I wanted to write a piece that would involve several voices, plus piano, but couldn't think of any text that was suitable. I phoned Patty Seyburn, "Do you know of any poem with three characters that would lend itself to a musical setting?" "I don't, but I've been thinking about writing a formal poem. Could we collaborate on this?" Patty chose the French composer Cécile Chaminade as her subject. Chaminade was a friend of the more famous composer, Camille Saint-Saëns. Patty invented a third character based on her grandmother as a young girl, the three characters corresponding by letters. It took nearly a year to complete the twenty-minute dramatic cantata, which she called *Flights of the Heart.*

The remainder of the program was to be made up of my art songs, and an abbreviated concert version of *Lost Empires,* which was to be performed primarily by students. We were finally getting our reading of this ill-fated musical. What I did not realize when I signed the contract was that the school was a Baptist college. Jocelyn Hagen had experienced no problems with this, but during the summer before my residency a new president was hired.

I got a call from Matthew Hoch, who was supervising the program,

"I'm sorry to say that you're going to have to cut one of the songs from *Lost Empires.*"

"Which one?"

"'That's Always Champagne.'"

"Why?"

"Because our new president objects to any reference to alcohol."

"What? Are you joking?"

"No, he reviewed all the material on the program, and that song must be cut."

"But the piece doesn't promote alcohol. It's a metaphor."

"Just the mention of it is offensive to him."

"Matt, to you it means just cutting a number. To me, that song completely defines the character of Uncle Nick, and without it he makes no sense in the plot at all."

"I'm sorry. We can't perform that number."

"I have never in my life had my work censored. I'm seriously considering canceling the residency. I'm going to have to speak to my collaborators about this."

When I told Todd, he was livid. "We worked so hard developing Uncle Nick. If that song's cut, I'm not going down there, and I don't think you should, either."

I phoned Patty in California. She couldn't believe it and joked, "What if I change the title to 'That's Always Cocaine?'"

"Todd's refusing to go, and I'm thinking of bailing out, too."

"But we've worked so hard on F*lights of the Heart*. It's easy for you and Todd to change your plans. You have no one else to consider, but I've arranged my leave from school and set up a baby-sitting schedule for my kids." "What in god's name are artists doing at a school like this?" I replied. "What's it going to be like working with these people." I relented but felt as though I was betraying all my political beliefs.

I phoned Matthew, "Todd refuses to attend, but Patty and I will come. I want to give you fair warning, however. Don't even think of introducing me to your president because I have no intention of being polite. I will tell him exactly what I think of him and his reactionary censorship policies."

Patty and I met at the Atlanta airport and drove to Rome. As we entered the town, we were struck by the sheer number of churches alternating with gun stores. Is there anything else in this burg, I wondered? How does this scene of gun-toters and evangelicals mesh with a program devoted to serious music. I hadn't been in the Deep South since the *Hello, Dolly!* tour, and nothing indicated to me that it had improved since then.

Shorter maintained a two-bedroom guest apartment with a private entrance in one of the dorm buildings. We assumed we would both stay there. But no. How dare you even think such sinful thoughts? We were not married. Imagine the scandal. Think how it would corrupt the students. Patty got the apartment, while I was exiled to some dreary motel on the edge of town, with nothing around it. Well, when in Rome. . .That became our maxim to laugh away the ridiculousness of the situation.

The rehearsal for *Flights of the Heart* was very encouraging. Matthew sang the baritone role and was quite wonderful, as were the soprano and mezzo. What became apparent was that everyone, students and faculty alike, was completely embarrassed by the president. They all apologized profusely to us. Rather than the rabid religious fanatics we anticipated, they were all nice, normal people. During the *Lost Empires* rehearsal, the head of the theater department approached me, "When I was introduced to the new president, the first thing he said to me was, 'I hate the theater.'" He also told me that the president, unseen by me, had peeked in on a rehearsal, no doubt to be certain there was no alcohol and no one was naked. "Is he a recovering alcoholic? Is that his problem?" I inquired. No one seemed to know.

The students did an admirable job with *Lost Empires,* but a reading requires top professional talent so one can ascertain that any evident problems are with the work itself, not the performances. We were uncertain, but the musical unsurprisingly appeared to require more work. Everyone was so gracious and grateful to Patty and me that we were glad we had decided to participate.

When I got back to New York, I learned that the president issued an edict requiring all faculty to sign a fealty oath stating that they had never committed adultery and never drank any alcohol. A rising-star theater composer was set to be their next resident artist, and when he learned of this, he canceled his engagement and wrote a scathing article in *Playbill* condemning the school. I wrote to Matthew and said, "For your career's sake, you must not stay at Shorter because the school is becoming a national laughing stock."

Most of the faculty we worked with refused to sign the oath and left the university. One remarkable tenor, Chuck Chandler, who sang two of my Whitman songs so magnificently, left to teach at Florida State University. A few years later, he included *Songs of the Poet* on a program he toured to several universities. He will soon release a recording of that program, giving me two commercial recordings of the cycle.

I'd never been very active politically, but I began paying closer attention beginning with the Clinton presidency, watching the country's rightward drift with increasing alarm. Todd and I were enthusiastic supporters of Obama. On election night, we watched the returns at the Shapiro's house. I cooked Julia Child's six-meat cassoulet for the occasion, and we all cheered as victory was announced. At last, America had come to its senses. When we left their house, we joined jubilant revelers in the Greenwich Village streets.

A year later, a dispiriting political reality dampened our enthusiasm. Obama called for a nonsensical troop surge in Afghanistan, ballooned the disastrous drone attacks and rendition of suspects to CIA black sites, expanded illegal surveillance, neutered habeas corpus, bowed to the pharmaceutical industry to kill the health care act's public option, imposed his neoliberal policies to bailout Wall Street, leaving the rest of America to fend for itself, and abandoned his promise to labor to renegotiate the NAFTA agreement. These despicable actions were taken despite the fact that during Obama's first two years in office the Democrats controlled the House of Representatives, held a sixty-vote supermajority in the Senate, and had enormous public support. What most disturbed Todd and me was how liberals, who condemned George W. Bush ("not in my name," they declared), seemed to be fine that Obama was continuing and expanding these horrors.

I chalked this up to a rising and debilitating tribalism—it's okay when our guy does it— which I view as one of the great menaces of modern times. It prompted me to write an article, "Time to Reset Our Moral Compass," which was published in the online progressive publication, *Common Dreams*. Tribalism was a crucial attribute in the prehistoric era, when loyalty to the group was a matter of life and death, affording protection against wild animals and warring tribes. Though this atavistic trait is obviously part of our DNA, we must learn to recognize its influence on our thinking and rein it in if we are to survive as a species. I firmly believe that if Obama's supporters had held him accountable and vehemently opposed his anti-progressive policies, we would not be saddled with the repugnant President Trump today.

Larry and I both learned two very important character traits from our parents, which I believe were their greatest gifts to us. First, from Mary Giovingo we learned the art of actively listening to other people. Everyone told her their troubles because she was sympathetic and interested in their concerns. When I suggested to Tony that he should seek therapy over his body-dysmorphic syndrome and family and boyfriend issues, his response was, "I don't need a therapist. I have you." It appeared that my students relied on me as much for my sympathetic ear as for my musical knowledge. Two psychiatrists I taught both said to me, "This is my therapy."

Second, both our parents gave Larry and me a deep commitment to fairness and justice, though Mary and Matt, both FDR Democrats, did not think specifically in political, but rather personal terms. "Don't ever take advantage of people. Don't accept gifts unless you can give something in return. Respect other people as you would be respected. Above all, be honest." These were the principles they lived by, and we were expected to follow suit.

"Norman," I said to myself, "you are not a political commentator, so if you have something to say, say it through your art." I am painfully aware that the political in art is extremely unfashionable today, and that with so much corporate sponsorship, organizations run at the sight of controversy. This was not always true. Mozart's and Beaumarchais's *The Marriage of Figaro* played a role in inciting the French Revolution. Picasso's "Guernica" and Benjamin Britten's *War Requiem* are among the great antiwar works of the 20th Century.

I learned that the Puffin Foundation gave grants to works of art that addressed social issues. I emailed Patty and asked if she'd be interested in writing the text for a piece on such a topic, so we could apply for the grant together. I was surprised that she never responded to me, especially since she made a point of how we must work together again after *Flights of the Heart.* This turned out to be a positive. Not hearing from her forced me into a whole new artistic endeavor—devising my own texts. In Howard Zinn's *People's History of the United States,* he discussed Percy Bysshe Shelley's poem *The Mask of Anarchy,* about workers who were slaughtered by industrialists for protesting unfair conditions.

I extracted the stanzas that applied to current issues and used Shelley's last line as the title for my work, *Ye Are Many—They Are Few, Cantata for a Just World,* which echoed all the current controversy about the ninety-nine percent versus the one percent. To this I added quotes from Zinn, George Bernard Shaw, Frederick Douglass, William Jennings Bryan, William Butler Yeats, and even Dorothy Parker, who said, "Which is worse—the perpetrators of injustice or those who are blind to it?" Woven between these quotes and the poem's stanzas, I added my own political commentary—particularly about the tribalism issue—and connected the elements into a dramatic arc. I set the work for four voices and piano, with additional unsung oratory by the bass-baritone, and it won a grant from the Puffin Foundation. The piece was given a stunning premiere by Vox3, a young operatic vocal group, at the beautiful Chicago Cultural Center, which boasts the largest Tiffany glass dome in the world. I was most pleased by audience members who told me after, "It's about time somebody said these things."

In 2010, Todd and I decided to explore my heritage more deeply. We began a series of excursions to Sicily. At first we stayed in hotels, but as our trips grew from two weeks to nearly six weeks long we began to rent apartments in Palermo. Almost immediately, I had the sense that this was my home, a place where I belonged, much as I had felt years earlier when I moved to New York. Todd seemed even more passionate about the island than I was.

Our first rental apartment in Palermo was in the center of the Ballaró market, a blocks-long series of outdoor stalls selling every conceivable food the island produces. Outside our door, were enormous carcasses of fresh-caught tuna and swordfish, *gamberi rosso* (the bright-red, succulent Mediterranean shrimp), perfect ripe tomatoes with unparalleled flavor, piles of three-feet-long *cucuzze*, long-stemmed artichokes, as well as hazardous, spiked-leaf baby-sized ones, sausages, cheeses, baked ricottas with savory toppings, and olives. Best of all, was that the prices were one-fourth what we pay in Manhattan. We rented the apartment primarily because we wanted to cook using these magnificent ingredients and to steep ourselves in the local culture. Tony joined us for several days to share in the experience and the fruits of the market.

Downstairs from our apartment was a turn-of-the century *farmacia*. Could this be the very one where my grandfather Ignazio worked? Why, as children, are we never curious enough to ask the questions we want desperately answered as adults? How I wished that I'd pressed my *Nonna* for details. Where did they live? I still saw evidence of the baskets hanging from balconies, to draw up food and other items, just as she had described. Had my grandparents ever sampled the exquisite pastries at Spinnato's? Did Ignazio ever get to see one of his cherished operas at the glamorous Teatro Massimo, the third largest in Europe? How sad. They are all gone, and I will never know.

The remarkable cultural heritage of the island is mind-boggling, from the heart-stopping majesty of the Greek temple at Segesta to the magnificent mosaics in the Martorano Chapel in Palermo. And this is what I and my parents were made to feel inferior about by the Swedes in Rockford? To appreciate or even be aware of the many layers of culture, one needs to know something about Sicily's history, how it was ruled by so many powers—Greeks, Romans, Arabs, Normans, Spanish, and French—each leaving its unique imprint. Only with such knowledge can one brush away the surface poverty and delight in the elements from each of those cultures, still evident in the architecture, the food, the language, and the Sicilian persona. Todd was my mentor in this knowledge, as he read every book on Sicilian history written in English, all in preparation for his writing about the island, and to distill its essence in his paintings. The deeper we bore into its history, the more Sicily became an inspiration for our artistic pursuits.

Sicily holds a crucial lesson for today's world, riven by religious and cultural wars, if only we'd make the effort to unlock its secrets. In 12th-Century Sicily, when the Normans gained power and as the Crusades raged elsewhere, "for one brief, shining moment" Christians, Muslims, and Jews, lived together in virtual harmony, each contributing its particular talents. Todd taught me that the Vikings swooped down from Scandinavia and conquered northern France, becoming Normans or men of the North It brings a smile to my face to think that with the Norman invasion of Sicily it's quite possible that I have some Scandinavian blood. Perhaps I'm part Swede.

We began toying with the idea of relocating to Palermo. I was born in the wrong town. New York, which I had so loved, has become abysmally Disneyfied to appeal to tourists. The city, so significantly changed from my early days, and America, with its recent neo-fascist leanings, no longer seem congenial to us. I hoped to end my days in the right town.

I learned that I might qualify for Italian citizenship through my paternal grandfather. Two years of arduous paper work finally led to my getting an Italian passport. Every document had to be translated by a government-approved translator and affixed with a state apostille. The various incarnations of my name posed innumerable difficulties and required me to change it legally. One benefit from the process was that I learned things about my grandparents I never knew: the correct spelling of Cangialosi; the names of their parents, where they were married; the ship that they emigrated on; and their date of embarkation at Ellis Island.

Todd and I began studying Italian, but learning a new language at age seventy can be daunting, with mental retention not what it was before I reached my dotage. As part of my studies, I read a book of Sicilian stories by Giovanni Verga in a dual-language edition. First I tried to read the Italian version, then the English, and back to the Italian to see what I had missed the first time. In the book was a four-page novella, *La Lupa,* the she-wolf, and my first reaction was how operatic it sounded. Verga, after all, was the author of *Cavalleria Rusticana,* which was, of course, turned into an opera by Pietro Mascagni.

Many singers had asked why I had not written an opera. I never seriously considered it because I was not much of an opera fan. Oh, I loved the music, but as a work of theater, the form had serious limitations. The libretti were often unspeakably inane, the acting was abysmal, the singers miscast, and I always felt that the form asked more of music than it could possibly deliver theatrically. And, why in heaven do they have to sing with such passion about the most mundane affairs in life? Perhaps, it was my background in musical theater, but I could never simply abandon myself to the music, ignoring all the other flaws.

Yet, here was this story, so dramatic, so compelling, so unexpected. Pina, La Lupa, is a thirty-five-year-old beautiful woman recently widowed, who falls deeply in love with Nanni, a handsome young soldier who works beside her as a wheat harvester in the fields near Mt. Etna. Sexually voracious, she throws herself at Nanni. To her horror, Pina learns that Nanni is enamored of her young daughter, Mara, who also works in the fields. Though it cut like a knife, she agrees to give her daughter to Nanni in marriage just to keep him in her life. Though Mara has no interest in Nanni, Pina forces the union, but not before seducing Nanni herself.

After the marriage of Nanni and Mara and the birth of their child, they live together in Pina's house. Mara comes to love Nanni, but Pina, who is jealous of her daughter, keeps the flame for Nanni ablaze. A weak-willed man who wants to please everybody, Nanni cannot resist Pina's overtures, yet is racked with guilt after every encounter. Mara catches her mother in an embrace with her husband and goes to the police. Pina is forced to leave her own house and keep away from Nanni, who atones for his sins through humiliation by a priest on the steps of the church. Pina, like a caged animal without Nanni, visits and seduces him one more time. He threatens to kill her if she ever comes near him again.

The stage picture in my mind of the final scene convinced me I must write this piece. Pina abandons her black, mourning garb and dons an alluring red dress from her youth. She walks resolutely and proudly, a bunch of red poppies in her hands, and bares herself to Nanni and his upraised axe. The story had elements of Greek tragedy, particularly *Phaedra* and the obsessive love of Sondheim's *Passion*.

Do I have the ability to write such a work? Except for a few verses in the Dorothy Parker musical, I had never written lyrics before. I decided that if I were going to write it, the major arias would have to be in rhyme to heighten the emotional experience and make them more immediately comprehensible to the audience, as Sondheim advises. Also, the bare-bones story, which gives little more information than my synopsis, required that I invent scenes and characters.

I studied Verga and learned that he was a major force in *verismo* literature, those works that dealt with real people, generally poor peasants or fishermen, and real situations. His writing had a major influence on the neo-realist Italian filmmakers of the mid-20th Century, such as Visconti and Fellini. D.H. Lawrence admired his work so much that he translated many of his stories into English. Verga had also turned *La Lupa* into a play, which I read in the hope that it would give me more to work with. It didn't. Except for a couple scenes and a bit of dialog, which I could use, the play dilutes the power of the story, and its second act degenerates into petty squabbling between the main characters. Despite its flaws, Visconti directed a production starring Anna Magnani in the 1950s, and the Royal Shakespeare Company produced the play in the 1990s.

Two Italian film versions of *La Lupa* were also produced. A problem I detected in all the previous dramatizations was that they depicted Pina as a nymphomaniac, making her very unsympathetic. Most psychologists dismiss the very idea of such a disorder as primarily a male fantasy, so I knew I needed to avoid that. In its place, I wanted Pina's love to be the dominating, albeit totally destructive, force. To develop her character, I turned to a statement from Verga's novella: "she never had her fill—of anything." Here was a woman who worked harder than any man, who seized life by the throat, and stopped at nothing to expand her world beyond the mundanity of her provincial village life and the oppressiveness of her serf-like existence.

My assessment of the story as being operatic was correct. I discovered that Puccini had worked with Verga to write an opera of the novella. Disagreement about the characterization of Mara, who Puccini felt needed to be more sympathetic, derailed the project. Some passages from *La Bohème* are thought to have been originally written for *La Lupa*.

I turned to Sondheim's two-volume work of his collected lyrics, *Finishing the Hat* and *Look I Made a Hat*, as my masterclass in lyric writing. But where to begin? I approached the work as though I were writing a musical. I needed to draw on everything I knew about musical theater, composing, and playwriting. I started with an aria that would define Pina's character, and I put something of myself into that aria. The world of my imagination, one of love and justice and equality, was so much more fulfilling to me than the real world, so I transplanted that imaginary world onto Pina, calling it "The World in My Head."

I put forth some of my leftist political beliefs in the opening scene, in which these farm laborers, slaving under the blazing Sicilian sun, are mercilessly exploited by their *padrone*. The whole piece began to look relentlessly dour, so I wrote a humorous choral "list" song, in which the women are on one side of the stage, enumerating (listing) the faults of

Pina, the whore who tries to steal their husbands and their sons. On the other side of the stage are the men, extolling the virtues of her ruby-red lips and the "pleasure that lies in those voluptuous thighs." I invented characters using my family's names, Cangialosi, Spera, and Giovingo, Still it lacked a sense of place, of connection to the land, of context. What was needed? Another trip to Sicily, of course.

Todd and I took the antiquated Circum-Etna railroad, studying the terrain and the villages, from the fertile fields at the base of the volcano to the barren, forbidding expanses of solidified lava. What emerged was that the volcano, with its ability to destroy life and yet sustain it through its fertile soil, is the perfect metaphor for the volatile personalities of the characters in *La Lupa*.

After visiting Verga's house in Catania, we settled in Taormina for two weeks of intensive study at the Babilonia Italian Language School. Our private tutor, Elisa Pianges, was a godsend, a brilliant woman, a scholar in both Italian and Russian literature and culture. From her I learned that Pina's importance as a literary character derives from the fact that a Sicilian woman of the late 1800s who controlled her own life, and particularly her own sexual passions, was an anomaly—a woman well ahead of her time. I was writing a lullaby that Mara sings to her infant son in Italian, and Elisa helped me correct some awkward phrases.

Through the school, we rented a simple and inexpensive studio apartment, which had a small terrace overlooking the Mediterranean. With the idyllic view of the sea and the countryside of the work's setting as inspiration, I composed two arias for the opera while basking on the terrace. We returned to New York and within two years I completed the opera. Now, what do I do with it? Putting together a reading of a two-hour opera with so much difficult music to learn is infinitely more complicated than a musical. I approached the music conservatories, but they have their own mandates to fulfill. Is this to be one more wasted effort, languishing unheard in my apartment?

On April 9, 2014, Todd and I were married. We had tried out the relationship for forty-six years and decided it might just work. Tony wanted us to have a large affair so he could assume one of his dream roles, wedding planner. However, we didn't want to make a big deal out of it at our age, so we had a simple ceremony at the City Clerk's Office, with Tony as our only witness and guest. Always trying to impart some class to our decidedly downscale life, Tony plied us with gifts, such as fine wines, a KitchenAid professional mixer, and Bottega Veneta wallets. Following the ceremony, he insisted on taking us for an extravagant dinner at David

Bouley's Japanese-inspired restaurant, Brushstroke. When we got home, I couldn't resist singing to Todd from *Cabaret*, "So you'll wake one day, Look around and say, 'Somebody wonderful married me.'" Amazing how musical theater provides a song for every occasion.

A few months later, Tony took a trip to Seville with two friends. While there he met a man, Eustaquio Limon, a handsome electrician who was so enthralled with him that he projected a life-sized photograph of Tony on his wall once he had left. They immediately began a bi-continental relationship, visiting each other whenever possible. Finally, Tony was connected with the sort of kind, good-hearted, considerate man that he deserved. We were fond of Eustaquio immediately and whenever he is in New York, he joins the Saturday-night dinner ritual. Otherwise he joins through a video-chat app.

Todd and I were concerned that after three years, the relationship was not moving past the periodic long-distance visits. We suspected that part of the problem was Tony's indecisiveness. From observation, we knew that when Tony was confronted with a decision about treatment options for his patients, there was never a moment of hesitation, he's the epitome of the take-charge person. On the other hand, making even a simple decision in his personal life is as arduous as climbing Mt. Everest. A full-hour can easily be spent choosing a seat on a flight or walking up and down streets trying to decide which restaurant is best for dinner. "These are not life-and-death decisions, Tony. You can actually choose one restaurant this week and the other next," I teased.

If these mundane choices are difficult, one can only imagine that committing to his boyfriend is an insurmountable obstacle. Do we live in New York or Seville? If in Seville, what would I do for a living? Should I change careers, start a business, what? Can I live on less money? Should we rent an apartment or buy a house? It all becomes a tangled web of too many options. Indecision rules.

Most disconcertingly, Tony claims that Eustaquio is equally indecisive. "You love each other. Why can't the two of you just sit down and discuss when you will be married?"

"He needs to ask me?"

"Why?"

"Because I want to be proposed to?"

This dilemma requires third-party intervention. As Dolly Levi said, "I put my hand in here." I emailed Eustaquio. "Todd and I view ourselves as Tony's foster parents. We adore both you and Tony and believe you make a terrific couple. We know that he loves you and would love to be married, but he has an old-fashioned, storybook idea about being proposed to. You know how indecisive he is. For him to take the initiative is probably impossible. He needs to be led by the hand."

The next time Eustaquio was in New York and came to our house for dinner, I noted how nervous and uncomfortable he was. Todd was unwell and went to bed before I served dessert.

Tony said to Eustaquio, "Are you ready to leave?" "Yes, yes." Still he was fidgeting about, pacing back and forth. Tony went into our bedroom to see how Todd was doing, and I followed him. "Where is Eustaquio?" Tony asked. I shrugged. Minutes later, wearing his coat, he enters the bedroom with a very sheepish look on his face. Several more painful minutes of discomfort pass by. The feeling of increasing tension is palpably felt by us all. Then suddenly, Eustaquio drops onto one knee and removes a box from his coat pocket.

"I know that this is your family, Tony, so I must do this in front of them." He removes the ring from the box. "Will you marry me?" "Yes." He puts the ring on Tony's finger. Todd and I are moved to tears. Finally, our child is going to be wed.

Very discouraged about the prospects for *La Lupa,* I noticed a call for scores for the Ft. Worth Opera's Frontiers Showcase of New Works, one of the most prestigious opera showcases in the country. A demo recording was optional, and unfortunately I did not have one. I submitted a thirty-minute segment of the score for consideration anyway. A few months later I received the notice that my opera had been rejected. Well, I'm not an opera composer, and it's probably not any good.

Let me try something totally different. I wrote a play—no music this time—called *Drone.* The impetus for the play came after reading the *Intercept's* "Drone Papers," which were leaked CIA reports, where the agency itself claimed that ninety percent of those killed in drone strikes are not the intended targets and that the program has led to more, rather than fewer, terrorists. I saw this as one of the great moral dilemmas of our time. I learned enough about playwriting to know that strictly didactic and polemical work would not resonate as theater. Instead, it must center around the personal, the dramatic, on how it affects our relationships. I researched everything I could on the subject and was inspired by some of the personal accounts of those involved in the program.

The play examines the human cost of using drones through two parallel families, the pilot's outside of Las Vegas and the victim's in the tribal areas of Pakistan, each with a soccer-playing son. The driving dramatic force is that the pilot observes the victim and his family for weeks, as they have tea, pray, dance, and even make love. This voyeuristic surveillance engenders an almost personal relationship with the victims, making the kill an extremely trauma-inducing act. Thus far, theaters shy away from the subject matter entirely, probably because a majority of Americans support drone warfare. However, Michele Pawk, who admires the play is preparing to direct a reading of it.

I hired three young singers and a pianist to record the segment from *La Lupa* I had submitted to Ft. Worth Opera, as well as two of Mara's arias. No one's interested in my opera, but, at least, I must hear it. I reserved a recording date at Opera America and paid for it in advance. About ten days before the scheduled recording, it became obvious that the mezzo hired to sing Pina was not going to be able to learn the extremely demanding part in time. I phoned Tracy Bidleman to see if she thought she could learn the role in ten days. She took a deep breath and said, "I'll try."

She, Adam Cannedy as Nanni, and Dasha Jensen as Mara did a first-rate job with minimal rehearsal. I sent the demo to the administrator of the program in Ft. Worth just for informational purposes. He wrote back and said, "Why don't you resubmit it for next year's showcase." I did and several months later I was notified that I was one of the winners. The demo recording made the difference. The selection panel, besides Ft. Worth's highly acclaimed artistic director, Darren Woods, was made up of people from the Metropolitan Opera, the Philadelphia Opera and G. Schirmer, the classical music publisher. This was finally affirmation for my work from some major figures in the business.

When they announced the casting, I went to each of the singers' websites with trepidation to see what I might expect from them. Anna Laurenzo will sing Pina; Trevor Martin, Nanni, and Christina Castro, Mara. I couldn't have been happier with the choices. All three have great voices, are good actors, and look terrific, which is important because the piece revolves so much on physical attractiveness. Frontiers is billed as "one of the most significant music events of the year," and I can scarcely believe I'm to be given such an opportunity at age seventy-five after so many years of struggle and disappointment. I'll be the Grandma Moses of opera, no doubt. My grandfather, Ignazio would be so pleased that the little boy who could not sit through Metropolitan Opera broadcasts with him had written an opera about his native land.

Todd made a connection at an online publication called the *Times of Sicily*, where he's a monthly contributor, writing such articles as how Sicily inspired his paintings, Sicilian dancing, a Sicilian family dinner, and various travel-inspired pieces. Through Todd, I met the publisher, Giovanni Morreale, who agreed to publish my article "Journey to a Sicilian Opera," and generously offered to connect me with opera directors in Sicily.

In her poem "The Little Old Lady in Lavender Silk," which is also the closing number in my musical, Dorothy Parker wrote:

> I was seventy-seven, come August
>   I shall shortly be losing my bloom.
> I've experienced zephyr and raw gust.
>   And (symbolical) flood and simoom.
>
> When you come to this time of abatement.
>   To this passing from summer to fall.
> It is manners to issue a statement
>   As to what you got out of it all.

So what did I get out of it all? Certainly not fame or fortune. But does that really matter? The journey is what's fulfilling. I did get the two things I declared in my youth to be most important to me: life-long love and in my own small way, a life in music theater (I use the term that encompasses both opera and musicals). No classical music stars have performed my work, but the performers who did were extraordinary talents who might have been stars with a bit more luck. I've never had a major production of my theatrical works, but many who saw my pieces in small venues told me they were touched by them. Like Mrs. Parker, I ask myself, "Do I expect too much of life?" Her answer was, "People who ask little, settle for it."

So I don't settle, I hope. I once read a treatise on pessimism versus optimism, and in chapter after chapter, I was harangued by how optimists display better mental and physical health. Okay, I'll buy that. Optimists do better in their careers. Yes, right. Optimistic presidential candidates have a far greater chance of being elected than pessimistic candidates. Okay, okay. I solemnly commit to develop a positive outlook on life. However, in the final chapter, the study conclusively demonstrates that pessimists have a significantly better grasp on reality. And the entire house of cards collapses before my eyes. So, like Mrs. Parker, I remain a confirmed pessimist who's "the biggest damned hoper you ever saw." I promised myself that I would never lie on my deathbed, lamenting, "If only I had tried a littler harder, I might have achieved more in life." No, I will die knowing I made every last effort.

If I let my imagination take flight, might I aggrandize my hopes a bit, strengthen my optimism? Let's try it. After my resounding success in Ft. Worth, I have the libretto for *La Lupa* translated into Italian so that it can be performed at the Teatro Massimo in Palermo, where Todd and I are now respected residents. The opening will be one of the theater's grand events, with a red carpet covering the imposing steps leading to the Greek-temple entrance, the doors flanked by handsome soldiers in 19th-Century-dress uniforms with red plumes in their hats, and carrying swords. At the end of the performance, the crowd screams, "Maestro, maestro," and I'm led onto the stage to deafening bravos. As with most pessimists, an undercurrent of optimism lies just beneath the surface, ready to burst forth at any moment.

Fifty-one years ago, a twenty-four-year-old man (well, technically a man; emotionally still a boy), lay on a lonely bed in a dreary room at the YMCA in New York. He's feeling very sorry for himself, indeed. He laments that he just missed out being hired for the corps de ballet at Lincoln Center because he happened to be standing on the wrong side of the room. Worse, he's racked with misery because a man he loved for nearly three years has thrown him out of his house and his life forever.

The boy holds a closed book in his hands, its dust jacket covered in plastic. It's a library book because the boy has no money to buy his own copy. The book is W. Somerset Maugham's *Of Human Bondage*. Reluctantly, he opens the book and returns to its final pages in an attempt to lose himself once again in the story. The main character, Philip Carey, is discussing life's meaning with his friend Cronshaw, who suggests that he examine the exquisite Persian carpets at the Musée de Cluny in Paris. What can a carpet reveal about life? Cronshaw tells him he must find the answer for himself in the carpet's exquisite patterns. Of course, the carpet is a metaphor, and a very good one. It gives the boy transitory solace.

A half-century later I examine the "carpet" that is Ignazio Norman Cangialosi Mathews, and what do I see? What meaning does it impart? No meaning. Merely an emerging design, embodied by the people, the events, the emotions, and the creations that compose his life. What kind of carpet is it? A prayer rug? No, I think not. He abandoned religion without regret too many years ago. A magic carpet? Hardly. Yet, there in the corner are the threads of Uncle Nick and Richard, performing their mesmerizing conjuring act.

It appears to be simply a decorative carpet, a small rug that doesn't try to dominate the room, but just asks to be noticed, to be given its due, for once, not to be underestimated. What is it made of? Here, touch it. You can feel it in the fine texture of the pile. It's mostly silk, which, because of its expense, necessitated the small size. Always quality over quantity. That's what its maker lived by. But what about that gold thread that weaves through the carpet like a beautiful haunting melody? That must be Walt Whitman's *Songs of the Poet*.

And there's Mary Giovingo, the large beige field—yes, that was her color, not dull, but solid, dependable—on which every other element rests. She has a clear view of the threads that surround her, those that represent her son: the editor, the dancer, the pianist, the teacher, the composer, and the playwright—the son who wore enough hats to fill a millinery shop. What would she say if she were here today? Can you hear her voice? I hear her clearly, "What are you, Norman, a jack of all trades and a master of none?" "Perhaps, mom. Yet, can't you agree that there is at least a modicum of competence in all of them?"

Green diamonds? They seem somewhat out of character here. Aren't there too many colors already? Maybe, but those are Matt Cancelose and his beloved Wrigley Field. He's still awaiting a Chicago Cubs World Series because he departed before its realization. And those little baskets. Those are my *Nonna,* still reminiscing about those culinary delicacies being delivered to her Palermo apartment.

The bright red? That's Pina with her bouquet of poppies, slowly approaching her doom. And the funny little repeated pattern in the corner? Dorothy Parker, of course, repeating over and over again her most famous epigram, as she searches for a way to use horticulture in a sentence. Ah, yes. "You can lead a whore to culture, but you can't make her think." That stack of disks is clearly Larry, still slogging his way through a pile of pancakes to save a buck.

The eye stops wandering and comes to rest on the most prominent and essential patterns of all, the identical ones on either side of the carpet in deep blue, those that resemble large TLs. They're matchless and lovingly formed. They anchor the design, give it weight and import. Without a doubt, they are Todd Lehman and Tony Lin.

Do all these disparate threads form a harmonious and pleasing whole? I'm standing too close. To judge requires distance and time. I need to move to the right side of the room. Over the remaining years, more threads will be added to the warp and woof—the warp being the threads that run lengthwise and the warp those that run crosswise. Who can know what they will be? Only then can one hope to determine whether this carpet, this tapestry of a life, reveals a hodgepodge of insignificant events or a coherent, focused, satisfying work of art.